THE CHRISTOLOGY OF THE NEW TESTAMENT

Books by Oscar Cullmann
Published by The Westminster Press

Baptism in the New Testament

Early Christian Worship

The Johannine Circle

The New Testament:
An Introduction for the General Reader

The Early Church (Abridged Edition)

Christ and Time:
The Primitive Christian Conception of Time and History (Revised Edition)

The Christology of the New Testament (Revised Edition)
(The New Testament Library)

Peter: Disciple, Apostle, Martyr
(Second Revised and Expanded Edition)
(Library of History and Doctrine)

OSCAR CULLMANN

THE CHRISTOLOGY OF THE NEW TESTAMENT

REVISED EDITION

Translated by
SHIRLEY C. GUTHRIE
and
CHARLES A. M. HALL

The Westminster Press
PHILADELPHIA

Translated from the German
Die Christologie des Neuen Testaments
(J. C. B. Mohr (Paul Siebeck) Tübingen 1957)
by Shirley C. Guthrie and Charles A. M. Hall

The English text of the manuscript was awarded first prize for 1955 by the Christian Research Foundation.

The chapters on the Messiah and the Son of Man were delivered in the present form for the first time in March 1955 as the Zenos Lectures of McCormick Theological Seminary.

LIBRARY OF CONGRESS CATALOG CARD NO. 59-10178

Published by The Westminster Press®
Philadelphia, Pennsylvania

PRINTED IN THE UNITED STATES OF AMERICA

1 2 3 4 5 6 7 8 9

TO THE
UNIVERSITY OF EDINBURGH
IN EXPRESSION OF THANKS
FOR THE CONFERRING OF THE DEGREE OF
DOCTOR OF DIVINITY

Contents

Part II

THE CHRISTOLOGICAL TITLES WHICH REFER TO THE FUTURE WORK OF JESUS

Part III

Part IV

CONTENTS

Abbreviations

ATANT	Abhandlungen zur Theologie des Alten und Neuen Testaments
BJRL	*Bulletin of the John Rylands Library*
BZAW	Beihefte zur *Zeitschrift für die alttestamentlichen Wissenschaft*
BZNW	Beihefte zur *Zeitschrift für die neutestamentliche Wissenschaft*
CNT	Commentaire du Nouveau Testament
DT	*Deutsche Theologie*
ET	English translation
ExpT	*Expository Times*
HNT	Handbuch zum Neuen Testament, ed. H. Lietzmann
ICC	International Critical Commentary
JBL	*Journal of Biblical Literature*
KNT	Kommentar zum Neuen Testament, ed. T. Zahn
Meyer	Kritisch-exegetisches Kommentar über das Neue Testament, begründet von H. A. W. Meyer
N.F.	Neue Folge
NTD	Das Neues Testament Deutsch
NTS	*New Testament Studies*
PG	Migne, *Patrologia Graeca*
PL	Migne, *Patrologia Latina*
RAC	*Reallexikon für Antike und Christentum*, ed. T. Klauser, 1950ff.
RB	*Revue Biblique*
RGG	*Die Religion in Geschichte und Gegenwart*
RHE	*Revue d'Histoire Ecclésiastique*
RHPR	*Revue d'Histoire et de Philosophie religieuses*
SEA	*Svensk Exegetisk Aarsbok*
SBT	Studies in Biblical Theology
SNTS	Studiorum Novi Testamenti Societas
Strack-Billerbeck	H. L. Strack and P. Billerbeck, *Kommentar zum Neuen Testament aus Talmud und Midrasch* I–IV, 1922–28
TB	*Theologische Blätter*
TLZ	*Theologische Literaturzeitung*

TR	*Theologische Rundschau*
TWNT	*Theologisches Wörterbuch zum Neuen Testament*, ed. G Kittel, 1933 ff.
TZ	*Theologische Zeitschrift*
ZAW	*Zeitschrift für die alttestamentliche Wissenschaft*
ZKG	*Zeitschrift für Kirchengeschichte*
ZNW	*Zeitschrift für die neutestamentliche Wissenschaft*
ZTK	*Zeitschrift für Theologie und Kirche*

Preface to the First Edition

THE WORK which I today (finally!) submit for publication has gone through a number of earlier unpublished 'editions' which I have repeatedly altered and extended in various lectures. The students to whom I first delivered them more than twenty years ago in Strasbourg will hardly recognize the present version, although the outline is for the most part the same. I have since then continued to work at the New Testament Christology along with my other publications. They have contributed to the present work, but anyone who knows my other New Testament investigations will see that conversely my Christological studies have also influenced them.

The chapters on 'The Messiah' and 'The Son of Man' were delivered in their present English form as the Zenos Lectures for 1955 at McCormick Theological Seminary in Chicago. In view of the present publication of the whole work, the Zenos Foundation graciously consented as an exception to forgo separate publication of these two chapters.

It is not for me to instruct my readers and critics how they should read my book, much less how they should discuss it. But I ask permission to express to them both a wish. To the reader: The structure of the book might suggest that it could be used as a work of reference on the Christology of the New Testament. But it should not be used in this way—at least not until the whole has been read—because, as I must emphasize again and again, the various parts are very closely connected. To the critics I should like to say beforehand that I am also willing to learn from their discussions precisely at the points where they differ with me. But I hope that they will not dispose of my interpretations with apodictic assertions and verdicts without exegetical grounds. Above all I hope that they will not place me in this or that category which they reject *a priori*, much less accuse me of not subscribing to this or that contemporary or earlier school. If my book is judged in terms of theological 'direction', none of the familiar 'schools of thought' will be satisfied with me.

This book is an exegetical work. I have expressed my conception of the exegetical method in various places. Dispensing with all profound methodological observations (and thus proving myself quite 'out of date'), I emphasize here only that I know no other 'method' than the proven philological-historical one. I know of no other 'attitude' toward the text than obedient willingness to listen to it even when what I hear is sometimes completely foreign, contradictory to my own favourite ideas, whatever they may be; the willingness at least to take the trouble to understand and present it, regardless of my own philosophical and theological 'opinions'; and above all the willingness to guard against designating a biblical statement a dispensable 'form' because it is unacceptable to me on the basis of my opinions.

For their valuable and selfless help, I am especially indebted to one of my theological students, Mr Karlfried Fröhlich, for the preparation of the German manuscript, and to Professors Shirley C. Guthrie (Columbia Theological Seminary) and Charles A. M. Hall (Wellesley College) for the English translation.

OSCAR CULLMANN

Chamonix, September 1956

Preface to the Second Edition

Now that a new edition is needed after only a few months, I do not feel called on to make any substantial changes; only a number of corrections and bibliographical additions have had to be incorporated in various passages. For most of the suggestions in these matters I have to thank most sincerely my esteemed friend and colleague Professor Dr. W. Baumgartner, who has read the book with his own careful attention to detail.

I shall have an opportunity later to define my position with regard to the other numerous observations of an objective kind which I have up to now received from my colleagues mainly in personal letters, and which are of value to me both in assent and in criticism.

OSCAR CULLMAN

Basel, February 1958

Translators' Preface

THE chapters of this translation were first prepared in Basel in frequent consultation with Professor Cullmann, and delivered by Professor Cullmann himself as lectures in various American universities and theological schools in 1955. We are grateful to him for his friendly and patient help with our original work and for his later suggestions for further revisions which led to this final version approved by him.

We have left the word *Heilsgeschichte* untranslated in the text, partly because it has become a technical term also in English, and partly because there is no single English equivalent which fully comprehends its meaning. Even in German its meaning has varied since it was first coined in the middle of the eighteenth century and taken up especially by J. T. Beck and J. Chr. K. Hofmann in the nineteenth century. As Professor Cullmann, with other contemporary biblical scholars, uses it, *Heilsgeschichte* has both the sense 'history of salvation' and 'saving history'; that is, it refers at the same time to the history of God's saving work among men, and to the redemptive character of that history as such. In both senses the term points to the fact that salvation is connected with the action of God rather than with abstract theological propositions about him. 'History' here means of course primarily the revelatory events of biblical history with its centre in the Christ event. But in a secondary sense *all* history is *Heilsgeschichte* in so far as its ultimate meaning must be understood and judged in terms of the continuous work and purpose of the same living and acting God, the Father of Jesus Christ, who once made himself uniquely known in his saving actions recorded in the Old and New Testaments. For a detailed discussion of Professor Cullmann's understanding of the term, see his *Christ and Time* (especially the Introduction).

Except in cases where Professor Cullmann has made his own translation, scripture quotations are from the Revised Standard Version of the Bible.

SHIRLEY C. GUTHRIE, JR.
CHARLES A. M. HALL

I

Introduction: The Christological Problem in Early Christianity

WE SHALL ASK FIRST what *place* Christology occupies in the theological thinking of the first Christians, then attempt to define the Christological *problem* in the New Testament, and finally speak of the *method* by which we shall approach this problem in the following chapters.

1. *The Role of Christology in the Theological Thinking of the First Christians*

If theo-logy is that science whose object is *God*, θεός, then Christology is that science whose object is *Christ*, his person and his work. Christology is usually considered as a sub-division of theology in the etymological sense. This custom has frequently influenced the historical representation of the first Christians' faith to the extent that one begins by stating their thoughts about *God*, and speaks only in the second place of their Christological convictions. That is the usual sequence of the older textbooks of New Testament theology.

This arrangement is still encouraged by the order of the two articles God-Christ in the later confessions of faith. That order does in fact imply that the early Church was interested first of all in God and only then in Christ. But the unequal length of the two articles shows that this is not really the case. Moreover, it can be shown that the oldest formulas which summarize the faith of the first Christians do not know the trinitarian division God-Christ-Holy Spirit of the later confessions. The oldest confessions are rather expressed exclusively in Christological terms. The separation between the first and second articles which is found in the later confessions does not yet exist.[1] The later separation is also the source of the erroneous belief that according to early Christianity the work of Christ is related only

[1] See O. Cullmann, *The Earliest Christian Confessions*, ET 1949.

to salvation, but not to creation. Actually the oldest formulas connect Christ with creation. Almost all of them contain only one article, the Christological. One of the few New Testament confessions which does mention both Christ and God the Father is in I Cor. 8.6, and it is characteristic of this that it does not know the separation between God as Creator and Christ as Saviour, but on the contrary speaks of creation both in the first article (God) and in the second (Christ): '. . . one God, the Father, from whom are all things and for whom we exist, and one Lord, Jesus Christ, through whom are all things and through whom we exist.' *Both* have to do with creation. The variation lies only in the prepositions: ἐξ and εἰς in connection with God; διά in connection with Christ, '*through* whom are all things' (δι' οὗ τὰ πάντα). Christ the Mediator of creation: not only do we find the idea in this ancient formula, but we can follow it through the whole New Testament (John 1.3; Col. 1.16). Its strongest expression occurs in Heb. 1.10, where the very foundation of the earth is attributed to Christ, and heaven designated as the work of his hands.

Other confessions of the early period mention God not as Creator, but as the 'Father of Jesus Christ'. He is introduced as the one who has resurrected the Christ (Polycarp, 2.1 ff.). This also proves that the theological thinking of the first Christians proceeds from Christ, not from God.

One may point out in the same way that all the elements which are connected with the Holy Spirit in the third article of the later formulas of faith are named as direct functions of Christ—for example, the forgiveness of sins and the resurrection.[1]

We should remember also that in the familiar liturgical formula at the end of II Corinthians the order is not God-Christ-Holy Spirit, but Christ-God-Holy Spirit: 'The grace of the Lord Jesus Christ and the love of God and the fellowship of the Holy Spirit . . .' (II Cor. 13.14).

The ancient formulas are especially important for knowledge about early Christian thinking, because, as short summaries of the theological convictions of the first Christians, they show what these Christians emphasized, which truths they regarded as central and which as derived. We can therefore say that early Christian theology

[1] *Ibid.*, pp. 39 f. Also baptism, which in later confessions is baptism of the *Church* in the third article, appears in the formula used by Ignatius of Antioch in *Smyrn.* 1.1 ff. as the baptism of *Jesus* by John. Also Ignatius, *Eph.* 18.2: 'He was baptized that by his passion he might purify the water' (see p. 68 below).

is in reality almost exclusively Christology. In so far as it concentrated its whole theological interest for several centuries on Christological discussions, the early Catholic Church remained close enough to the early Church.

But we must now ask whether these later discussions put the question in the same way as we find it in the New Testament.

2. *What is the Christological Problem in the New Testament?*

We have described Christology as the science whose object is the person and work of Christ. Now we ask to what extent a *problem* confronted the first Christians in this respect and exactly what it is. The later so-called Christological controversies refer almost exclusively to the *person* or *nature* of Christ. They refer on the one hand to the relation between his nature and that of God; on the other hand, to the relation which exists in Christ himself between his divine and his human nature. If we are to avoid the danger of seeing the Christological problem of the New Testament in a false perspective from the very beginning, we must attempt first of all to disregard these later discussions. It must be acknowledged from a historical point of view, of course, that it was necessary for the Church at a certain period to deal with the precise problems resulting from the Hellenizing of the Christian faith, the rise of Gnostic doctrines, and the views advocated by Arius, Nestorius, Eutyches and others. That is, it was necessary for the Church to deal with the question of the natures and attempt to answer it. We may say, however, that although the Church attempted a solution to the problem by reference to the New Testament, its statement of the problem was nevertheless oriented all too exclusively in a direction which no longer completely corresponds to the manner in which the New Testament itself states it.

The New Testament hardly ever speaks of the person of Christ without at the same time speaking of his work. Even the prologue to the Gospel of John connects the one statement that 'the Logos was with God, and the Logos was God' immediately with the second statement that through this Logos 'all things were made'. He is the Mediator of creation. These introductory verses as a whole speak of the being of the Word only in view of the revelatory action of him who became flesh—of him who is the subject of all twenty-one chapters of this Gospel. When it is asked in the New Testament 'Who is Christ?', the question never means exclusively, or even primarily, 'What is his nature?', but first of all, 'What is his function?'[1] Therefore, the various answers given to the question in the New Testament (answers which are expressed in the various titles we shall investigate one after the other) visualize both Christ's person and his work. This applies even to the titles of honour referring to the pre-existent Christ, with whom the last part of this book deals: Logos, Son of God, and God. We shall see of course that these various titles implicitly raise also the question concerning the relationship between God and the person and origin of Christ. But the problem is not really a 'problem of natures' even here.

There is thus a difference between the way in which the first Christians and the later Church understood the Christological problem. It must of course be granted that Athanasius and other defenders of orthodoxy in the later battle which came to a temporary halt with the Council of Chalcedon emphasized the redemptive character of the nature of Christ and showed that the conception of the accomplished work of Christ is dependent upon how one understands his nature. To this extent they took his work into consideration, but they did so, nevertheless, only from the point of view of his natures.

As a result of the necessity of combating the heretics, then, the Church fathers subordinated the interpretation of the person and work of Christ to the question of the 'natures'. In any case, their emphases, compared with those of the New Testament, were misplaced. Even when they did speak of the work of Christ, they did so only in connection with discussion about his nature. Even if this shifting of emphasis was necessary against certain heretical views, the discussion of 'natures' is none the less ultimately a Greek, not a Jewish or biblical problem.

In order to answer the question 'Who is Jesus?', the first Christians had at their disposal certain concepts which were already present in Judaism, especially in Jewish eschatology. Therefore the Christological question was presented in the earliest period in the following way: To what extent did Jesus fulfil what these concepts implied? To what extent did his actual work go beyond what they implied? At what point does his work stand in contradiction to analogous

[1] In saying this, I do not think of the function of Christ in Bultmann's sense as only an event in the '*kerygma*,' but as a real Christological event. On this point see Karl Barth, *Rudolf Bultmann, ein Versuch ihn zu verstehen*, 1952, pp. 16 ff.; O. Cullmann, 'Le mythe dans les écrits du Nouveau Testament', *Numen* 1, 1954, pp. 120 ff.

concepts and views which may have been attached to the same expression in Judaism? When the first Christians in a Hellenistic environment answered the question about Jesus with a title which in Greek culture designated a divine mediator, one must investigate from the point of view of the New Testament to what extent the early Church connected with that title the same or different ideas.

One must certainly react from the very beginning against the erroneous notion lying behind many representations of early Christian Christology, that this Christology had necessarily to conform to the conceptual scheme already present in Judaism or Hellenism. Although the viewpoint of comparative religions is justified in itself, an exaggeration of it undoubtedly leads to such a way of thinking. But as scholars we simply cannot neglect to take Jesus' own self-consciousness into consideration. For one must reckon *a priori* with the possibility—even with the probability—first, that in his teaching and life Jesus accomplished something new from which the first Christians had to proceed in their attempt to explain his person and work; second, that their experience of Christ exhibited special features not present in every obvious analogy to related religious forms. It is simply unscholarly prejudice methodically to exclude from the beginning this possibility—this probability.

The Christological question emerges for the first time as a problem even during the lifetime of Jesus. In Mark 8.27–29 Jesus himself gives it what may be called a classical formulation. We must investigate this text in detail later; now we are interested in it only with regard to the way it states the problem: '... and on the way he asked his disciples, "Who do men say that I am?" And they told him, "John the Baptist; and others say, Elijah; and others one of the prophets." And he asked them, "But who do you say that I am?" Peter answered him, "You are the Christ."'

Here we see that the problem as such already existed both for the people and for the disciples who lived every day in close fellowship with Jesus—those who 'saw him with their eyes and heard him with their ears'. We see also that both among the people and among the disciples various answers were given, answers in the form of familiar *titles*, each describing at the same time a function and a work to be accomplished. (It is precisely this that justifies the approach of the present work to the problem.) All these answers have in common the fact that they do not simply place Jesus in a general human category, but attempt rather to explain his *uniqueness*. This uniqueness alone is in question in what we have called the 'Christological problem', not for instance a biographical-statistical identification. Therefore, the designation of Jesus as 'Rabbi' or 'Teacher' or 'Physician' (titles certainly important for describing the life of Jesus) is not important for the Christological problem.[1] Although the assertion that he is one of the prophets seems also to place him only in a particular human occupational category, we shall see that in reality 'prophet' is a title which represents one solution to this problem.

The titles listed in Mark 8.27 ff. are not by any means the only ones conferred upon Jesus in the New Testament. Still others are ascribed to him in order to express who he is and in what his work consists. The reason for his being described in so many different ways is that no one of these titles by itself can comprehend all the aspects of his person and work. Each of them shows only one particular aspect of the whole wealth of convictions of faith about him which we find in the New Testament. Only when we investigate all the different titles which the first Christians conferred upon him shall we most nearly approach what we can call 'the Christology of the New Testament'. We must not forget for a moment that all the various concepts are united in Jesus himself.

The expressions 'Christology' and 'Christological' in this work are not used in the restricted sense to refer exclusively to the designation Christ-Messiah, which is only one of many titles. We use these expressions in a general sense to comprehend everything which refers to the uniqueness of the person and work of Jesus Christ.

3. *The Method to be Followed*

Although we are striving for a total picture of the Christological conceptions of the New Testament, we shall proceed in a purely analytical way. This does not mean that we shall investigate in turn each New Testament writing with all the different titles which appear in it, but rather that we shall examine in its precise meaning each Christological title for itself as it appears throughout all the New Testament books.[2] In this way, despite the analytical method,

[1] E. Lohmeyer, *Galiläa und Jerusalem*, 1936, p. 73, observes that the address διδάσκαλος in Mark does not simply recognize Jesus as belonging to the class of rabbis, but actually distinguishes him from that class. This is correct, but in these cases the designation 'Teacher' is only an attribute of another title of honour to which we shall devote our first chapter, the title '*the* Prophet'. On this connection see C. H. Dodd, 'Jesus as Teacher and Prophet', *Mysterium Christi* (ed. G. K. A. Bell and A. Deissmann), 1930, pp. 63 ff.

[2] This methodology, which follows from the given Christological titles as such and then seeks to differentiate by analysis, seems to me preferable to that of

we shall be able to identify the principal characteristics of each title. Before we investigate its use in the New Testament, we shall speak of each title's significance in Judaism and (when the concept exists there) in the general history of religion, particularly in Hellenism. For the reasons given above we shall ask in each case within the New Testament: first, if and in what sense Jesus applied this or that Christological designation to himself (a question which seems to me warranted today also in the light of form criticism); then, how it was understood by the different New Testament writers.

It seems to me that the time has actually come when the very results of form criticism require us to raise again the question of the historical Jesus—in a different way of course from that in which it was considered before the work of form criticism.[1] It was certainly proper for the question to have been deliberately ignored for the past few decades, but to abandon it permanently seems to me to be a false consequence of past mistakes. The knowledge that the Gospels are confessions of faith and that the early Church's faith in Christ is the real creator of the Gospel tradition does not justify an absolute historical scepticism which refuses to use these confessions of faith as historical sources at all. On the contrary, this knowledge should encourage us to use the Church's faith in Christ positively as a means of discovering historical reality.[2]

In order to arrive at Jesus' self-consciousness, we shall make use of the form-critical examination of the Gospel tradition in that we shall attempt to distinguish between the places where the Gospel writers obviously express their own view and the places where they report the words of Jesus himself. If there should be within a Gospel a certain discrepancy between the Christological titles which the writer uses and those which Jesus applies to himself, we shall have found an objective criterion for this distinction.

G. Sevenster in his worthwhile *Christologie van het Nieuwe Testament*[2], 1948. Nevertheless, in his interpretation, which deals with the Christology of the various New Testament writings one after the other, Sevenster does always attempt to understand correctly the 'unity and difference' of the New Testament's preaching of Christ.

[1] Essays such as the following show that this has recently gained recognition: E. Käsemann, 'Das Problem des historischen Jesus', *ZTK* 51, 1954, pp. 125 ff.; T. W. Manson, 'The Life of Jesus. Some Tendencies in Present Day Research', *The Background of the New Testament and Its Eschatology* (volume in honour of C. H. Dodd), 1956, pp. 211 ff.; E. Fuchs, 'Die Frage nach dem historischen Jesus', *ZTK* 53, 1956, pp. 210 ff.

[2] It seems to me that at this point also G. Bornkamm in his brilliantly written little book, *Jesus of Nazareth*, ET 1961, goes somewhat too far in his scepticism about ascribing any kind of messianic title of majesty to the historical Jesus.

Concerning the question whether Jesus conferred the title under consideration upon himself, we shall have to be careful to hold ourselves free from every *a priori*—including that present in the thought of R. Bultmann. Faithful to his earlier position, Bultmann consistently maintains in his *The Theology of the New Testament* I, ET 1952, pp. 26 f., the opinion that Jesus by no means considered himself as one with a special divine commission in a unique sense—least of all in any of the forms which we shall investigate here. According to Bultmann, Jesus only proclaimed God the Father and his Kingdom. Bultmann himself may have perceived that only the denial of Jesus' messianic self-consciousness (a denial which, incidentally, goes methodically beyond the neutral point of view of Bultmann's own conception of form criticism) can justify the omission of the possibility that the Christology of the early Church could have been decisively influenced by a new interpretation first made by Jesus. In the final analysis Bultmann's denial agrees with the well-known thesis of Harnack that only the Father and not the Son belongs to the gospel of Jesus. Bultmann differs from Harnack, of course, in so far as he asserts that this conclusion by no means influences our own faith in Christ. *We* can nevertheless believe that Jesus is the Messiah and thus share the Christological convictions of the early Church. With this position Bultmann does go far beyond the position of earlier liberalism. But is it not illusion to think that we can have the same faith as the early Church if we accept its Christological views, but still assert that Jesus himself had no 'self-consciousness' of being what we confess him to be? In reality an essential characteristic of the early Church's faith in Christ was its conviction that Jesus believed himself to be the divine Son of Man, the Servant of God, and conferred on himself this or that title of which we shall have to speak. The early Church believed in Christ's messiahship only because it believed that Jesus believed himself to be the Messiah. In this respect Bultmann's faith in Christ is fundamentally different from that of the early Church.

The New Testament titles are numerous, each of them presenting a particular aspect of the problem. No single title is sufficient to comprehend the infinite fullness disclosed in Christ. I enumerate here only the most important of them: Prophet, High Priest, Mediator, Servant of God, Lamb of God, Messiah, Son of David, Son of Man, Judge, Holy One of God, Lord, Saviour, King, Logos, Son of God, God.

We need not devote a special chapter to all these titles. It will be obvious that some can be explained within the framework of another Christological concept. Thus the discussion of 'Mediator' will be found in the chapter on the High Priest, 'Lamb of God' in the chapter on the Servant of God, 'Son of David' and 'King' in that on the Messiah,

'Judge' in that on the Son of Man, 'Holy One of God' in that on the Son of God.

With which one shall we begin, and how shall we classify them? We shall speak first of those which designate primarily the *earthly* work of Christ; secondly, of those which relate primarily to his *future*, eschatological work; then, of those which explain primarily his *present* work; and finally, of those which explain primarily the work completed in his *pre-existence*. This will be the arrangement of our book. It involves an unavoidable schematic classification, for as a rule each title or Christological concept is related not only to one of these four different functions of Jesus, but at the same time to two or even three of them. Moreover, a mutual assimilation of meanings and connotations may have taken place in the consciousness of the first Christians, who often applied different titles to Jesus simultaneously. We must take into account the fact that early Christianity by no means always distinguished so sharply between the titles as we shall in our phenomenological investigation. These had a mutual influence on each other; in fact, they often go back to the same source.

Our arrangement of the material is based on the chronological principle characteristic of all New Testament Christology that 'Jesus Christ is the same yesterday and today and forever.'[1] We have seen that it is characteristic of New Testament Christology that Christ is connected with the total history of revelation and salvation, beginning with creation. There can be no *Heilsgeschichte* without Christology; no Christology without a *Heilsgeschichte* which unfolds in time. Christology is the doctrine of an 'event', not the doctrine of natures.

At the end of the phenomenological investigation of the different titles, we shall see that from all the variety of individual New Testament books and individual concepts there emerges in the thinking of early Christianity one total picture of the Christ-event from the pre-existence to eschatology. It is not as if the New Testament were a series of monographs like Kittel's theological wordbook.

On the other hand, when we see which titles shaped the beginning point of the early Church's Christological thinking, we shall also derive from our analytical consideration a history of the development of early Christian Christology. The order in which the material is arranged in our book is by no means identical with that

[1] See O. Cullmann, *Christ and Time*, ET 1950.

of this history; that is, with the chronological order of Christological solutions suggested by the first Christians themselves.

We begin with the Christological designations whose special purpose is to explain the earthly work of Jesus which took place in the past, in the centre of the time of salvation.

PART ONE

The Christological Titles which Refer to the Earthly Work of Jesus

2

Jesus the Prophet

WE HAVE already raised the question whether an investigation of the designation 'Prophet' belongs at all in a work devoted to the Christological problem as we have defined it. Did not those who called Jesus a prophet simply want thereby to place him in a particular general human category of his time? Was he not in this way simply identified according to his purely human appearance? One could suppose that Jesus was called 'Prophet' just as he was called 'Rabbi' (Teacher) in order to specify his human profession.[1] We should note, however, that prophecy as a profession no longer existed in New Testament times. In fact, there were rarely prophets at all any longer in the specifically Israelitic sense of spiritually inspired men who had received a special calling from God. Prophecy had died out more and more until by this time it really existed only in the written form of the prophetic books. This consideration alone indicates that to call Jesus 'Prophet' was not simply to place him in a human professional category. Further, it is significant that in most passages in which he is called by this title, Jesus appears not only as *a* prophet but as *the* Prophet, the final Prophet who should 'fulfil' all prophecy at the end of time. We shall see that the expectation of such a prophet with a very definite task to perform at the end of time was widespread in Judaism at the time of Jesus.

We are concerned now with a specifically Jewish conception, and in this respect this title differs from the others we shall investigate. In the case of 'Son of Man' or 'Logos', for instance, we find parallels in oriental religions and Hellenism.

It is therefore unnecessary to speak here of the concept 'Prophet' in the Greek world. We encounter it in the Greek poets, where it means primarily 'proclaimer', the meaning 'foreteller' being only a rare

[1] See p. 6 n. 1 above.

exception. The prophetic figures here are impersonal, and their only function is to satisfy human curiosity. Apart from the term itself, no lines of connection can be drawn to Israelitic prophecy, which does lay the foundation for the Christian concept of the prophet. Also the Egyptian priest-prophet forms at best a formal parallel to the Israelitic prophet and corresponds rather to the later apocalyptic figures than to the genuine prophets. This question has been thoroughly investigated by E. Fascher, ΠΡΟΦΗΤΗΣ. *Eine sprach- und religionsgeschichtliche Untersuch ung*, 1927, although he treats the chapter on the prophet in the New Testament somewhat summarily.

1. *The Eschatological Prophet in Judaism*

Ancient Israelitic prophecy explains the expectation of the eschatological prophet. The original concept *nabi* is ambiguous in Israelitic religion.[1] It designates on the one hand an ecstatic; on the other hand, a professional, oracular prophet. But these conceptions are not characteristic of specifically Israelitic prophecy, the uniqueness of which lies in its concept of the one prophet of the end time (*der endzeitliche Prophet*). The decisive thing for the classical prophets of Israel is the fact that their function does not rest on a mere profession, but on a concrete calling. Further, the prophet makes his proclamation under a certain compulsion—a compulsion which does not destroy but intensifies his personality. Yahweh makes use of the prophet's capacity of judgment in order to speak to his people through him. In this activity the prophet does not limit himself as does the fortune-teller to isolated revelations, but his prophecy becomes preaching, proclamation. He explains to the people the true meaning of all events; he informs them of the plan and will of God at the particular moment; if necessary he predicts the judgment of God. As we have said, this living prophecy in Israel has faded out long before the New Testament period. The authority of the ancient prophets' writings has taken the place of the spoken prophetic word. As Joel 2.28 ff. (Heb. 3.1 ff.) makes clear, the prophetic gift was seen more and more as an eschatological phenomenon which would become a reality again only at the end of days, and then in a particularly obvious way. There would therefore be prophets in the early Church.[2] As a result of his absence at that time, the Spirit was looked upon in Judaism as an eschatological element. There

[1] A summary is given by H. H. Rowley, 'The Nature of Old Testament Prophecy in the Light of Recent Study', *The Servant of the Lord and other Essays on the Old Testament*[2], 1954, pp. 91 ff.

[2] I Cor. 12.28; Eph. 4.11; Acts 11.27 f.; 13.1; 21.10; Rev. 22.9; *Did.* 11–13.

had been prophets in the past, and there would be prophets again at the end of days. Thus prophecy became more and more the subject of eschatological expectation.

For this reason the very appearance of John the Baptist was considered an eschatological event. Here again appears a living prophet like the ancient prophets. Probably his baptizing also was widely understood as a prophetic act of the same kind as the symbolic deeds undertaken by Old Testament prophets in particular situations—deeds like those of Jeremiah, Elijah, Elisha, Isaiah, and especially Ezekiel.[1]

Luke 3.2 shows that John was considered a prophet according to the Old Testament pattern. It says exactly as it was said of the ancient prophets, ἐγένετο ῥῆμα θεοῦ ἐπὶ Ἰωάννην. We shall speak of the Baptist in the next section; we are concerned now only to show in a preliminary way that in him a prophet again appeared after a long interruption, and that this indicates his *eschatological* significance. Of similar significance was the faith of the Qumran sect in the 'Teacher of Righteousness', or the faith of various fanatics in certain Jewish miracle workers and political heroes of this period.[2] The end time has come, because God speaks through his prophets again. What was fulfilled now in John had long been the subject of Jewish hope for the revival of prophecy at the end of days. This hope is attested by the Books of Maccabees[3] and also by Ps. 74.9.

This general expectation had already taken also the concrete form of the conviction that *a* prophet would appear at the end who would be the fulfilment, so to speak, of all earlier prophecy.[4] This specific Jewish expectation of one final prophet is what interests us in our investigation. Although the fact itself that Jesus (like John) was looked upon as a prophet in this period gave him a unique eschatological dignity, what is *Christologically* important is first the fact that this particular view of *a* prophet of the end was referred to him. The expectation of the prophet who would appear at the end of days must have been common in New Testament times. In view of the

[1] See H. Wheeler Robinson, *Old Testament Essays*, 1927, pp. 1 ff.; W. F. Flemington, *The New Testament Doctrine of Baptism*, 1948, pp. 20 ff.; and especially G. Fohrer, *Die symbolischen Handlungen der Propheten* (ATANT 25), 1953.

[2] Josephus, *Bell. Jud.* II, 68; II, 261 f.; *Ant.* XX, 97 f. See also R. Meyer, *Der Prophet aus Galiläa*, 1940, pp. 41 ff.

[3] Cf. I Macc. 4.44 ff.; 14.41.

[4] See P. Volz, *Die Eschatologie der jüdischen Gemeinde im neutestamentlichen Zeitalter*[2], 1934, pp. 193 ff.

success of the Baptist, the Jews ask him in John 1.21, 'Are you *the* prophet?' It is assumed that everyone knows who is meant thereby.

The idea that a single prophet would represent the whole of prophecy may have another root besides eschatology in Judaism, one which rests more on a theological speculation. It is the idea that since all prophets have proclaimed basically the same divine truth, the same prophet was successively incarnated in different men. Thus the idea arose that actually the same prophet always appeared and that each time he merely took a different form.

We find this idea in the Pseudo-Clementine writings (about which we shall speak in connection with the Christian concept of Jesus the Prophet)[1] and also in the so-called *Gospel of the Hebrews*; that is, in writings which are actually Jewish-Christian, but which nevertheless may be used as sources for the Judaism of the New Testament age. According to the Pseudo-Clementine writings, the 'true Prophet' has appeared repeatedly since Adam through the centuries, changing his name and form, until he comes at the end in the Son of Man.[2] According to the fragment of the *Gospel of the Hebrews* cited by Jerome in his *Commentary on Isaiah*,[3] the Holy Spirit says to Jesus when he comes out of the water after his baptism, 'In all prophets I have awaited you, that you might come and that I might rest in you.' Here the eschatological conception is united with the speculation concerning the reincarnation of the one prophet realized many times in the past. The prophet appears in his final form and prophetic fullness only at the end of time, when he achieves the goal of all prophecy.

The thought of the return of the same prophet to the earth certainly facilitated the Christian view originating with Jesus himself that he himself, who has already been on earth, will one day come a second time to earth. The Jewish Messiah does not come again, but the Prophet does. This fact in itself makes the concept of the reappearing prophet Christologically important. A common idea of contemporary Judaism thus at least prepared the way for Jesus' prophecy of his own return.

The Jewish belief in a returning prophet took the particular form of an expectation of the return of a particular Old Testament prophet at the end of days. This expectation arises already with the words in Deut. 18.15: 'The Lord your God will raise up for you a prophet like me from among you . . .' This text, which of course does not

[1] See pp. 38 f. below.

[2] *Hom.* III, 20.2; *Recogn.* II, 22.

[3] Jerome on Isa. 11.2 (*PL* 24, 145).

yet point to a return of Moses himself but to the eschatological appearance of a prophet similar to him, plays an exceptionally important role in the concept of the prophet.[1] Philo cites the passage and emphasizes the eschatological character of this prophet.[2] Acts 3.22 and 7.37 apply it to Jesus. The Pseudo-Clementine *Preaching of Peter* likewise cites it.[3] On the other hand, belief in the return of Moses himself arises on the basis of it.[4] The recently suggested view[5] that the Suffering Servant of God in Second Isaiah is to be regarded as *Moses redivivus* is not an impossible one.[6]

Above all, however, the return of *Elijah* was expected. This is a relatively old conception. Already in Mal. 4.5 (3.23 in the Hebrew Bible) Elijah is identified with the messenger who is sent to prepare the way for Yahweh. Jesus ben Sirach[7] and the rabbinical texts[8] attest the same belief. Elijah's task is to 'establish' the future community of believers and right teaching at the end.

Occasionally the return of *Enoch* is also mentioned.[9] It is understandable that it is precisely Elijah and Enoch who should be taken as the ones who would come back to earth, since according to the

[1] See H. J. Schoeps, *Theologie und Geschichte des Judenchristentums*, 1949, pp. 87 ff.; J. Jeremias, 'Μωυσῆς', *TWNT* IV, pp. 862 ff. It is also significant that this verse, along with other Old Testament passages, is cited in a collection of messianic testimonies of the Qumran sect. See J. M. Allegro, 'Further Messianic References in Qumran Literature', *JBL* 75, 1956, pp. 174 ff.

[2] *De Spec. Leg.* I, 65.

[3] *Recogn.* I, 43; Peter says that the Jews 'often sent for us to talk with them about Jesus, in order to find out whether he was the Prophet whom Moses had predicted would come'.

[4] *Sibylline Oracles* V, 256 ff. See also the passages listed below. On the late rabbinical texts see P. Volz, *op. cit.*, p. 195; J. Jeremias, 'Μωυσῆς', *op. cit.*, pp. 860 ff. In connection with the return of Moses one must also consider the idea of a return of the Mosaic age at the end. On this point see H. Gressmann, *Der Messias*, 1929, pp. 181 ff.

[5] A. Bentzen, *King and Messiah*, ET 1955, pp. 65 ff. Bentzen agrees in part with T. H. S. Nyberg, 'Smärtornas man', *SEA* 7, 1942, pp. 75 f. Sellin in his *Mose*, 1922, had already identified the *ebed Yahweh* with Moses. Although Bentzen accepts this thesis, he rejects Sellin's theory of Moses' supposed martyrdom in Transjordan.

[6] Whereas S. Engell, *SEA* 10, 1945, understands the *ebed Yahweh* figure on the basis of the idea of kingship, it is just the concept of the prophet that A. Bentzen, *op. cit.*, pp. 48 ff., would like to emphasize much more strongly.

[7] Ecclus. 48.10 f. Here the returned Elijah shares with the *ebed Yahweh* of Isa. 49.6 the task of 'restoring' the tribes of Israel.

[8] See Strack-Billerbeck IV, pp. 779 ff.

[9] Enoch 90.31. Here Enoch returns together with Elijah. His function is not defined in detail.

Old Testament, both were taken up directly to heaven without dying. We also hear that *Baruch* will be preserved alive in order to bear witness against the heathen at the end of time (Apocalypse of Baruch 13.1 ff.).

Finally a combination of these names took place so that *two* returning prophets were named. In the Book of Enoch, *Enoch* and *Elijah* will come again.[1] According to the Midrash Deut. rabba 3.10.1 (which is of course of late date),[2] *Moses* and *Elijah* will come—an expectation certainly presupposed in the New Testament account of the transfiguration (Mark 9.2 ff.)[3] and perhaps also in the appearance of the 'two witnesses' in Rev. 11.3 ff.

In any case, this is the usual explanation of the passage in Revelation. Moses and Elijah are to return at the end to preach repentance. J. Munck, *Petrus und Paulus in der Johannes-Apokalypse*, 1950, has tried to shake this hypothesis, which P. Volz, *op. cit.*, p. 197, had already called 'questionable'. Munck believes that the two witnesses are really the apostles Peter and Paul.[4] This opinion was advocated for the first time by the Jesuit Mariana, *Scholia in Vetus et Novum Testamentum* (1619, pp. 1100 f.). Recently the thesis has been advocated by L. Herrmann, *L'Apocalypse johannique et l'histoire romaine* (*Latomus* VIII, 1948, pp. 23 ff.), and by M. E. Boismard, *L'Apocalypse* (La Sainte Bible), Jerusalem, 1950, pp. 21 f., 53 f. Munck defends the thesis with partially convincing arguments. He admits that the two witnesses have much in common with the prophets of the end time (especially with the returning Elijah), since they too are preachers who call for repentance. But he emphasizes that the two witnesses in Rev. 11.3 ff. are not forerunners of the Messiah, but introduce the coming of the Antichrist. He adds (p. 13) that we nowhere find precisely two forerunners of the Messiah. This point, however, is not true of the texts mentioned above, since Elijah appears there in one case with Enoch, in another case with Moses, even though the pairs are not forerunners of the Messiah. Munck then attempts to show (p. 21) that what is said in Rev. 11.5 f. does not fit Elijah and Moses.

Certainly only *one* prophet was originally expected. The variations (among which we should also mention the prophet Jeremiah)[5] may

[1] See the passage mentioned above, Enoch 90.31. Also the Apocalypse of Elijah (ed. Steindorff, 1899), p. 163.

[2] 'God said to Moses: "When I send the prophet Elijah, both of you shall go together."' See also the Jerusalem Targum to Ex. 12.42.

[3] See J. Jeremias, *TWNT* II, p. 941; H. Riesenfeld, *Jésus transfiguré*, 1947, pp. 253 ff.; E. Lohmeyer, 'Die Verklärung Jesu nach dem Markus-Evangelium', *ZNW* 21, 1922, pp. 188 ff.

[4] See O. Cullmann, *Peter; Disciple, Apostle, Martyr*, ET 1953, pp. 88 f.

[5] See Matt. 16.14. The Jewish texts do not directly attest the return of Jeremiah,

be explained by the fact that it was not certain with which of the ancient prophets the coming one should be identified.

That the expectation of an eschatological prophet was widespread is shown by the fact that religious groups on the periphery of Judaism also expected such a prophet—the Samaritans, for instance, and especially the sect which has become better known through the recently discovered Qumran texts.

On the basis of Deut. 18.15 ff. the Samaritans awaited the coming of *Ta'eb*. He is clearly identified as *Moses redivivus* and has the characteristic features of the prophet: he performs miracles, restores the law and true worship among the people, and brings knowledge to the other nations. Like Moses, he dies at the age of 120. He is called the 'Teacher' or also *Ta'eb*, which is to be translated either 'the Returning One' or, more probably, 'the Restorer'.[1] For the Samaritan woman in John 4.19,25 the Messiah is at the same time a prophet.

The concept 'prophet' was still more central for the Jewish sect which, through the Damascus manuscript discovered in Cairo in 1896 and published in 1910,[2] was first known by the name 'Community of the New Covenant'.[3] We are now more familiar with the teaching and organization of this sect since the highly significant cave discoveries in Khirbet Qumran on the Dead Sea. We may consider as definitely established that this was an Essene sect.

Almost all scholars who are interested in the history of Judaism in the New Testament period have rightly recognized the importance of the various sensational discoveries which have followed one after another since early 1947. The evaluation of these in all their abundance is not yet complete. The publication and annotation of the texts will require years. Old Testament as well as New Testament scholarship will have to investigate them thoroughly during the coming decades. The literature has already grown so large that I can here name only some of the especially important works. For general orientation I recommend H. Bardtke, *Die Handschriftenfunde am Toten Meer*, 1952; A. Dupont-Sommer, *Aperçus*

but II Macc. 15.13 ff. ascribes to him a special role of mediation as the 'Prophet of God' in the present era.

[1] See A. Merx, *Der Messias oder Ta'eb der Samaritaner*, 1909.

[2] S. Schechter, *Documents of Jewish Sectaries*, Vol. I, *Fragments of a Zadokite Work*, 1910.

[3] See L. Rost's edition of the Hebrew text, *Die Damaskusschrift*, 1933. German: W. Staerk, *Die jüdische Gemeinde des Neuen Bundes in Damaskus*, 1922. English: R. H. Charles, *The Apocrypha and Pseudepigrapha of the Old Testament* II, 1913, pp. 799 ff. The best commentary is: Chaim Rabin, *The Zadokite Documents*, 1954 (2nd edition, 1957).

préliminaires sur les manuscrits de la Mer Morte, 1953, and *Nouveaux aperçus sur les manuscrits de la Mer Morte*, 1953; G. Vermès, *Les manuscrits du désert de Juda*, 1953; and especially Millar Burrows, *The Dead Sea Scrolls*, 1955, and O. Eissfeldt, *Einleitung in das AT*[2], 1956, pp. 788 ff. For the best orientation in the whole literature see the essays of W. Baumgartner, '*Der palästinische Handschriftenfund*', which have appeared periodically since 1948/49 in the *Theologische Rundschau*, and the same author's reports in the *Theologische Literaturzeitung*: '*Der gegenwärtige Stand der Erforschung der in Palästina neu gefundenen hebräischen Handschriften*' (first report in *TLZ* 74, 1949). The latter series offer investigations of individual texts. Also indispensable are the conscientious and thorough reports which Père de Vaux, director of the French archeological school in Jerusalem, has published from time to time in the *Revue Biblique* on the locality and place where the discoveries have been made. Finally we should point out the particular evaluation of the texts for New Testament research. First, K. G. Kuhn, 'Die in Palästina gefundenen hebräischen Texte und das Neue Testament', *ZTK* 47, 1950, pp. 194 ff. See also S. E. Johnson, 'The Dead Sea Manual of Discipline and the Jerusalem Church of Acts', *ZAW* 66, 1954, pp. 110 ff.; O. Cullmann, 'The Significance of the Qumran Texts for Research into the Beginnings of Christianity', *JBL* 74, 1955, pp. 213 ff. (these two articles are reprinted in *The Scrolls and the New Testament*, ed. K. Stendahl, 1958, pp. 129 ff. and 18 ff.); A. Metzinger, O.S.B., 'Die Handschriftenfunde am Toten Meer und das NT', *Biblica* 36, 1955. More comprehensive is H. Braun, *Spätjüdisch-häretischer und frühchristlicher Radikalismus: Jesus von Nazareth und die essenische Qumransekte* (Beiträge zur historischen Theologie 24), 2 vols., 1957. A 'Bibliographie zu den Handschriften vom Toten Meer' is given by C. Burchard in *BZAW* 76, 1957.

For our question, besides the already known Damascus fragment, the most important of the new texts published to date is the *Commentary on Habakkuk*.[1] By means of allegorical exposition it relates the words of the prophets to the situation of the sect in such a detailed way that it can actually be used as a source of information about the external history and the theology of this remarkable group. In this commentary the man who is probably the founder of the sect, and to whom the highest veneration is offered, is called 'Teacher of Righteousness', מוֹרֶה צֶדֶק, a title of honour which is bestowed upon Elijah in later Jewish literature.[2] The expression

[1] The text has been published by Millar Burrows, J. C. Trever, and W. H. Brownlee, *The Dead Sea Scrolls of St Mark's Monastery* I, *The Isaiah Manuscript and the Habakkuk Commentary*, 1950. See also especially K. Elliger's thorough monograph with commentary and translation, *Studien zum Habakuk-Kommentar*, 1953 (with a supplement containing the text in Hebrew).

[2] L. Ginzberg, *Eine unbekannte jüdische Sekte*, 1922, pp. 303 ff., especially p. 316.

could be translated equally well by 'Teacher of Truth' or 'the true Teacher'.[1] According to the *Habakkuk Commentary*, God has revealed to him all the secrets of the words of his servants, the prophets.[2] He is appointed to proclaim these words.[3] His whole proclamation points to the end.[4] With regard to the end, he is especially inspired to interpret correctly the prophecies of the prophets. His adversary is 'the Man of the Lie', the 'Prophet of Falsehood'.[5] In correspondence with the destiny of the prophets, the 'Teacher' also must suffer injustice.[6] It is not certain, however, whether he suffered martyrdom after his condemnation.[7]

If the identity of the Teacher-Prophet who has already appeared with the one still expected could be assumed with certainty,[8] we would have a parallel to the early Christian hope of the return of Christ, since the return of a recently dead prophet would also be expected in this Commentary. But this is quite uncertain. The *Manual of Discipline* 9.11, moreover, distinguishes between the coming of the prophet and the coming of the two Messiahs of Aaron and Israel.[9]

Probably *The Testaments of the Twelve Patriarchs*, which have always been difficult to place in their setting, also originate in the same milieu

[1] See K. Elliger, *op. cit.*, p. 245 (following J. L. Teicher). According to T. H. Gaster, *The Scriptures of the Dead Sea Sect*, 1957, p. 6, it does not indicate a historical person at all, but an office (as *m^e baqqēr*).

[2] *Hab. Com.* VII, 5: II, 9.

[3] *Hab. Com.* II, 8.

[4] *Hab. Com.* II, 10; VII, 1 f.

[5] *Hab. Com.* II, 1 f.; X, 9. On the connection with the 'True Prophet' and the 'Prophet of Falsehood' of the Pseudo-Clementine writings, see O. Cullmann, 'Die neuentdeckten Qumrantexte und das Judenchristentum der Pseudoklementinen', *Neutestamentliche Studien für Rudolf Bultmann* (BZNW 21), 1954, pp. 39 f.

[6] *Hab. Com.* IX, 1 ff.

[7] The statements of the *Habakkuk Commentary* do not allow us to answer this question. It is also not certain whether the 'Teacher' is still alive at the time of the writing of the commentary. See K. Elliger, *op. cit.*, pp. 202 ff., 264 ff. It is just in this regard that the hymns must be considered (German ed., H. Bardtke in *TLZ* 81, 1956, pp. 149 ff., 589 ff.; ET of the hymns, T. M. Gaster, *The Scriptures of the Dead Sea Sect*, 1957, pp. 131 ff.), but these seem to offer as little support to the hypothesis of an execution as do the fragments not yet published.

[8] Opinions still differ radically on this point. Already S. Schechter, *op. cit.*, p. xii, maintained against Staerk that this identity exists in the *Damascus Document*. Staerk, *op. cit.*, p. 5, believed that there are two different teachers, the founder of the community, and another who is still expected. The question has been considered again in connection with the new discoveries. With the exception of A. Dupont-Sommer, *Nouveaux aperçus*, pp. 81 f., most scholars today seem to reject the thesis which postulates an identity.

[9] See p. 23 n. 3, and p. 86 below.

as that of this sect.[1] If so, it is noteworthy that in the *Testament of Levi* the expected Messiah himself, the 'Renewer of the Law' (*Test. Levi 16*), is called the 'Prophet of the Highest' (8.15).

It seems to me justified, simply because of its temporal proximity to early Christianity, to give greater consideration to the belief of this sect of the New Covenant in the coming (perhaps the coming again) of the Prophet. Moreover, the consideration is factually justified because attributes of the Messiah and especially of the High Priest[2] are united in the Prophet. In any case these circumstances help us to understand that when the question of the identity of John the Baptist and Jesus arose, the theological category of '*the* Prophet' naturally suggested itself to the people.

Everywhere in Judaism at this period the hope of the end was united with the expectation of the revival of prophecy—a prophecy which assumes final form and is concentrated in the one true Prophet who makes an end of all false prophecy.[3]

Summarizing all the different versions of the same faith, we may describe the function of the Prophet as follows: He preaches, reveals the final mysteries, and above all restores revelation as God had given it in the law of Moses. But he does not simply preach as did the earlier prophets; his proclamation announces the end of this age. His call to repentance is God's very last offer. Thus his coming and his preaching as such constitute an eschatological act which is a part of the drama of the end. Although by its very nature the principal function of the Prophet is to reveal the will of God, his function is also to establish the tribes of Israel (Ecclus. 48.10). The task of the Elijah *redivivus* is to overcome the world powers and to redeem Israel.[4] He has to battle with the Antichrist.[5] He shares the fate of suffering with the ancient prophets.[6] The same conclusion can also be drawn from Mark 9.13 (paralleled by Matt. 17.12): 'They did to him whatever they pleased, as it is written of him.'[7]

[1] See especially A. Dupont-Sommer, 'Le Testament de Lévi (XVII–XVIII) et la secte juive de l'Alliance', *Semitica* 4, 1952, pp. 33 ff., and *Nouveaux aperçus*, pp. 63 ff.

[2] See p. 86 below.

[3] Taxo, in the *Assumption of Moses* 9.1 ff., is probably also a figure related to this prophet of the end time. S. Mowinckel, in an interesting essay, *Vetus Testamentum*, Suppl. I, 1953, pp. 88 ff., associates him with the *m^eḥōqēq* of the *Damascus Document*.

[4] See Strack-Billerbeck IV, pp. 782 ff.; J. Jeremias, ''Ηλ(ε)ίας' *TWNT* II, p. 933.

[5] Apocalypse of Elijah (ed. Steindorff), p. 169.

[6] See H. J. Schoeps, *Aus frühchristlicher Zeit*, 1950, pp. 126 ff. ('Die jüdischen Prophetenmorde').

[7] See J. Jeremias, *TWNT* II, p. 944.

Originally the eschatological Prophet is not merely a forerunner of the Messiah; faith in the returning Prophet is sufficient in itself, and to a certain extent runs parallel to faith in the Messiah. The Messiah actually requires no forerunner, since he himself also fulfils the role of the Prophet of the end time. Thus it can happen that Prophet and Messiah are united in the same person.[1] It is possible that the two concepts may ultimately be traced back to a common source.[2] Nevertheless, we do well to differentiate between the 'prophetic' and 'messianic' lines. The eschatological Prophet of Jewish expectation originally prepares the way for Yahweh himself, since he appears at the end of days. Later the connection of the idea of the returning Prophet with that of the Messiah not only developed so that this Prophet is at the same time the Messiah, but also so that the returning Elijah is only the forerunner of the Messiah, and thus no longer the direct forerunner of God.[3] We must maintain a clear distinction between the concept of the Prophet who is the forerunner of God and the concept of the Prophet who is the forerunner of the Messiah. We find both of them in the New Testament and must therefore evaluate them differently.

2. *The Eschatological Prophet in the New Testament*

A. *John the Baptist*

In the Gospels not only Jesus but, before him and even more prominently, John the Baptist is designated 'the Prophet'. We have seen that by this title John is above all placed in the line of the Old Testament prophets. Thus Luke 3.2 says in a manner quite analogous to the introductory formulas of the Old Testament prophetic books: 'The word of God came to John.' On the other hand, we have seen

[1] As New Testament evidence for the popular connection of the eschatological Prophet with the Messiah H. Riesenfeld, 'Jesus als Prophet', *Spiritus et Veritas*, 1953, pp. 135 ff., cites John 6.14 f., Mark 13.22 par., and the mocking before the crucifixion in which the Messiah crowned with thorns is told to 'prophesy' (προφητεύειν).

[2] The so-called Uppsala School (Engnell) would make the 'idea of kingship' the common denominator. A Bentzen, *King and Messiah*, pp. 47 ff., would make it the idea of the Son of Man or Original Man.

[3] See Strack-Billerbeck, IV, pp. 784 ff.; J. Jeremias, *TWNT* II, p. 933 n. 20. In Justin Martyr, *Dialogue with Trypho* 8.4 and 49.1, he is actually commissioned to anoint the Messiah. Also the passage in the Qumran *Manual of Discipline* 9.11 expressly distinguishes the prophet's coming and the coming of the two Messiahs (of Aaron and Israel). See K. G. Kuhn, 'The Two Messiahs of Aaron and Israel', *The Scrolls and the New Testament*, p. 63.

that, because of the expiration of the prophetic gift, the 'coming of the word' to the Baptist marks him as the one who introduces the end time in which this gift is to appear again.

Beyond the general classification of John as a prophet, we now have further to investigate to what extent he is identified with the peculiarly eschatological figure of the returning Prophet. This identification took place in a double way: on the one hand, he is identified as the returning Elijah in the later sense of a forerunner of the Messiah; on the other hand, he is identified as the returning Elijah in the original sense of a forerunner of God himself.

The later Jewish interpretation is probably present in Matt. 11.7 ff., where Jesus himself speaks of John as the returned Elijah: 'What did you go out into the wilderness to behold? A reed shaken by the wind? Why then did you go out? To see a man clothed in soft raiment? Behold, those who wear soft raiment are in kings' houses. Why then did you go out? To see a prophet? Yes, I tell you, and more than a prophet . . . For all the prophets and the law prophesied until John; and if you are willing to accept it,[1] he is Elijah who is to come.' When Jesus says that John is more than a prophet, this must mean that he is *the* Prophet who is to come at the end of time. It is not entirely clear in this passage whether John fulfils this prophetic role as a forerunner of the Messiah or as a forerunner of God himself. According to the context in which Matthew has placed these words (which includes also the saying in v. 11 about the 'least' who is greater in the kingdom of heaven, whereby Jesus publicly places himself above the Baptist),[2] one must certainly say that in any case the evangelist interpreted the words to mean that the Baptist is the forerunner of the Messiah. This interpretation is the only possible one if Jesus considered himself the Messiah.

Matt. 17.10 ff. (parallel, Mark 9.11 ff.) yields the same conclusion: 'And the disciples asked him, "Then why do the scribes say that first Elijah must come?" He replied, "Elijah does come, and he is to restore all things; but I tell you that Elijah has already come, and they did not know him, but did to him whatsoever they pleased. So also the Son of Man will suffer at their hands."' Jesus here clearly identifies the Baptist as the returned Elijah. If the connection of Jesus with the Son of Man goes back to Jesus himself, John the re-

[1] On the condition implied in εἰ θέλετε δέξασθαι, see p. 36 below.

[2] The usual translation, 'the least in the kingdom of heaven' is certainly not correct. The words ἐν τῇ βασιλείᾳ τῶν οὐρανῶν do not belong with ὁ μικρότερος See p. 32 below.

turned Elijah in this passage is the forerunner of Jesus the Son of Man. In addition, these words of Jesus, corresponding to the Jewish expectation, tell us that the eschatological Prophet fulfils also the destiny of all earlier prophets: he is persecuted.[1] His role thus consists not only in preaching repentance but also in suffering, and from here a line leads to the Suffering Servant of God, a title to which we shall devote a special chapter. We have already mentioned that the different messianic or Christological concepts have mutually influenced each other.[2]

Further we find a whole series of New Testament passages in which John the Baptist is seen as the eschatological Prophet in the sense of the forerunner of God himself. We must consider in this context first of all Proto-Luke, which very probably contains independent traditions about John originating in the circles of his followers. We read in Zechariah's hymn of praise in Luke 1.76 that the Baptist will be called 'the prophet of the Most High', for he will 'go before the Lord to prepare his ways'. 'Lord' in this passage undoubtedly refers to Yahweh. The announcement of the angel in 1.17 indicates the same conception of the coming prophet: 'and he will go before him in the spirit and power of Elijah, to turn the hearts of the fathers to the children and the disobedient to the wisdom of the just, to make ready for the Lord a people prepared'. One must of course reckon here with the possibility that the evangelist, as in the case of other Old Testament citations, applied the phrase 'for the Lord' to Jesus.[3]

Thus it is certain that the Synoptic Gospels consider John the Baptist to be the Prophet of the end time—in some passages as the forerunner of God; in others as the forerunner of the Messiah.

We may ask whether the Baptist himself was conscious of being the eschatological Prophet. The question cannot be unequivocally answered from the Synoptics, since John nowhere gives an explanation of his own person. It is always others who ascribe the role of the Prophet to him. But it may be said at least that the Baptist did not think of himself as the Prophet of the end time in the sense of one preparing the way for God. That is evident from the certainly

[1] See p. 22 above.

[2] If the thesis advocated by Scandinavian scholars is correct (see p. 23 n. 2 above), we would have to assume that the different concepts were originally united in a single concept, became separated, but at the same time tended toward a new fusion.

[3] Cf. Ph. Vielhauer, 'Das Benedictus des Zacharias', *ZTK* 49, 1952, pp. 255 ff.

genuine opening verses of Matt. 11, in which the Baptist sends his disciples to ask Jesus whether he is the one who is to come, or whether they should look for another. The way in which the question is formulated shows in any case that the Baptist expects still another sent from God who should come after himself. This is clear also from John's sermons when he baptized. He speaks of the 'mightier one' (ἰσχυρότερος) who will come after him and especially emphasizes the paradox that he who comes later, who is subordinate to or the servant of the one who comes before, is in this case endowed with the greater divine power.[1] We may conclude from this that in any case John did not consider himself the Prophet in the sense of the forerunner of God himself.

On the other hand, in view of Matt. 11.3, it is not certain whether John thought of himself as the eschatological prophet in the sense of the forerunner of the Messiah. If he meant that 'he who is to come' (ὁ ἐρχόμενος) and the 'mightier one' is the Messiah, the question could be answered affirmatively. But we must allow for the possibility that John expected the coming one to bear the characteristics of the Prophet of the end—in fact that by the ἐρχόμενος he referred to that Prophet himself.[2] In this case, the Baptist would have ascribed to himself the modest role of *a* prophet, but not that of the final Prophet. We have seen that even if this were so, he would still be the one who introduced the end, since it was he who realized for the first time after a long interruption the revival of prophecy which had been predicted for the future. If he thought of himself only as *a* prophet, then his disciples and Jesus were the first to recognize him (after his death) as the final Prophet of the end time.

However that may be, it is certain that according to the Synoptic tradition the first Christians and even Jesus regarded the Baptist as *the* Prophet who was the forerunner of the Messiah. The disciples of the Baptist, on the other hand, considered him the final Prophet who prepared the way for God himself. The Pseudo-Clementine writings confirm the existence of the latter belief. We read here[3] that the later sect of John's disciples believed the Baptist to be the Messiah. According to Luke 3.15 this is a view already considered during his lifetime. But this sect evidently understood 'Messiah' to mean the same as 'eschatological Prophet'. According to the original conviction of the Baptist's disciples, then, John is actually

[1] See O. Cullmann, 'ὁ ὀπίσω μου ἐρχόμενος', *The Early Church*, 1956, pp. 177 ff.

[2] Thus J. Héring, *Le royaume de Dieu et sa venue*, 1937, p. 71.

[3] *Recogn.* I, 60.

the Prophet of the end time, whose function is sufficient in itself and requires no Messiah to come after him, since he himself prepares the way for God to establish his kingdom.

Very probably this sect of the Baptist's disciples eventually merged with another sect of Jewish origin, the Mandaeans, whose religious organization still exists today, and in whose sacred writings Jesus appears as an impostor, a 'false Messiah', while John appears as 'the Prophet' in the absolute sense.[1] In the account of the birth of John in Mandaean literature, we read several times: 'John will take the Jordan and he will be called Prophet in Jerusalem.'[2]

We summarize our findings to this point. Both from the Synoptic Gospels and from Mandaean texts we may say with certainty: (1) After his death, his own disciples considered the Baptist to be *the* Prophet (above all the returned Elijah), and indeed, in the sense

[1] According to M. Lidzbarski and R. Bultmann, 'Die Bedeutung der neuerschlossenen mandäischen und manichäischen Quellen für das Verständnis des Johannes-Evangeliums', *ZNW* 24, 1925, pp. 100 f., the Mandaean texts go back to the pre-Christian era. This position was shaken by E. Peterson, 'Bemerkungen zur mandäischen Literatur', *ZNW* 25, 1926, pp. 216 ff.; 'Urchristentum und Mandäismus', *ZNW* 27, 1928, pp. 1 ff.; 'Der gegenwärtige Stand der Mandäerfrage', *TB* 7, 1928, col. 12; and especially by H. Lietzmann, *Ein Beitrag zur Mandäerfrage* (SB Preuss. Ak. d. Wiss., Phil.-Hist. Kl.), 1930. Also the use of the Mandaean texts for the exegesis of the New Testament fell into discredit, because they had become for a time really a matter of 'fashion' among New Testament scholars. Such fashions often play a far too important role in the history of theology and also in New Testament research. During the years 1925–1930 one could hardly pick up a book or an article in which the Mandaeans were not quoted at least once. M. Goguel rightly spoke at that time of a 'Mandaean fever' which had gripped New Testament scholars (*Jean-Baptiste*, 1928, p. 113). As is always the case with fashions, however, this one too disappeared, and for fear of appearing 'out of date', scholars then completely ignored the Mandaeans. But this complete silence is just as unjustified as indiscriminate quotation. Only recently has the study of the Mandaeans begun again. See especially H. Schlier, *TR*, N.F. 5, 1933, pp. 1 ff.; H. Puech, 'Le Mandéisme—Le Manichéisme', *L'histoire générale des religions* III, 1945, pp. 67 ff. W. Baumgartner, at the International Congress of Comparative Religions in Amsterdam, 1950, reported on this new work, showing that the pre-Christian origin of the Mandaeans may be considered as proven, and that therefore the use of the Mandaean texts for the explanation of the New Testament is quite legitimate. See Baumgartner, 'Der heutige Stand der Mandäerfrage', *TZ* 6, 1950, pp. 401 ff. We may add that the Qumran texts give evidence of a pre-Christian Jewish Gnosticism (see p. 39 n. 2 below). The relationship between the Mandaeans and Qumran should also be investigated in the light of the new texts. F. M. Braun, 'Le Mandéisme et la secte essénienne de Qumran', *L'Ancien Testament et l'Orient*, Louvain 1957, pp. 193 ff., makes a first attempt in this direction. He believes that the Mandaeans emerged from the Essenes.

[2] See M. Lidzbarski, *Johannesbuch der Mandäer*, 1915, p. 78.

of a direct forerunner of God, so that the role of another Messiah becomes superfluous. (2) The disciples of Jesus and even Jesus himself also considered the Baptist to be *the* Prophet, but in the sense of a forerunner of the Messiah. (3) It is impossible that the Baptist considered himself the Prophet in the first sense. On the other hand, it is possible—but only possible—that he considered himself the Prophet in the sense of a forerunner of the Messiah.

We must now investigate the attitude of the Fourth Gospel in this connection. According to it, the Baptist himself expressly refuses the honour of being considered *the* Prophet, even in the second sense. He does not want to be regarded as the eschatological Prophet; he rejects every comparison with Elijah, and is content to be a simple 'voice' (φωνή) crying in the wilderness like the prophet of old. In other words, he wants to be only *a* prophet like the Old Testament prophets.[1] This is expressed as clearly as possible in John 1.21. The Jews ask John, 'Are you Elijah?' He answers, 'No'. John thus rejects for himself the title which Jesus gives him in the Synoptics.

It can be demonstrated that the whole of the Fourth Gospel, and especially the prologue, carries on a polemic not against the Baptist himself, but against the sect of the Baptist, which after his death considered him to be the final Prophet, the forerunner of God, and thus bestowed upon John a role which excluded the coming of the Messiah after him. It can be shown[2] that the whole prologue is directed against those who wish to set the Baptist in opposition to Jesus; that is, against the predecessors of the Mandaeans. For this reason the prologue emphasizes that John was not himself the light. It combats at the same time one of the main arguments of the adherents of this sect of the Baptist, the chronological argument that John came before Jesus and is therefore greater than he. The prologue quotes a saying of the Baptist himself which contains the answer to this objection: 'He who comes after me ranks before me, for he was before me' (John 1.15). John alludes here to the preexistence of Christ.[3]

Other parts of the Gospel also exhibit this polemic tendency against the sect of John's disciples (not against John himself). We find, for example, in John 1.20 the strikingly strong emphasis on the fact that John himself rejected the title 'Christ': 'He confessed, he

[1] The writer of the Gospel thinks also of the contrast between this 'voice' and the 'Word' of the prologue.

[2] See W. Baldensperger, *Der Prolog des Johannesevangeliums*, 1898.

[3] See O. Cullmann, 'ὁ ὀπίσω μου ἐρχόμενος', *op. cit.*

did not deny, but confessed' (ὡμολόγησεν καὶ οὐκ ἠρνήσατο, καὶ ὡμολόγησεν). This could have meaning only if there were those who maintained that John was the Christ. We have already shown that there were such people. In Luke 3.15 they debate whether John is the Christ. And we saw further in the Pseudo-Clementine writings that the disciples of John affirmed that he was the Christ. The disciples of John must have been especially widespread in the area where the Gospel of John was written. For this reason the Fourth Evangelist is the only one who reports certain sayings in which the Baptist himself expresses his subordination to Christ. In John 3.28 the Baptist says, 'You yourselves bear me witness, that I said, I am not the Christ.' In 3.31 he designates Jesus as the one who comes from above, himself as one who comes from the earth: 'He who comes from above is above all; he who is of the earth belongs to the earth and of the earth he speaks.' The Baptist thus rejects once again every claim to be God's eschatological emissary.

The Fourth Gospel, therefore, undoubtedly has a tendency strongly to underline the fact that John the Baptist is not *the* Prophet. We understand this tendency even better when we note that this same Gospel emphasizes that *the* Prophet is Jesus. In the Johannine Jesus all the functions of all those sent from God are united. We have seen that in this Gospel, the Baptist refuses not only to be considered the Messiah; but even to be considered the eschatological Prophet, the returning Elijah. This representation of him could very well correspond to the facts of the case. At any rate, it does not contradict the view of the Synoptics. We saw that according to the first three Gospels the Baptist certainly did not consider himself the forerunner of God himself. And concerning the application of the designation 'Prophet' in the sense of a forerunner of the Messiah, we recall that we can derive nothing certain from the Synoptics. Perhaps this uncertainty is removed in a way corresponding to the real situation by the Gospel of John, in which the Baptist simply refused the title 'the Prophet'.

We shall see that there was a debate at the beginning of the second century between the disciples of John and the Jewish Christians.[1] Not the title 'Christ', but the title 'Prophet' stood at the centre of this controversy. The Jewish Christians designated Jesus 'the true Prophet', and went so far as to picture John the Baptist as a representative of false prophecy. The subject of the first Christological discussions thus took the form not so much of Christology as of

[1] See pp. 38 ff. below.

'Prophetology', and the battle was fought out not between Jews and Christians, but between the disciples of the Baptist and Christians. This shows the importance of the concept Prophet.

B. *Jesus*

We come now to the texts in which the title 'the Prophet' is applied to Jesus. First we must make a preliminary remark. We have already mentioned that one must distinguish between the passages in which Jesus is designated simply *a* prophet like many others who had arisen in the past, and the passages in which he is considered *the* Prophet—the one eschatological Prophet. Only this second category directly concerns the Christological problem as we have defined it—the question of the uniqueness of Jesus. The functions which Jesus has in common with other men are only indirectly connected with the Christological problem so understood. However, since the conception of the one eschatological Prophet is very closely connected with the general Israelitic prophetic concept, we shall nevertheless consider briefly also the first category of texts. What is true for John the Baptist in this respect is also true of Jesus: the very fact that a prophet appeared again after the long interruption of prophecy was considered in itself a sign that the end time was breaking in. The appearance of Jesus, of course, may have caused less of a sensation in this respect after the appearance of John as a prophet shortly before him.

Nevertheless, we read in Luke 7.16 at the end of the account of the raising of the young man of Nain: 'Fear seized them all; and they glorified God, saying, "A great prophet has arisen among us."' In the Greek there is no article before the noun προφήτης, and it is even accompanied by an adjective. This indicates that the remark of the crowd does not point to *the* eschatological Prophet; that prophet does not need the description 'great'. Jesus is simply placed in the prophetic category, a category in which also others have belonged. Still, a miracle like the one reported in this passage does show that the Spirit of God is now at work again in an especially powerful way, just as he was earlier at work in the prophets. The judgment of the crowd, of course, does not directly express the eschatological significance of this fact; Jesus is not designated *the* Prophet of the end time.[1]

[1] It would be a different matter if ἠγέρθη were to be translated more literally as 'resurrected'. Then we would be dealing with the conception of the eschatological return of an ancient prophet. But this translation is undoubtedly false here.

In Matt. 21.46 the chief priests and the Pharisees would have arrested Jesus had they not feared the multitudes 'because they held him to be a prophet'. Again no mention is made of *the* eschatological Prophet. In Mark 6.4 Jesus calls himself only *a* prophet when he says after his failure in Nazareth, 'A prophet is not without honour, except in his own country, and among his own kin, and in his own house.' Jesus expresses a similar thought in his lamentation over Jerusalem who 'kills the prophets' (Matt. 23.37). This passage also confirms our observation that suffering is a characteristic of the destiny and indeed of the eschatological function of the prophets in general.[1]

Much more important are the passages in the New Testament in which Jesus is designated *the* Prophet, the one expected at the end of time, the returned Prophet.

We begin with Mark 6.14 ff. 'Some said, "John the baptizer has been raised from the dead; that is why these powers are at work in him." But others said, "It is Elijah." And others said, "It is a prophet like one of the prophets of old." But when Herod heard of it he said, "John, whom I beheaded, has been raised."'

This passage gives three statements by which the people and Herod attempted to answer the question who Jesus is. They are all the more valuable to us because they were expressed during the lifetime of Jesus himself. We find here one of the *oldest* explanations of the puzzle of Jesus' person and work. It is noteworthy that the primary Christological titles for Jesus (Messiah or Christ, and Son of Man) do not appear among them. The first of these three opinions (and that of Herod also) is that Jesus is *John the Baptist* risen from the dead. This is a Christological explanation which deserves more attention than it usually receives, first historically because of its early date; secondly, because of the remarkable presuppositions it implies. The second opinion is that Jesus is *Elijah*. The third, according to most manuscripts, is that 'he is a prophet like one of the prophets'; according to the Western text, that 'he is one of the prophets'.

We begin with a closer investigation of the first of these Christological statements: Jesus is John the Baptist risen from the dead. One might think at first that this very peculiar conception is no more surprising than the second, that Jesus is Elijah. But there is a great difference between them, for Elijah belonged with the ancient prophets to the distant past, and it is therefore relatively easy to

[1] See p. 22 above.

explain the belief in his return. But according to the Gospel of Luke, John the Baptist was only a few months older than Jesus. The belief that Jesus is the risen Baptist can be explained only on the basis of several presuppositions. First, in so far as their relationship is concerned, the activity of Jesus and of the Baptist must be both chronologically and spatially separated. Those who held Jesus to be the risen Baptist could not have seen the two of them working together. So long as John was baptizing and preaching, therefore, at least a part of the people must not have noticed Jesus. This agrees also with what the Synoptics tell us about the date of Jesus' beginning his public activity: he began it for the first time when the Baptist was sent to prison. Between the time of his baptism and John's imprisonment Jesus seems to have worked in the shadow of the Baptist. Perhaps he appeared at first more or less as a disciple of the Baptist.

In agreement with Franz Dibelius [1] and the older Church Fathers,[2] and in grammatical accordance with the text itself, I translate Matt. 11.11: 'He who is least (i.e., Jesus as a disciple of John) is greater than he (i.e., John) in the kingdom of heaven.' [3]

According to the Gospel of John, of course, there was a period during which Jesus and John worked simultaneously but independently. Whatever the nature of this situation may have been according to the Fourth Gospel, the duration of this period cannot have been long, and in any case Jesus' activity cannot have been very closely observed during it. This is proved precisely by the opinion of the people recorded in the passage we are considering, according to which Jesus is none other than the risen Baptist. The people have an impression of succession, not of contemporaneousness, regarding the chronological relationship between John and Jesus.

We must assume that the belief of the people in Jesus as the risen John was shared only by those who lived neither in the immediate company of John nor that of Jesus; otherwise they would have had the opportunity of seeing the two together at least once—when John baptized Jesus. Or at least they would have heard of this event. Had the people seen or heard of this meeting of the two, they could not possibly have considered Jesus to be John risen from the dead.

[1] F. Dibelius, 'Zwei Worte Jesu', *ZNW* 11, 1910, pp. 190 ff.

[2] In his *Commentary on Matthew* (*PL* 26, 74A), Jerome writes: 'Multi de Salvatore hoc intelligi volunt, quod qui minor est tempore, maior sit dignitate.' This exegesis is also given by Origen (*PG* 17, 293B), Hilary (*PL* 9, 981A), and Chrysostom (*PG* 57, 422).

[3] See O. Cullmann, 'ὁ ὀπίσω μου ἐρχόμενος'; *The Early Church*, p. 180.

Mark 6.14 ff. was the occasion of an observation of Origen which hardly has a historical foundation, but rests rather on a speculative reflection. He writes that there must have been a physical resemblance between Jesus and the Baptist.[1] This does not necessarily follow from the text, but we can at least say that their *behaviour* apparently displayed common features.[2] This assumption is not contradicted by Matt. 11.18, in which the people say that John came as an ascetic (μήτε ἐσθίων, μήτε πίνων), but that Jesus is a 'glutton and drunkard'. On the contrary, the distinction in regard to their way of life shows that the people compared them because they resembled each other in regard to their public activity.

The belief that Jesus is the risen John presupposes also a particular popular conception of resurrection which must have been common among the people at the time of Jesus. According to the interpretation of Paul in I Cor. 15.35 ff., the resurrection at the end of time will be a resurrection of a spiritual body (σῶμα πνευματικόν), not of a physical, earthly body. The popular view we are considering conceives of the resurrection in a completely different way: that of the physical body, not of a spiritual one. The resurrection does not mean Paul's conception of a transformation of the physical body into a spiritual one, but simply the continued life of the same physical body.

Another question implicitly raised by Mark 6.14 ff. is the problem of resurrection and reincarnation. The resurrection cannot mean here the reincarnation of the soul in a new body, as if the soul of the Baptist had passed over into another physical body, the body of Jesus. This explanation is ruled out by the verb ἐγήγερται, which always presupposes an awakening from the sleep of death, a revival.[3] The belief in the resurrection of John is distinguished from the later belief in the resurrection of Jesus by the fact that John was not raised *to be with God*. In John's case, not ἀνάστασις but only ἔγερσις is applicable. Above all, we cannot think in this context of John's being taken up to heaven after his death.

The belief of the people that Jesus is the risen John, then, has to do with an actual miraculous return of John in the body which he had at the time of his death. This not only presupposes that those who shared this belief had never seen John and Jesus together, but that they had never even seen or known of Jesus alone before his public appearance. They obviously had to suppose that he had appeared

[1] Origen, *In Joan.* VI, 30 (*PG* 14, 285).

[2] Against E. Lohmeyer, *Das Evangelium des Markus* (Meyer 1.2), 1937, p. 116 n. 2, one should probably conclude from this that John also worked miracles.

[3] For the meaning of ἐγείρειν and its distinction from ἀνίστασθαι, see E. Lichtenstein, 'Die älteste christliche Glaubensformel', *ZKG* 63, 1950, pp. 26 ff.

suddenly on earth, probably immediately or at least very soon after the death of the Baptist. Nothing had essentially changed in John, therefore, except his name; his earthly body simply continued to live by the name Jesus. Strack-Billerbeck record examples of such a Jewish faith in the miraculous return of a prophet with the same body he had at the moment of his death.[1]

We can draw still another conclusion from this opinion of the people. The contemporaries of Jesus were apparently interested only in his public activity; his earlier life presented no problem for them. We may conclude that his earlier life (about which the Gospels report nothing) aroused their curiosity so little because they supposed that Jesus' earlier life was that of the Baptist.

Since, as we have seen, John the Baptist was considered to be a prophet, his appearance consequently being regarded as an eschatological revival of ancient prophecy, the identification of Jesus with John means in the final analysis the identification of Jesus as the eschatological Prophet. The particular significance of Jesus' being identified with John is that the prophet appearing as Jesus is not a prophet from the remote past who had now come again to earth, but a prophet who had died in the immediate past, already in the end time, and immediately or very soon thereafter risen again.

The second opinion about Jesus which was widespread among the people is that he is *Elijah* (Mark 6.15). We need not consider this point in detail, since it also deals basically with the belief in the eschatological return of the Prophet who prepares the way for Yahweh.

Concerning the third opinion of the people (Mark 6.15b), there are two different ways of reading the text. We must first of all speak of this problem of textual criticism. Most manuscripts read, 'a prophet like one of the prophets' (προφήτης ὡς εἷς τῶν προφητῶν). According to this reading of the text, this opinion of the people would be different from the first two. It would make only the general assertion that ancient prophecy is again alive. This interpretation is quite possible. Nevertheless, it seems to me that, contrary to the usual assumption, the reading of the Western text (represented by D and a few other witnesses) possibly offers the better text in this case. Here the passage reads, 'he is one of the prophets' (εἷς τῶν προφητῶν). The third group of the people does not compare but directly identifies Jesus with one of the ancient prophets. In other

[1] See Strack-Billerbeck I, p. 679.

words, according to the Western text, the third opinion corresponds to the first two; indeed, it is basically the same. We would have here, then, simply a third variation of the same popular belief. In each case it concerns the eschatological Prophet. In the first case he is designated the returning Baptist; in the second, the returning Elijah; in the third, the name of the returning prophet is withheld, since, as we have seen, the actual name changes: at one time it is Elijah who returns, at another Moses, or Enoch, or even Jeremiah.

The parallel text in Luke 9.8 indicates that Luke read this report in the form we have it in the manuscript D of Mark 6.15.[1] It is conceivable that a copyist subsequently inserted the words προφήτης ὡς into Mark's text, and in this way gave the third opinion the meaning that Jesus is *like* one of the ancient prophets. Apparently the copyist did not know of the belief in the return of *the* Prophet which had formerly been widespread. We shall see that the Christological interpretation of Jesus as the Prophet of the end time disappeared very early from the Church's theology. The copyist wanted to clarify a text which was not understandable to him, but he actually robbed it of its original meaning. Thus the reading in D would be the *lectio difficilior*, and therefore the preferable one.

Mark 8.28 substantiates the above conclusion. In an entirely different context, this passage gives precisely the same three Christological explanations as popular opinions about Jesus. It says also that some see in Jesus John the Baptist; others, Elijah; others, 'one of the prophets' (εἷς τῶν προφητῶν).

Again in Matt. 21.10 f., on the occasion of Jesus' entry into Jerusalem, the multitude expressed the same opinion found in Mark 6.14 ff. and 8.28: 'This is the prophet (ὁ προφήτης) Jesus from Nazareth of Galilee.' In the context of the homage offered Jesus shortly before as the 'Son of David', it is probable that *the* Prophet of the end time is meant here, although the other interpretation, that he is only *a* prophet, cannot be excluded.

The texts we have cited from the Synoptic Gospels show therefore that during his lifetime a part of the people considered Jesus to be the Prophet expected at the end of time. This is all the more significant in view of the fact that the Synoptic writers themselves did not make use of this title to express their own faith in Jesus. They themselves did not consider Jesus as *the* Prophet, the returned Elijah. They repeat this interpretation only as the opinion of others. For this reason, their report of this conviction which was widespread among a part of the people merits that much greater confidence.

[1] Luke 9.8: προφήτης τις τῶν ἀρχαίων ἀνέστη.

We might suppose that this opinion of the people was particularly widespread in Galilee—especially when we recall that the Samaritans had a very strong hope of a return of the Prophet. This conclusion would be relevant to the discussion of the problem of the relationship between Galilee and Jerusalem raised by E. Lohmeyer in his *Galiläa und Jerusalem*. We have already suggested that the concept of the 'eschatological Teacher', which Lohmeyer claims for Galilean Christology, is identical with that of the Prophet.

Now we ask whether Jesus thought of himself as the eschatological Prophet who should come at the end of time. We remember that he ascribed this title and its corresponding function to John the Baptist: 'If you are willing to accept it, he is Elijah who is to come' (Matt. 11.14). The condition 'if you are willing to accept it' probably means only that it does not make any difference whether the name of the returning prophet is Elijah or that of one of the other ancient prophets. The essential thing for Jesus is that in John the eschatological Prophet 'has already come' and that 'they did to him whatever they pleased' (Matt. 17.12; Mark 9.13). We can therefore conclude with certainty that according to the Synoptics Jesus did not think of himself as *the* Prophet. The Synoptic tradition also indicates that his disciples did not believe him to be this Prophet. In the texts we have mentioned, it is never the disciples but always a section of the people who advocate this opinion. The disciples remembered only too well that Jesus designated not himself but the Baptist as the Prophet. The Gospel of John confirms the result of our investigation of the Synoptics. Here again only the crowd applies the title 'the Prophet' to Jesus. The people who have experienced the miraculous feeding of the 5000 say, 'This is indeed the prophet who is to come into the world!' (John 6.14). It is clear that they do not mean an ordinary prophet who could be placed on the same level with the other Jewish prophets, but *the* particular Prophet who should come into the world at the end of time: ὁ ἐρχόμενος εἰς τὸν κόσμον. It is interesting to note that ὁ ἐρχόμενος is exactly the same expression used in the already mentioned question of the Baptist to Jesus: 'Are you the ἐρχόμενος?' (Matt. 11.3). This appears to confirm our previous conjecture that this expression (הַבָּא in Hebrew) was a *terminus technicus* to designate the eschatological Prophet. Once again, it is the people in this passage who make the Christological—or more accurately, 'Prophetological'—confession.

We conclude that according to all four of the Gospels a section of the people expressed their faith in Jesus by the title 'the Prophet' and by the thoughts which were connected with it in the Jewish eschatological hope. But Jesus himself did not identify himself in this way. We should repeat here, however, that the prediction of his own return is at least foreshadowed in the conception of the return of the Prophet.[1]

The Synoptic writers did not express their personal faith in Jesus by means of this conception. On the other hand, it does seem to have had a certain meaning for the writer of the Fourth Gospel. His particular emphasis of the fact that the Baptist rejected for himself the title of the Prophet, the returned Elijah, suggests that the writer of John wants to reserve this title for Jesus—along with other Christological designations and concepts, of course. Nicodemus, for example, calls Jesus the 'teacher come from God' (John 3.2). G. Bornkamm has shown that the figure of the Paraclete in the Gospel of John includes the essential features of the Prophet, who also is to 'lead into all truth'. This is done in such a way, of course, that the forerunner and the perfecter are one.[2] For the Fourth Gospel there can be no title of honour which is not fulfilled in Jesus Christ. It is precisely for this reason that this Gospel contrasts Jesus so sharply with a figure like Moses. If Jesus is at the same time the Prophet as well as the Logos and the Christ, then Moses can no longer be regarded as the absolute Prophet. This explains the vigorous denial of the assertion that Moses is the dispenser of the 'bread from heaven' (John 6.32; see also 1.17).

With regard to the rest of the New Testament writings, we have already seen that the first part of the Book of Acts, the very part which contains Jewish Christian traditions, twice (Acts 3.22; 7.37) mentions the saying that Jesus is the prophet foretold by Moses in Deut. 18.15. We know that this very important Old Testament passage played a decisive part in establishing the Jewish faith in the eschatological Prophet. In the second part of Acts, which deals with the missionary activities of Paul, and also in the letters of the New Testament, the concept of the Prophet applied to Jesus does not occur at all.

If my explanation of κατέχων in II Thess. 2.6 ff. is right, we could find there the assumption that a particular preacher of repentance will be active at the end—but this relates to the apostle, not to Jesus. In my article,

[1] See p. 16 above.

[2] G. Bornkamm, 'Der Paraklet im Johannesevangelium', *Festschrift R. Bultmann*, 1949, pp. 12 ff.

'Le caractère eschatologique du devoir missionaire et de la conscience apostolique de S. Paul. Etude sur le κατέχων de II Thess. 2.6–7' (*RHPR* 16, 1936, pp. 210 ff.), I attempt to show that this passage, as well as others in the New Testament, presupposes that the Gospel must be preached to the heathen before the end can come.[1]

Except for the Gospel of John and the first (Jewish Christian) part of Acts, no New Testament writing considers Jesus the eschatological Prophet who prepares the way for God. The solution to the riddle of the person and work of Jesus by means of the expectation of the Prophet of the end time was not long common, although it did at first circulate among the people. Other solutions soon took its place. We shall have to ask later why this one had so little success. But first we must consider a branch of early Christianity whose Christology was built entirely on this concept.

3. *Jesus the 'True Prophet' in Later Jewish Christianity*

Apart from the group of people mentioned in the Gospels who regarded Jesus as the returned Baptist or Elijah or as the Prophet, there is only a single school of thought in the history of the solution to the Christological problem which consistently conceives of Jesus as the Prophet: Jewish Christianity. The rapid disappearance of the early Christological conception of Jesus as the True Prophet is connected with the disappearance of Jewish Christianity. We find the conception first of all in the *Gospel of the Hebrews*, which we know was used by the Jewish Christians. Unfortunately we possess only a few fragments of this gospel.[2] The fragment preserved in Jerome's *Commentary on Isaiah* containing the close of the report of Jesus' baptism[3] shows that the fundamental Christological concept in this apocryphal gospel was that of the Prophet. In this passage the Spirit says to Jesus, 'In all prophets I have awaited you, that you might come and that I might rest in you.' These words of the Holy Spirit to Jesus were undoubtedly further developed in the *Gospel of the Hebrews*.

The gap in our knowledge of the remaining contents of this gospel, however, is filled by the ancient Jewish Christian literary source, *The Preaching of Peter* (*Kerygmata Petrou*), which is preserved in the

[1] J. Munck, *Paulus und die Heilsgeschichte*, 1954, pp. 28 ff. (ET, *Paul and the Salvation of Mankind*, 1959, pp. 36 ff.) follows my thesis.

[2] Collected by E. Klostermann, *Apocrypha II* (Kleine Texte 8)[3], 1929, pp. 5 f.

[3] Cf. p. 16 n. 3 above.

Pseudo-Clementine novel.[1] Here the primary title for Jesus is 'the True Prophet', ὁ ἀληθὴς προφήτης, and the whole Christology of this writing is oriented toward that title. The ancient interpretation of Jesus as the Prophet is further developed to the extent that the old eschatological element is pushed more or less into the background, while a speculative and Gnostic element is emphasized. The adjective 'true', which is always connected with the noun 'Prophet', is in itself an indication of this fact. The emphasis in this speculation does not lie so much on the fact that the Prophet introduces the end time and thus means the fulfilment of all previous prophecy; the emphasis lies rather on the fact that he represents in its perfection the truth proclaimed by all prophets. There is a certain relationship here with the Gospel of John, in which Christ, the Logos, stands in the foreground as the bearer of true revelation. As we have seen, the Fourth Gospel also shows a particular interest in the title 'Prophet'. It probably originated in a region in which there was speculation concerning this concept. But whereas this conception in the Gospel of John is embedded in a Christology resting on genuine biblical views, in the Jewish Christian *Preaching of Peter* it takes the form of a typically Gnostic speculation. This whole writing has a pronounced Gnostic character.[2]

It is altogether false to set Jewish Christian theology and Gnosticism over against one another as two opposite poles, so to speak, between which the theology of the early Church moved. The Jewish Christian Christology especially is usually considered the antithesis of Gnostic-Docetic Christology. In reality, the sources reveal that it is precisely the earliest Christian Gnosticism, which we can trace back into the New Testament itself, that bears a Jewish Christian character. The letters of

[1] See the German translation by H. Waitz (H. Veil) in Hennecke's *Neutestamentliche Apokryphen*[2], 1924, pp. 153 ff.; 215 ff. A critical edition of the text was not then possible. A critical edition of the homilies has since appeared in the series *Griechischen Christlichen Schriftsteller*, published by the Kirchenväterkommission in Berlin: *Die Pseudoklementinen*. I: *Homilien* (ed. B. Rehm), 1953. For literature on the Pseudo-Clementine writings see H. Waitz, *Die Pseudoklementinen, Homilien und Rekognitionen*, 1904; O. Cullmann, *Le problème littéraire et historique du roman pseudo-clémentin*, 1930; H. J. Schoeps, *Theologie und Geschichte des Judenchristentums*, 1949. See also the discussion between G. Bornkamm, *ZKG* 64, 1952/53, pp. 196 ff., and R. Bultmann, *Gnomon*, 1954, pp. 177 ff.

[2] H. J. Schoeps attempts to show against my thesis that there is no Gnosticism here. But we differ only in our choice of words. Schoeps seems to recognize only a narrow concept of Gnosticism. In reality, it is just the new Qumran discoveries which show that there was Gnosticism already in Judaism. Schoeps later revised his opinion (see p. 146 n. 1 below).

Ignatius, which contain the oldest definite statements we possess about Docetism, leave no doubt about the Jewish Christian origin of the Christological heresy Ignatius combats.

The very first chapter of the *Preaching of Peter* has to do with the 'True Prophet'. The world with its sins and errors is compared with a house full of smoke. The people who are inside vainly try to reach the truth, but the truth cannot get in to them. Only the True Prophet is able to open the door and let it into the house. This prophet is the Christ, who entered the world for the first time in the person of Adam. Thus already Adam is the True Prophet and as such he announces the future world. In our chapter on the Son of Man, we shall see that the Jewish Christians in this way combined the concept of the Prophet with that of the Son of Man.[1] Since the creation of the world, the True Prophet hastens through the centuries, changing his name and form of appearance. He incarnates himself again and again—in Enoch, Noah, Abraham, Isaac, Jacob and Moses. Moses renewed the eternal law which Adam had already proclaimed. By extending the law to permit the practice of sacrifices, he made a concession to the stubbornness of the people in order to prevent worse outgrowths of that stubbornness. But this permission was only provisional. In Deut. 18.15 Moses himself proclaims a future prophet, and this passage plays an important role in the *Preaching of Peter*, as it does in all Jewish texts which speak of the Prophet. But in this writing the particular task ascribed to the True Prophet is to forbid the practice of sacrifices which Moses allowed. The Jewish Christians laid particular emphasis on this point; thus for them the prohibition of sacrifices is one of the most important functions of the True Prophet.[2] As in the fragment of the *Gospel of the Hebrews* mentioned above,[3] so in the *Preaching of Peter* the True Prophet finally comes to rest in this coming Prophet. He is the Christ, who both completes and corrects the work of Moses by abolishing sacrifices. Thus a direct line runs from Adam to Jesus—the line of the Prophet. Jesus is the true incarnation of this Prophet.

According to this remarkable Jewish Christian theory the line of the False Prophet runs parallel through history to that of the True

[1] See pp. 47 f. below.

[2] The situation is somewhat different, although along the same line, in the *Epistle of Barnabas*, in which the author argues against Jewish sacrifices by appealing to the real intention of the *ancient* prophets. They were already 'true prophets' through whom the Lord made known his will.

[3] See p. 16 n. 2 above.

Prophet. Good and evil are seen from the standpoint of true and false prophecy. Here we see that the whole doctrine of salvation is actually dominated by the prophetic concept. The whole of history runs in conjoined pairs (συζυγίαι), the first or left member of which represents false prophecy, the second or right member of which represents true prophecy. This antithesis was directed especially against the sect of the disciples of the Baptist which is implicitly combated also in the Gospel of John. Apparently this sect, which was later absorbed into the Mandaeans,[1] represented particularly dangerous competition for early Christianity at the end of the first and beginning of the second century. It must have represented dangerous competition above all for the Gnostic Jewish Christianity we meet in the Pseudo-Clementine *Preaching of Peter*.

We recall that the disciples of the Baptist regarded their master as the final Prophet, who needed no one sent from God to follow him. Expositions of the Pseudo-Clementine teaching have not sufficiently noted that the intention behind the whole system of conjoined pairs is to oppose the teaching of the Baptist's followers that John is the True Prophet. The Jewish Christian speculation claimed that a number of pairs of men, representing true and false prophecy in their pure form, appear through the history of the human race. This speculation took over Gnosticism's popular dualistic conception of the principle of good and the principle of evil, and adapted it to serve completely the prophetic concept. Thus in the first pair Adam, the first representative of true prophecy, stands in opposition to Eve, the principle of false prophecy. The pairs Isaac and Ishmael, Jacob and Esau, Moses and Aaron are related in the same way as the contrast between true and false prophecy. The pair which concerns our present investigation sets Jesus the Son of Man, the True Prophet, over against John the Baptist, the False Prophet.

We see how the polemic against the disciples of John overshoots its mark and degenerates into a polemic against the Baptist himself, whereas the Gospel of John only combats the false opinion that the Baptist is the Christ or *the* Prophet. The Fourth Gospel does not direct its polemic against the person of the Baptist himself, but on the contrary, refutes the false conception of his person by his own words. Thus the evaluation of the person of the Baptist changed in the course of the polemic against his disciples: in the Synoptic Gospels he is still acknowledged as *the* Prophet; in the Fourth Gospel he is denied this

[1] See p. 27 above.

title; in the Pseudo-Clementine writings he actually appears as the False Prophet—as does Elijah, whose identity with the Baptist is probably acknowledged.[1]

It is also interesting to note how the Jewish Christian theory of pairs is used to combat the chronological argument that since he is older the Baptist is superior to Jesus. We have found traces of this discussion also in the Gospel of John. But whereas the evangelist answers by pointing to the pre-existence of Jesus and thus to his absolute priority, the Jewish Christians proceed differently in the *Preaching of Peter*. They admit without debate the temporal priority of John over Jesus, but assert that this is precisely what proves his character as a false prophet, since, beginning with the second pair, the first member chronologically always represents false prophecy, while the second member chronologically always represents true prophecy. Cain comes before Abel, Ishmael before Isaac, Esau before Jacob, Aaron before Moses, John the Baptist before Jesus the Son of Man, Paul the Apostle to the Gentiles before Peter, the Antichrist before the returning Christ.[2]

We see that this whole Jewish Christian teaching orients its positive as well as its polemic element around the concept of the Prophet. Despite the fact that the eschatological character which clings to this concept in Judaism and also in the New Testament recedes to a great extent, nevertheless we discover here the only explicitly developed Christology which rests on the old conception of the returning Prophet. It is without doubt one of the oldest Christologies we possess.

The future did not belong to this Christology, however, but to other explanations of the person and work of Christ. The 'prophetological' solution of the *Preaching of Peter* disappeared from the scene with Jewish Christianity. It exerted scarcely any influence at all on the historical development of Christian theology. On the other hand, it did have a remarkable influence on another religion, Islam, in which the Prophet is the central figure.[3]

We shall see that the concept of the Prophet of the last days as such—not to mention the Gnostic-Jewish-Christian speculation about this figure—is too narrow to comprehend the whole fullness of the person and work of Christ. This leads us to our final question.

[1] *Hom.* II, 17.1. He is thus placed on the same level with the prophets of the Old Testament, who are also rejected by the *Preaching of Peter.*

[2] *Hom.* II, 16–17; *Recogn.* III, 61. On the reconstruction of the list see O. Cullmann, *Le problème littéraire et historique du roman pseudo-clémentin*, p. 89.

[3] See pp. 49 f. below.

4. *The Conception of Jesus the Prophet as a Solution to the Christological Problem in the New Testament*

What are the advantages and disadvantages of the prophetic concept for explaining the uniqueness of the person and work of Christ in view of the total witness of the early Christian faith?

There are incontestable advantages. On the one hand, this concept takes into consideration the unique and unrepeatable character of the person and work of Jesus in so far as its application to Jesus treats the decisive if not the final appearance of the Prophet. On the other hand, it takes the human character of Jesus fully into account: the eschatological Prophet expected by Judaism appears on earth as a man.

Moreover, concerning the content of the task to be fulfilled by the Prophet, this concept is quite adequate to express one side of the earthly work completed by Jesus. At least it does not contain anything which contradicts the nature and goal of the work of Jesus as it is presented in the Gospels. In this respect, the concept of the Prophet without doubt has advantages over the concept of the Messiah. We shall see that at least the authoritative Jewish circles at the time of Jesus expected the Messiah to play a political role, to fight and conquer the enemies of Israel, and to make Jerusalem the centre of his government, which was understood in a purely this-worldly sense. Such a conception completely contradicts the role which Jesus ascribed to himself.

The function of the eschatological Prophet in the Jewish texts consists primarily in preparing the people of Israel and the world by his preaching for the coming of the Kingdom of God. He fulfils this function, not simply as the former Old Testament prophets did, but in a much more direct way as the immediate Preparer of the way for the Kingdom of God itself. He comes endowed with unique eschatological authority. His call to repentance is final and requires final decision. This gives his preaching a final, absolute character such as the preaching of the ancient prophets did not have. As we hear in the Gospel of John (3.18), in which the concept of the Prophet achieves a particular importance, judgment is actually executed already in the present with the decision of each individual in response to this prophet. When this prophet speaks (he who comes at the end of days, the ἐρχόμενος), he brings the last word, the final possibility offered to men. For when he speaks, he points to the Kingdom of God already approaching.

This function exactly corresponds to the earthly vocation of Jesus as he actually conceived and executed it. The authority, ἐξουσία, with which Jesus proclaimed his Gospel was in fact not that of any ordinary prophet, but that of the final Prophet: 'But *I* say to you . . .' (ἐγὼ δὲ λέγω ὑμῖν). And the content of his preaching corresponded to this authority: 'Repent, for the kingdom of heaven is at hand.' This is the beginning point of his proclamation. He wants to prepare men to become members of the coming Kingdom. No one contests the eschatological aim of Jesus' preaching.

The application of the concept of *the* Prophet to Jesus explains perfectly, then, both his preaching activity and the unique authority of his eschatological vocation and appearance in the end time.

Besides this advantage, we may further note that the concept Prophet lends itself to combination with other essential Christological concepts which were applied to Jesus. It combines with the concept *Messiah*, since the Messiah also appears at the end of days and is the one who directly prepares the way for God's Kingdom. It combines also with the Johannine concept *Logos*, which unites the work and person of the Prophet by identifying them: Jesus is himself the Word. We may recall also the beginning of the Letter to the Hebrews, where a similar thought is expressed, although the emphasis is not the same: 'In many and various ways God spoke of old to our fathers by the *prophets*; but in these last days he has spoken to us by a *Son*.' Here the concept Prophet is connected also with that of the *Son of God*. Again, we have seen that a direct line leads from the concept Prophet to that of the *Suffering Servant of God*, since it is the eschatological fate of the Prophet to suffer in the fulfilment of his function. Finally, we should not forget the fact we have already emphasized[1] that of all the early Christian titles of honour conferred upon Jesus, the title Prophet is the only one which suggests the expectation of a *second coming* of Jesus to earth.

But over against these incontestable advantages are a series of important disadvantages which result from conceiving the person and work of Christ exclusively in terms of the concept of the eschatological Prophet. We may divide these disadvantages into four categories: (1) the earthly life of Christ, (2) the present Christ at the right hand of God, (3) the future Christ who will come again, (4) the pre-existent Christ.

[1] See pp. 16 and 37 above.

(1) We have seen that in some respects the concept Prophet conceives the *earthly* work of Christ in a complete way, and that the merit of the concept lies precisely here. Nevertheless, it is inadequate even in this regard. It emphasizes too strongly only one side of Christ's earthly work, his preaching activity, and thus misplaces the emphasis. We have of course heard of other acts of the Prophet in the Jewish writings: he is to raise up the nation of Israel, overthrow the world powers, struggle against the Antichrist, work miracles.[1] But these tasks are not his specific function; they are rather functions which were transferred to him subsequently from other concepts, perhaps from that of the Messiah. The earthly work of Jesus as the first Christians understood it is not exhausted by his eschatological proclamation, but is fulfilled first of all by his forgiving sins, and above all by the act which represents the crowning of this activity, his atoning death. According to the witness of the Gospels, this is the way Jesus himself conceived of his work, and the early Church saw his prophetic preaching in the light of this act.

We have indeed seen that a direct line leads from the Prophet to the Suffering Servant of God. But conscious, vicarious suffering and dying is not a characteristic function of the eschatological Prophet. His suffering and dying is an unavoidable consequence of his preaching, but not really his eschatological *vocation* as in the case of the Suffering Servant. The Prophet is, at bottom, simply the preacher of repentance at the end of days. Everything else about his person and work is subordinate to this function. The situation is exactly the opposite in the actual life of Jesus, however: his teaching activity is completely dependent upon his consciousness that he must suffer and die for his people. Therefore, another concept which concerns the earthly life of Jesus, and which is much more central in the New Testament than that of the Prophet, must be brought into the foreground: precisely that of the Suffering Servant of God, the Christological application of which, as we shall see, originates with Jesus himself. The concept of the Prophet may be applied to Jesus' earthly life only in connection with the Suffering Servant concept. Without this connection it would be insufficient, giving a false picture of the person and work of the earthly Jesus as it is represented in the writings of the New Testament.

(2) The insufficiency of the prophetic concept emerges to a still higher degree when we attempt to explain the present and future work of Christ. There is no room at all for a present function of the

[1] See p. 22 above.

eschatological Prophet, since this concept does not provide for a temporal interval between an earthly activity (which is itself eschatological) and a second coming of the Prophet. We have indeed seen that the Prophet expected by Judaism has been on earth previously, and to that extent the prophetic concept prepares for the thought of a twofold coming of Jesus. But the difference lies in the fact that according to the Jewish view, the first coming of the Prophet did not have an eschatological character, whereas for the early Christian faith both appearances of Jesus are eschatological. According to the Jewish expectation, the Kingdom of God will come immediately after the returned Prophet has finished his preaching of repentance. It does not foresee a further temporal extension of his function. For this reason the prophetic concept cannot be applied at all to the work of the risen Christ, whom the early Church confessed especially with the title Lord, *Kyrios*. This means that it is precisely one of the most important Christological functions in the New Testament that remains and must necessarily remain entirely disregarded by the concept Prophet.

From the point of view of Jewish eschatology, we can and in fact we must speak of a 'delay' of the parousia. In Christian thought, there is indeed a delay of the completion expected by Judaism to the extent that the Christian faith believes in a fulfilment already present in a world not yet freed from sin and death. It is just this that is the new element in the Gospel. What distinguishes the Gospel of Jesus from Judaism, even from the highest form of prophetism, is the conviction that 'the kingdom of God has come upon you' (Matt. 12.28); that Satan is fallen 'like lightning from heaven' (Luke 10.18); that 'the blind receive their sight and the lame walk, lepers are cleansed and the deaf hear, and the dead are raised up, and the poor have good news preached to them' (Matt. 11.5). When the present is seen in this light, the whole eschatological process as taken over from Judaism must be prolonged, for a time of fulfilment is now inserted which is not yet consummated.

The discussion of 'consistent eschatology' should therefore take place in terms of the question whether the 'delay of the parousia' is a decisive theological motif in early Christianity [1] (as A. Schweitzer and his dis-

[1] This is by no means to deny that later also within early Christianity the delay of the parousia was recognized. I maintain, however, that the theological-chronological description of salvation did not first originate from this, but existed from the very beginning; and that the de-eschatologizing consists precisely in reducing the tension between present and future. With regard to E. Grässer, *Das*

ciples, and more recently R. Bultmann,[1] believe), or whether this concept does not rather mark exactly the boundary line between Judaism and the gospel of Jesus. Eschatology in the New Testament is neither 'realized' (Dodd) nor 'only future' (Schweitzer). From the very beginning there is a *tension* between 'already fulfilled' and 'not yet consummated'. For early Christianity the delay of the parousia resulted at most in a stronger emphasis on the 'already fulfilled'. On this question see my discussion with F. Buri in 'Das wahre durch die ausgebliebene Parusie gestellte neutestamentliche Problem', *TZ* 3, 1947, pp. 177 ff. and 422 ff. The crucial question is whether Jesus himself believed in a fulfilment already in the present without thereby excluding the expectation of a consummation to take place in the near future, but yet only after his death. The words of Jesus cited above show that this question is to be answered affirmatively. In this connection see especially W. G. Kümmel, *Promise and Fulfilment*, ET (SBT 23), 1957.

The title Prophet thus proves to be inadequate as a solution to the Christological problem when we consider that it is precisely the exalted present Christ who stands at the centre of the faith of the early Church as it is attested in the New Testament. It is true that Judaism reckons with the idea that the Prophet was previously on the earth, but it does not reckon with the idea that he has a further task to perform after the fulfilment of his eschatological work. It actually excludes a continuation of his work in the present. The exclusively preparatory character of the Prophet of the end time simply makes a prolongation of his function impossible.

(3) For this reason, it is also difficult to apply the concept of the Prophet to the third, the *future, eschatological* phase, which the early Church expected as the consummation of the work of Jesus. The very nature of the Prophet of the end time in Judaism requires that his role cease precisely where the Kingdom of God begins. We have indeed seen that the coming of the Prophet is the object of hope in Judaism and that he is even a totally eschatological figure. But he is explicitly expected only as one who prepares the way and not as one who completes. For this reason he can appear a second time at the end after he has already earlier spent a time on earth as a prophet, but he cannot come again as the Completer, because completion is by definition not his task. Here we see again the difficulty which

Problem der Parusieverzögerung in den synoptischen Evangelien und der Apostelgeschichte (BZNW 22), 1957, in which all texts must bow to the thesis that the emphasis on the present was first called forth by the parousia's non-appearance, see my essay 'Parusieverzögerung und Urchristentum', *TLZ* 83, 1958, col. 1 ff.

[1] See his 'History and Eschatology in the NT', in *NTS* 1, 1954/55, p. 5 ff.

arises as soon as we attempt to express the early Christian interpretation of the person and work of Jesus in terms of the Prophet. Only those who expected the Kingdom of God to come immediately, during the lifetime of Jesus, did not need to visualize a prolongation of the function of Jesus and could be satisfied with the belief in him as the eschatological Prophet. The early Christian faith, which lies at the basis of all the books of the New Testament, on the other hand, begins with the death and resurrection of Christ and is related to the present and the returning Christ. One can show that the historical Jesus himself thought of a continuation (although a brief one) of his work as Mediator before the end.[1]

'The Prophet of the end time' failed to include the activity of the 'living' Christ after Easter, although it was just this, as we shall see, which was *the* fundamental Christological experience for the early Church which gave birth to all New Testament Christology. The failure of this concept to comprehend that central Christological experience is certainly the primary reason for the fact that 'Prophet of the end time' did not persist as a title and explanation for the person and work of Christ.

(4) Finally, we mention the *pre-existent being* of Christ as various New Testament passages witness to it. No direct lines lead from the concept of the Prophet to this concept. At most one could think of the idea that the Prophet was previously on earth in other forms, and find in this way a sort of 'prototype' which suggests a kind of preexistence. This concept is basically different, however, from that which the New Testament writings apply to Jesus, because the New

[1] Albert Schweitzer's theory that Jesus himself believed at first that the Kingdom of God would come during his lifetime, and then later that it would break in immediately with his death, is a hypothesis which does indeed remain worthy of consideration and as such has been fruitful in New Testament scholarship. But it is nevertheless only a hypothesis, and Schweitzer himself is too serious a scholar not to attempt to justify it. No New Testament scholar today, of course, advocates it in the form he suggested, and it was at least severely shaken especially by W. G. Kümmel, *Promise and Fulfilment*. This does not prevent the disciples of Schweitzer in Basel and Bern who represent the so-called 'consistent eschatology' school (among whom there is no New Testament scholar) from a remarkable dogmatism. They ascribe scientific insincerity (work informed by 'embarrassment') or Catholicizing tendencies to all those who do not accept Schweitzer's hypothesis, but believe that Jesus himself thought that the Kingdom of God would come very soon, but only after his death. See F. Buri, 'Das Problem der ausgebliebenen Parusie', *Schweizerische Theologische Umschau*, 1946, pp. 97 ff. and my discussion cited on p. 47 above, as well as my essay in *TLZ*, mentioned on p. 47 in note 1 to p. 46. See also pp. 205 f. and 233 f. below.

Testament thinks of an eternal existence with God. One could at most see the possibility of a connecting line between the concepts if a connection were supposed between the Johannine Logos (the 'Word which was in the beginning with God'), which emphasizes the pre-existence of Jesus as a being with God; and the Prophet, who in his deepest being is the incarnation of the divine Word.

We must conclude, then, that the concept of the eschatological Prophet is too narrow to do justice to the early Christian faith in Jesus Christ. It fully comprehends only one aspect of the earthly life of Jesus, and even in this aspect it can be supplemented by other more central concepts such as that of the Suffering Servant of God. Moreover, the concept of the Prophet cannot be united at all with those Christological titles of honour which refer to the present Lord, since it excludes by definition an interim following Easter. It is fundamentally incompatible with the perspective in which the whole New Testament sees the event of salvation. The New Testament regards the historical Christ and his work as the central event, the midpoint of time. A theology based on the Prophet cannot be harmonized with this perspective, since by his very nature the Prophet can only be preparation, not fulfilment, and his work therefore cannot be the centre of time. So far as the Prophet is concerned, the decisive thing has not yet happened, but is yet to come. The prophetic concept thus allows no room for the present work of Christ. For as early Christianity understands it, faith in the present Christ and the Christ who is coming again presupposes that New Testament perspective in which the decisive thing has already happened in the incarnate Jesus, but the consummation is yet to come. It is therefore not surprising that the centre of the New Testament event of salvation, the death of Christ, has no theological meaning at all for Jewish Christian Christology.

We have seen that neither Jesus himself nor his immediate disciples applied the concept of *the* Prophet to his person and work, that this concept expresses rather an opinion about his person which was widespread among the people during his lifetime. After his death, the Gospel of John and the Letter to the Hebrews took up its valuable elements and incorporated them into other Christological concepts. The only Christological system which was built entirely upon the foundation of faith in the Prophet is the Jewish Christian one which we have found in the Pseudo-Clementine *Preaching of Peter*—that is, a heretical branch of early Christianity. But although the future did not belong to this part of Christianity, its Christology had a real historical role to play again at a later time—not in Christianity, but in Islam.[1] Specialists in the study of this religion now acknowledge that it was founded under the influence of Jewish Christianity. Not orthodox but heretical Jewish Christianity as it was spread in the Syrian area (precisely the branch which had no influence on the further development of Christianity) had a part in the founding of Islam. There the figure of the Prophet lives on in a new form. Much research remains to be done, however, concerning the links which join Islam with Jewish Christianity.

In later Christian theology we find remnants of the Christology of the Prophet in the essentially altered form of the so-called *munus propheticum Christi*, prophetic office of Christ.

[1] See W. Rudolph, *Die Abhängigkeit des Qorans vom Judentum und Christentum*, 1922; A. J. Wensinck, 'Muhammed und die Prophetie', *Acta orientalia* II, 1924; Tor Andrae, 'Der Ursprung des Islams und das Christentum', *Kyrkohistorisk Arsskrift*, 1923/25; J. Horovitz, *Qoranische Untersuchungen*, 1926; W. Hirschberg, *Iüdische und christliche Lehren im vor- und frühislamischen Arabien*, 1939; H. J. Schoeps, *Theologie und Geschichte des Judenchristentums*, pp. 334 ff.

3

Jesus the Suffering Servant of God

(*Ebed Yahweh*, παῖς θεοῦ)

WE COME straight to the heart of New Testament Christology with the title *ebed Yahweh*, although scholars have not usually given it its proper place. Its importance is obvious simply from the fact (which we must of course validate) that its application as well as the application of the title 'Son of Man' originates with Jesus himself. Moreover, it is especially important because the main thought behind it, vicarious representation, is the principle by which the New Testament understands the whole course of *Heilsgeschichte*. We cannot understand the New Testament's view of history beginning with creation itself without the thought of the representation of the many by a minority, progressing to the representation by the One. The figure of the Suffering Servant of God is the exemplary embodiment of this idea of representation. The 'Servant of God' is one of the oldest titles used by the first Christians to define their faith in the person and work of Christ. Like that of the Prophet, this title disappeared quite early—for reasons we must investigate.

Scholars have often investigated the meaning of the *ebed Yahweh* figure as an Old Testament problem,[1] but seldom its application to Jesus. Both the older work of A. Harnack [2] and the more recent work of E. Lohmeyer [3] deal with the question only from the point of view of the early Church, without investigating whether Jesus himself had not already considered himself the one who was called to fulfil the function of the

[1] See H. H. Rowley, 'The Servant of the Lord in the Light of Three Decades of Criticism', *The Servant of the Lord and Other Essays on the Old Testament*[2], 1954, pp. 1–58.

[2] A. Harnack, *Die Bezeichnung Jesu als Knecht Gottes und ihre Geschichte in der alten Kirche* (SB Berliner Akademie der Wissenschaften), 1926, pp. 212 ff.

[3] E. Lohmeyer, *Gottesknecht und Davidsohn*, 1945.

'Servant of God' of whom Deutero-Isaiah speaks. The full scope of the problem for the New Testament has been recognized only very recently and dealt with in various monographs. I mention, besides my own study,[1] especially the work of H. W. Wolff[2] and J. Jeremias' work in *The Servant of God*, which appeared originally as the article on *Pais* in the *Theologisches Wörterbuch*.[3]

The problem raised by the application of this title to Jesus is all the more important because it throws new light on the much-discussed question of the relation between Jesus and the Apostle Paul.

We shall discuss also this designation in the following sequence: (1) its meaning in Judaism, (2) Jesus and the *ebed Yahweh*, (3) the faith of the early Church in Jesus the *ebed Yahweh* (παῖς θεοῦ), (4) a criticism on the basis of the total Christological witness of the New Testament.

1. *The* Ebed Yahweh *in Judaism*

As in the case of the eschatological Prophet, we are dealing here with a Jewish concept. We shall ask first what it means in the Old Testament, and then what role it plays in Judaism. In the present context, we must limit ourselves to the formulation of the problem. The Old Testament passages which relate to this figure are Isa. 42.1–4; 49.1–7; 50.4–11; 52.13–53.12. The texts which especially interest us in view of their later application to Jesus are the first verses of ch. 42 and the famous ch. 53. According to the Revised Standard Version they read:

Isa. 42.1–3: Behold my servant, whom I uphold, my chosen, in whom my soul delights; I have put my spirit upon him, he will bring forth justice to the nations. He will not cry or lift up his voice, or make it heard in the street; a bruised reed he will not break, and a dimly burning wick he will not quench; he will faithfully bring forth justice.

[1] O. Cullmann, 'Gésu, Servo di Dio', *Protestantesimo* 3, 1948, pp. 49 ff. (In French, 'Jésus, Serviteur de Dieu', *Dieu vivant* 16, 1950, pp. 17 ff.).

[2] H. W. Wolff, *Jesaja 53 im Urchristentum*², 1950.

[3] See W. Zimmerli and J. Jeremias, *The Servant of God*, ET (SBT 20), 1957, pp. 43 ff. (The article on παῖς θεοῦ is in *TWNT* V, pp. 636 ff.) The work of T. W. Manson, *The Servant-Messiah. A Study of the Public Ministry of Jesus*, 1953, investigates the presuppositions of the idea of the Servant of God in the life of Jesus, and contains interesting references to their connection with Jesus' conception of his work, but it does not deal especially with the relationship to the Old Testament *ebed Yahweh*. A thorough investigation by C. Maurer, 'Knecht Gottes und Sohn Gottes im Passionsbericht des Markusevangeliums', *ZTK* 50, 1953, pp. 1 ff., attempts to prove the influence of the *Pais* Christology on Mark.

These verses are important both for understanding the baptism of Jesus, and because they are quoted in Matt. 12.18 ff.

Isa. 52.13–53.12: Behold, my servant shall prosper, he shall be exalted and lifted up, and shall be very high. As many were astonished at him—his appearance was so marred, beyond human semblance, and his form beyond that of the sons of men—so shall he startle many nations; kings shall shut their mouths because of him; for that which has not been told them they shall see, and that which they have not heard they shall understand. Who has believed what we have heard? And to whom has the arm of the Lord been revealed? For he grew up before him like a young plant, and like a root out of dry ground; he had no form or comeliness that we should look at him, and no beauty that we should desire him. He was despised and rejected by men; a man of sorrows, and acquainted with grief; and as one from whom men hide their faces he was despised, and we esteemed him not. Surely he has borne our griefs and carried our sorrows; yet we esteemed him stricken, smitten by God, and afflicted. But he was wounded for our transgressions, he was bruised for our iniquities; upon him was the chastisement that made us whole, and with his stripes we are healed. All we like sheep have gone astray; we have turned every one to his own way; and the Lord has laid on him the iniquity of us all. He was oppressed, and he was afflicted, yet he opened not his mouth; like a lamb that is led to the slaughter, and like a sheep that before its shearers is dumb, so he opened not his mouth. By oppression and judgment he was taken away; and as for his generation, who considered that he was cut off out of the land of the living, stricken for the transgression of my people? And they made his grave with the wicked and with a rich man in his death, although he had done no violence, and there was no deceit in his mouth. Yet it was the will of the Lord to bruise him; he has put him to grief; when he makes himself an offering for sin, he shall see his offspring, he shall prolong his days; the will of the Lord shall prosper in his hand; he shall see the fruit of the travail of his soul and be satisfied; by his knowledge shall the righteous one, my servant, make many to be accounted righteous; and he shall bear their iniquities. Therefore I will divide him a portion with the great, and he shall divide the spoil with the strong; because he poured out his soul to death, and was numbered with the transgressors; yet he bore the sin of many, and made intercession for the transgressors.

The expressions the prophet uses to describe the *ebed* figure are at the same time precise and enigmatic. We learn fairly accurately what the nature of his work is, and we hear a few details about his fate. And yet we still do not know *who* this 'Servant of Yahweh' is. The prophet tells us neither when nor under what circumstances he will appear. I. Engnell explains the main motive of these hymns by reference to the Jewish idea of kingship.[1] E. Lohmeyer relates the title to the 'Son of David'.[2] A. Bentzen explains the figure by means of the Jewish views of the fate of prophets, and above all by means of the conception of the *Moses redivivus* (i.e., by the views we discussed in the last chapter).[3] Old Testament scholars today still ask the same question asked in Acts 8.34 by the eunuch who was reading Isa. 53: 'About whom does the prophet say this, about himself or about someone else?' The prophet could assume that his readers knew this figure; but it will probably never be possible without hypotheses for us to solve the puzzle which these hymns present. Old Testament scholarship has already suggested many such theories.

An orientation in the present state of the question is provided by the following: C. R. North, *The Suffering Servant in Deutero-Isaiah*², 1956; H. H. Rowley, 'The Suffering Servant and the Davidic Messiah', *Oudtestamentische Studiën* 8, 1950, pp. 100 ff.; W. Zimmerli, 'παῖς', *TWNT* V, pp. 655 ff. (ET, *The Servant of God*, pp. 9–42). For further literature see O. Eissfeldt, *Einleitung in das AT*³, 1957, pp. 399 f.

We can reduce the problem to the question whether we are dealing in the Old Testament with an individual personality or with a collective one. The question is not easy to answer. On the one hand, there are passages in the *ebed Yahweh* hymns which appear to identify the *ebed* with the whole of Israel: 'You are my servant, Israel, in whom I will be glorified' (Isa. 49.3). On the other hand, some passages see him only as a part of the people, probably the 'remnant'. Again, there are passages which reduce the collective still further to a single man, an individual personality.

Our task here is not to consider this complex problem in detail. We must emphasize from the very beginning, however, that any solution which takes into consideration only one category of passages cannot be correct. Moreover, the three explanations are by no means mutually exclusive. The identification of collective and individual representatives is quite common in Semitic thinking.[4] It is thus

[1] I. Engnell, *Studies in Divine Kingship in the Ancient Near East*, Uppsala 1943, p. 48. See also his 'The Ebed Jahwe Songs and the Suffering Messiah in Deutero-Isaiah'. *BJRL* 31, 1948, pp. 54 ff.

[2] See E. Lohmeyer, *Gottesknecht und Davidsohn*.

[3] A. Bentzen, *King and Messiah*, pp. 48 ff. The author develops his thesis in opposition to the position of Engnell and Engnell's criticism of his views.

[4] See among others C. R. North, *op. cit.*, pp. 103 ff.; H. Wheeler Robinson, 'The Hebrew Conception of Corporate Personality', *BZAW* 66, 1936, pp. 49 ff.; A. R. Johnson, *The One and the Many in the Israelite Conception of God*, 1942, pp.

actually characteristic of the central theological idea of the *ebed Yahweh* hymns (that is, the idea of *representation*) that a plurality is progressively reduced as an always decreasing minority takes over the task which was originally that of the totality. I have tried to show, in my book *Christ and Time*,[1] how the biblical *Heilsgeschichte* unfolds from beginning to end according to the principle of representation in a progressive reduction: the way proceeds from the whole creation to humanity, from humanity to the people of Israel, from the people of Israel to the 'remnant', from the 'remnant' to a single man, Jesus. The *ebed Yahweh* figure is symptomatic of this development of *Heilsgeschichte*; he is at the same time the whole people, the 'remnant', and the One. He is so to speak the personification of the complexity which is definitive for the idea of the representation central in these hymns. Therefore this figure is of exceptional significance for understanding biblical *Heilsgeschichte*.

The most important essential characteristic of the *ebed Yahweh* in these texts is that his vicarious representation is accomplished in suffering. The *ebed* is the *suffering* Servant of God. Through suffering he takes the place of the many who should suffer instead of him. A second essential characteristic of the *ebed Yahweh* is that his representative work *re-establishes the covenant* which God had made with his people. We shall have to consider both characteristics when we come to the question of Jesus and the *ebed Yahweh*.

In Judaism the main problem concerning the *ebed* is his relation to the Messiah.[2] Here also we must guard against giving an answer which oversimplifies the problem. The encounter of the two concepts within Judaism was inevitable. Both the *ebed Yahweh* and the Messiah have the task of restoring the destroyed or distorted relationship between Yahweh and his people, of leading the people back to the vocation which God had given them through his election. Lohmeyer[3] emphasizes in this connection that as Jewish concepts the *ebed Yahweh* and the Messiah are more closely related than the *ebed Yahweh* and the 'Son of Man', since the Son of Man is not an exclusively Jewish figure. According to Lohmeyer the Servant of God is 'anointed' with the spirit. In any case it is certain that the *ebed Yahweh* and the 'Messiah' came into contact. Engnell believes

1 ff.; in our context especially O. Eissfeldt, *Der Gottesknecht bei Deuterojesaja (Jes. 40–55) im Lichte der israelitischen Anschauung von Gemeinschaft und Individuum*, 1933.

[1] *Christ and Time*, pp. 115 ff.

[2] See S. R. Driver and A. Neubauer, *The Fifty-third Chapter of Isaiah according to the Jewish Interpreters*, 1876.

[3] *Op. cit.*, pp. 98 ff.

that this meeting is clarified by their common connection with the idea of kingship. From various linguistic considerations, one may conclude that the Septuagint seems to interpret Isa. 52.13–53.12 messianically.[1]

The Book of Enoch, the Apocalypse of Ezra and the Apocalypse of Baruch identify the Messiah indirectly with the *ebed Yahweh* by ascribing to the Messiah the epithets of the *ebed*.[2] It is characteristic of Judaism at the time of Jesus, however, that this identity remained purely external. The *ebed's* essential task of vicarious suffering was not transferred to the Messiah. If the passage in the *Testament of Benjamin* (3.8) is really pre-Christian, we would have here before the time of Jesus the idea of a Messiah from the tribe of Joseph-Ephraim who will die for the godless.[3] But this idea is not typical of the main stream of contemporary messianism. One can at best find faint traces of a suffering Messiah in Judaism.[4]

We have seen that suffering is also of the essence of the *Prophet*. But he does not consciously suffer *vicariously*, voluntarily take upon himself the suffering of the people as atonement. He suffers because suffering is the inevitable fate of the prophet. In so far as the Prophet of the end time was identified here and there with the Messiah, we can perhaps speak of a 'suffering Messiah'. When we consider the mutual influence of the various concepts at the disposal of Judaism for designating the mission of a special emissary of God, it is possible that the idea of a suffering Messiah may have emerged occasionally already in Judaism.

We may add that the kingship cult led to both concepts—to that of the Messiah and to that of the Suffering Servant of God. Also H. H. Rowley quite rightly accepts this common root,[5] although he does not otherwise

[1] See K. F. Euler, *Die Verkündigung vom leidenden Gottesknecht aus Jes. 53 in der griechischen Bibel*, 1934, pp. 122 ff. The question must still be asked how this is related to the fact noted by Jeremias, *The Servant of God*, pp. 43 ff., that Hellenistic Judaism, in contrast to Palestinian Judaism, knew only the collective interpretation of the *ebed Yahweh* songs.

[2] See H. W. Wolff, *Jesaja 53 im Urchristentum*, pp. 42 ff. With reference to Enoch, see also Jeremias, *The Servant of God*, pp. 56–60.

[3] Those who favour this theory of the pre-Christian origin include Jeremias, *op. cit.*, pp. 57 ff.; G. H. Dix, 'The Messiah ben Joseph', *JTS* 27, 1926, p. 136; J. Héring, *Le royaume de Dieu et sa venue*, p. 67 n. 1. It is questionable whether the 'prophecy of heaven' refers to Isa. 53.

[4] See the careful discussion of the relevant passages by W. D. Davies, *Paul and Rabbinic Judaism*, 1948, pp. 247 ff.

[5] H. H. Rowley, 'The Suffering Servant and the Davidic Messiah', *Oudtestamentische Studiën* 8, p. 133.

believe in the identity of the two concepts in Judaism and projects also all speculation about a *Messiah ben Ephraim* into the post-Christian era. The kingship cult leads to two parallel but not identical figures.

The kernel of truth in the thesis advocated by J. Jeremias[1] is that there was some kind of mutual influence. M. Buber[2] and H. Riesenfeld[3] also accept this thesis, Riesenfeld basing his argument primarily on the Jewish explanation of Gen. 22.

A problem in itself is the relation between the *ebed Yahweh* and the Teacher of Righteousness in the recently discovered Qumran texts. We have seen that the Teacher too has to suffer, but that it is not certain whether he died a martyr's death.[4] In any case, suffering plays a great role in the texts, above all in the recently published Psalms. There is much to be said for the thesis of W. H. Brownlee[5] that the function of the Suffering Servant of God was ascribed to the sect as such, and that this function was concretely realized in the Teacher of Righteousness.[6] Brownlee does not of course assume the identity of the Teacher with the Messiah.[7]

Nevertheless the suffering of the Teacher of Righteousness fits better in the category of prophetic suffering—the suffering which is

[1] J. Jeremias, 'Erlöser und Erlösung im Spätjudentum und Urchristentum', *DT* 2, 1929, pp. 106 ff. Appealing to several passages of late Jewish literature, he attempts to prove that rabbinic Judaism already in the pre-Christian era had a messianic interpretation of Isa. 53, and therefore also the conception of a suffering Messiah. See also his 'ἀμνὸς τοῦ θεοῦ–παῖς θεοῦ', *ZNW* 34, 1935, pp. 115 ff.; and 'Zum Problem der Deutung von Jes. 53 im palästinischen Spätjudentum', *Aux sources de la tradition chrétienne*. Mélanges offerts à M. Maurice Goguel, 1950, pp. 113 ff. He has attempted to undergird the thesis anew with a careful exegesis of the texts in his *The Servant of God*.

[2] M. Buber, 'Jesus und der Knecht', volume in honour of G. van der Leeuw, 1950, p. 71.

[3] H. Riesenfeld, *Jésus transfiguré*, 1947, pp. 81 ff.

[4] See p. 21 above.

[5] W. H. Brownlee, 'The Servant of the Lord in the Qumran Scrolls', *Bulletin of the American Schools of Oriental Research* 132, Dec. 1953, pp. 8 ff.; 135, Oct. 1954, pp. 33 ff. See also his 'Messianic Motifs of Qumran and the New Testament', *NTS* 3, 1956/57, pp. 12 ff.

[6] Millar Burrows, *The Dead Sea Scrolls*, p. 267, is critical of this thesis. M. Philonenko, 'Interpolations chrétiennes dans les Testaments des douze Patriarches', *Diplôme de l'Ecole pratique des Hautes Etudes, Sect. des Sciences Religieuses*, 1955, following A. Dupont-Sommer, thinks that the so-called 'Christian' interpolations in the Testaments of the Twelve Patriarchs come from the milieu of the Qumran sect. If this is true, it of course has far-reaching implications for this question.

[7] See W. H. Brownlee, 'Messianic Motifs of Qumran and the New Testament', *op. cit.*, pp. 21 ff.

the unsought consequence of prophetic proclamation. Even if it is true that in Israel all suffering has a more or less representative character,[1] one should not negate the distinction between the voluntary atoning suffering of the *ebed Yahweh* and the fate forced upon the prophet. May it not be that we find in John 10.17 f. a deliberate delimitation of the death of Jesus over against that of all other prophetic martyrs—above all over against the fate of the Zealot leaders (the probable identity of the 'thieves and robbers' who 'come before' Jesus in John 10.8 and who, according to John 10.12 f., are not concerned for the life of their followers)? No one takes the life of the true Shepherd; he gives it of his own free will for the sheep (John 10.18).[2]

Even if it were possible to find in the Judaisin of the New Testament period the conception of an eschatological saviour of Israel who consciously assumes the role of the *ebed Yahweh*, it would be a conviction which arose on the periphery of Judaism. The thought that the Messiah has to suffer is foreign to the official expectation at least. The Targum of Isaiah 53 (investigated by P. Humbert,[3] G. Kittel,[4] P. Seidelin,[5] and H. Hegermann,[6] as well as by Jeremias) shows that it was in any case difficult for the Rabbis to accept the idea of a *suffering* Messiah. The author of this Targum does identify the *ebed Yahweh* of Isa. 53 with the Messiah, but by means of a curious and highly arbitrary exegesis he eliminates precisely everything which

[1] E. Schweizer, *Erniedrigung und Erhöhung bei Jesus und seinen Nachfolgern* (ATANT), 28 1955 (Eng. ed., rev., *Lordship and Discipleship*, 1960), has again emphasized this. See p. 71 n. 1 below concerning the conclusions he draws from it. Also J. A. Sanders, *Suffering as Divine Discipline in the Old Testament and Post-Biblical Judaism* (Colgate Rochester Divinity School Bulletin 28), 1955, with a thorough investigation of the texts, shows the atoning character of all suffering in Israel. E. Lohse, *Märtyrer und Gottesknecht, Untersuchung zur urchristlichen Verkündigung vom Sühnetod Jesu Christi*, 1955, is of the same opinion. On the other hand, Lohse, *ibid.*, p. 110, rightly emphasizes that this *general* atoning value of suffering never means final forgiveness. The idea that God himself could intervene for the sins of men is also foreign to Judaism.

[2] See O. Cullmann, 'The Significance of the Qumran Texts for Research into the Beginnings of Christianity', *The Scrolls and the New Testament*, pp. 18 ff.; *The State in the New Testament*, ET 1957, p. 22.

[3] P. Humbert, 'Le Messie dans le Targoum des prophètes', *Revue de Théologie et Philosophie* 43, 1911, pp. 5 ff.

[4] G. Kittel, 'Jesu Worte über sein Sterben', *DT* 9, 1936, p. 177.

[5] P. Seidelin, 'Der Ebed Jahve und die Messiasgestalt im Jesajatargum', *ZNW* 35, 1936, pp. 197 ff.

[6] H. Hegermann, *Jesaja 53 in Hexapla, Targum und Peschitta*, 1954, comes to other conclusions, as does Jeremias.

concerns the *suffering* of the *ebed*, and twists the text to mean just the opposite of what it says.

I cite here only a few examples of this strange exegesis. Verse 2b in the Old Testament reads, 'He had no form or comeliness that we should look at him, and no beauty that we should desire him.' The Targum explains this passage in the following way: 'The appearance of the *ebed* is not commonplace, and the fear which he inspires is not ordinary; his splendour is a holy splendour. Who considers him, considers him with reverence.' The Rabbi clearly makes the text say just what it does not say in order to avoid the suffering of the Messiah whom he identifies with the *ebed*.

In Isa. 53.3 the prophet writes: 'He was despised and rejected by men; a man of sorrows, and acquainted with grief; and as one from whom men hide their faces he was despised, and we esteemed him not.' The rabbinical interpretation reads: 'Although he is an object of contempt for the people, he will make an end of all the kingdoms.[1] They will be made weak and sorrowing like a man of grief who is familiar with sickness. As if God had turned his face from them, so are we despised and mocked.' The exegete simply changes the subject of the verse in a completely arbitrary way. Whereas the text says that the *ebed Yahweh* is despised, the Rabbi makes it say that *we* are despised; whereas the text says that we hide our faces before him because we despise him, the Rabbi interprets it to say that *God* has turned his face from us. This strange exegesis continues by the same method, but these examples are enough to show that its one aim is to apply the title *ebed Yahweh* to the Jewish Messiah in such a way that the Servant of God is relieved of his most essential characteristic, his vicarious suffering. According to the rabbinical view, suffering is simply incompatible with the real mission of the Messiah.

There is of course a possibility that this Targum in its present form is directed against the Christian identification of the *ebed Yahweh* with Jesus.[2] But there is no certain evidence of an anti-Christian polemic here.

[1] P. Seidelin, *op. cit.*, p. 207, on the basis of a different reading (p. 211), translates, 'Therefore the honour of all kingdoms will be held in contempt and disappear.' Jeremias, *The Servant of God*, pp. 168 f., believes there is a trace of an older messianic interpretation here which the secondary reading accepted by Seidelin later referred to the kingdoms. But even if we accept the usually preferred reading which relates 'being held in contempt' to the Messiah, the above translation does not necessarily imply a trace of the concept of a suffering Messiah. Jeremias himself admits that also the Targum to Isa. 53.12 ('. . . he poured out his soul to death') does not necessarily refer to death.

[2] Jeremias in his contribution to the volume for M. Goguel (see also *The Servant of God*, p. 71) emphasizes this, as G. Dalman already had in *Jesus-Jeshua*, ET 1929, pp. 172 f., although in an earlier work, *Der leidende und der sterbende Messias der Synagoge im ersten nachchristlichen Jahrtausend*, 1888, pp. 43 ff., Dalman had taken a different position. See also H. Hegermann, *op. cit.*, p. 121.

The Rabbi's interpretation of Isa. 53 is not so stated that it suggests the rejection of an opposing conception. He appears rather to be interested in the positive messianic use of the text. One cannot prove J. Jeremias' thesis that an original text is here reworked from an anti-Christian point of view. The fact (about which we shall speak later) that early Christian circles did not long explain the person and work of Christ on the basis of Isa. 53 suggests that a polemic on this point was not particularly urgent.

We may say in conclusion that official Judaism at the time of Jesus—even in Palestine—did not include atoning suffering as a necessary part of the messianic idea, and that even if one can actually show the existence of the conception of a suffering Messiah, it was at best marginal and weak. The manuscripts from Qumran can at present be taken at most as indirect evidence for such a view, since in the manuscripts which have been published to date we have to do with a suffering Prophet rather than with an *ebed Yahweh* who voluntarily suffers for the atonement of others. This is not to deny, however, that there is a connection between the suffering Prophet and the Suffering Servant of God.

2. *Jesus and the* Ebed Yahweh

Since the primary task of the Suffering Servant of God is vicarious suffering and death, we shall ask first what importance suffering and death have in the proclamation of Jesus in general, without speaking of the relation of Jesus to the Old Testament figure of the *ebed Yahweh*. Then with that foundation we shall investigate secondly whether Jesus did not consider his divine mission to be quite precisely the fulfilment of the work of the *ebed Yahweh* as the Old Testament prophets described it. That is, we shall first examine the sayings of Jesus which mention the necessity of his death in general, without direct reference to Isaiah; then, those sayings which refer directly to the *ebed*.

Did Jesus think of his suffering and death as an essential part of the task he had to fulfil in carrying out the divine plan of salvation? Most representatives of so-called theological 'liberalism' usually answer this question *a priori* in the negative: Jesus himself did not believe his death to be of atoning significance; the Apostle Paul was the first to introduce this idea.

R. Bultmann in his *Theology of the New Testament* answers this question in one sentence: 'Can there be any doubt that (the predictions of the passion) are all *vaticinia ex eventu*?'[1] Bultmann's thesis that the early Church invented the prophecies of Jesus about his death in order to explain it afterwards is contradicted by the fact alone (which Bultmann himself admits) that the Christology of the *ebed* was not at all widespread in the early Church.

It is true of course that Jesus did not place his own person, especially his suffering and death, so centrally in his preaching of the Kingdom of God as the Apostle Paul later did in his proclamation. But that is because Jesus was conscious during his earthly life of being called first of all to live, not to teach, the work of atonement. Thus he did not only teach the Father's forgiveness of sins; in healing the sick he actually forgave sins. This is extremely important for the Jesus-Paul problem; here lies the connection between the two. The Synoptic writers too connect Jesus' act of forgiving sins with his own person in so far as they speak of the fact that he himself forgives sins. This is an indisputable fact. But the question must then be asked, how Jesus could attribute this authority (ἐξουσία) to himself. If we take this question seriously, we must ascribe to Jesus the consciousness of having been sent to fulfil this very task of forgiving sins.

Even apart from this preliminary observation, however, we may point out a whole series of Jesus' sayings which unequivocally count his suffering and death as a part of the work he knows he had to fulfil in accordance with the divine plan of salvation.

There is of course a simple—all too simple—method of disposing of all these passages: one may assert *a priori* that they are not genuine and consider each and every one of them as the invention of the early Church, which wanted in this way to bring the teaching of the Apostle Paul into harmony with that of Jesus. But this all too arbitrary method is inadmissible—not on apologetic grounds, but on objective and scholarly ones.

We consider briefly the most important sayings of Jesus which are relevant here. First we may mention in the Synoptic Gospels Mark 2.18 ff. on fasting while the bridegroom is present. Verse 20 ('the days will come when the bridegroom is taken away from them')[2] clearly presupposes the conviction of Jesus that he must die. Since his presence is so important that it can release the disciples from the duty of fasting, it is clear that with the picture of the bridegroom Jesus considers himself the one divine Emissary. And in saying that

[1] R. Bultmann, *Theology of the New Testament* I, p. 29.

[2] E. Lohmeyer, *Das Evangelium des Markus*, p. 60, considers the possibility that this passage is an allusion to Isa. 53.8: αἴρεται ἀπὸ τῆς γῆς ἡ ζωὴ αὐτοῦ.

as such he must be taken away from men by death, he assumes that this death belongs to his messianic mission. Against the assertion that this passage is a *vaticinium ex eventu* to explain why the members of the early Church fasted whereas the companions of Jesus had not,[1] we may answer that the members of the early Church were not conscious of living in a time of mourning, but in the time of salvation. Thus they could hardly have invented v. 20 in Mark 2.[2]

In Luke 13.31 ff. Jesus places himself in the human category of prophet ('for it cannot be that a prophet should perish away from Jerusalem'), but the Greek verb τελειοῦμαι in v. 32 may indicate that beyond this he ascribes to himself a special divine mission which consists in his death. The same verb in Luke 12.50 is related to the accomplishment of his death, which (as in Mark 10.38) is described as 'baptism': 'Are you able to be baptized with the baptism with which I am baptized?' These words indicate that Jesus' death is not just an epilogue, but an integrating essential part of his work.

In the saying about the sign of the prophet Jonah in Matt. 12.39 ff.[3] Jesus proclaims not only his death but also (if v. 40 is genuine) his resurrection: 'For as Jonah was three days and three nights in the belly of the whale, so will the Son of man be three days and three nights in the heart of the earth.' There are reasons worth mentioning for accepting as genuine only the first part of the saying, v. 39, in which Jesus says that an evil and adulterous generation will be given no sign except the sign of Jonah. According to this interpretation the sign of Jonah has to do with the prophet's preaching of repentance.[4]

[1] Cf. E. Klostermann, *Das Markus-Evangelium* (HNT)[3], 1936, *ad. loc.*; E. Lohmeyer, *Das Evangelium des Markus, ad loc.*; R. Bultmann, *Die Geschichte der synoptischen Tradition*[2], 1931, pp. 17 f.

[2] H. J. Ebeling, 'Die Fastenfrage (Mk. 2.18–22)', *Theologische Studien und Kritiken* 108, 1937/38, pp. 387 ff., also calls attention to this fact. For this reason he does not relate the time of mourning and fasting to the time of the Church (which did *not* fast), but to the time of future 'messianic woes'; but he therefore rejects the whole saying of Jesus. On the other hand, W. G. Kümmel, *Promise and Fulfilment*, pp. 75 ff., sees no other possibility than to relate the contrast between Mark 2.19a and 2.20 to the time before and after the death and resurrection of Jesus, so that even if the report has been amplified at the end by the Church's interpretations, it expects a longer or shorter period of separation of Jesus and his disciples after his death.

[3] See the careful work of P. Seidelin, 'Das Jonaszeichen', *Studia Theologica* 5, 1951, pp. 119 ff.

[4] Thus E. Klostermann, *Das Matthäus-Evangelium*[2], 1927, *ad loc.* See also W. G. Kümmel, *op. cit.*, pp. 68 ff. A different solution is given by J. Jeremias, "Ἰωνᾶς', *TWNT* III, pp. 412 f. Among others who accept the genuineness of v. 40 see:

Nevertheless, it is not easy to explain v. 40 as a later interpolation. If the Christians really wanted subsequently to introduce in this way an allusion to the death and resurrection of Jesus, this particular interpolation would not be very apt. The 'three days and three nights' of which the verse speaks do not really fit the Gospels' reports of Jesus' resurrection, since they presuppose only *two* nights. This consideration could actually speak in favour of the genuineness of the whole saying of Jesus, the 'three days and three nights' then being understood not in the sense of chronological precision, but as a general designation of a very short period of time. But this question of genuineness must remain open.[1]

Further, we may mention the three times Jesus prophesied his death following Peter's confession in Caesarea Philippi: Mark 8.31; 9.31; 10.33 f. We mention all these passages, despite the fact that they represent a certain schematization on the part of the evangelist. In the first of these texts Jesus corrects what is usually called the confession of Peter at two points: (1) For the title Χριστός which Peter conferred upon him, Jesus substitutes the title υἱὸς τοῦ ἀνθρώπου. We shall see later that this corresponds to a general tendency of Jesus. (2) Jesus adds that this Son of Man, who, according to Daniel will come on the clouds of heaven, must first suffer many things. This radically new thought is offensive to Peter, as it must be for every Jew. The supposition that the *kerygma* of the early Church subsequently invented these prophecies of Jesus would necessarily result in also considering as legendary the whole scene (certainly not an invented one) in which Jesus says sharply to Peter, 'Get behind me, Satan'.[2]

Still further, we may cite Mark 12.1 ff., the parable of the evil tenants ('This is the heir; come, let us kill him . . .');[3] and Mark 14.8,

A. Schlatter, *Der Evangelist Matthäus*², 1933, *ad loc.*; J. Schniewind, *Das Evangelium nach Matthäus* (NTD), 1937, *ad loc.*; M.-J. Lagrange, *Evangile selon S. Matthieu* (Etudes Bibliques), 1941, *ad loc.*; W. Michaelis, *Das Evangelium nach Matthäus* II, 1949, *ad loc.* See also A. T. Nikolainen, *Der Auferstehungsglaube in der Bibel und ihrer Umwelt*, II, 1946, p. 49.

[1] It would even be understandable if v. 40 had later been *eliminated* because of this discrepancy with the Gospel reports. Lagrange suggests that precisely this consideration caused Justin, *Dial.* 107.1, to omit this verse from his quotation of the passage.

[2] Also E. Schweizer, *Erniedrigung und Erhöhung*, p. 16 (ET, p. 19), correctly points out the unity of this scene, which makes the assumption of a later insertion of the prophecy of suffering impossible. He also rejects the hypothesis that the *whole* scene is to be regarded as unhistorical.

[3] See W. G. Kümmel, 'Das Gleichnis von den bosen Weingärtnern', *Aux sources de la tradition chrétienne*, pp. 120 ff. See also p. 289 below.

in which Jesus says when the woman of Bethany pours ointment over his head, 'She has anointed my body beforehand for burying.' Many exegetes also deny of course that these two sayings are genuine.

We find only one direct quotation from Isa. 53 in a saying of Jesus: 'For I tell you that this scripture must be fulfilled in me, "And he was reckoned with transgressors"; for what is written about me has its fulfilment' (Luke 22.37). According to the Hebrew text (not according to the Septuagint), Jesus quotes Isa. 53.12 here. The genuineness of this saying also has been contested. But the fact that it is not included in Mark and Matthew is no conclusive reason for questioning its authenticity. H. W. Wolff rightly observes that the writer of Luke himself nowhere connects the suffering of Jesus with Isa. 53.[1]

Besides this single direct quotation, however, there are a number of allusions to Isa. 52–53 which can hardly be questioned as such. The clearest are in the sayings of Jesus about the Lord's Supper.[2] They indicate indirectly that the thought of Isa. 53 also lies behind most of the passages we have mentioned above in which Jesus speaks more generally of the necessity of his death. We need not compare the four versions of Jesus' institution of the Lord's Supper handed down to us in Mark 14.24, Matt. 26.28, Luke 22.20 and I Cor. 11.24. The differences between them are quite considerable in details, but all four passages agree in the most important point: when Jesus distributed the supper, he announced that he would shed his blood *for many*. The very fact that these different reports do not agree in other respects makes this fundamental agreement all the more significant.

It is difficult to contest the unanimous tradition that at this moment Jesus predicted his atoning death 'for many' and accompanied the prediction with the sacramental act. All four reports (with the exception of the D manuscript in Luke) use either the expression ὑπὲρ ὑμῶν, ὑπὲρ πολλῶν, or περὶ πολλῶν. Moreover, the fact that all four contain the word διαθήκη is also important for our problem, since we have seen that the ideas of *representation* and *covenant* are precisely the two main elements of the work which according to the Old Testament the *ebed Yahweh* must accomplish. The preposition

[1] H. W. Wolff, *Jesaja 53 im Urchristentum*, p. 57.

[2] Independently of me, E. Lohse, *Märtyrer und Gottesknecht*, pp. 122 ff., arrives at conclusions similar to mine, if not the same in all details. This relationship is rejected by F. J. Leenhardt, *Le sacrement de la S. Cène*, 1948, p. 27 n. 1; and by E. Schweizer, *RGG*[3] I, col. 13 f.

'for' or 'instead of', which is basic to the idea of representation, plays an important part in Isa. 53. Isa. 42.6 and 49.8 ascribe to the *ebed* the task of re-establishing the covenant between God and his people[1]—in fact, in this context the *ebed* himself *is* the *berith* in person.[2]

Thus when Jesus took the last meal with his disciples, he announced what he would accomplish the next day on the cross.[3] These words consequently throw light also on the other sayings we have mentioned. We shall see that by the time the Synoptic Gospels were written, the *ebed Yahweh* as a title for Jesus was no longer common in the early Church. The Gospels prefer other titles for him, above all 'Christ'. It is all the more remarkable that not only Paul but also all three Synoptics in relating the story of the Last Supper recall that Jesus at this decisive moment ascribed to himself the role of the *ebed Yahweh*.[4]

There is therefore no valid argument for contesting the genuineness of Mark 10.45, another saying of Jesus which is a clear reference to Isa. 52–53, and for describing it with R. Bultmann as a 'Hellenistic-Christian doctrine of salvation'.[5] Jesus says here, 'For the Son of man also came not to be served but to serve, and to give his life as a ransom (λύτρον) for many.' Here we hear the central theme of the *ebed Yahweh* hymns, and this is a clear allusion to Isa. 53.5.[6] It is as if Jesus said, 'The Son of Man came to fulfil the task of the *ebed Yahweh*.' Jesus consciously united in his person the two central concepts of the Jewish faith, *barnasha* and *ebed Yahweh*.

[1] In the words of the Lord's Supper we must think of this διαθήκη, not of the blood of circumcision, which the rabbis can also call the blood of the covenant. See Strack-Billerbeck I, p. 991. Jer. 31 was also referred to only later. It is precisely the mention of *blood* which shows that this passage did *not* originally refer to Jer. 31.

[2] See G. Dalman, *Jesus-Jeshua*, p. 170; H. W. Wolff, *op. cit.*, p. 65.

[3] It is regrettable that even W. G. Kümmel, who (in contrast to many of his German colleagues) does not usually give a contrary opinion *ex cathedra* without foundation, can be content simply to write (*Promise and Fulfilment*, p. 73), 'Nor do the eucharistic words constitute a link between Jesus' death and the atoning death of the servant of God.'

[4] Inasmuch as we presuppose that the words of institution refer to the concept of the *ebed Yahweh*, it is unnecessary to call the whole scene an 'aetiological cultic legend'.

[5] Cf. R. Bultmann, *Geschichte der synoptischen Tradition*, p. 154.

[6] W. G. Kümmel, *op. cit.*, p. 73, also admits that 'doubtless ideas of Isa. 53 are to be found' here. But why then does he reject *a priori* any allusion to Isa. 53 in other words of Jesus? According to E. Lohse, *op. cit.*, pp. 117 ff., we are dealing in this saying with the earliest Palestinian tradition.

We must speak of still another very important passage, one which allows us to go a step further in our investigation and at the same time to answer the question we have mentioned before: at which point in his earthly life did Jesus reach the consciousness that he had to realize the task of the *ebed*? The key to the solution of this problem is the voice from heaven which Jesus hears when he is baptized by John in the Jordan (Mark 1.11 and parallels). The saying, 'Thou art my beloved Son; with thee I am well pleased,' is a quotation from Isa. 42.1. In the Old Testament these words are addressed to the *ebed Yahweh*; indeed, they are the introduction to the *ebed Yahweh* hymns.

We may consider it certain that the words of the voice from heaven are really a citation of this passage in Isaiah.[1] Nothing to the contrary may be deduced from the fact that Mark 1.11 translates the Hebrew *ebed* with υἱός instead of παῖς, the translation in the Septuagint and in Matt. 12.18. παῖς means both 'servant' and 'son' (and this is relevant also for the translation of *ebed*).[2] Moreover, the word *bachir*, which is connected with *ebed* in Isa. 42.1, and which in Matt. 12.18 is translated ἀγαπητός, suggests the idea of son. The Septuagint uses ἐκλεκτός for *bachir* in Isa. 42.1. According to a very well documented and probably original reading,[3] the Gospel of John in reporting the words of the voice from heaven also translates *bachir* with ἐκλεκτός. This shows that the Fourth Gospel recognizes these words from Isaiah in the voice from heaven.[4] We must of course reckon with the possibility that the thought of Ps. 2.7 ('You are my son, today I have begotten you') suggested itself as a parallel, and facilitated the translation υἱός. This possibility is supported by the Western text reading of Luke 3.22, according to which the voice from heaven simply quotes Ps. 2.7.

The voice from heaven so understood thus comes to Jesus as a summons to accept the task of the one who is addressed in the same way at the beginning of the *ebed Yahweh* hymns in Isa. 42.1. Jesus therefore became conscious at the moment of his baptism that he

[1] See O. Cullmann, *Baptism in the New Testament*, ET (SBT 1), 1950, pp. 16 ff.; J. Jeremias, *The Servant of God*, pp. 81 f.; C. Maurer, *ZTK* 50, 1953, pp. 30 ff.

[2] Following Jeremias, *op. cit.*, pp. 43 f., Maurer, *op. cit.*, pp. 25 ff., refers especially to Wisd. 2.13–20, and believes that it is even possible to draw from this far-reaching consequences for the question of the high priest in Mark. 14.55 ff.

[3] Thus A. Harnack, *Studien zur Geschichte des Neuen Testaments und der Alten Kirche*, 1931, pp. 127 ff.; A. Loisy, *Le quatrième Evangile*[2], 1921, *ad loc.*; C. K. Barrett, *The Gospel according to St John*, 1955, pp. 148 f. See also my *Early Christian Worship*, ET (SBT 10), 1953, p. 64.

[4] Also E. Lohmeyer, *Gottesknecht und Davidsohn*, p. 9, emphasizes that 'Son' and 'Servant' belong together.

had to take upon himself the *ebed Yahweh* role. The words of the heavenly voice also answer a question the first Christians later asked: What is the meaning of baptism for forgiveness of sins for Jesus himself?[1] The other Jews went to John the Baptist to be baptized for their own sins. But when Jesus is baptized just as all the others were, he hears a divine voice which implicitly says to him, 'You are not baptized for your own sins, but for those of the whole people. For you are the one whose vicarious suffering for the sins of others the prophet predicted.' This may also be the sense of Jesus' words in Matt. 3.15 about 'fulfilling all righteousness'.[2] But this means that Jesus is baptized in view of his death, that on the cross he will accomplish a general baptism of his people. He takes on himself all the sins which the Jews bring to the Jordan. In this way the whole plan of salvation which he has to realize is openly laid before him.

This explanation of Jesus' baptism is confirmed by the only two sayings of Jesus which contain the verb βαπτισθῆναι, Mark 10.38 and Luke 12.50. For Jesus, 'to be baptized' means the same as 'to die'.[3] This is the reason he no longer baptized with water after he began his work independent of the Baptist. After he heard the voice from heaven, there was only one more baptism for him, his own death.

The strongest support for this interpretation lies in the way the Gospel of John reports the baptism of Jesus through the witness of the Baptist himself. In John 1.29 ff. we have what might be called the oldest commentary on the event of Jesus' baptism. There can be no doubt that the fourth evangelist understood the voice from heaven as a summons for Jesus to take on himself the task of the *ebed Yahweh*. This is the only way we can understand the witness of the Baptist when he says, 'Behold the Lamb of God, who takes away the sin of the world' (vv. 29 and 36). These words clearly relate Jesus' baptism and his vicarious suffering. The connection lies in the words of the voice from heaven. As we have seen, it is even clearer in the Gospel of John than in the Synoptics that this voice uses the

[1] On the following discussion see O. Cullmann, *Baptism in the New Testament*, pp. 18 ff.

[2] This possibility is discussed fully by H. Ljungmann, 'Das Gesetz erfüllen. Matth. 5.17 ff. und 3.15 untersucht', *Lunds Universitat Arsskrift*, new series, 50, 1954, pp. 97 ff.

[3] W. G. Kümmel, *TR* 18, 1950, pp. 37 ff., seeks to weaken this argument by saying that a similar way of speaking may be found in the Old Testament. But the passages usually cited (Ps. 42.7 ff.; 69. 1f., 14 f.; Isa. 43.2) can hardly be seriously considered as parallels.

words of Isa. 42.1 addressed to the *ebed Yahweh*, because the original reading of this account of Jesus' baptism depends more closely on the Old Testament text.[1]

The connection between the baptism and death of Jesus appears even more clearly in the statement of Ignatius (*Eph.* 18.2): 'He (Jesus) was born and baptized, that by his passion he might purify the water.' Ignatius uses here ancient Christian confessional material. But even if in this form the statement is coloured by his own thoughts, it still indicates a remembrance of the Church that there is a connection between the baptism of Jesus and his atoning suffering.

I refer with particular emphasis to this witness of John and Ignatius in defence of my thesis. Various scholars have all too quickly, almost automatically, reacted negatively to it as I presented it in my *Baptism in the New Testament*, pp. 18 ff.; and in my *Early Christian Worship*, pp. 63 ff. This reaction is typical of the common suspicion of any thesis which harmonizes the different elements of the New Testament. My critics accuse me of supporting my argument by a construction derived from a 'desire for synthesis'. (See for example W. G. Kümmel, *TR* 18, 1950, pp. 39 f.; and L. Cerfaux, *RHE* 44, 1949, p. 586.) One should certainly reject forced attempts at harmonization, and let actual discrepancies in the New Testament stand. But do we New Testament scholars not run the risk of falling into a 'professional destruction' which expresses itself in our taking an almost sadistic pleasure in finding unbalanced texts and in our objecting to every thesis which indicates lines of connection at any point—even between Jesus and Paul, for instance? With reference to the particular problem which concerns us here, J. A. T. Robinson has attempted to prove by relevant texts that the connection between the baptism and death of Jesus is a motif which runs through all the New Testament.[2]

We have seen that the *ebed* consciousness of Jesus came to him very probably at the time of his baptism. He realized at that time that he was the *ebed Yahweh*, and from that time on the way he should go was clear to him. It is permissible to set a definite date for the origin of this consciousness in the life of Jesus? We shall see in our next chapter that the writer of the Letter to the Hebrews at least did not hesitate to speak of an 'inner development' in Jesus' life.[3]

We conclude that the concept 'Jesus the *ebed Yahweh*' has its origin with Jesus himself, just as does the concept 'Jesus the Son of

[1] See p. 66 above.

[2] J. A. T. Robinson, 'The One Baptism as a Category of New Testament Soteriology', *Scottish Journal of Theology* 6, 1953, pp. 257 ff., reprinted in *Twelve New Testament Studies* (SBT 34), 1962, pp. 158 ff.

[3] See pp. 97 f. below.

Man'. Thus it is not the early Church which first established a connection between these two fundamental Christological concepts. Now we must investigate the place the application of the title *ebed Yahweh* did occupy in the early Church.

3. *Jesus the* Ebed Yahweh *in Early Christianity*

We have already mentioned that the principal Christology of the Gospel writers is not that of the *ebed Yahweh.* We find only a few passages in which the authors of the *Synoptic Gospels* relate Jesus directly to the figure of the Servant of God. Nevertheless in Matt. 8.16 f., which deals with the healing of the sick, the evangelist remarks: 'He cast out the spirits with a word, and healed all who were sick. This was to fulfil what was spoken by the prophet Isaiah, "He took our infirmities and bore our diseases."' Following the usual introductory phrase ὅπως πληρωθῇ (that it might be fulfilled), the evangelist here cites verbatim a part of Isa. 53.4. What interests him first of all in this quotation is of course not the vicarious suffering which is the central thought of Isa. 53. He sees Jesus' healing of the sick, not his death, as the fulfilment of this prophecy. Whereas the prophet thinks of the *ebed's* taking the disease of others upon himself through his own suffering and death, Matthew obviously interprets the text to mean that the *ebed* has 'taken away' diseases. This explanation is correct to the extent that in the light of early Christian theology the healing which Jesus accomplished represents an anticipation, so to speak, of the final work he will accomplish through his death. But it seems remarkable that Matthew does not cite Isa. 53 with reference to the central saving act accomplished by Jesus, his atoning death. In the passion story too, Matthew, who quotes the Old Testament so often and with such pleasure, never refers to the Suffering Servant of God of Isa. 53. In Matt. 12.18–21 he does indeed quote once again a passage from the *ebed Yahweh* hymns (Isa. 42.1 ff.), but here also he is only interested in a secondary element, the fact that Jesus forbade the sick whom he had healed to make him known publicly.

In the Gospel of Mark we find no allusion to the *ebed Yahweh* or the Servant hymns by the author himself.

C. Maurer does point out that the constitution and formation of Mark's passion story indicate the influence of the Servant of God concept.[1] But

[1] C. Maurer, *op. cit.* on p. 65 n. 3 above; V. Taylor, 'The Origin of the Marcan Passion Sayings', *NTS* 1, 1954/55, pp. 159 ff., comes to the same conclusion.

as Maurer himself says, this is not due to the Evangelist himself, but rather to the tradition handed down to him.[1]

Did the writer of the *Fourth Gospel* attach a greater significance to the idea that Jesus fulfilled the role of the Servant of God? At first glance one would be tempted to think that he knew nothing at all of the identification of Jesus with the Servant of God. We may legitimately object in general, however, to the prejudice which holds that in the Fourth Gospel the idea of glorification forces the idea of the atoning death completely into the background.[2] We need cite only a few passages to show that the reverse is true. We recall the explanation the author himself gives of the saying about the temple in John 2.19 ff. ('... he spoke of the temple of his body'.). Again we think particularly of the lifting up of Christ (on the cross!) in John 3.14 ('And as Moses lifted up the serpent in the wilderness, so must the Son of man be lifted up'). Then in 3.16 we read, 'For God so loved the world that he *gave* his only Son ...' The verb ἔδωκεν (gave) is used at the same time in the sense of παρέδωκεν (delivered). We could also mention the account of the wedding at Cana in ch. 2, in which the 'hour' which has not yet come without doubt refers to Jesus' death.[3]

Besides these texts there is still more direct evidence that the fourth evangelist did not force the idea of the atoning death into the background. There is for example John 10.11: 'I am the good shepherd. The good shepherd lays down his life for the sheep.' This and the following verses can have only one meaning. Verses 17 f. are especially important: 'For this reason the Father loves me, because I lay down my life, that I may take it again. No one takes it from me, but I lay it down of my own accord.' This seems to emphasize just the distinction between the suffering of the prophet and that of the *ebed Yahweh*. We could even ask whether this verse is not to be taken together with v. 8 of the same chapter ('all who came before me are thieves and robbers'), which reminds us of men like Judas the Galilean or the 'Teacher of Righteousness' of the Qumran texts—even if the latter did not suffer martyrdom in the form of execution.[4]

[1] C. Maurer, *op cit.*, p. 2.

[2] See for example R. Bultmann, *Theology of the New Testament* II, ET 1955, pp. 53 f; *Das Evangelium des Johannes* (Meyer 2)[11], 1941, p. 293.

[3] See O. Cullmann, *Early Christian Worship*, pp. 66 ff.

[4] It is certainly not correct to think of 'Herodians, Rabbis, and party leaders' at the time of Jesus as does R. Schlatter, *Der Evangelist Johannes*, 1930, p. 236. R. Bultmann, *Das Evangelium des Johannes*, p. 286, rightly rejects this idea. See O. Cullmann, *The State in the New Testament*, p. 22.

But even the Fourth Gospel does not deal only with the necessity of the death of Jesus in general.[1] It contains direct and precise reference to Isa. 53 in 1.29 and 1.36 in the testimony of John the Baptist: 'Behold, the Lamb of God, who takes away the sin of the world.' (We have already seen that this whole section of John confirms the explanation I have given of the Synoptic account of Jesus' baptism.)[2] The works of C. F. Burney [3] and J. Jeremias [4] have shown that the Aramaic phrase טַלְיָא דֶּאלָהָא which means both 'Lamb of God' and 'Servant of God', very probably lies behind the Greek expression ἀμνὸς τοῦ θεοῦ. Since the expression 'Lamb of God' is not commonly used in the Old Testament as a designation for the paschal lamb, it is probable that the author of John thought primarily of the *ebed Yahweh.* The translation ἀμνός is all the more easily explained when one considers that the idea of the *ebed Yahweh* is related to that of the paschal lamb and that Isa. 53.7 compares the *ebed* with a lamb. The use of the verb αἴρειν (take away), which seems applicable only to the paschal lamb and not to the *ebed*, could be explained by the fact mentioned in Strack-Billerbeck [5] that the Aramaic verb נְטַל can be translated in Greek either as αἴρειν or as φέρειν. Thus we may consider the designation ἀμνὸς τοῦ θεοῦ in John 1.29 and 1.36 as a variant of παῖς θεοῦ, the Greek equivalent of the Hebrew *ebed Yahweh.*

Even if one could not prove that the concept 'Jesus the Lamb of God' in these verses is derived from the Aramaic *taljā dē'lāhā*, it still represents a variation of 'Jesus the *ebed Yahweh*'. It does seem at first glance that the paschal lamb (which is also related to Jesus in I Cor 5.7 and I Peter 1.19) denotes a different idea, and there is in fact at least a subtle difference. For the Jews the purpose of sacrificing the paschal lamb is to achieve atonement for the sins of the people (Ex. 12). The Jewish idea of sacrifice brought to God lies in the background here. The *ebed Yahweh* concept

[1] E. Schweizer, *Erniedrigung und Erhöhung*, pp. 57 f., does not deny that the death of Jesus as the consummation of his path of obedience is also important for the Gospel of John. But he believes that for the thought of the early Church the 'Servant of God' title is not limited to Jesus' atoning death, but describes him quite generally as the suffering Righteous One (pp. 84 f.). Therefore Schweizer can state that the idea of Jesus' atoning death is almost completely missing in the Fourth Gospel.

[2] See pp. 67 f. above.

[3] C. F. Burney, *The Aramaic Origin of the Fourth Gospel*, 1922, pp. 107 f.; and already before him, C. J. Ball, *ExpT* 21, 1909/10, p. 92.

[4] J. Jeremias, 'ἀμνὸς τοῦ θεοῦ–παῖς θεοῦ', *ZNW* 34, pp. 115 ff.

[5] Strack-Billerbeck II, p. 370.

also includes the idea of a sacrifice, but the idea of a voluntary representation dominates this concept. The paschal lamb is by nature purely passive; it takes away sins by its being passively offered up. The *ebed Yahweh*, on the other hand, voluntarily takes the sins of others upon himself and only in this active manner takes them away. We are therefore concerned with very closely related concepts, each of which emphasizes a particular aspect of the atoning death. We could say that the concept of the lamb emphasizes more strongly the goal, while the concept of the *ebed Yahweh* emphasizes the means (voluntary vicarious suffering) by which the goal is reached. The two ideas are so closely related, however, that we may assume that the prophet had also the paschal lamb in mind in his description of the *ebed Yahweh* in ch. 53, and that for this reason he introduced the comparison with a lamb in v. 7 ('like a lamb that is led to the slaughter'). Such a close relationship would explain especially well the Fourth Gospel's use in 1.29 and 1.36 of an expression which could have both meanings. The presupposition of this thesis is of course that an Aramaic text lies behind this section of John, or that the author at least thought in Aramaic terms.

It must be admitted, however, that another passage in the Gospel of John, 19.36, thinks only of the paschal lamb. The subject in the text is the crucified one, whose bones, contrary to the general custom, were not broken. The evangelist explains this fact by reference to Ex. 12.46 and Num. 9.12, which relate directly to the paschal lamb. But this does not prove that the idea of the *ebed Yahweh* could not predominate in John 1.29 and 1.36. Precisely in view of the close connection between the two concepts, it is entirely possible that the evangelist bears witness to *both* of them. He could even have had both in mind in the same passage.[1]

We have already seen [2] that it was the Gospel of John that most clearly preserved the memory that the saying of the voice from heaven at the baptism was a quotation from the beginning of the *ebed Yahweh* hymns. Only this Gospel with its use of the word ἐκλεκτός

[1] C. H. Dodd, *The Interpretation of the Fourth Gospel*, 1953, pp. 235 f., thinks that the term ἀμνός refers here rather to the Messiah as the king of Israel. Otherwise, however, he too emphasizes that the idea of the Suffering Servant of God had a very special significance for the fourth evangelist, although he does not accept the explanation of C. F. Burney and C. J. Ball. On the concept of the 'lamb of God', see also C. K. Barrett, 'The Lamb of God', *NTS* 1, 1954/55, pp. 210 ff., who begins from Dodd's connection of the lamb and the messianic king, but in the context of early Christian theology and liturgy strongly emphasizes the idea of the Passover. On the central Christological significance of the lamb in Revelation, see P. A. Harlé, *L'agneau de l'Apocalypse et le Nouveau Testament* (Etudes théologiques et religieuses), 1956, pp. 26 ff., who shows the link with Isa. 53 and with the early Christian liturgy.

[2] See p. 66 above.

correctly reproduces the Hebrew word in Isa. 42.1. The writer of the Fourth Gospel knows that the calling of Jesus at his baptism was a summons to fulfil the task of the *ebed Yahweh*.

Finally, we may mention that in John 12.38 we find a direct quotation from Isa. 53.1: 'Lord, who has believed our report, and to whom has the arm of the Lord been revealed?'

The Acts of the Apostles offers us the strongest proof of the fact that in the most ancient period of early Christianity there existed an explanation of the person and work of Jesus which we could characterize somewhat inaccurately as an *ebed Yahweh* Christology—or more exactly as a 'Paidology'. We may even assert that this is probably the oldest known solution to the Christological problem. The account of the conversion of the Ethiopian eunuch (Acts 8.26 ff.) shows that in the first century Jesus was explicitly identified with the *ebed Yahweh*, and that apparently the memory remained alive that Jesus himself understood his divine mission in this way.[1]

Besides this account, however, there are other passages in Acts which do not actually contain a direct quotation from Isaiah, but are still extremely important for our question. These passages openly give Jesus the actual title παῖς τοῦ θεοῦ, the Septuagint's translation of Deutero-Isaiah's expression *ebed Yahweh*. We find this title four times in Acts. It is significant that all four occur in the same section, chs. 3 and 4, and that Jesus is designated παῖς τοῦ θεοῦ in no other book of the New Testament.[2] Jesus is called this first in Acts 3.13, which refers to Isa. 52.13; then again in Acts 3.26, which actually deals with a Christological title: Jesus is called *Pais* exactly as he later is commonly called 'Christ'. One gains the clear impression also in the next chapter (4.27, 30) that παῖς is used almost as a *terminus technicus* which has a tendency to become a proper name—as did happen in the case of 'Christ'. This confirms the existence of a very old Christology on the basis of which Jesus was called the *ebed Yahweh*. This Christology later disappears, but it must extend back to the very earliest period of the Christian faith, since the author of Acts preserved its traces precisely in the first part of his book.

[1] Those passages in Acts which, following Isa. 53.11, designate Jesus δίκαιος also come into consideration here: Acts 3.14; 22.14; and especially 7.52. Cf. J. Jeremias, 'ἀμνὸς τοῦ θεοῦ—παῖς θεοῦ', *ZNW* 34, p. 119.

[2] We emphasize with H. W. Wolff, *Jesaja 53 im Urchristentums*, pp. 86 ff., and in opposition to R. Bultmann, *Theology of the New Testament* I, pp. 50 f., and E. Schweizer, *Erniedrigung und Erhöhung*, pp. 47, 83, that precisely the context here points directly to Deutero-Isaiah. So also J. Jeremias, *op. cit.*, p. 119.

Unfortunately we know nothing exact about this Christological—or more properly 'Paidological'—doctrine. The context in which Acts places this ancient designation, however, perhaps allows us to guess what early Christian group commonly used the title. It is probably no accident that of the only four passages in the New Testament which call Jesus *pais*, two occur in a speech attributed to the Apostle *Peter*, and two are spoken in prayers of the Church in the presence of Peter. Acts itself, which contains 28 chapters, uses this expression in no other passage. It is probably not venturing too much to draw the conclusion that the author may have preserved the precise memory that it was the Apostle Peter who by preference designated Jesus the 'Suffering Servant of God'. Of course one cannot prove this hypothesis. But it would at least be quite consistent with everything else we know about Peter. According to Mark 8.32 he was the very one who in Caesarea Philippi showed so little understanding of the necessity of Jesus' suffering. It was he who took Jesus aside to tell him, 'This shall never happen to you,' so that Jesus, who saw in Peter the same Tempter who once before tried to divert him from his way, had to rebuke him with the words, 'Get behind me, Satan!' We can understand that the same apostle, who according to I Cor. 15.5 was later the first to see the risen Christ, was also the first after this experience to proclaim in the light of the resurrection the necessity of the suffering and death of Jesus. He, who had wanted to hear nothing of it during the lifetime of Jesus, made Jesus' suffering and death the very centre of his explanation of Jesus' earthly work.[1]

It is also interesting to note in this connection that I Peter cites with very particular emphasis the passages from Isaiah which relate to the *ebed Yahweh* (2.21 ff.). This fact retains its significance for our problem quite apart from the question whether or not the letter is genuine. Even if it was not written by Peter, the anonymous author who ascribed it to him would nevertheless have known just as did the author of Acts that Peter preferred to speak of Jesus in terms of the Suffering Servant of God.

If Papias is right in connecting the oral tradition behind the Gospel of Mark with the preaching of Peter, we can take yet a further step. We saw that C. Maurer has attempted to show that the Marcan tradition was shaped to a great extent by the *ebed Yahweh* concept.[2] Could not this point to Peter as the source of such an emphasis?

[1] Reflection on Peter's denial of Christ also suggests this. See O. Cullmann, *Peter*, pp. 65 ff.

[2] See p. 53 n. 3 above.

We may conjecture, by way of summary, that the *ebed Yahweh* concept very probably dominated the Christology of the Apostle Peter—if we may really speak of a 'Christology' of Peter in spite of the small amount of direct information we possess about his thought. If this is the case, he, who had wanted to divert Jesus from the way of suffering, who had denied him at the decisive moment of the passion story, would be the first after Easter to grasp the necessity of this offence. He could not express this conviction better than with the designation *ebed Yahweh*, especially since he must have known what great importance Jesus himself had attributed to the ideas related to it. Subsequent periods of the Church were often unjust to Paul by placing him in the shadow of Peter. Are we not perhaps unjust to Peter when we place him in the shadow of Paul?

Another indication of the very great antiquity of the title 'Jesus the Servant of God', which was very soon forced into the background, is the fact that it was maintained longest in the documents which by their very nature preserve the oldest elements of early Christianity: the *ancient liturgies*. We read several times in the ancient liturgy of the Roman Church contained in *I Clement* 59.3–61.3, 'Jesus thy servant', or, in still closer connection with the *ebed Yahweh* hymns, 'through Jesus Christ, thy beloved servant' (59.2, 3, 4). Again, we read in the famous eucharistic prayers of the *Didache*: 'We give thanks to thee, our Father, for the Holy Vine of David, thy servant, which thou hast made known to us through Jesus thy servant' (9.2); and 'We give thanks to thee . . . for the knowledge and faith and immortality which thou hast made known to us through Jesus thy servant' (10.2). We observe that it is precisely *eucharistic* prayers which designate Jesus as *Pais*. Does this not preserve the recollection that the Last Supper was the decisive moment when Jesus openly told his disciples that his task was that of the Suffering Servant of God? We have seen that the words which Jesus spoke then could not be otherwise understood.

It is no accident that at the end of the first and beginning of the second century we find the designation *Pais* for Jesus only in these liturgies. It had already disappeared from other Christian writings by this time.

We still have one final question to ask: What is the attitude of the Apostle *Paul* to the *ebed Yahweh* concept and its application to Jesus? The central place which the death of Christ occupies in his theology suggests that the identification of Jesus with the 'Servant of God' in Isaiah should be very important to him. But as a matter of fact, while we do find the designation 'Paschal Lamb' (I Cor. 5.7),[1] there are remarkably few actual quotations from Isa. 53. Only Isa. 53.12 is directly quoted—in Rom. 4.25. II Cor. 5.21 concerning him who 'knew no sin' clearly refers to Isa. 53.6. The quotations from Isa. 52–53 in Rom. 10.16 and 15.21 refer to the missionary preaching, not to the peculiar work of the Servant of God. Although these passages are sufficient to prove that the application of the *ebed Yahweh* concept to Jesus was not unknown to Paul, the absence in his writings of other citations from the *ebed Yahweh* hymns and of the title *Pais* demands an explanation.

First we should observe that only direct quotations are absent. In three of the most important Christological passages of the letters of Paul (I Cor. 15.3; Phil 2.7; Rom. 5.12 ff.), the *idea* of the vicarious suffering of the Servant of God is undoubtedly present.

I Cor. 15.3 contains an ancient confession which Paul himself did not compose, but which he expressly says he had received through tradition. This is probably the oldest Christian creed; Paul has simply taken it over and further developed it.[2] The assertion mentioned first here is that 'Christ died for our sins in accordance with the scriptures'. There is little doubt that 'the scriptures' must refer to Isa. 53.[3] Paul's citation of an already existent confession of the early Church confirms the fact that the *ebed Yahweh* Christology extends back into the earliest period of the Christian faith, and that Paul is not the creator of the doctrine of the atoning death of Christ.

The same conclusion may be drawn from the second of the three basic Christological texts, if Lohmeyer is correct in his thesis that in Phil. 2.6–11 Paul quotes an ancient psalm of the Church.[4] We shall consider this passage in detail in our chapter on the Son of Man[5] and again in connection with the title *Kyrios*.[6] We mention it now because Phil. 2.7 certainly includes the idea of the *ebed Yahweh* in the

[1] See p. 71 above.

[2] See O. Cullmann, *The Earliest Christian Confessions*, pp. 23, 45, 53.

[3] J. Héring, *La première Epître de S. Paul aux Corinthiens* (CNT), 1949, pp. 134 f., still maintains that this only refers to Holy Scripture as a whole. This interpretation is possible, but not probable. E. Lichtenstein, 'Die älteste christliche Glaubensformel', *ZKG* 63, 1950, pp. 17 ff., also assumes that this refers primarily to Isa. 53.

[4] E. Lohmeyer, *Kyrios Jesus. Eine Untersuchung zu Phil. 2.5–11* (Sitzungsberichte der Heidelberger Akademie der Wissenschaften, phil.-hist. Klasse), 1927/28; J. Héring, *Le royaume de Dieu et sa venue*, pp. 159 ff.

[5] See pp. 174 ff. below.

[6] See pp. 217 ff. below.

humiliation of Christ's incarnation: μορφὴν δούλου λαβών ('taking the form of a servant'). *Ebed* is translated here by δοῦλος.[1]

Although Paul also in this passage uses material handed down to him, he certainly has made its ideas his own. This is proved by the third of the three texts, Rom. 5.12 ff., in which the apostle does not reproduce an older formula, but formulates his Christological solution in his own words. Like Phil. 2.6 ff. this passage unites (as did Jesus) both of the most important concepts which go back to Jesus himself: 'Son of Man' and 'Servant of God'. Verse 19 shows clearly that the apostle had in mind the 'Servant' of Isaiah: '. . . by one man's obedience many will be made righteous'. This is a reference to Isa. 53.11: 'My servant shall make many to be accounted righteous.' Perhaps we could also mention in this context the familiar and controversial ἱλαστήριον of Rom. 3.25.

But the question remains: Why did Paul not use the title *Pais* to express his faith in Jesus? The answer lies, as we shall see in the last section of this chapter, in the fact that this title explains primarily the earthly work of the incarnate Jesus; but Paul's Christology is just as interested in the work which Christ fulfils as the *Kyrios* exalted to the right hand of God.

It is true that Isa. 52.13 ff. says, 'Behold, my servant shall prosper, he shall be exalted and lifted up, and shall be very high.' And the following verses speak of the astonishment of nations and of kings. This passage is one extremely important point of contact for the Christian idea that the *ebed Yahweh* is at the same time the Son of Man who will come on the clouds of heaven.[2] But Deutero-Isaiah gives us no details about the future work the *ebed* will accomplish in glory, and the main theme of the *ebed* hymns remains the Servant of God's vicarious suffering, through and only after which he will come into glory. In any case it was this idea of atoning death which was suggested by the *Pais-ebed* name in New Testament times.

For this reason, this title is primarily applicable only to the earthly work of Jesus. But since Paul can see Christ only in the light of the

[1] E. Lohmeyer, *Gottesknecht und Davidsohn*, pp. 3 ff., correctly emphasizes that this translation is possible. V. Taylor, *The Atonement in New Testament Teaching*[2], 1945, pp. 65 f., even uses the expression μορφὴν δούλου as proof for his assumption that Paul avoided the *title* of the Suffering Servant of God, although he was thoroughly acquainted with the *idea*, because he believed the word 'slave' was inappropriate as a designation of his *Kyrios*.

[2] H. W. Wolff, *op. cit.*, p. 31, following G. von Rad, *Zur prophetischen Verkündigung Deuterojesajas* (Verkündigung und Forschung), 1940, p. 62, emphasizes that Deutero-Isaiah speaks of suffering and dying *only from the standpoint of exaltation.*

event of the resurrection, he must make use of another title to designate Christ's person and work—the title *Kyrios*, which points to the exalted Lord who allows his Church to take part in the fruits of his atoning death and who at the same time continues his function as Mediator.

This is also the reason for the fact that even the thoughts relative to the *ebed Yahweh* are pushed more and more into the background of early Christian writings. We have seen that the title was preserved for a short time only in liturgies. We do find frequent quotations from Isa. 53 applied to Jesus,[1] but they have no central significance, and the specific Christological idea of the *ebed Yahweh* is not prominent in them. We see this quite clearly in the Apostolic Fathers.

We find for example a very long quotation from Isa. 53 in *I Clement* 16. All of the important sections of ch. 53 are assembled here and applied to Jesus. But their purpose is not so much to explain the person and work of Christ as to summon the Christians of Corinth to be as humble as Jesus was. We read in ch. 16: 'For Christ is of those who are humble-minded, not of those who exalt themselves over his flock. The sceptre of the greatness of God, the Lord Jesus Christ, came not with the pomp of pride or of arrogance, for all his power, but was humble-minded, as the Holy Spirit spake concerning him. For it says . . .'. Then follows a quotation of Isa. 53.1 ff. about the external form of the *ebed Yahweh* and the contempt to which he is subjected. At the end of the quotation the author adds: 'You see, beloved, what is the example which is given to us; for if the Lord was thus humble-minded, what shall we do, who through him have come under the yoke of his grace?'—Thus we do not find here a real Christological application of the *ebed Yahweh* concept. The author uses the quotation from Isaiah only as a proof-text for the humility of Jesus.

We find a more important passage in the *Epistle of Barnabas*. Throughout the letter the author repeatedly compares Jesus with the sacrifice which the Jews offer for reconciliation (7.6; 8.1). In 5.2 he connects this idea with an allusion to the *ebed Yahweh*, and cites Isa. 53. But this is an isolated element in the *Epistle of Barnabas*.

* * *

We summarize our conclusions:

(1) Judaism in the New Testament period did connect the name *ebed Yahweh* with that of the Messiah. In some (perhaps esoteric) circles the conception of a suffering Messiah may also have arisen. But official Jewish messianism lacked the principal idea of the *ebed Yahweh* hymns, the idea of vicarious suffering and atoning death.

[1] See H. W. Wolff, *op. cit.*, pp. 108 ff.

(2) Jesus did not designate himself by the *title* 'Suffering Servant', but according to the Synoptics and the Gospel of John he applied to himself the idea of vicarious suffering and death, and also the idea of the *ebed's* restoration of the covenant between God and his people. Probably he gained the conviction that he had to fulfil his earthly work in this way at the time of his baptism.

(3) Early Christianity preserved the memory that Jesus himself was conscious of having to realize the work of the *ebed Yahweh*. In the Gospel of John we find Jesus designated 'Lamb of God', the Aramaic equivalent of which also means 'Servant of God'. Acts 3 and 4 use the title παῖς τοῦ θεοῦ, the Greek translation of *ebed Yahweh*, as a real Christological title. This use presupposes a very old Christology which was built entirely on the idea of the *ebed Yahweh*. It seems to have been particularly characteristic of the Apostle Peter's Christology, which possibly influenced the formation of the oral Gospel tradition, particularly that of the passion story.

(4) Paul gives the atoning death of Jesus a central place. He does not actually use the title *ebed Yahweh*, but according to two of the most important Christological texts in his writings which he took from the ancient tradition of the Church and made his own (I Cor. 15.3 and Phil. 2.7), Jesus fulfilled the task of the Servant of God. Also in Rom. 5.12 ff. Paul makes use of ideas relative to the *ebed Yahweh* and his atoning work.

(5) Although the *ebed Yahweh* Christology is one of the oldest and most important Christologies, extending back to Jesus himself, it very soon receded into the background. After the New Testament period, we encounter the title *Pais* applied to Jesus only in the liturgical texts of the *Didache* and the prayer of the Church in *I Clement*. Its early disappearance may be connected with the limitation to which we have already referred with regard to Paul and which we must now examine more closely.

4. *The Conception of Jesus the* Ebed Yahweh *as a Solution to the Christological Problem in the New Testament*

We have seen that the Christological concept of the Prophet of the end time is applicable to the earthly vocation of Jesus presented in the New Testament, but that it fully describes only one side of this work, Jesus' preaching and healing activity. We remember further that this concept is not broad enough to comprehend the present and future function of Jesus. In the case of the *ebed Yahweh* we are dealing with an explanation belonging to the New Testament itself, not, as with the Prophet, with an opinion of the people which the New Testament does not adopt but only repeats. Consequently we can expect from the outset that our evaluation from the New Testament point of view will be more positive in dealing with the *ebed Yahweh*—the more so, since Jesus himself understood his earthly work in terms of the *ebed's* task.

Concerning the *earthly* work of Jesus, we can say that the *ebed Yahweh* concept comprehends the central Christological event in a way which does full justice to the total witness of the New Testament. The atoning death of Jesus is not only the central act of his earthly life, but also the central act of the total history of salvation from the first creation at the beginning of time to the new creation at the end of time. To this extent the *Pais* Christology is a very important solution to the New Testament Christological problem. It understands Jesus as the one who at the decisive point in time carried out the decisive work of the total plan of salvation. This is the classical expression of the principle of the whole New Testament *Heilsgeschichte*. At most one could object that this concept does not take into consideration the preaching of the earthly Jesus. But except for the Gospels, the rest of the New Testament also either places that activity in the background or thinks of it as implied in the work of reconciliation. We can therefore conclude that the concept *ebed Yahweh* characterizes the person and work of the historical Jesus in a way which completely corresponds to the New Testament witness to Christ.

Concerning the *present* and *future* function of Jesus, it must be said that an extension of the work of the *ebed Yahweh* into the present and future is not prominent in the Old Testament *ebed* figure. Nevertheless the Old Testament does foresee such an extension. It is just the central hymn about the suffering of the Servant of God which looks forward to the time when the servant shall 'prosper', 'be exalted and lifted up' (Isa. 52.13). And at the end of the hymn we hear that 'he shall see his offspring, he shall prolong his days' (Isa. 53.10), and that he will be given 'a portion with the great' (53.12). All this, however, does not actually indicate so much a continuation of the work of the *ebed* as an epilogue to it. Nevertheless, everything the New Testament says about Christ's present rule can find a point of contact here. Whereas the Prophet of the end by his very nature has only a preparatory character, the work accomplished by the *ebed*

Yahweh has in itself a decisive character. It brings salvation. It marks the pivotal point of *Heilsgeschichte*. On the basis of this fact, we can draw a line from his work both backwards and forwards in time. Although the action accomplished by the *ebed* is complete in itself as an earthly action, just by virtue of this decisive character it points to consequences which lie beyond the time of the earthly Jesus. In other words, the concept of the *ebed Yahweh* can very easily be connected with other concepts which emphasize the work of the present or returning or pre-existent Christ.

One might think, then, that in principle the designation Jesus-*Pais* could have succeeded as an expression of the New Testament solution to the Christological problem. For on the basis of the early Christian understanding of the saving death of Christ as the central element of salvation, it would have been quite possible to consider the present and future work of Christ as included in this title. Indeed, we can even say that this would have corresponded especially well with early Christian theology and its understanding of history and time, according to which the death of Christ represents the centre of the whole history of salvation. The fact that the *Pais* Christology nevertheless disappeared so early is connected with the fact that it was actually faith in the *present* Christ which directly determined the life of the early Christian Church and led it to express its faith in Jesus primarily by reference to thoughts connected with the present *Kyrios*. Although the work of Jesus accomplished in the historical past to a large extent maintained the central place in early Christian thought, faith in the consequences of this work (i.e., faith in the exalted Lord at the right hand of God, and in his lordship over the Church and the world) meant more for the everyday life of the individual Christian and the Church—even more than the action itself upon which the present Lord's office as Mediator rests. The early Christian and the early Church prayed to the present Lord; and in their breaking of bread, joy at his presence was more prominent than remembrance of his death. This is the reason that, despite the central theological importance which continued to be attributed to the death of Christ, the title *ebed Yahweh* as a designation for Jesus had to take a subordinate place.

Nevertheless, this Christological designation deserves more attention in contemporary theology than it usually receives, not only because it is one of the oldest answers to the question who Jesus is, but also because it goes back to Jesus himself and therefore opens to us most clearly the secret of his self-consciousness. In this respect it would be even more correct to speak of a *Pais*-consciousness of Jesus than of his messianic-consciousness. But we shall see in one of the following chapters that another concept also is fundamental to Jesus, that even for him himself the *ebed* concept does not comprehend his whole work. For this reason he conferred upon himself the title 'Son of Man', which he of course related to the idea of the *ebed Yahweh*.

But we must speak now of still another New Testament designation which refers primarily to the earthly work of Christ: 'High Priest'. It was conferred upon Jesus only after his death, of course, and served only in certain circles as an answer to the Christological question.

4

Jesus the High Priest

(ἀρχιερεύς)

APPLIED TO JESUS, the concept High Priest is closely related to that of the Suffering Servant of God. In a certain sense one could actually understand it as a variant of the Suffering Servant concept. Nevertheless it is proper that we devote a special chapter to the High Priest, first because its application to Jesus in early Christianity has a completely different historical origin, and secondly because it has aspects which are foreign to the *ebed Yahweh* concept. We shall see that we are now dealing with a more complex Christological conception than that of the Prophet or Servant of God, since our present title does not concern exclusively the historical work of Jesus.

Contrary to the titles we shall consider in the following chapters, the title High Priest does not require us to investigate parallels from non-biblical religions.

1. *The High Priest as an Ideal Figure in Judaism*

The High Priest is an essentially Jewish figure. But at first glance it might seem superfluous to devote a special section to this concept in Judaism as we have reason to do in dealing with most of the other Christological titles. The expected Jewish redeemer does not at first appear to have the characteristics of the High Priest. And yet there are traces in Judaism of a connection between the Messiah-king and the High Priest. We mention first the speculations about the mysterious King Melchizedek of Gen. 14.17 ff. and Ps. 110.4.

Gen. 14.17 ff. tells how Abraham freed his nephew Lot from Chedorlaomer, the king of Elam, and his allies. When Abraham came back from the battle, King Melchizedek met and blessed him, and Abraham gave Melchizedek a tenth of the booty. Genesis tells us nothing more of this mysterious king before whom Abraham humbled himself in this way. For this reason the figure of Melchizedek very early stimulated the imagination of the Jews.

We read in v. 4 of the well-known Ps. 110 which the early Christians repeatedly quoted, 'You are a priest for ever after the order to Melchizedek.' The psalm addresses the words to the king on whom are conferred the high priestly functions of this high order. As an external framework it presupposes the enthronement ceremony of the king.[1] Just as the mysterious king of the ancient history of Canaan was also a priest, so shall the new king again perform a priestly office—an office highly exalted above any empirical priesthood, one which will not pass away but is eternal. If Ps. 110 connects kingship with an ideal priesthood—this was a familiar conception to the whole of the ancient East—while on the other hand the idea of kingship is the basis of messianism, we have here the starting-point for a messianic formulation of the figure of the High Priest.

When Jesus quotes Ps. 110 in Mark 12.35 ff. to show that the Messiah's Davidic sonship is problematical, he clearly presupposes that the king addressed in the psalm (the king who is at the same time a priest for ever after the order of Melchizedek) is to be understood as the Messiah.[2] The Septuagint also interprets the psalm in this way. It is true that before the second half of the third century after Christ we find no evidence in the rabbinical texts for such an identification,[3] but this may be connected with the fact that because of its anti-Christian polemic, Judaism tended to devaluate the figure of Melchizedek.[4]

Because Melchizedek names Abraham before he names God in Gen. 14.19 ff., later Judaism took the high priestly office away from him and transferred it to Abraham (Ned. 32b; Sanh. 108b).[5] The treatise Aboth R. Nathan 34 expressly makes the Messiah superior to the High Priest: 'You, Messiah, are a prince over Melchizedek and are therefore more beloved by God than this messianic High Priest Melchizedek.'

[1] SeeH. Schmidt, *Die Psalmen*, 1934, p. 203; and A. Weiser, *The Psalms*' ET (Old Testament Library), 1962, pp. 693 ff. Concerning the relationship between Melchizedek and Zadok, see H. H. Rowley, 'Melchizedek and Zadok', *Festschrift für A. Bertholet*, 1950, pp. 461 ff.

[2] This statement retains its value even if Mark 12.35 ff. is an invention of the early Church, as R. Bultmann maintains, *Geschichte der synoptischen Tradition*, pp. 145 ff. This thesis is not probable, however (see p. 132 below).

[3] With reference to the whole discussion here see the entire excursus, 'Der 110. Psalm in der altrabbinischen Literatur', Strack-Billerbeck IV, pp. 452 ff.

[4] See M. Simon, 'Melchisédech dans la polémique entre juifs et chrétiens et dans la légende', *RHPR* 17, 1937, pp. 58 ff.

[5] Strack-Billerbeck IV, pp. 453 f.

Not only must there have been messianic interpretations of Ps. 110 at the time of Jesus, but there must also have been speculations in Judaism which identified Melchizedek himself, if not with the Messiah, at least with other eschatological figures. The seventh chapter of the Epistle to the Hebrews, and later patristic attempts to see in Melchizedek the prototype of Christ, presuppose a Jewish tradition which utilized the priest-king concept eschatologically. Thus in a Midrash to the Song of Solomon (a late one to be sure) he becomes almost a messianic mediator.[1] In other writings the returned Elijah sometimes appears both as prophet and as High Priest of the end time.[2] In certain speculations about Adam, the priest-king assumes also the characteristics of Adam conceived as the ideal man.[3] Sometimes an eschatological priest appears independently beside Elijah as *Kohen zedek* (Priest of Righteousness).[4] We may also mention that Philo identifies the Logos with Melchizedek and calls him the 'Priest of God'.[5]

Older Jewish motifs may have merged with Gnostic ones in the Gnostic-Christian Melchizedek speculations of the Church Fathers.[6] In any case E. Käsemann is right in finding a Melchizedek speculation before the Epistle to the Hebrews which is of partly Jewish, partly Christian-Gnostic origin.[7] He points out that this speculation identifies the High Priest with figures related to the beginning and to the end of time—figures such as Shem, the Archangel Michael, the Original Man, Adam, Metatron.[8]

[1] Midrash to the Song of Solomon (100b); cf. Pesiq. 51a.

[2] See J. Jeremias, ''Ηλ(ε)ίας', *TWNT* II, pp. 934 f. See also Strack-Billerbeck IV, pp. 462 f.

[3] See F. J. Jerome, *Das geschichtliche Melchisedek-Bild und seine Bedeutung im Hebräerbrief*, 1920.

[4] Strack-Billerbeck IV, pp. 463 f. This reminds us of the Qumran sect's 'Teacher of Righteousness', who is also a priest. See pp. 86 and 116 below.

[5] Philo, *Leg. Alleg.* III, 79; *De Congressu* 99.

[6] Ambrose, *De fide* III, 11; Jerome, *Ep.* 73; Epiphanius, *Haer.* 55.5; 67.3, 7. Hippolytus, *Refut.* VII, 36; X, 24, and others even speak of 'Melchizedekians' who place Melchizedek above Christ. See G. Bardy, 'Melchisédek dans la tradition patristique', *RB* 35, 1926, pp. 496 ff.; 36, 1927, pp. 25 ff.

[7] E. Käsemann, *Das wandernde Gottesvolk*, 1939, p. 130.

[8] In addition to the studies already mentioned, the following are important for the Melchizedek speculations: M. Friedländer, 'Melchisédec et l'épître aux Hébreux', *Revue des Etudes Juives* 5, 1882, pp. 188 ff.; 1883, pp. 186 ff.; G. Wuttke, *Melchisedech, der Priesterkönig von Salem. Eine Studie zur Geschichte der Exegese* (BZNW 5), 1927; H. Stork, *Die sogenannten Melchisedekianer*, 1928; H. W. Hertzberg, 'Die Melchisedeqtraditionen', *Journal of the Palestine Oriental Society*, 1928, pp. 169 ff.; O. Michel, 'Μελχισεδέκ', *TWNT* IV, pp. 573 ff., and *Der Brief*

In this connection we may certainly mention also the 'Teacher of Righteousness' of the Qumran sect. He has eschatological characteristics, and (as the *Habakkuk Commentary* shows) he is a priest.[1] We may also refer to the *Testaments of the Twelve Patriarchs*, above all to the *Testament of Levi*, which predicts the rise of a 'new priest' (ch. 18).[2] If Dupont-Sommer's thesis is correct, this 'new priest' is the 'Teacher of Righteousness' himself.[3] In any case the Qumran texts (*Manual of Discipline* 9.11; *Serek ha'eda* 2.12 ff.), the *Damascus Document* (12.23; 14.19; 19.10; 20.1), and the *Testaments of the Twelve Patriarchs* (*Reub.* 6.7 ff.; *Sim.* 7.2, etc.) distinguish between a priestly and a political-royal Messiah, between a Messiah of Levi and one of Judah, between the 'Messiah of Aaron' and the 'Messiah of Israel'. In each of these cases the priestly Messiah is superior to the royal one.[4] The important thing is that the identification of the High Priest with the Messiah is accomplished in these texts.

We conclude that Judaism knew of an ideal priest who, as the one true priest, should fulfil in the last days all the elements of the Jewish priestly office. The Jewish conception of priest was bound sooner or later to lead to this expectation. Because of his office, the High Priest is *the* proper mediator between God and his people, and as such assumes from the very beginning a position of divine eminence. Judaism had in the High Priest a man who could satisfy already in the present the need of the people for divine mediation in a cultic framework. But the weaker became the correspondence between the reality of the empirical priesthood and their high expectations, the stronger became the Jews' hope for the end when all things would be fulfilled. This hope included also the concept of priest, so that the figure of a perfect High Priest of the end time moved ever nearer that of the Messiah.

The natural consequence of this was that the expected High Priest

an die Hebräer, 1949, p. 160; J. Jeremias, *TB* 16, 1937, col. 309. For further literature see C. Spicq, *L'Epître aux Hébreux* II, 1953, p. 213 f.

[1] *Habakkuk Commentary* II, 8; K. Elliger, *Studien zum Habakuk-Kommentar vom Toten Meer*, 1953, p. 168.

[2] See also 8.11–18. J. Jeremias, *TWNT* II, p. 934 n. 30, cites a number of other passages whose foundation he rightly considers pre-Christian.

[3] A. Dupont-Sommer, *Nouveaux aperçus sur les manuscrits de la mer morte*, pp. 63 ff. In this connection we may mention that M. Friedländer, *op. cit.*, had already expressed the opinion that the speculations about Melchizedek and even the sect of Melchizedekians originated in the Essene sect.

[4] K. G. Kuhn, 'The Two Messiahs of Aaron and Israel', *The Scrolls and the New Testament*, pp. 54 ff.; E. Stauffer, 'Probleme der Priestertradition', *TLZ* 81, 1956, pp. 135 ff. See below, p. 107 n.1. and p. 116.

not only had to fulfil positively the idea of all priesthood, but above all had to overcome the insufficiencies of the empirical priesthood. Thus his task came to be defined as being also actually in contradiction to that of the temporal high priest. This is important for the application of the concept to Jesus.

2. *Jesus and the Idea of the High Priest*

Is it possible to speak of Jesus' own attitude toward the idea of the High Priest in a Christological sense? We might be tempted to dismiss the question as irrelevant and to proceed directly to the concept Ἰησοῦς ἀρχιερεύς in early Christianity. Jesus' position regarding the temple does indeed seem at first to exclude the possibility of his ascribing to himself a high priestly function. Even if the cleansing of the temple means only the purging and not the rejection of it, there are still sayings of Jesus which clearly call in question the temple cult itself—such as that in Matt. 12.6 ('something greater than the temple is here'), for example. A genuine saying of Jesus about the disappearance of the temple very probably lies behind the words which, according to the Synoptics, were a 'false witness' at his trial (Mark 14.57 ff. and parallels), but in the Gospel of John are reported in a somewhat different form, as words actually spoken by Jesus (John 2.19). In John's interpretation of his saying (2.21) Jesus actually appears as one who takes the place of the temple.

Whether or not Jesus himself conceived of his task as John interprets it here, it is certain that he was convinced that with his coming (a coming which introduces the end) the temple cult would not simply continue as before. So he must probably have taken a critical attitude also toward the continuation of the high priestly office. If we hear in the Gospels primarily of Jesus' polemic against the Pharisees, we can by no means therefore conclude that he was somehow more sympathetic toward the priestly party of the Sadducees. However much the Synoptic reports of the so-called trial of Jesus may have been influenced by tendencies of the early Church, they have without doubt preserved the recollection that the enemies who desired Jesus' death were to be found especially in priestly circles. John 11.47 confirms the fact.

But we cannot conclude from Jesus' critical attitude toward the priesthood that he therefore could not have included the idea of the High Priest in his conception of his task. On the contrary, we have seen that even in Judaism criticism of the empirical priesthood and belief in an ideal priesthood conditioned each other. In addressing the king as a High Priest after the order of Melchizedek, Ps. 110 not only places him above the empirical priesthood, but at the same time sets him over against it almost as an opponent. This consideration makes it conceivable that Jesus on occasion applied to himself the idea of an ideal High Priest 'after the order of Melchizedek', if not the title itself.

But we can go still further; we have two sayings of Jesus in which he expressly relates Ps. 110 to the Messiah. The first is the discussion about the Son of David in Mark 12.35 ff. and parallels. Jesus himself quotes Ps. 110, which, as we shall see,[1] became so very important for all early Christian theology that it is cited in the New Testament more often than any other Old Testament passage. Jesus' explanation of this psalm in Mark 12.35 ff. is one of the most difficult of his sayings reported in the Synoptics. It is by no means certain that he here rejects Davidic sonship for himself. Some scholars have even questioned whether he speaks of himself at all, or only makes a statement about the Messiah without relating it to himself. We shall return to this passage later and see that the key to its meaning may lie in Mark 3.33.[2] Bultmann's assumption that it is a formulation of the early Church[3] is in any case not probable, since it is hardly likely that the early Church would have attributed a saying to Jesus which necessarily presented such great difficulties precisely from the viewpoint of early Christian theology. For Jesus' interpretation of the meaning of the psalm clearly suggests that he speaks of himself. If so, it is very important for an understanding of his self-consciousness that he applied to himself this psalm in which the messianic king appears as High Priest after the order of Melchizedek. Then we would have to reckon with the probability that the idea was not foreign to Jesus that he had also to fulfil the office of the true high priesthood.

The second passage in which Ps. 110 is cited is clearer and increases this probability. When Jesus answers the high priest in Mark 14.62, he combines a reference to Dan. 7 with the reference to Ps. 110: 'You will see the Son of man sitting at the right hand of Power, and coming with the clouds of heaven.' 'Sitting at the right hand' is inseparably connected with the thought of the priest-king after the order of Melchizedek. Is it not significant that Jesus applies to himself a saying about the eternal High Priest precisely when he

[1] See pp. 222 f. below. [2] See p. 132 below.

[3] Cf. Bultmann, *Geschichte der synoptischen Tradition*, pp. 145 f.

stands before the Jewish high priest and is questioned by him concerning his claim to be the Messiah? He says in effect that his messiahship is not that of an earthly Messiah—indeed, that he does not even attribute to himself on an earthly level the role of the earthly high priest standing before him—but that he is the heavenly Son of Man and the heavenly High Priest. This saying is thus parallel to that in the Gospel of John in which Jesus tells Pilate that his kingship is not of this world (John 18.36). He tells the earthly ruler that his government is not earthly; he tells the earthly high priest that his priesthood is not earthly.

We conclude, then, that Jesus considered it his task to fulfil the priestly office. This opens perspectives which are of far-reaching importance for the self-consciousness of Jesus. It is in any case important that a later Christological interpretation such as that of the Epistle to the Hebrews could find a point of contact in these two citations of Ps. 110 by Jesus himself.

3. *Jesus as the High Priest in Early Christianity*

We must speak now first of all of the Epistle to the Hebrews. Ἀρχιερεύς is not the only Christological title applied in this epistle; he is also called *Kyrios* (Lord) and especially υἱὸς τοῦ θεοῦ (Son of God). But Jesus the High Priest stands in the foreground, and the whole letter deals with him in this role.

The title μεσίτης, Mediator, a *terminus technicus* of legal language designating an arbitrator or guarantor, also appears in this letter (8.6; 9.15; 12.24) as well as in I Tim. 2.5. Since it is only a variant of the concept High Priest, we need not devote a special chapter to it.

The seventh chapter is the centre of the Epistle to the Hebrews. It uses scriptural proof (Gen. 14 and Ps. 110) to describe Jesus as the true High Priest. Whereas other Christians at this time sought to prove by means of the Old Testament that Jesus is the Messiah expected by the Jews, the writer of Hebrews seeks to show that Jesus fulfils absolutely the high priestly function of the Jews. For this writer the office of high priest in Judaism has only a transitory and imperfect character but in its very insufficiency points beyond itself.

The argument of ch. 7 rests on a typological interpretation of the Old Testament which, as we have seen,[1] probably makes use of an

[1] See p. 85 above.

already familiar Jewish tradition about Melchizedek.[1] The writer seeks justification in the Old Testament itself for the idea we have mentioned several times, that the priesthood of the Old Covenant is not the 'last word', but must be replaced by a final priesthood of the New Covenant. He sees this new priesthood as realized in Jesus Christ, who is *the* Priest in an absolute and final sense, the fulfilment of all priesthood. In his temporal and qualitative uniqueness Jesus *the* High Priest makes all other high priests superfluous.

In connection with the Jewish tradition we have mentioned, the writer finds this absolute—we could say 'fulfilled'—priesthood of Jesus already foreshadowed in the Old Testament in the puzzling figure of Melchizedek in Gen. 14. We need not expound Heb. 7 in detail, but it is important to see the broad outlines of its speculation about Melchizedek. We must of course guard against limiting the Christology of Hebrews to this figure, which as the type of Christ was especially to occupy the Christian imagination of the ancient Church after there had been much reflection about it already in Judaism.

Having given various arguments (which seem to us rather arbitrary from an exegetical point of view) to show the connection between Melchizedek and Jesus, the author then seeks to show the superiority of this Melchizedek, who points to Jesus, over the Levites, the priests of the Old Covenant. This is the reasoning: The ancestor of the Levites and thus of the Jewish priesthood is Levi. But Levi is the descendant of Abraham. According to the Jewish theory of ancestry which the writer presupposes, Levi already existed in the 'loins' of Abraham, so that what happened to Abraham therefore happened also to him. That Abraham received a blessing from Melchizedek is a sign of his inferiority to Melchizedek; he who blesses is superior to him who is blessed. Therefore Levi and the whole Israelitic priesthood which stems from him are inferior to Melchizedek. Melchizedek is the true priest. He blesses and he receives the tithe. He is *the* high priest. Since Christ realized this true priesthood, he is finally the true High Priest, the true Mediator between God and man. This whole line of reasoning (which some scholars think was a Midrash to Gen. 14.17 ff. and Ps. 110.4) [2] seems peculiar to us, especially in its details. But behind it lies the deep theological thought that as the

[1] G. Schille, 'Erwägungen zur Hohenpriesterlehre des Hebräerbriefes', *ZNW* 46, 1955, pp. 81 ff., assumes on the basis of the interchange of ἱερεύς and ἀρχιερεύς the utilization of a *Christian* tradition.

[2] See H. Windisch, *Der Hebräerbrief* (HNT)², 1931, p. 59.

true High Priest, Jesus Christ not only sets aside the Old Testament priesthood, but also fulfils it.

We see that the concept High Priest is not far removed from that of the *ebed Yahweh* when we recall the essentially voluntary nature of the *ebed's* sacrifice. In his transformation of the Old Testament conception of sacrifice, the writer of Hebrews emphasizes the voluntary character of the sacrifice brought also by this High Priest: 'he offered up himself' (Heb. 7.27). Now the writer is no longer dependent upon Jewish speculations about priests. When Jesus is designated the High Priest, this idea must inevitably be related to that of the *ebed Yahweh*. In the exercise of his office the high priest offers up sacrifices; that is his function. But Jesus himself is the sacrifice; he is at the same time sacrificer and sacrificed. Therefore he necessarily becomes the one who offers up himself.

The statement in Heb. 9.28 that Christ was offered once 'to bear the sins of many' is a direct reference to Isa. 53.12. The Old Testament concept of high priesthood yields only the idea of *sacrifice* brought by the mediator for the atonement of the sins of the people; it does not contain the idea of the high priest's self-sacrifice.[1] In this respect the *ebed Yahweh* concept is more suitable than that of the High Priest to express the New Testament view of what Jesus and the early Church considered his work to be. Only by connection of the High Priest concept with that of the *ebed Yahweh* is the insufficiency of the Jewish high priestly office overcome.

Nevertheless a new and valuable element is introduced into Christology with the Jewish concept of high priesthood. It is the idea that in his very self-sacrifice Christ manifests his high priestly *majesty*. This removes even more radically than the *ebed Yahweh* concept the passiveness we discovered in the idea of the paschal lamb. It is precisely in offering himself and taking the greatest humiliation upon himself that Jesus exercises the most divine function conceivable in Israel, that of the high priestly Mediator. This consideration explains the close connection between the ideas of the High Priest and the Son of God in Hebrews. In the light of the High Priest concept, the atoning death of Jesus demonstrates the true

[1] The idea of a priestly self-sacrifice for the atonement of others may have arisen in isolated cases already in Judaism. The martyr Eleazar, who conceived of his death as an atoning sacrifice for his people (IV Macc. 6.29), is a priest. Also the possible martyrdom of the Qumran sect's 'Teacher of Righteousness' becomes particularly significant by virtue of the fact that he is a *priest*. These sacrifices are of course basically connected rather with the general idea of an atoning effect of the suffering of the righteous.

New Testament dialectic between deepest humiliation and highest majesty. That is the great significance of the Christological concept of Jesus the High Priest. This dialectic also makes clear that Jesus' atoning death both fulfils all Old Testament priesthood and thereby dispenses with it. Therefore in 10.1 ff. the author emphasizes that the blood of bulls and goats cannot take away sin. In the true high priestly work completed by Jesus, the High Priest is identical with the sacrifice.

But we must note also a further point involved in Hebrews' formulation of the High Priest concept. Because he himself is 'perfect', Jesus as the High Priest brings humanity to its 'perfection'. Beside and through the task of atonement, we thus see another goal and effect of the high priestly calling Christ fulfils. The covenant with God is renewed in such a way that humanity is made 'perfect'. The expression τέλειος and words from the same root play a very important part in the Christology of Hebrews. With them we approach at times very close to the Son of Man concept. Since the task of the High Priest is to be the Mediator between God and man, the crowning of his work is the realization of the perfect man. For this reason τέλειος refers both to that which is *perfect* and to that which is *complete*.[1]

The commentaries correctly emphasize the cultic-sacral character of this 'perfection'. It has this character in the language of the mystery religions, and the Septuagint actually gives it the meaning 'dedication'.[2] It is certainly correct to think in terms of a cultic significance in a context such as ours where the figure of the High Priest stands at the centre of attention. But we should not do justice to the riches of the Christology of Hebrews if we sought to exclude every thought of moral perfection or moral maturity, or if we were only willing to speak of an 'ethically neutral' conception.[3] Hebrews says on the one hand that Jesus Christ is made perfect by the Father (2.10; 5.9; 7.28), and on the other hand that the High Priest Jesus Christ makes his brothers perfect (2.10 ff.; 10.14). In both cases the cultic interpretation alone is too narrow and

[1] C. Spicq, *L'Epître aux Hébreux* II, p. 39, connects τελειοῦν in Hebrews with the Johannine report of Jesus' saying from the cross, τετέλεσται (John 19.30).

[2] For example Ex. 29.9 ff.; Lev. 4.5 ('fill the hand'). Concerning the concept in general, see the commentaries of Windisch and Michel on Heb. 5.9, and especially the extensive excursus in Spicq, *op. cit.*, pp. 214 ff. Spicq's book also contains a detailed bibliography.

[3] Thus J. Kögel, 'Der Begriff τελειοῦν im Hebräerbrief', *Theol. Studien f. M. Kähler*, 1905, pp. 35 ff.

represents an abridgement of the statement.[1] Just as the High Priest concept applied to Jesus is so fulfilled that the purely cultic in general must be raised to a higher level, so must the purely cultic concept τελειοῦν applied to him necessarily include also the sense of making morally perfect. This happens in a really human life—in Jesus, the High Priest, who is made perfect; and in the brothers, the sanctified, who are made perfect by him (Heb. 2.11).

I cannot share the timorousness of many theologians who do not venture to speak of the 'moral perfection' of Jesus because they fear that this would automatically mean falling back into the liberal view of the life of Jesus. We shall see that the author of Hebrews, as perhaps no other early Christian theologian, had the courage to speak of the man Jesus in shockingly human terms—although at the same time he emphasized perhaps more strongly than any other the deity of the Son.[2]

In order to lead humanity to its completion, the High Priest himself must go through the various stages of a human life. It is true that Hebrews naturally thinks primarily of the final phase of that life, the passion, as 'completion'. But in connection with its emphasis on the necessary humanity of the High Priest, it nevertheless considers Jesus' life in its entirety. The High Priest must realize the τελείωσις through his whole life until the final sacrifice of his voluntary death. Although he lived under the very same human conditions as we, he was the one human being without sin: 'in every respect tempted as we are, yet without sinning' (Heb. 4.15).

Precisely on the basis of the High Priest concept, the author of Hebrews is bound to be particularly interested in the sinlessness of Jesus which both earlier and contemporary writers had asserted. He mentions it not only in 4.15 but also in 7.26 and 9.14. It is also either expressly mentioned or at least presupposed in II Cor. 5.21; I Peter 1.19; 2.22; 3.18; John 7.18; 8.46; 14.30. The Synoptic writers must also have been convinced of it, since they wrote that Jesus had the power to forgive the sins of others. We can say with certainty that Matthew must have had a theory about the sinlessness of Jesus; otherwise he would not have changed the question of Jesus in Mark 10.18, 'Why do you call me good?', to read 'Why do you ask me about what is good?' (Matt. 19.17). Apparently he thought the

[1] H. Windisch rightly expresses this idea in his commentary on Hebrews (5.9), p. 45.

[2] This side is neglected even in the otherwise quite valuable essay of M. Rissi, 'Die Menschlichkeit Jesu nach Hebr. 5.7 und 8', *TZ* 11, 1955, pp. 28 ff.

question in Mark made Jesus' sinlessness problematical, so he changed it. Did he interpret the question correctly? It does indeed stand in a certain tension with the assertion of Jesus' sinlessness. The tension can only be resolved if we understand the 'weakness', ἀσθένεια (in the sense of 'ability to be tempted'), which Hebrews ascribes to Jesus despite his sinlessness to mean 'not good'. Mark may have interpreted Jesus' question in this way, although he was convinced of Jesus' sinlessness.

The fact that Jesus was tempted is a definite element of the Gospel tradition. But whereas in the Synoptics Jesus never even lets temptation approach him (except possibly at Gethsemane), Hebrews significantly presupposes even more strongly the possibility of his sinning precisely by mentioning it together with his sinlessness. This alone is enough to show that the ability of Jesus to be tempted is much more important in Hebrews than in the Synoptics. We shall see that at this point Hebrews understands the humanity of Jesus in a more comprehensive way than the Gospels or any other early Christian writing. This follows from the idea that the High Priest not only completely enters the realm of humanity, but within that realm must participate in everything that is human. When we consider Hebrews' strong emphasis on the susceptibility of Jesus to temptation, it is clear that the idea of a moral 'perfection' within the concept τελειοῦν was not in the least offensive to the author.

On the other hand, Hebrews' claim that Jesus was sinless becomes really meaningful only in connection with the strong emphasis on his susceptibility to temptation. Unless he was really tempted, the claim that Jesus was without sin is fundamentally meaningless.[1] The difference between Jesus and other men achieves its full significance in Hebrews only because he was first of all completely one of them. The 'High Priest' presents the dialectic of all Christology in its complete sharpness.

As a result of this connection between sinlessness and susceptibility to temptation, 'without sin' appears less dogmatic in Heb. 4.15 than in any other passages we have quoted about Jesus' sinlessness—although even here in the background is the thought of the sacrificial lamb without blemish (as in I Peter 1.19 and Heb. 9.14), and the thought of the *ebed Yahweh* (as in I Peter 2.22). We can understand the full scope of the words 'without sin' in Heb. 4.15 only when we

[1] At this point I thus advocate precisely the opposite view from that of H. Windisch, *op. cit.*, p. 39. He writes: 'Can we really assert in the strictest sense the sinlessness of one who was attracted by temptations exactly as we are?'

first read the beginning of the sentence: 'For we have not a high priest who is unable to sympathize with our weaknesses, but one who in every respect has been tempted as we are.' The full significance of this description of Jesus' humanity is rarely appreciated. The assertion that Jesus had to withstand the same temptations as we is extraordinarily far-reaching. It obviously does not think only of the Synoptics' report of the temptations following Jesus' baptism. After all, they were messianic temptations which could be imposed only upon the Christ. I believe that the emphatic statement that Jesus was tempted in every respect as we are (πεπειρασμένον κατὰ πάντα καθ' ὁμοιότητα) goes far beyond both the temptations in the wilderness and the temptations presented by Jesus' opponents in doctrinal debates (Mark 8.33; 12.15; John 8.1 ff.). The words added to πεπειρασμένος are so strongly emphasized that they actually rule out a restriction of Jesus' temptations to such as these. The author of Hebrews really thinks of the common temptations connected with our human weakness, the temptations to which we are exposed simply because we are men. 'In every respect as we are' refers not only to form but also to content.

This statement of Hebrews, which thus goes beyond the Synoptic reports of Jesus' being tempted, is perhaps the boldest assertion of the completely human character of Jesus in the New Testament. It is a short but very important remark which casts a special light on the life of Jesus, leading us to consider aspects of his life with which we are not acquainted and with which the author of Hebrews was probably not acquainted. Of course we must guard against trying to discover material for a historical novel here. We know nothing exact about these temptations κατὰ πάντα and all that is Christologically important is the fact itself that Jesus was tempted in every respect as we, but without sinning.

Heb. 2.17 also emphasizes the High Priest's full participation in the humanity of all men: 'Therefore he had to be made like his brethren in every respect, so that he might become a merciful and faithful high priest in the service of God, to make expiation for the sins of the people. For because he himself has suffered and been tempted, he is able to help those who are tempted.'

The idea of Jesus' weakness manifested in his susceptibility to temptation dominates also the beginning of ch. 5. In 5.7 f. the author mentions a concrete temptation: 'In the days of his flesh, Jesus offered up prayers and supplications, with loud cries and tears, to him who was able to save him from death, and he was heard in his fear. Although he was a Son, he learned obedience through what he suffered.'

It still seems to me by far the most probable explanation of this passage that it is a reference to Gethsemane.[1] The expressions 'cries' and 'tears' are so concrete that they must refer to a definite event when Jesus pleaded for rescue from death. The description does not fit Golgotha, despite the cry from the cross. It can refer only to the actual great temptation of Jesus in Gethsemane, when he still had the possibility of going another way than that assigned him, the way of the cross and of obedience.[2]

I do not understand why some translators choose to translate the phrase εἰσακουσθεὶς ἀπὸ τῆς εὐλαβείας 'He was heard for his godly fear (reverence),' when it can just as accurately be translated, 'He was heard in his fear (anxiety).'[3] The whole context forces upon one the sense of ordinary human fear as the meaning of εὐλάβεια.[4] This is just what the *temptation* is. The ἀσθένεια of Jesus shows itself precisely in the fact that he was afraid, that he had the ordinary human fear of death! And he was heard because he conquered his fear when he prayed 'not my will . . .'.

These verses dealing with Jesus' fear are Christologically extremely important. They show no trace of Docetism. Jesus was really a man, not just God disguised as a man. The author uses expressions which indicate that, as he sees it, the fear which the tempted Jesus experienced was more terrible than the Gospel descriptions lead us to suppose. To the scene in Gethsemane as we know it from the Gospels, Hebrews adds that in his fear of death Jesus cried out loud and wept. He did not, with Stoic resignation, view death as a very natural transition, but as something horrible, not willed by God—in Paul's words 'the last enemy' (I Cor. 15.26).[5]

[1] So also J. Héring, *L'Epître aux Hébreux, ad loc.* M. Rissi, *op. cit.*, p. 39, does not agree. In my essay, *Immortality of the Soul or Resurrection of the Dead? The Witness of the New Testament,* ET 1958, I have emphasized the fear of Jesus precisely in view of this passage in Hebrews.

[2] See O. Cullmann, *The State in the New Testament*, pp. 31 f.

[3] Out of context both translations are of course possible. O Michel and C. Spicq decide in favour of the first translation in their commentaries. (Both authors also give a survey of the history of the exegesis of this passage.) So also M. Rissi, *op. cit.*, p. 38. On the other hand, the commentaries of H. Windisch (with a question mark) and J. Héring translate it as I have proposed.

[4] Harnack's often cited conjecture, the addition of οὐκ, is neither justified nor necessary to explain the text when it is translated in this way.

[5] Christ's resurrection will be taken seriously only when his death is taken this seriously. See *Immortality of the Soul . . .*, p. 26.

It is not certain whether the author of Hebrews really had at his disposal a tradition independent of the Gospels we know. But another passage in Hebrews also suggests that he might have known definite facts preserved only by oral tradition. In 12.3 he writes, 'Consider him who endured from sinners such hostility against himself, so that you may not grow weary or faint-hearted.' Of course this could refer to one of the episodes reported in the canonical Gospels.

The most important confirmation of Hebrews' conception of Jesus' full humanity, however, is the statement that he *learned* obedience (5.8). This expression, which has never been successfully explained away, presupposes an inner human development. The life of Jesus would not be really human if its course did not manifest a *development*. Such a growth is also quite clearly attested in a completely different New Testament writing, Luke 2.52: 'Jesus increased (προέκοπτεν) in wisdom and in stature, and in favour with God and man.'

The word ἔμαθεν (learned) in Heb. 5.8 casts light also on the word τελειοῦν, which we have already discussed and which appears again in the very next verse. Parallel to the 'learning' of obedience through suffering, Heb. 2.10 says that through suffering Jesus was made perfect. This obviously also implies a certain development which finds its completion only after the way ends in the obedience of atoning suffering. Jesus had to 'learn' this obedience. He had to 'learn' to carry out the task of the *ebed Yahweh* to its end. 'Obedience' in Heb. 5.8 reminds us of the same expression in Phil. 2.8: '. . . obedient unto death, even death on a cross.' The word μέχρι (even unto) indicates a climax and thus also a certain development within Jesus' humiliation.

Hebrews is not so much interested in Jesus' becoming man as in his being man. That is what really characterizes the high priestly office. The question *Cur deus homo* is answered here solely on the basis of the idea of the High Priest: he must be able to suffer with men in order to suffer for them.

The idea of an inner human development is even more unbearable to some theologians than that of moral perfection.[1] They see here also the ghost of the justifiably notorious liberal picture of Jesus. But to draw the final consequences of the Son's becoming man for his being man as Hebrews does is not in itself to fall into the error of psychologizing. Instead of yielding to the unjustified fear of these consequences, it would be more appropriate to guard against the

[1] See pp. 92 f. above.

opposite danger of Docetism, which from the New Testament period on has been the Christological arch-heresy. He whose faith in Christ is endangered by Christ's completely human features shows that he has not understood what the New Testament means by 'faith in Christ'. The essence of faith in the New Testament is faith despite the scandal of humanity. We shall see that it is just those New Testament writings which most strongly emphasize the deity of Christ which also take his humanity most seriously. Thus we find precisely in Hebrews the boldest of all assertions of Christ's deity: it could not be asserted more strongly than in Heb. 1.10, in which the Son is addressed directly as Creator of heaven and earth.

The writer of Hebrews also does not hesitate to ascribe to Jesus human attributes and conduct in a laudatory sense. In 2.17 he says that Jesus had to become a 'merciful and faithful high priest'. In 12.2 he even speaks of Jesus' *faith*. When he calls Jesus the 'pioneer and perfecter' of our faith, he means, according to his conception of the High Priest in the whole letter, both that Jesus himself believed [1] and that he brought men to faith in his work.

It belongs to the basic doctrine of Hebrews that through his humanity Jesus the High Priest 'sanctifies' and 'perfects' our humanity. We have already seen this in connection with the concept τελειοῦν. E. Käsemann therefore rightly sees at this point a connection with the figure of the heavenly Original Man.[2] We may mention as a parallel the Gnostic myth in which the redeemer is himself redeemed and by this means becomes the leader of others.

But before we examine more closely this correspondence between the perfection of the High Priest and the perfection of the brothers, we must first consider an aspect of Jesus' high priestly work which, despite the parallel just mentioned, indicates the chasm between the theology of Hebrews and all Gnosticism and mythology. We think of the *once-for-all character* (ἐφάπαξ) of the high priestly work. It stands in express opposition to the necessity of the continual repetition of the Old Testament priest's work. We see again in this respect how Jesus not only *fulfils* the Old Testament priesthood, but also overcomes all its inadequacies.

The writer of Hebrews emphasizes the ἐφάπαξ so strongly in order to demonstrate this opposition. He describes a final and decisive act which in its very uniqueness brings salvation to men. This uniqueness points primarily to the idea that the act of salvation will not be

[1] The preceding chapter, Heb. 11, also suggests this explanation.

[2] E. Käsemann, *Das wandernde Gottesvolk*, p. 90.

repeated by Jesus the High Priest himself, but it also suggests that the brothers cannot repeat the act, despite the solidarity of the High Priest with their humanity. This 'one time' means 'once for all time': '. . . he entered once for all into the Holy Place, taking not the blood of goats and calves but his own blood, thus securing an eternal redemption' (Heb. 9.12); '. . . he has appeared once for all at the end of the age to put away sin by the sacrifice of himself' (9.26); '. . . we have been sanctified through the offering of the body of Jesus Christ once for all' (10.10). Corresponding to 'once for all', we read in 10.14, 'for all time' (εἰς τὸ διηνεκές). The saving character of this historically unrepeatable fact is decisive and unending. What the High Priest Jesus completed on the human level is therefore the centre of all events, the decisive midpoint of time. Every cultic event from now on is concentrated on the historical event of this High Priest's human life, lived at one single time, with its one crowning climax in his atoning death.

Christian worship is therefore possible only on the basis of unreserved respect for this ἐφάπαξ. As I have previously pointed out,[1] Protestants are incorrect in describing the Catholic mass as a 'repetition' of the sacrificial act of Jesus. Catholic theologians have always rejected this interpretation. They speak rather of 'making present' Christ's act. But does not also this description of the mass violate the ἐφάπαξ of Hebrews—above all when one designates the mass a 'sacrifice'? It is just the sacrifice as such which cannot be made present in the way it is supposed to happen in the Catholic mass. The danger of falling back to the level of Old Testament priesthood arises when the high priest must always present the sacrifice anew. Christian worship in the light of that 'one time' which means 'once for all time' is possible only when even the slightest temptation to 'reproduce' that central event itself is avoided. Instead, the event must be allowed to remain the divine act of the past time where God the Lord of time placed it—at that exact historical moment in the third decade of our chronology. It is the saving consequences of that atoning act, not the act itself, which become a present event in our worship. The Lord present in worship is the exalted *Kyrios* of the Church and world, raised to the right hand of God. He is the risen Lord who continues his mediating work on the basis of his unique, completed work of atonement. The words εἰς τὴν ἐμὴν ἀνάμνησιν (in remembrance of me) describe the connection between his crucifixion and the celebration of the Lord's Supper. This means 'in remembrance of that which I have completed, on the basis of which I now dwell among you as the resurrected Lord'.

It is because of the once-for-all character of Jesus' atoning act that

[1] See O. Cullmann, *Christ and Time*, p. 169.

the writer of Hebrews emphasizes so strongly that as High Priest Jesus mediated a *New Covenant* with God. 'Therefore he is the mediator of a new covenant' (Heb. 9.15). 12.24 too refers to him as διαθήκης νέας μεσίτης. In this respect the concept of High Priest comes into contact again with that of the *ebed Yahweh*, whose function is also the re-establishment of the covenant with God.

This brings us to the continuing effect on believers of the once-for-all act. Christ becomes the ἀρχηγός (leader) of a new humanity, the αἴτιος (source) of salvation for all who obey him (Heb. 5.9). The correspondence is complete: the faithful obey Christ as he himself obeyed the Father. We have already seen that Christ makes them to be τέλειοι just as he himself has become the τέλειος. On a higher level, he makes them able to come before God just as the high priest of the Old Covenant made them qualified to worship. 'For by a single offering he has perfected for all time those who are sanctified' (10.14). τελειοῦν (to make perfect) is almost a synonym for ἁγιάζειν (to sanctify). Thus 2.11 reads, 'For he who sanctifies and those who are sanctified have all one origin.'

Apart from the faith of the individual, Hebrews does not say how it is possible to think of the connection between the once-for-all act of Jesus and the sanctification of those perfected. The fact of the connection itself is seen as effect. The analogy in Rom. 5.12 ff. of the relation between Adam and sinful humanity might be considered a parallel, but in Romans too that relation is only stated as a fact, not explained.[1] Augustine's explanation is not explicitly to be found in the New Testament.

Because of the strong emphasis on the humanity of Jesus, his high priestly solidarity with us, one might be tempted to understand the connection as an *imitatio Christi*. Expressions like ἀρχηγός do in fact point in this direction, and one may indeed find faint traces of the later Christian concept of the 'imitation of Christ' in Hebrews. But it is just the idea of ἐφάπαξ which this book so strongly emphasizes which shows that an imitation of Christ is possible only when we are first of all aware of the fact that we are not able to imitate him. He is sinless; we are not. He offers the sacrifice of atoning death; we cannot. It is precisely the decisive act of obedience which effects our perfection which we cannot imitate.[2] In Hebrews and in Paul the connection between our perfection and the perfection of the High

[1] See pp. 170 ff. below.

[2] It may be that already Ignatius of Antioch has the erroneous idea that the martyr who loses his life for Christ's sake is able to do this.

Priest can be understood only as happening in faith in the ἐφάπαξ of the high priestly act.

In Heb. 6.20 we find another designation which expresses the relation between the High Priest and the faithful: πρόδρομος (forerunner). With this expression we come to a new aspect of Jesus' high priestly work—his work as the Exalted One. To this point we have considered Christ as the source (αἴτιος, ἀρχηγός) of salvation by virtue of his human life and death; now we must add that by entering the 'inner shrine behind the curtain' as 'forerunner', he draws with him those who are his into his *resurrection* and its consequences. This second aspect is of course fully subordinate to the first. For this reason we have placed the chapter on Jesus as High Priest in the first group of the Christological explanations of the New Testament, those which concern primarily the earthly work of Jesus. Parallel with 6.20, 9.12 thus emphasizes first of all the atoning death: '. . . he entered once for all into the Holy Place, taking not the blood of goats and calves but his own blood.' But this refers *also* to the act of resurrection. And the expression πρόδρομος is not far removed from the idea in the writings of Paul[1] and in the Revelation[2] that through his resurrection Jesus has become the πρωτότοκος τῶν νεκρῶν (first-born of the dead). Paul's description in I Cor. 15.12 ff. of the connection between Jesus' resurrection and ours is similar to that of Hebrews.

Hebrews further emphasizes that the High Priest remains in the Holy Place and there continues his work in the present. This is also meant when it is said that he is a priest εἰς τὸν αἰῶνα (6.20) or εἰς τὸ διηνεκές (7.3)—a priest 'for ever'. 'After the order of Melchizedek' is synonymous with 'for ever' as a description of the priest. The expression 'for ever' is the major theme of the second half of ch. 7.[3] It corresponds to the other major theme of 'once-for-all' (ἐφάπαξ). Jesus the High Priest thus fulfils a double office: that of the once-for-all act of atonement, and that of the extension of this work continued into eternity. Actually it is not a double function, but only one, for everything rests on the one act of sacrifice. 'But he holds his priesthood permanently, because he continues for ever' (7.24). This verse describes his priesthood as ἀπαράβατος, permanent. Hebrews thus considers also the present lordship of Christ as a high priestly office. As a result of this conception of the High Priest, the author

[1] Rom. 8.29; Col. 1.18. See I Cor. 15.20: ἀπαρχὴ τῶν κεκοιμωμένων.

[2] Rev. 1.5.

[3] See also Heb. 10.13 f.

connects as closely as possible Christ's present work and his once-for-all act. 'Consequently he is able for all time to save those who draw near to God through him, since he *always lives* to make intercession for them' (7.25). This quite clearly indicates a high priestly office which Christ continues to fulfil in the present since his resurrection, and εἰς τὸ παντελές (throughout all time).

The phrase προσερχόμενοι δι' αὐτοῦ τῷ θεῷ (those who draw near to God through him) expresses in a classical way the idea of the high priestly mediation in view of the present office of Christ. This mediation also rests completely on the sacrificial act of Jesus in the past, of course, but the author nevertheless thinks now of its continuation; that is, of the work Jesus the High Priest exercises as the one exalted to God's right hand.

What is the work of mediation which Christ fulfils for us in the present? He who 'always lives' makes intercession for us (ἐντυγχάνειν, 7.25). According to 9.24 he appears 'in the presence of God on our behalf'. In other words, his work consists in his *intercession* for those who are his. Hebrews emphasizes especially that it is the present Christ who executes this work; the words πάντοτε ζῶν ('since he always lives', 7.25) are the classical designation for the present Christ.[1] Christ's intercessory activity, which is always effective because of his once-for-all work, is a genuine high priestly act. As the one who 'always lives' in the present, Christ intercedes for us no longer simply in a collective sense as he did in his unique atoning death; now he intercedes in every moment for each individual. Again we see how both the once-for-all and the continuing aspects of the high priestly office of Jesus are intimately related and yet represent two different sides of his work. 'Jesus Christ is the same yesterday and today . . .' (Heb. 13.8).

The living Christ who intercedes for us now can do so only because he is the same Christ who was on earth, was man, was tempted in all respects as we are. Only for that reason, too, can he today sympathize with each individual. The necessity of his being man is thus related not only to his unique act of sacrifice, but also to his present intercession for us. The idea that Christ intercedes for us also in the present is Christologically very important and ought to be

[1] The Old Testament expression 'the living God', which often occurs in Hebrews (3.12; 9.14; 10.31; 12.22), points to the fact that God acts *constantly*. Although the word ζῆν applied to Jesus in Heb. 7.8 (as in Luke 24.5 and Rev. 1.18) emphasizes more strongly his triumph over death through the resurrection, Heb. 7.25 visualizes the constantly continuing work of Christ.

given a more central place also in systematic theology than is usually the case. We shall see that the significance attributed to this present aspect of the high priestly work of Christ is by no means an isolated idea of the Epistle to the Hebrews in the New Testament, but one characteristic also of Paul's writings, and even more clearly of the farewell discourses in the Gospel of John.

But now we must ask whether Hebrews relates the concept of Jesus' high priesthood to a third aspect, the *eschatological* side, of his work as the New Testament understands it. At first glance one is tempted to answer negatively. It is true that the idea of Jesus' fulfilling a special high priestly office at the end when he comes again does not appear prominently in Hebrews. Nevertheless 9.28 shows that the author has not neglected this side of Christ's work either: 'So Christ, having been offered once to bear the sins of many, will appear a second time, not to deal with sin but to save those who are eagerly waiting for him.' The expression ἐκ δευτέρου (a second time) is important here. It points clearly to the return of Christ.

Some scholars have wrongly claimed that the New Testament nowhere speaks of a 'return' of Jesus. Heb. 9.28 contains not only the idea but also a literal reference to the 'second' coming of Jesus.[1]

The expression ἐκ δευτέρου describes the eschatological work of the High Priest just as the expression ἐφάπαξ describes his earthly work and εἰς τὸ διηνεκές describes his present work. Hebrews does not further explain the particular meaning of the high priestly work of Jesus at the end of time; it only indicates its nature with the words 'not to deal with sin'. Perhaps the positive significance of this work has to do with our perfection. When all things are completed, humanity will once again need Jesus' high priestly office of mediation. We have seen that Judaism thought of the ideal High Priest precisely in terms of an eschatological hope. It is therefore not surprising that the New Testament book which offers a complete Christology of the 'High Priest' also considers this side of his mediatorial work, the eschatological completion of the reconciliation of humanity with God.

We have seen that Hebrews' development of the High Priest concept offers a full Christology in every respect. It includes all the three fundamental aspects of Jesus' work: his once-for-all earthly

[1] The idea, already mentioned, of the return of the Prophet, especially *Elijah*, proves that a return to earth was familiar in Jewish thought already before Christ's death and resurrection. See pp. 16 ff. above.

work (ἐφάπαξ), his present work as the exalted Lord (εἰς τὸ διηνεκές), and his future work as the one coming again (ἐκ δευτέρου). 'Yesterday, today, for ever' (13.8). At most it could be objected that this concept does not especially take into account the work of the pre-existent Christ. But, besides the bold reference in 1.10 to Christ as the Creator of earth and heaven, we can find at least starting-points for such a consideration in the Melchizedek speculation. Moreover the author especially emphasizes another Christological title, 'Son of God', which refers precisely to Jesus' pre-existence.

Further, Hebrews' concept of the High Priest is related to the pre-Christian (Old Testament) history of salvation in a way which corresponds closely to the thinking of the whole New Testament. Christ both fulfils all Old Testament priesthood and replaces the temple. With his coming the priest of the Old Covenant becomes superfluous. Christ's person summarizes the whole cultic development of the chosen people. This is the meaning of the statement in Matt. 27.51 that at the moment of Jesus' death the curtain of the temple was torn in two. The evangelist must have thought of the fact that Jesus is the High Priest who now goes into the Holy Place.

We may say that of the Christological views we have investigated to this point, the High Priest concept describes most fully and adequately the New Testament understanding of Jesus. The very fact that this concept takes account of all three aspects of Jesus' work is a big advantage, even if the third aspect, the second coming of Christ, is only mentioned and not fully developed. Moreover the concept describes the relation of the three aspects in a way which corresponds to the total witness of early Christian thought: the centre of the high priestly work is Jesus' earthly act of sacrifice, but the present office of mediation emphasizes the work of the risen Lord, the aspect which actually interested the Church above all.

We have said that Hebrews contains the only detailed Christology of the High Priest in the New Testament. However we find the ideas developed in Hebrews either expressed or implied in other New Testament writings.[1] The Book of Revelation figuratively describes

[1] The interesting attempt of G. Friedrich ('Beobachtungen zur messianischen Hohepriestererwartung in den Synoptikern', *ZTK* 53, 1956, pp. 265 ff.) to find traces of a High Priest Christology throughout the Synoptic Gospels makes visible a number of connecting lines between the 'High Priest' and the rest of New Testament Christology. But this suggested connection must remain questionable for many of the passages cited. Friedrich begins with the assumption that

the Son of Man who appears in the midst of the seven lampstands as the High Priest: 'clothed with a long robe and with a golden girdle around his breast' (1.13). The author does not dwell on this figure, of course, since the figure of the 'Lamb' is more important to him.

The Gospel of John emphasizes the High Priest concept much more strongly. This book is more closely related to Hebrews in other respects too than any other New Testament writing, so it is not surprising that this same concept of the High Priest appears here also. C. Spicq points out that according to John 18.15 the beloved disciple was acquainted with the high priest.[1] That would explain his particular interest in the idea that Jesus represents the fulfilment of the Old Testament priesthood.[2] It is of course uncertain whether Spicq is correct in his thesis that the author of Hebrews actually took over the concept of Jesus as the High Priest from the Johannine writings. The thesis is not impossible. But when we consider that the concept goes back to Jesus himself, and that early Christianity in general had a special predilection for applying Ps. 110 to Jesus, it is probably not necessary to assume a direct dependence of one of these writings on the other.

It is certain at any rate that the author of the Gospel of John also pursues this concept with particular interest. We think first of all of ch. 17. This whole chapter, a part of Jesus' farewell discourses, is actually known in theological scholarship as the 'high priestly prayer'. True, this description is not as old as we are inclined to think. It does not even date back to the Church Fathers, although Cyril of Alexandria commented on John 17.9 that Jesus appears in this chapter as High Priest.[3] Chytraeus, a Protestant theologian of the sixteenth century, was the first to coin the description 'high priestly prayer', and from his time on both Protestant and Roman Catholic theologians have used it.

Jewish messianic thought was to a large extent determined by the idea of the messianic High Priest.

[1] C. Spicq, 'L'origine johannique de la conception du Christ-prêtre dans l'Epître aux Hébreux', *Aux sources de la tradition chrétienne* (volume in honour of M. Goguel), pp. 258 ff. On the same theme see O. Moe, 'Das Priestertum Christi im Neuen Testament ausserhalb des Hebräerbriefs', *TLZ* 72, 1947, col. 335 ff.; E. Clarkson, 'The Antecedents of the High-Priest Theme in Hebrews', *Anglican Theological Review* 29, 1947, pp. 92 ff.

[2] With others Spicq also suggests that the Fourth Gospel's reference to Jesus' 'seamless' robe (John 19.23) reminds one of the high priest's robe.

[3] See *PG* 74, 505. See C. Spicq, 'L'origine johannique de la conception du Christ-prêtre dans l'Epître aux Hebreux', *op. cit.*, p. 261 n. 4.

But even if the designation is of relatively recent origin, there is no doubt that Chytraeus was exegetically quite correct in using it. For it is a fact that one can explain the whole prayer only on the basis of the high priestly consciousness of the one who spoke it. Jesus directs this prayer to the Father before he brings his offering, asking that those given him may be sanctified by the Father in order to be able to receive the fruits of the offering brought by the High Priest. The petition for the sanctification of his own (17.17) and their separation from the world (17.11 ff.) is a typical high priestly prayer. But whereas in the Old Testament the petition is only cultically understood, here, in view of the concept of the High Priest fulfilled in Christ, it is understood ethically. Just as Christ himself is sanctified by the Father (10.36), so shall his own be sanctified. Spicq correctly emphasizes that Heb. 10.10 contains the same concept of sanctification.[1]

The farewell discourses in John also develop especially the second idea we discovered in Hebrews—the idea that Jesus as 'leader' (ἀρχηγός) and 'forerunner' (πρόδρομος) goes before his people and thus continues his high priestly office of mediation in the present. Thus in John 17.24 Jesus prays that those whom God has given him may be with him where he is. The saying about preparing a place in his Father's house (14.2 ff.) corresponds, as Spicq shows, to the preparing of a city mentioned in Heb. 11.16.

With the exception of Hebrews, no other New Testament writing emphasizes so strongly as the Johannine literature the sinlessness of Jesus: 'Which of you convicts me of sin?' (John 8.46); '. . . in him there is no sin' (I John 3.5); 'He who does right is righteous, as he is righteous' (I John 3.7).

It seems to me that the concept of the Paraclete is especially related to the High Priest concept. The judicial character of the Paraclete has been rightly pointed out.[2] But this is connected with the high priestly role of mediation: '. . . if any one does sin, we have an advocate with the Father, Jesus Christ the righteous' (I John 2.1). Heb. 7.25 and 9.24 describe the office of Jesus in the same way. According to the application of Ps. 110 to him, Jesus continues to work in the present from the right hand of God; according to the Gospel of John, he comes to earth in the Paraclete for his own. It is his highest high priestly function, the summary of all the high priestly prayers he

[1] See C. Spicq, *L'Epître aux Hébreux* I, 1952, pp. 122 f.

[2] T. Preiss, 'Justification in Johannine Thought', *Life in Christ*, ET (SBT 13), 1954, pp. 9 ff.

brings before God in the present, that he 'will pray to the Father, and he will give you another Counsellor, to be with you for ever' (John 14.16). This Counsellor fulfils on earth the mediation of sanctification. He is the 'Spirit whom the world cannot receive', who will lead those who belong to Christ into all truth. On the other hand, the command to the disciples in the Johannine discourses to pray 'in Jesus' name' shows that Christ continues his high priestly work after his ascension by bringing their prayers before God in heaven. This is what is meant when Christians end their prayers with διὰ Ἰησοῦ Χριστοῦ.

Thus we see that, contrary to the usual assumption, the High Priest concept is not only present in Hebrews, but lies also behind the Christological statements of other New Testament passages. It is of course true that no other writing has so concentrated all the Christological assertions in the High Priest concept as has Hebrews. Also in subsequent times it has never again been made the centre of a whole Christology. On the other hand, the concept has never completely disappeared and has in any case played a much larger role in the history of doctrine than the ancient *ebed Yahweh* Christology. The High Priest concept has served to emphasize one Christological aspect among others.[1] Theologians have often devoted a special chapter in their Christologies to the *munus sacerdotale* of Christ. The reason the concept has been preserved to this extent is the fact that it is clearly the central theme of a canonical writing of the New Testament.

Having completed our investigation of the High Priest concept, we come to the end of the first part of our work, the examination of the Christological titles which relate primarily to the earthly work of Jesus.

[1] Especially interesting is the distinction which Hippolytus makes between the Messiah from Judah and the Messiah from Levi, both of whom are united in the person of Jesus. This distinction gains importance through the Qumran texts, which (like the *Damascus Document* and the *Testaments of the Twelve Patriarchs*) attests the expectation of two Messiahs, one from Aaron and one from Israel (see p. 86 above). L. Mariès, 'Le Messie issu de Lévi chez Hippolyte de Rome', *Mélanges J. Lebreton* I, *Recherches de Science Religieuse*, 1951, pp. 381 ff., has convincingly shown that Hippolytus must have known the tradition contained in the *Testaments of the Twelve Patriarchs*. See also J. T. Milik, *RB* 60. 1953, p. 291.

PART TWO

The Christological Titles which Refer to the Future Work of Jesus

IN ORDER TO AVOID any misunderstanding, especially at the beginning of this part of our work, we emphasize once again that our general classification of the various Christological titles according to the various periods of *Heilsgeschichte* is by no means intended to force them into categories too narrow to contain them. The titles and concepts we have now to consider relate *primarily* to the eschatological work of Christ. We underline the word 'primarily'. Rarely does a title actually relate only to one of the four Christological aspects we have distinguished. We have already seen, for example, that the High Priest concept refers above all to the earthly work of Christ, but that it also includes the present office of the risen Christ, and even points to his future work. The division we have made between the various aspects of Christ's work would be misunderstood if it became a rigid schematism forced upon the Christology of the New Testament. Such a division can only serve the purely practical purpose of classifying the various Christological concepts in a way consistent with early Christian theology itself. It is a way of preventing an arbitrary determination of the sequence of the concepts considered and of working from the basis of the New Testament itself instead of from later theological points of view.

We must also emphasize again that the various concepts we investigate are not really so sharply distinguished as our phenomenological division of them might seem to indicate. In point of fact, they have to a large extent mutually influenced one another—sometimes already in Judaism even before they were applied to Jesus. Often a single title not only implies the specific views essentially connected with it, but also includes the views originating from other titles.

Nevertheless, despite the fact that we cannot draw exact lines of separation, we may legitimately distinguish between the concepts and analyse them one after another in order better to understand the Christology of the New Testament. With the express reservation that in doing so we do not exclude a mutual influence, we continue our method of division and turn now to the titles which concern especially the *future*, not yet completed, work of Christ.

It is especially important to remember the qualification of mutual influence when we discuss the title Messiah. I agree for the most part with the thesis of Jean Héring (which is similar to that of A. F. v. Gall, mentioned on p. 139 below), but it seems to me that in his important book, *Le royaume de Dieu et sa venue*,[1] which is important especially for this part of our work, Héring has not escaped the danger of the schematism we have mentioned.

[1] See also Héring's additions to this work in his article, 'Messie juif et Messie chrétien', *RHPR* 18, 1938, pp. 419 ff.

5

Jesus the Messiah

(Χριστός)

WE ARE DEALING NOW with a title which had its origin above all in the Jewish hope for the future. With its application to Jesus it was inevitably influenced by other Christological aspects of the New Testament and by the early Christian conception of time with its characteristic tension between present and future. Nevertheless it is first and foremost an eschatological concept. We need only recall that the adjective 'messianic' is almost a synonym for 'eschatological'.

On the other hand, the title Messiah has a special place among all the other Christological titles. It became more or less the crystallization point of all New Testament Christological views. Externally seen, almost all other concepts are subordinated to this one. Thus we speak simply of 'Christology', although in so doing we by no means think only of the New Testament views related to the Messiah-Christ.

We have seen that even before the New Testament period, Judaism had the tendency to connect all views and even titles having to do with the end time with the one title 'Messiah' and to make them all special attributes of this figure—despite the fact that many of the conceptions were hardly compatible.

Just at the time of Jesus there were in Judaism many varied conceptions of the coming Mediator of the end time, some of which differed radically from one another. We must not forget that at this time Judaism had by no means a single fixed concept of the Messiah. We are accustomed to think of the Jewish Messiah as if he were an unambiguous, clearly defined figure. In general it is true that the Jews expected a saviour with certain nationalistic and Jewish characteristics. But this common form could hold the most widely varying content.[1] In the New Testament period the prevailing

[1] Thus rightly F. J. Foakes Jackson and K. Lake, *The Beginnings of Christianity* I, 1920, p. 356. See also A. E. J. Rawlinson, *The New Testament Doctrine of the Christ*, 1926, pp. 12 ff.; W. Manson, *Jesus the Messiah*, 1946, especially pp. 134 ff.

Messiah type was of course more and more that which we roughly designate the 'political Messiah', or simply the 'Jewish Messiah'. In the interests of simplicity we shall make use of this usual terminology in our investigation, but we must not forget that the expression 'Messiah' was not a *terminus technicus* for this one conception, but was only in the process of becoming that.

Certain Jewish conceptions of the expected saviour were actually conscious contradictions of the prevailing Messiah type, and yet they still belong under the common denominator 'Messiah'. In the realm of New Testament thought it is precisely the Jewish Christological views and title which did not have to do with a political Messiah which are particularly significant. Despite this fact, even the very first Christians adopted the designation Messiah.

In order to grasp the importance the first Christians attached to this title, we have only to remember that *the* Christological title for Christians from New Testament times until today has been the title Messiah. The Greek Χριστός (derived from χρίω, to anoint) is nothing more than a translation of the Hebrew *mashiach*, 'anointed one'. From a very early date Christians were accustomed to connect the designation 'Christ' with the name Jesus. Jesus-Christ means Jesus-Messiah. Already the letters of Paul, the oldest Christian writings we possess, have a tendency to fix the word Christ as a proper name, although the passages in which Paul writes 'Christ' before Jesus (i.e., 'Christ Jesus') serve as a reminder that he is still aware of its real meaning. Christians of the New Testament period did not completely forget the meaning of the title Messiah as we often do today when we say 'Jesus Christ'. We should remember in reading the New Testament that its authors were still at least partly aware of the significance of 'Jesus-Messiah'.

But it would be quite a mistake to conclude that the specific ideas which Judaism connected with the title had especially great significance for the writers who applied it to Jesus. If that were the case, we should have to give the present chapter a very central place. The fact is, however, that the Christians took over only certain important elements of the predominating picture of the Messiah, and did not apply to Jesus other quite essential aspects of the Jewish Messiah. The most obvious explanation of the fact that the title Messiah nevertheless was so successful that it almost excluded all other titles is that the early Christians were aware that it could include many different conceptions and that they had to adopt it if they hoped at all to make clear to the Jews the Christological role of Jesus.

But in view of the strong political stamp of the Jewish title, this explanation is probably not a sufficient reason to explain the exclusive value of the title in Christian thought. The few elements which the first Christians could take over from the prevailing Jewish conception of the Messiah and which did lend themselves to be applied to Jesus must have been theologically very important to them. We must therefore carefully single out these particular elements.

The great success of the designation Messiah-Christ is all the more remarkable in light of the fact that Jesus himself always showed a peculiar reserve in accepting it as a description of his calling and person, although he did not fully reject it. One might consider it really ironical that the title Messiah ('Christ' in Greek) should have been deliberately, permanently connected with the name Jesus. The designation even gave the new faith its name. Its followers were called Christians ('Messianites') for the first time in Antioch (Acts 11.26). Because they themselves chose to emphasize the title, they cannot have rejected completely the fixed, nationalistically limited picture of the Messiah.

In order to confirm the fact that Jesus himself never ascribed to himself the characteristic task of the Messiah expected by the Jews of his time, we must first investigate more closely the Jewish concept which was such an essential part of the thought and hope of the large majority of the people at the time of Jesus. At the same time we shall discover in how far other aspects of the same politically coloured picture of the Messiah are nevertheless applicable to Jesus, and how they may at least to some extent justify the success of the title in the Church.

1. *The Messiah in Judaism*[1]

The Hebrew participle *mashiach* means 'anointed one'. In this sense it designates in particular the *king of Israel*. He is called 'the anointed

[1] Among other important works on this subject see the following: P. Volz, *Die Eschatologie der jüdischen Gemeinde im neutestamentlichen Zeitalter*[2], 1934, especially pp. 173 ff.; H. Gressmann, *Der Messias*, 1929; W. Küppers, 'Das Messiasbild der spätjüdischen Apokalyptik', *Int. Kirchl. Ztschr.* 23, 1933, pp. 193 ff.; 24, 1934, pp. 47 ff.; J. Héring, *Le royaume de Dieu et sa venue*, 1937. Unfortunately I was unable to consult the newest comprehensive work on the Jewish messianic hope, S. Mowinckel, *He That Cometh*, ET 1956. See also A. Bentzen, *King and Messiah*, 1954, and, with extensive references to the literature, O. Eissfeldt, 'Christus I', *RAC* II, col. 1250 ff.

one of Yahweh'—an allusion to the rite of anointing the king (I Sam. 9.16; 24.6). But the title is not reserved only for the king of Israel; anyone to whom God assigns a special mission for his people can bear it. In Ex. 28.41 the priest is 'the anointed one', *mashiach*, and in I Kings 19.16 Elisha is to be 'anointed' to the prophetic office. Even a foreign heathen king can bear the title when God commissions him with a special task, when he is the organ for executing the divine plan of salvation. In Isa. 45.1 Cyrus is 'messiah', 'anointed one'.[1]

But the one special divinely commissioned person during the time of the Israelitic monarchy is the king himself. 'Anointed one of Yahweh' is a common description of the king, who is considered the representative of God in a special sense. The king has a divine character, because kingship in Israel is 'by the grace of God'. Consequently we find as synonyms for 'anointed one of God' various titles which express the divine origin of his function. In II Sam. 7.14 he is the 'Son of God'. The idea is that Yahweh is the true king of Israel and that the earthly king exercises this divine function in his place.

According to II Sam. 7.12 ff., God promised David that his kingship would last for ever. History denied the realization of this prophecy in a brutal way, but the Jewish eschatological hope held fast all the more energetically to this unfulfilled expectation so that 'the anointed one of Yahweh', the 'Messiah', gradually became an eschatological figure (although strangely enough the expression *mashiach* does not appear in the Old Testament itself as an eschatological designation).

We must emphasize, however, that this does not mean that this 'anointed one' would appear in an other-worldly setting. The word 'eschatological' is to be understood here only in its etymological (i.e., temporal) sense. The Jews took it for granted that an earthly kingship would be necessary in order to introduce future salvation. We read in Ps. 89.3 f.: 'I have made a covenant with my chosen one, I have sworn to David my servant: 'I will establish your descendants for ever, and build your throne for all generations."' Here is an eschatological hope to be fulfilled in a completely earthly framework.

It was probably first during the exile, when the throne of David no longer existed, that the Jews postponed the promise made to him to the distant future, a time when salvation would still be realized in an earthly setting, but in a final way. Jeremiah writes, 'And it shall come to pass in that day, says the Lord of hosts . . . they shall serve

[1] See E. Jenni, 'Die Rolle des Kyros bei Deuterojesaja', *TZ* 10, 1954, pp. 241 ff.

the Lord their God and David their king, whom I will raise up for them' (Jer. 30.8 f.). Pss. 2 and 72 proclaim that all nations will have to subject themselves to the king appointed by Yahweh.

During the exile Ezekiel especially conferred upon the future king the exact characteristics which also later described the figure of the Messiah. According to Ezek. 37.21 ff. the whole kingdom of Israel will one day be united under David, who will rule eternally.

The hope of the eschatological appearance of a king of Davidic descent became particularly active as Jewish nationalism developed under the rule of Greece. During this time the Jews expected a completely earthly, political king, not some heavenly being who would appear on earth in a miraculous way. Some of them—the prophet who wrote Zech. 9.9 f., for example—expected him to be a peaceful king, but still one who would play a completely political role. Others—by far the majority—expected him to be a warring ruler who would conquer all Israel's enemies. The Psalms of Solomon emphasize especially the second expectation. Psalms 17 and 18 of this book call the king of the future, a descendant of David, χριστός.[1]

The prayer in Psalms of Solomon 17.21 ff., a classical expression of the prevailing messianic expectation in New Testament times, is quite characteristic:

> Behold, O Lord, and raise up unto them their king, the son of David, at the time in which Thou seest, O God, that he may reign over Israel Thy servant. And gird him with strength, that he may shatter unrighteous rulers, and that he may purge Jerusalem from nations that trample her down to destruction . . . With a rod of iron he shall break in pieces all their substance, He shall destroy the godless nations with the word of his mouth; at his rebuke nations shall flee before him, and he shall reprove sinners for the thoughts of their heart. And he shall gather together a holy people, whom he shall lead in righteousness, and he shall judge the tribes of the people that has been sanctified by the Lord his God . . . And neither sojourner nor alien shall sojourn with them any more . . . And he shall have the heathen nations to serve him under his yoke; And he shall glorify the Lord in a place to be seen of all the earth; And he shall purge Jerusalem, making it holy as of old . . .
>
> (Translated by G. B. Gray in *The Apocrypha and Pseudepigrapha of the Old Testament*, ed. R. H. Charles, vol. II, 1913.)

[1] Foakes Jackson and Lake, *op. cit.*, p. 356, emphasize that 'Messiah' appears here for the very first time in its technical eschatological sense. Although the date of the Qumran texts is not yet certain, the use of the Messiah designation in them must of course be taken into consideration.

These messianic hopes were widespread among the Pharisees of Jesus' time.

Besides this 'classical' messianic expectation, we find also (but not until the Jewish apocalypses of the first Christian century) the idea that the expected king will not bring in the final kingdom but only a provisional one, while God himself will bring in the permanent kingdom.[1] In this case, the messianic king becomes the *forerunner of God*. Two originally separate conceptions are obviously combined here. According to one the messianic king brings in the final kingdom; according to the other, probably older, Yahweh himself brings it in. When the two concepts are combined, the Messiah-king, who now clearly is an earthly ruler, introduces an era which is no longer that in which we live but is not yet the coming aeon. It is rather a kind of eschatological interim time. It is important for the specifically Christian concept of time that Judaism too knew of a 'between times' such as this.

The *Apocalypse of Ezra* shows clearly the political character of the messianic kingdom.[2] The messianic king destroys the evil and deals graciously with the good who wait for the last things. Also in the *Apocalypse of Baruch* the king destroys the enemies of Israel. He establishes a condition of perfection on earth: nature is more fruitful, animals are no longer vicious, the elect enjoy long life and good health.[3] Many writings of late Judaism do not mention the Messiah in their descriptions of the future, but they probably presuppose his function.

We have very roughly described the characteristic Jewish ideas of a political Messiah-king. We must not forget, of course, that these conceptions often appear in connection with thoughts originating in other Jewish concepts of an expected saviour. Besides the Messiah from Judah, there appears in the *Damascus Document* and in the *Qumran texts* also the 'Messiah from Aaron (Levi)', who has obvious features of the 'priest'. *The Testaments of the Twelve Patriarchs* indicate the same connection.[4] It is especially important that in this context *two* Messiahs are expected—the priestly and the political, the former being superior to the latter. This subordination of the political Messiah-king is a Jewish analogy to Jesus' evaluation of the political messianic ideal, although Jesus' opposition to political kingship is not based on the priestly concept.

[1] II (4) Esd. 7.26 ff.; 11–14; Baruch 29;30; 40. See also Sanh. 96b ff.

[2] See II (4) Esd. 11 f.; 13; 7. 27 ff.

[3] Baruch 72 ff.

[4] See p. 86 above and the articles by K. G. Kuhn and E. Stauffer cited there.

We summarize the main points of the Jewish conception of the Messiah: (1) The Messiah fulfils his task in a purely earthly setting. (2) According to one view, which we find in the Psalms of Solomon, he introduces the end time; according to an earlier conception, he introduces an interim period. In any case the aeon in which he appears is no longer the present one. This temporal consideration distinguishes the Messiah from the Prophet. (3) Whether it is of peaceful or warlike character, the work of the Jewish Messiah is that of a political king of Israel. He is the national king of the Jews. (4) The Jewish Messiah is of royal lineage, a descendant of David. For this reason he also bears the title 'Son of David'.

2. *Jesus and the Messiah* (*Son of David*)

The question whether Jesus had a 'messianic self-consciousness' is one of the major problems for understanding both his life and teachings. We have already mentioned that Christians today usually think of the adjective 'messianic' in a quite general sense and not usually in terms of a strongly marked concept of the Messiah such as we find in the Psalms of Solomon. In the present chapter, however, we use the expression precisely in this limited sense. Our purpose now is to discover in how far Jesus applied to himself or rejected the particular Jewish ideas connected with the title Messiah.

Three Synoptic passages are especially important for our problem: Mark 14.61 f. and parallels, Mark 15.2 ff. and parallels, and Mark 8.27 ff. and parallels. We begin with the first, in which the question is most clearly stated. During the trial of Jesus, the high priest Caiaphas asks him, 'Are you the Messiah, the Son of the Blessed?'[1] Caiaphas obviously asks the question in order to set a trap; whatever answer Jesus gives will be to the high priest's advantage. Caiaphas probably expects an affirmative answer, for he must know that Jesus appeared with a particular claim about himself. For Caiaphas this claim can only be that Jesus considers himself the Messiah, and he needs a messianic declaration from Jesus himself to support the complaint brought against him. If Jesus answers affirmatively, Caiaphas could turn him over to the Romans as a political rebel. To claim to be a Messiah who will establish the throne of David is to declare oneself for an autonomous government, and thus to be guilty of treason. On the other hand, a negative answer from Jesus

[1] Concerning the relationship between 'Messiah' and 'Son of God', see pp. 279 ff. below.

(a possibility with which after all Caiaphas had also to reckon) would also not be necessarily to the high priest's disadvantage. In that case, he thinks, Jesus would be discredited among the people. In their disappointment they would at least abandon him, and perhaps they would even turn against him. Whether his answer be 'Yes' or 'No', Jesus must therefore compromise himself.

But how did he answer? We have here a philological and exegetical problem. According to the usual and most obvious interpretation, Jesus answered with an unmistakable, unqualified affirmation. We shall see, however, that this interpretation is not so self-evident when we consider the parallel Synoptic texts and go back to the Aramaic original, which we must presuppose for Jesus' answer at least in Matthew. Moreover, Jesus added another sentence to his answer, in which he clearly ascribed to himself a role which does not agree with that of the Messiah according to the expectations of the traditional political Jewish conception of him. According to the Greek text of Mark, Jesus answered ἐγώ εἰμι.[1] That certainly means 'Yes'. But the parallel texts in Matthew and Luke read differently. In Matt. 26.64 Jesus says σὺ εἶπας, 'You have said so.' On the basis of the Greek these words would also signify an affirmative answer. But the corresponding Aramaic word אֲמַרְתְּ (presupposing that we may assume here a literal translation from the Aramaic) by no means indicates a clear affirmation. It is rather a way of avoiding a direct answer and can even mean a veiled denial. In that case, the sense of Jesus' words would be, '*You* say so, not I.' If we may understand his answer to the high priest's trick question in this way, then Jesus neither clearly affirmed nor clearly denied that he was the Messiah.

This understanding of the phrase, which has important consequences also for other New Testament passages,[2] has been given very little attention in the commentaries. In recent times it has been defended by A. Merx, who very carefully investigated all the relevant material. See his '*Das Evangelium Matthaeus nach der syrischen im Sinaikloster gefundenen Palimpsesthandschrift*', Vol. II/1 of the total work, *Die vier kanonischen Evangelien nach ihrem ältesten bekannten Texte*, 1902, pp. 382–84. In his *Le royaume de*

[1] The text variant σὺ εἶπας ὅτι . . . probably rests upon a harmonization with Matthew. Some exegetes (for example, Lohmeyer and Taylor), however, consider it very early, and hold that the texts of Matthew and Luke may be explained from it. In this case, also Mark would have known of an evasive answer of Jesus.

[2] A. Merx does not begin with the passage we are considering, but with Jesus' answer to Judas' question at the last supper, 'Is it I, Master ?' (Matt. 26.25). Here also an evasive answer by Jesus ('*You* say so') fits the context surprisingly well.

Dieu et sa venue, pp. 112 f. J. Héring agrees with Merx's interpretation. But even the Church Fathers did not all interpret Jesus' answer as an affirmation. Origen, for instance, in his *Commentary on Matthew* (*PG* 13, 1757) writes expressly that Jesus' answer is neither positive nor negative: 'He neither denies that he is God's Son, nor does he expressly confess that he is.' Thus Origen also assumes that Jesus gave an evasive answer.

We cannot be absolutely certain, of course, that the exact Aramaic equivalent אֲמַרְתְּ lies behind the Greek σὺ εἶπας. But the assumption is probable, and the sense of the Aramaic expression is clear at least to the extent that it does not mean 'Yes'. Moreover, as we have already mentioned, the sentence Jesus added to these words quite clearly contains a conception which does not correspond to the common official picture of the Messiah. In Matthew this sentence is obviously more than a simple qualification; it is a direct contrast. The sentence begins with the conjunction πλήν, '*But* I tell you, hereafter you will see the Son of man seated at the right hand of Power, and coming on the clouds of heaven.' πλήν means an emphasized 'but', which sets one statement over against another which is rejected.[1] It suggests that the preceding answer of Jesus was probably negative. According to Matthew, then, Jesus says in effect, 'I will not answer this question, but I will tell you something else.' And then follows characteristically not a statement about the Messiah the Jews expected, but a statement about the Son of Man, with whom Jesus openly identified himself.

We shall speak in the next chapter of the Son of Man concept, which Jesus here contrasts with that of the Messiah. Now we are only interested in his attitude toward the application of the Jewish conception of the Messiah to himself. His saying about the Son of Man sitting on the right hand of God and coming again on the clouds of heaven is not derived from the concept of the Messiah we have described in the last section. The Son of Man is a heavenly being, not an earthly king who will conquer the enemies of Israel and exercise an earthly sovereignty. The contrast is clear in the form Matthew reports Jesus' answer. Matthew thus actually does seem to have translated the Aramaic original more faithfully than the other Synoptic writers. The correct translation of Jesus' answer is probably, 'That is what you say, but I tell you . . . ,' followed by the statement about the Son of Man.

[1] According to Blass-Debrunner, *Gramm. d. neutest. Griechisch*[7], 1943, par. 449, the word means *jedoch, indessen* (yet, however) in Matt. and Luke; *jedenfalls* (in any case) in Paul. See also W. Bauer, *Wörterbuch*[4], 1952 (translated and edited by W. F. Arndt and F. W. Gingrich, *A Greek-English Lexicon*, 1957, p. 675).

It is true that one would expect an emphasizing ἐγώ in this case. Perhaps its omission may be explained by the fact that the Greek-writing evangelist himself no longer correctly understood the words σὺ εἶπας in their Aramaic sense. It is quite certain that Mark did not reckon with the possibility of a negative meaning. His translation ἐγώ εἰμι implies a simple affirmation.[1] But that does not in itself contradict the assumption that the Aramaic sense lies behind the text of Matthew and perhaps even of Mark.

The parallel passage in Luke 22.67 ff. supports the interpretation which assumes that Matthew preserved a literal translation of the Aramaic phrase. According to Luke, Jesus says in answer to the high priest's question whether he is the Messiah: 'If I tell you, you will not believe, and if I ask you, you will not answer. But from now on the Son of man shall be seated at the right hand of the power of God.' Luke clearly preserves the memory that Jesus refuses to answer directly. He evades the high priest's question and, as in Matthew's report, continues with an explanation not about the Messiah but about the Son of Man. Thus Luke's report of this scene clearly confirms our interpretation of Matthew's report: Jesus refuses to claim for himself the title Messiah in this form. But on the other hand, he does not answer with a direct 'No'. This must be said especially in the light of the probability that at the time of Jesus the Son of Man concept was somehow connected with that of the Messiah.

The most important conclusion to be drawn from an investigation of the passages in Matthew and Luke is that in any case—even apart from the argument concerning the Aramaic original—Jesus deliberately corrected the high priest's question by substituting the 'Son of Man' for the 'Messiah'. Jesus knows that the specific ideas relating to the Jewish Messiah are of a political nature, and nothing is more foreign to his conception of his calling. In order to prevent all misunderstanding from the very beginning, he purposely avoids the title Messiah. But in order to make it clear that he does not thereby give up his conviction that he has to fulfil in a special sense God's plan of salvation for his people and therefore for all humanity, he adds immediately the sentence about the 'Son of Man'. Since he is a heavenly being, the Son of Man is actually more closely related to

[1] That Mark understands Jesus' answer in this way may also be connected with the fact that in the total outline of his Gospel the messianic confession of Jesus has an important place in this passage: first the demons recognize him as Messiah, then his disciples, and now as a climax also his enemies. On this overall plan of Mark see the instructive book of J. M. Robinson, *The Problem of History in Mark* (SBT 21), 1957.

God than the Messiah. Jesus' rejection of the Messiah title, therefore, by no means indicates a rejection of his claim to an elevated position. On the contrary, the claim to be the Son of Man in the sense of Daniel's heavenly being coming on the clouds may be considered even more radical than the claim to be a political Messiah. Jesus rejects only the political role of the Messiah-king.

When the high priest asks him if he is the Messiah, Jesus takes the same attitude he takes at other times when his opponents try to trap him by asking cunning questions which he could not answer either negatively or positively without compromising himself. That is certainly the purpose of the high priest's question. But as in all such 'temptations' Jesus does not compromise himself in this case. He answers neither 'Yes' nor 'No'. He is not insincere in avoiding the question, because, as in other cases, his answer actually lies beyond the question put to him.

The second important text concerning Jesus' attitude toward the concept 'Messiah' is Mark 15.2 ff. and parallels. Here Jesus stands before Pilate, who asks him, 'Are you the King of the Jews?' Pilate translates the designation Messiah into the Roman terminology, for only on this basis can the whole affair interest him.[1] Perhaps the Jews themselves had already used the word 'king' in denouncing Jesus to the Romans. Jesus answers Pilate, 'You say so (σὺ λέγεις).' Matthew and Luke report the same answer. The evangelists probably understood the Greek words σὺ λέγεις in this case also to mean 'Yes'. But here also it is possible that Jesus intended an evasive answer. The dialogue about the 'kingdom not of this world' which follows Pilate's question in the Gospel of John (18.33 ff.) could point in this direction, and such an interpretation would then agree with our conclusions about Jesus' answer to the high priest. It is worth noting that in Mark 15.2 ff. and parallels Pilate does not react at all to Jesus' 'You say so.' He would certainly have done so, had he understood Jesus' answer to be an affirmation. It is especially significant that after Jesus' answer in the Lucan text, Pilate issues the verdict, 'I find no crime in this man' (Luke 23.4). Could he have said this if he had understood Jesus' answer as a direct affirmation? Would he not have ended the hearing immediately, since the complaint was already proved? In the name of the Roman state, would he not have had to suppress and punish any illegal claim to authority in the province he governed?

[1] On the role of the Romans in Jesus' trial see O. Cullmann, *The State in the New Testament*, pp. 24 ff.

The third text having to do with Jesus' attitude toward the title Messiah is the well-known scene in Caesarea Philippi, Mark 8.27 ff. and parallels. In v. 29 Peter confesses, 'You are the Christ (Messiah).' According to the usual interpretation of this passage, Jesus explicitly accepts Peter's messianic proclamation. But Matthew's report of the incident (16.15 ff.) has influenced this interpretation because of the words it attributes to Jesus about Peter's being the 'Rock' on which the Church will be grounded; and it is almost certain that these words do not belong in this context.[1] Despite the usual interpretation and the support the text of Matthew gives it, we must therefore examine more closely Jesus' reaction to Peter's confession in Mark. Mark 8.30 f. reads: 'And he charged them to tell no one about him. And he began to teach them that the Son of Man must suffer many things, and be rejected by the elders and the chief priests and the scribes, and be killed, and after three days rise again.'

It is usually said that in forbidding Peter and the other disciples to speak of it, Jesus implicitly accepted the messianic title Peter conferred upon him, and only added that he must suffer many things. But we have already seen in our investigation of the *ebed Yahweh* concept that it is difficult to connect suffering with the Jewish messianic expectation.

The fact is that Jesus neither affirms nor denies Peter's messianic confession. He says nothing at all in answer to this explanation, and (as in the other passages we have considered) speaks instead of the *Son of Man* who must suffer many things. When Peter rebukes him for such an idea, Jesus flings at him the terrible accusation, 'Get behind me, Satan' (Mark 8.33). This means nothing less than that Jesus considered as a satanic temptation the conception of the Messiah which Peter implied by his rebuke and clearly intended when he confessed Jesus to be the Messiah. The same Satan who met Jesus openly in the wilderness after his baptism and tried to impose upon him the role of a political Messiah—that Satan now uses the disciple Peter to prevent him from fulfilling his real task and again to persuade him to play the role of a Jewish political Messiah.[2] The extraordinary vehemence with which Jesus rejects this demand in Caesarea Philippi indicates how deeply the temptation of Peter affects him. He does not want to be the king of Israel in this way; he has the firm conviction (probably since his baptism) that he must fulfil his task in suffering and dying, not in establishing a political kingdom.

[1] See O. Cullmann, *Peter*, pp. 170 ff., and pp. 280 f. below.

[2] See also J. M. Robinson, *op. cit.*, p. 51.

It is no accident that according to the Synoptics Satan appears immediately after Jesus' baptism with his messianic temptation. All three Synoptic Gospels agree in connecting the two events. If we gave the correct interpretation of Jesus' baptism in our chapter on the *ebed Yahweh*, Jesus became certain at that moment that the divine calling he had to fulfil was to die for his people. Satan comes immediately to resist this conviction. He knows that the fulfilment of that task means the end of his own rule; and on the other hand, he knows that the other way, the way of the political Messiah-king, would really make Jesus his obedient servant. Therefore Satan 'showed him all the kingdoms of the world and the glory of them; and he said to him, "All these I will give you, if you will fall down and worship me"' (Matt. 4.8 ff.). Matthew rightly set this at the end of the three individual temptations as the climax and meaning of the whole scene. Just as Jesus later answers Peter in Caesarea Philippi, he answers here with the words, 'Begone, Satan!' Satan's offer to give Jesus sovereignty over all the kingdoms of the world corresponds exactly to the official Jewish hope for their expected Messiah.

The fact that Jesus himself considered this political conception of his work of salvation an especially great temptation indicates how attractive it must have been to him. A man is only tempted by something to which he feels drawn. Thus the common view of the Messiah cannot have been completely inconceivable to Jesus.[1] Just for this reason he fought all the more energetically against this temptation from the time of his baptism on. On the other hand, the fact that Peter wants to force a political role on his master indicates also how common—even self-evident—this conception was even in Jesus' immediate environment. As in all things, Peter is only the representative of the other disciples in this case. Mark had good reason for writing that Jesus looked at the other disciples when he answered Peter with the strong words, 'Get behind me, Satan' (Mark 8.33). Jesus knew very well that all his disciples had the secret hope that he would assume the political Messiah's glorious kingly role. That function also had consequences for the role his disciples would then play. The disciple of a powerful Messiah-king is quite different from the disciple of one condemned to death. The argument of the sons of Zebedee concerning their rank in the future kingdom is enough to show what thoughts were in the heads of the disciples. Their desertion of their master when he was arrested and their flight

[1] I show how Jesus had constantly to deal with the Zealot question in *The State in the New Testament*, pp. 8 ff.

was not only the result of an understandable human cowardice, but also the result of disappointment that Jesus did not resemble in the slightest the expected Messiah-king.

It is probably not incorrect to seek the subjective reason for Judas Iscariot's betrayal in this disappointment.[1] The Synoptic accounts show that according to the oldest tradition, greed for money was not his primary motive. If disappointment were the real motive, we would have to consider Judas the extreme example of the same sin of which all the disciples were guilty. According to the Synoptic account of the event in Caesarea Philippi, Satan worked not only in Judas but also in Peter, the representative of all the disciples. Judas is the personification of the sin of all of them. Satan is behind all the disciples, but he seems to celebrate his triumph in Judas. The explanation of Judas' betrayal on the basis of disappointment is even more understandable if he were really a Zealot and the word 'Iscariot' is derived from the Latin *sicarius*, assassin.[2]

In any case, it is important that according to the Gospel tradition Jesus saw the hand of Satan at work in the contemporary Jewish conception of the Messiah. This is probably the basis for explaining what has been known since W. Wrede as the 'messianic secret'—Jesus' repeated command that he be not proclaimed the Messiah.[3] Wrede himself is therefore not correct in explaining it as a later speculation inserted into the Gospels to answer the first Christians' question why Jesus was not recognized as the Messiah during his lifetime.[4]

The principle of form criticism, which Wrede used long before the actual school of form criticism, should not be so exaggerated that the question is no longer even asked whether this or that theme appearing in

[1] For the history of the explanations of Judas' betrayal see K. Lüthi, *Judas Iskariot in der Geschichte der Auslegung von der Reformation bis in die Gegenwart*, 1955.

[2] See *The State in the New Testament*, p. 15.

[3] W. Wrede, *Das Messiasgeheimnis in den Evangelien*, 1901. See also H. J. Ebeling, *Das Messiasgeheimnis und die Botschaft des Marcus-Evangelisten*, 1939; E. Percy, *Die Botschaft Jesu*, 1953, pp. 271 ff. See also p. 141 n. 2, and p. 154 n. 3 below.

[4] Ebeling, *op. cit.*, pp. 167 ff., emphasizes a parallel literary motive of the evangelist: the disciples' lack of understanding, which serves to emphasize the glory of the divine revelation of Jesus. E. Percy, *op. cit.*, follows Wrede on the whole, but alters Wrede's thesis in that he reckons with a messianic tradition about Jesus from the very beginning. Percy thinks that this was later changed by means of the theory of the 'messianic secret', which served as a basis for the later understanding of Christ in the light of the cross and resurrection. But the Synoptic writers exhibit no clear trace of this consideration; it is represented only later by the author of the Fourth Gospel. See my *Early Christian Worship*, pp. 38 ff.

the Gospels (the 'messianic secret', for instance) cannot actually be founded on *history*. After all, history should not simply be dissolved into apologetic 'theories' of the early Church.

Jesus himself, not the early Church, is the source of the command not to proclaim him the Messiah. He was afraid that such a proclamation would lead to a false conception of his task, the conception he recognized and fought as a satanic temptation. That is the reason for his restraint to the very end with regard to the title Messiah.[1]

Precisely the fact that we have to do here with restraint and not with rejection seems to me the best proof of the fact that we are concerned with history, not with early Christian theory. We emphasize this also in opposition to R. Bultmann, who in his *Theology of the New Testament* I, p. 32, completely accepts Wrede's thesis.[2] Bultmann is not right in saying that the restraint of Jesus appears only in 'editorial sentences'. He cannot ascribe to Jesus himself the replacement of the messianic idea with the idea of the Son of Man, because he also rejects Jesus' consciousness of being the Son of Man in any form.

The three Synoptic passages we have examined are in complete agreement. In all three Jesus demonstrates an attitude at least of extreme restraint toward, if not direct rejection of, the *title* 'Messiah'. This is confirmed by the fact that in almost no passage in the Synoptics in which the expression Χριστός appears does Jesus apply it to himself; it is always others who speak of him as the Christ.[3]

The Gospel of John yields the same conclusion as the Synoptics.[4] Besides the dialogue with Pilate in which Jesus emphasizes that his kingdom is not of this world, the writer of John reports in 6.15: 'Perceiving then that they were about to come and take him by force to make him king, Jesus withdrew to the hills by himself.'

[1] Percy, *op. cit.*, p. 272, like Wrede, rejects the interpretation I have suggested. But his reasons are very general and therefore not convincing: he says that Jesus usually did not let himself be influenced by considerations of expediency. In view of the New Testament passages cited above, I especially cannot understand the following argument: '... we must ask with Wrede why Jesus did not simply say that he was not the political Messiah.' Jesus did indeed make it quite clear that he was not—and not only according to the Gospel of John. If he did not directly reject the title, it is because the title is not necessarily connected with the idea of the political Messiah. Therefore reserve, not rejection!

[2] See also R. Bultmann, *Geschichte der synoptischen Tradition*, pp. 371 ff.

[3] See V. Taylor, *The Names of Jesus*, p. 19.

[4] *Ibid.*, p. 20. Only one passage seems to contradict this: John 4.26, Jesus' answer to the Samaritan woman. But here the evangelist himself probably makes use of the designation *Christos* which was familiar to him, and attributes it to Jesus.

By way of summary: (1) Jesus showed extreme reserve toward the *title* Messiah. (2) He actually considered the specific ideas connected with the title as satanic temptations. (3) In decisive passages he substituted 'Son of Man' for 'Messiah', and even set the one in a certain opposition to the other.[1] (4) He deliberately set the ideas relative to the *ebed Yahweh* over against the Jews' political conceptions of the Messiah. All these points indicate the irony of the fact that Jesus was crucified by the Romans as a political Messiah.

In subordinating the kingly to the priestly Messiah, the Jewish Qumran sect also seems to have opposed the political messianic idea.[2] The reason for Jesus' opposition is of course quite different.

We come now to a further question: Is there nothing at all in the Jewish conception of the Messiah which Jesus could apply to himself? We have seen that we can speak of Jesus' radical rejection only of the *Jewish understanding* of the title; with regard to the *title itself* we have found strong reserve but no direct rejection.

That Jesus rejected the title as radically as he did the Jewish conceptions connected with it is improbable simply for the reason that in his time the title no longer referred exclusively to the real messianic idea in the strict sense. But more positively, there is at least *one* aspect of the Jewish conception of the Messiah which we can reconcile with Jesus' consciousness of his calling: the title expresses a continuity between the task he had to fulfil and the Old Testament. The Messiah represents the fulfilment of the role of mediation which the whole of God's chosen people should have realized. This idea lies behind most of the Christological titles originating in Judaism and thus is a common element in the messianic and other eschatological figures. But it finds a particularly powerful expression in the Messiah title; the idea that the Messiah comprehends and fulfils the whole history of Israel has a special significance, precisely because of its strong national emphasis. The only valuable and Christologically relevant element here, however, is the *fact* that the Messiah fulfils the task of Israel. The Jewish conception of *how* he does this is not applicable to Jesus. Despite all its inadequacies, therefore, the idea of the Messiah is important to the extent that it establishes a continuity

[1] E. Stauffer, 'Messias oder Menschensohn?', *Novum Testamentum* 1, 1956, pp. 81 ff., like J. Héring before him, advocates a similar thesis, but he does so in a greatly exaggerated form: Stauffer holds that Jesus *never* called himself 'Messiah', neither in the political nor in the non-political sense. The self-designation 'Son of Man' completely excludes the antithetical 'Messiah'.

[2] See pp. 86 and 116 above.

between the work of Jesus and the mission of the chosen people of Israel.

There are many sayings of Jesus which indicate that he thought of his task as that of carrying out the role of Israel. Such passages offer the possibility of interpreting his attitude toward the messianic description at this one point as one of consent, although of reserved consent. At least they make it plausible to assume that instead of completely rejecting the title, he only consciously avoided it.

One must ask further if Jesus could not accept some elements of the Jewish conception of the Messiah with regard to his future, eschatological work which he had radically to reject for his earthly work. His citation of Ps. 110 in his answer to the high priest (Mark 14.62 and parallels) suggests that he probably expected a future rule over the world. This is true, of course, only in so far as even this expectation excludes all purely political elements. The fact remains that in his answer to the high priest, Jesus described his future work too, not as that of the Messiah, but as that of the 'Son of Man', and spoke of his coming at the end in terms of Daniel's picture of a completely other-worldly heavenly being.

In connection with the question of Jesus' application of the concept Messiah to himself, we have to speak of another designation which is a variant of that concept, or rather a description of the origin of the Messiah-king: *Son of David.*

Two separate questions are involved here: (1) Did Jesus' family really have the tradition that it stemmed from the royal family of David? (2) Did Jesus consider Davidic descent an essential qualification for the task he had to fulfil? Only the second question is actually of Christological importance, but since the first is related to it, we must consider it also.

Since in this section we are investigating Jesus' own attitude toward the concept, we shall not be primarily concerned with the further question how far the early Church attributed a fundamental significance to his Davidic sonship, or how it connected this assertion with his virgin birth. The question comes into consideration only in so far as the Church's theology may have influenced the Gospel tradition of Jesus' own sayings on this point.

We ask first, then: Did Jesus' family trace its family tree back to David? We can put the question only in this form, of course; it is clear that a historical validation of such a tradition would not be possible.

Most scholars believe that even the question whether Jesus' family had the *tradition* of Davidic descent must be answered negatively.[1] They usually argue that the Christians invented the tradition as an apologetic answer to the Jews, who commonly believed that the Messiah must be of Davidic descent. But the assumption that the early Church invented this idea is not so obvious as some scholars have claimed.

We cannot depend upon the genealogies in Matthew and Luke for an answer, because they differ from one another at decisive points and draw quite different lines of connection between Jesus and David. Since Annius of Viterbo (*c.* 1490), the usual solution to the contradiction is to assert that Luke's genealogy is that of Mary; Matthew's, of Joseph. This presupposes that Mary too is a descendant of David. We know that this presupposition was common in the second century,[2] but we possess no earlier evidence of it. In any case, a comparison of the two genealogies involves difficulties which can be resolved only by complicated hypotheses and combinations.[3] One may ask whether the assertion that Mary as well as Joseph was of Davidic lineage was not a later solution conceived to harmonize the New Testament passages about the Davidic sonship of Jesus 'after the flesh' on the one hand, and those about his virgin birth on the other.[4] In addition to these difficulties there is the fact that certain rabbinic circles already had other genealogies of the expected Messiah. In view of these complications, it is better not to begin with the genealogies of the two Gospel accounts in order to answer the question whether Jesus' family had the tradition that it descended from David.

Nevertheless these genealogies are important for our question in so far as they prove at least that between the years 70 and 90 such a

[1] See for instance the explanations of M. Goguel, *Jésus*[2], 1950, pp. 195 ff.

[2] For evidence see W. Bauer, *Das Leben Jesu im Zeitalter der neutestamentlichen Apokryphen*, 1909, pp. 13 ff.

[3] A very early attempt to harmonize the two genealogies is a text of Julius Africanus preserved in Eusebius, *Hist. Eccl.* I, 7. On the historical value of the genealogical traditions used here, see G. Kuhn, *ZNW* 22, 1923, pp. 225ff.

[4] K. Bornhäuser, *Die Geburts- und Kindheitsgeschichte Jesu. Versuch einer zeitgenössischen Auslegung von Matthäus 1 and 2 und Lukas 1–3*, 1930, pp. 22 ff., rejects the possibility that the Gospel of Luke gives the genealogy of Mary. But the solution he offers in order to recognize both genealogies as historically 'correct' and to harmonize them by reference to levirate marriage seems very artificial to me.

tradition was fixed. It must in fact be considerably older than that. Paul clearly presupposes it in Rom. 1.3, and since he is very probably citing an older confession of the Church,[1] we must without doubt reckon with a very early date. This early existence of the tradition is important, because we know that at that time members of Jesus' family still lived. It is of course not impossible, but it is highly improbable that the tradition could have been invented in their presence without some kind of information from the time of Jesus himself. On the basis of this consideration, it is quite possible that Jesus' family did indeed trace its origin to David.[2] It may not have occurred to any member of the family to prove an unbroken line of descent. And it may well be that it was first the early Church which later constructed genealogies of Jesus. Perhaps the lineage was originally nothing more than a family tradition (such as other families may also have had), which no one took the trouble to prove. We should remember that tribal membership was an important factor in the place of every Jewish family occupied in Israelitic society.[3] During the reigns of the emperors Domitian and Trajan at the end of the first and beginning of the second centuries, we hear of relatives of Jesus who were commonly considered descendants of David.

Hegesippus was a Jewish Christian author of a history of the very early Church of which we possess only a few fragments. According to Eusebius [4] he tells the following story: Despite the destruction of Jerusalem in A.D. 70, Domitian wanted to satisfy himself that the Jews were loyal. So one day he commanded that all the descendants of David be sought out and brought before him. Apparently he knew that messianic revolts among the Jews were connected with their expectation that a descendant of David would rise against the Romans, claiming to be king. One of those denounced and arrested was the grandson of Judas, a brother of Jesus. The emperor asked the group whether they were of Davidic lineage, and they answered 'Yes'. Then he inquired about their financial condition. They answered that they had only 9,000 denarii among them, and that they had to work the land in order to live. To prove that they themselves had to work, they showed him the calluses on their hands.

[1] See O. Cullmann, *The Earliest Christian Confessions*, p. 55. Also O. Michel, *Der Brief an die Römer* (Meyer 4^{10}), 1955, pp. 30 f.

[2] Among those who agree with this are J. Weiss, *Das Urchristentum*, 1917, p. 89; G. Dalman, *The Words of Jesus*, ET 1902, pp. 319 ff.; E. Stauffer, *New Testament Theology*, ET 1955, pp. 281 f.

[3] We may also recall in this context that Paul also possessed a family tradition of his descent from the tribe of Benjamin (Phil. 3.5).

[4] Eusebius, *Hist. Eccl.* III, 19 f.

That convinced Domitian that these descendants of David were quite impoverished and harmless, and he contemptuously let them go.—I tell this story only to show that the Davidic tradition in Jesus' family was not contested.

This story comes from the end of the first century, of course—a time in which the relatives of Jesus by virtue of their kinship with him were highly respected in the Jewish Christian community of Transjordan.[1] One could therefore explain the claim of Davidic origin as the later product of a wrongly understood 'dynastic' interest on the part of the Jewish Christians. But Rom. 1.3 proves that already long before this, even before Paul's time, there was no question of Jesus' Davidic sonship. It was assumed, then, even at the time when, to be sure, James the brother of Jesus was playing an important role in the Christian community; but he can hardly have presumed upon his Davidic descent to guarantee his position there. It would be strange if Jesus' Davidic descent were asserted at such an early date without James' knowing of it, for the claim affected him personally also. Although this argument is not necessarily decisive, it does seem to me to speak in favour of the assumption that Jesus' family had an oral tradition, if not a formal genealogy,[2] according to which it came from the lineage of David. As we have said that was certainly nothing out of the ordinary. There may have been many other families who also traced their ancestry to David.[3]

We come to the more important question: Did Jesus designate himself the 'Son of David'? There is only one passage, Mark 12.35 ff. and parallels, which gives us any information on this subject: 'And as Jesus taught in the temple, he said, "How can the scribes say that the Christ is the Son of David? David himself, inspired by the Holy Spirit, declared, 'The Lord said to my Lord, Sit at my right hand, till I put thy enemies under thy feet.' David calls him Lord; so how is he his son?" ' This is one of the most difficult of Jesus' sayings to explain, and it has been interpreted in many different ways. The

[1] See H. J. Schoeps, *Theologie und Geschichte des Judenchristentums*, 1949, pp. 282 ff.

[2] Josephus, who gives detailed information about his ancestors on the first page of his *Vita*, proves that there were families in which full genealogies must have existed.

[3] See T. Zahn, *Das Evangelium des Matthäus* (KNT)[2], 1905, p. 43 n. 6.—As a kind of curiosity I mention here the example of various aristocratic families of Basel who trace their genealogy back to Charlemagne. The parallel is of course not exact, because the question of descent in Judaism did not serve a historical and antiquarian interest, but, as we have said, was theologically important for the position of a family in the Jewish community.

difficulty lies in the all too marked brevity of Jesus' words here as all three Synoptic Gospels report them. One almost has the impression that the evangelists themselves did not know how to explain them.

One common interpretation is that with this saying Jesus expressly denied his Davidic sonship.[1] But that is not so certain as it might seem. The evangelists who reported it at least can hardly have understood it in that sense. They themselves were convinced of Jesus' Davidic descent, and would hardly have included in their Gospels a saying which they thought denied it. It is possible, then, to interpret the passage differently. What Jesus rejected is not necessarily his descent from David, but the Christological significance the Jews attached to this descent for the work of salvation he had to accomplish.

Jesus uses here the method of proof of his time. He cites the familiar Ps. 110, of which we have spoken in another context and of which we shall speak again.[2] The psalm glorifies the king. King David traditionally composed all the Psalms, and this tradition is the foundation of Jesus' argument. According to the original intention of the Psalmist, the *Kyrios* in the nominative case designates God; the *Kyrios* in the dative, the king—'my Lord'. Thus the psalm originally meant, 'God spoke to my king: sit at my right hand . . .' The meaning of the psalm changes, however, as soon as one is convinced that it was not written in honour of the king, but was composed by him, by David himself. The *Kyrios* in the nominative remains God, but the *Kyrios* in the dative can no longer be the king, since he himself is speaking. The words 'my Lord' then come to mean the Messiah.

At least this much is certain therefore: Jesus argues against the idea that the Messiah must be of the physical lineage of David. He refutes this false conception by indicating that David would not have called the Messiah his 'Lord' if the Messiah were his own physical descendant; no one calls his descendant, his own son, 'Lord'. The Messiah whom David calls his Lord must be greater than David; his decisive origin cannot be from David, but must be from someone higher than David. In this case, the idea developed more fully in the Gospel of John would be in the background—the idea that in reality Christ came from no man at all, but from God.

If this interpretation is correct, Jesus' attitude toward the title 'Son

[1] Note for example the way in which B. E. Meyer, *Ursprung und Anfänge des Christentums* II, 1921, p. 446, treats this interpretation as a foregone conclusion.

[2] See pp. 88 f. above and p. 222 f. below.

of David' is quite analogous to his attitude toward the title 'Messiah' in general. Contrary to the usual messianic expectation, he rejects also in this case the political messianic ideal which the claim to be the descendant of David the king especially emphasizes.

R. Bultmann thinks that the saying of Jesus about Davidic sonship is not genuine, but an interpolation of the early Christian community.[1] But if Bultmann were right, it would be impossible to explain in which circles the saying originated. In view of the emphasis on Jesus' descent from David 'according to the flesh' which seems generally to have belonged to the early Christian confession (Rom. 1.3), even the claim that the saying is of Hellenistic origin presents more difficulties than the assumption of its genuineness. Moreover, would not its meaning have been expressed less ambiguously if it were the result of a later interpolation?

We can make clear the fact that Mark 12.35 ff. does not necessarily mean Jesus' denial of the fact of his Davidic sonship by comparing this passage with another saying in which he does not dispute the fact of his physical relations, but does deny that they have any fundamental significance. Mark 3.31 ff. reads: 'And his mother and his brothers came; and standing outside they sent to him and called him. And a crowd was sitting about him; and they said to him, "Your mother and your brothers are outside asking for you." And he replied, "Who are my mother and my brothers?" And looking around on those who sat about him, he said, "Here are my mother and my brothers! Whoever does the will of God is my brother, and sister, and mother."'

Here also Jesus assumes a kinship different from the physical; sonship and brotherhood are not understood in a natural, physical sense. This confirms the possibility that also in Mark 12.35 ff. Jesus can refute any Christological value of the Davidic sonship, without necessarily denying the fact itself. In this case, he would have demonstrated the same reserve toward the title 'Son of David' which we have seen he showed toward the title 'Messiah'. In both cases, however, he would not have categorically rejected the title as such.

This interpretation rules out also the psychological explanation of the self-consciousness of Jesus as derived from the presence of a family tradition of Davidic sonship.[2] If he attaches no significance to his physical

[1] R. Bultmann, *Geschichte der synoptischen Tradition*, pp. 145 f. See also his *Theology of the New Testament* I, p. 28.

[2] A. E. J. Rawlinson, *The New Testament Doctrine of the Christ*, p. 42 n. 3. B. F. Spitta had earlier defended this thesis.

descent, it can by no means have been decisive for the origin of his so-called messianic self-consciousness.

We conclude, then, that Jesus probably did not directly deny other people's application of the title Son of David to himself,[1] but that he did vigorously reject the idea of a political kingship connected with that title. With regard to this title, however, we must add a remark similar to that we made with regard to the title Messiah: in so far as Jesus was conscious of having to fulfil the task of the people of Israel, it does not contradict his conception of his vocation if he did accept also the concept of kingship in such a way that it had a new content for him—if he thought in terms of a 'kingdom not of this world', as the Gospel of John describes it.

3. *The Early Church and the Messiah*

We have already mentioned that the title Messiah was so successful that it superseded all other titles, or at least that they were subordinated to it. No other title we investigate in this book has received the honour of being permanently and intimately joined to the name of Jesus.

The original Palestinian Church was far from sharing Jesus' reserve toward the title Messiah. On the contrary, in the light of the Easter experience and in the expectation of the approaching end, it elevated the expression 'Jesus is the Messiah (Christ)' to a confession. The Gospel of Mark seldom refers to Jesus as Christ-Messiah, but Matthew and Luke and Acts use the term much oftener.[2] We must observe, however, that in these writings the expression has not yet become fixed as a proper name, that the original sense of the word Christ persists. This is true even of Acts, which is probably influenced by its older sources in this respect.

The fixing of 'Christ' as a proper name is a sign that the specific Jewish messianic ideas are again receding. This development may have taken place particularly in Hellenistic Churches where there was no messianic interest in the original sense of the term. It is paradoxical that precisely as a result of its becoming fixed as a proper

[1] It is true that Mark and Luke have only one reference which indicates this: Mark 10.47 (Luke 18.38). Matthew has five others: 9.27; 12.23; 15.22; 21.9; 21.15.

[2] See V. Taylor, *The Names of Jesus*, pp. 19 f.

name so that it was used more and more frequently, the title lost its national and political colouring and approximated to Jesus' own attitude toward it.

We can see at least the beginnings of this development in Paul's writings, although his occasional practice of putting 'Christ' before 'Jesus' shows that he was still clearly aware that the title is not a proper name.[1] The fixation progresses rapidly throughout the other New Testament writings.

But how can we explain the fact that contrary to Jesus' own attitude the original Palestinian Church deliberately preferred the designation Messiah? We must mention first the discussion between the first Christians and the Jews. The disciples were probably able to make their faith in Jesus understandable to the Jews of their time only by using this title.[2] But there were also theological reasons. Even though the memory was still alive that Jesus himself had emphatically substituted the designation Son of Man for the title Messiah—and the Synoptic Gospels prove that this memory remained alive for a long time—in the light of the events of the death and resurrection of Jesus, the early Church felt justified in proclaiming him as the Christ. The idea we have traced to Jesus himself, that he is the accomplisher of Israel's task, must have been seen in such a bright new light that the political Messiah expected by the Jews seemed pale in comparison to the figure of Jesus the Son of Man.

Since the early Church was conscious of living already in the time of fulfilment and of being itself the chosen 'people of God', the idea must have forcefully arisen that Jesus had also fulfilled the role of the Messiah in *Heilsgeschichte*. In order to emphasize the continuity between the Old and New Covenants, the Church then stressed also the Davidic sonship of Jesus,[3] to which he himself had attached so little importance. In the light of the fulfilment, the designation Son of David also attained such great significance that it was even included in confessional statements (Rom. 1.3; Ign. *Smyrn.* 1.1; *Trall.* 9.1). The deep meaning of the Davidic rule was fulfilled in the king-

[1] Therefore I cannot agree with Taylor, *ibid.*, p. 21 n. 1, that Rom. 9.5 (and that with a question mark) is the only passage in which Paul uses 'Christ' in the sense of 'Messiah'. A. Stuiber, *RAC* III, col. 25, also uses the criterion of the appearance of the title 'Christ' before 'Jesus' in order to find a continuation of the original meaning of this title in the ancient Church.

[2] Note the role which the concept Messiah plays for example in Justin's apologetic *Dialogue with Trypho*.

[3] See pp. 295 ff. below concerning the connection between the Davidic sonship and the virgin birth.

ship which Jesus exercised when he was exalted to the right hand of God. There he achieved the goal of the Israelite monarchy.

On the basis of its conviction of this fulfilment, the early Church could also take over some of the features of the political picture of the Messiah. Since the people of God was now no longer a political entity but the community of believers, these political features were of themselves purified. The kingship of the Son of David was now primarily a kingship over the Church.

The more intense the faith in Jesus' fulfilment became, the stronger became the hope of its completion, for like Jesus himself early Christianity was aware of the tension between 'already fulfilled' and 'not yet completed'.

The early Church never identified the kingship of Christ with the ecclesiastical institution. Eschatological expectation, the early Christian corrective for this tendency, was too strong to allow the removal of tension. That happened only later in the Catholic Church. The thesis advocated by J. L. Leuba in his *L'institution et l'évènement*, 1950, that the ideas of the 'institution' and of the prophetic 'event' are parallel in the New Testament, should probably be tested from the standpoint of the temporal tension between fulfilment and completion.

The early Church believed that the kingship of Jesus would become visible only in the future. The danger of a political interpretation of Jesus' messianic role can arise at this point, and perhaps the early Church did not always completely avoid this danger with regard to its conception of the second coming of Christ. The writings of Paul certainly show no traces of this misunderstanding. Paul does expect a final event in which Christ will visibly appear, but he never allows Christ's eschatological work to take a political form. But when the idea of Jesus' future kingship is concentrated in the so-called thousand-year reign as in Rev. 20.4, the conception of his earthly calling which Jesus himself rejected can emerge again, though of course in a form altered to fit the visible Church of the end time.[1]

We conclude that the early Church not only took over the terminology relative to the Messiah, but in the light of the 'fulfil-

[1] As opposed to A. Schweitzer, I agree with J. Héring, 'Saint Paul a-t-il enseigné deux résurrections?', *RHPR* 12, 1932, pp. 300 ff., that it is impossible to find in Paul's future hope the belief in a 'thousand-year reign'. Above all it seems to me that a 'second' resurrection to judgment is incompatible with Paul's doctrine of the resurrection in I Cor. 15.35 ff. Paul knows only *one* resurrection, that with the σῶμα πνευματικόν. The argument of H. Bietenhard, *Das tausendjährige Reich. Eine biblischtheologische Studie*, 1944, pp. 65 ff., is also not convincing at this point.

ment', and with a Christian transformation, also applied to Jesus certain specific ideas taken from the Jewish messianic expectation. It emphasized that Jesus appeared on earth as the Son of David, that he exercises kingship over his Church and that he will appear on earth as Messiah at the end. These ideas give way to other Christological views as soon as 'Christ' is used as a proper name. This is particularly true in the Hellenistic Church.

6

Jesus the Son of Man

(*Barnasha*, υἱὸς τοῦ ἀνθρώπου)

Along with the concept *ebed Yahweh*, the Son of Man is the most important concept we have to investigate. Its Christological use also goes back to Jesus himself. Surprisingly, systematic theologians have never dealt as exhaustively with its important Christological implications as it deserves. In official systematic theologies, particularly those involved in the Christological controversies of the fourth and fifth centuries, the Logos concept plays such an important role that all other titles are more or less suppressed. This is one reason why we possess no real Christology founded on the Son of Man. We have seen that the *ebed Yahweh* concept explains the Christological work of the incarnate Jesus in an exhaustive way. Above all it explains the central act of salvation, his death. We shall see that the idea of the Son of Man is even more comprehensive; it embraces the total work of Jesus as does almost no other idea.

The great significance of this designation is shown by the fact that according to the Gospels it is the only title Jesus applied to himself. We have seen that he never calls himself 'Messiah'; now we shall see that he openly and purposefully replaced that designation with 'Son of Man'. This is all the more important because the Gospel writers themselves do not use this title to express their own faith in Jesus. The messianic designation 'Christ' already prevailed by the time they wrote. The fact that they nevertheless use 'Son of Man' when they introduce Jesus as the speaker indicates that they are very probably handing down an already established tradition that Jesus called himself by that name.[1]

1. *The Son of Man in Judaism*

Our practice of beginning with the meaning of each title in Judaism is especially appropriate here, for when Jesus designates himself

[1] See p. 155 below.

the Son of Man, he establishes a direct contact with a particular view current in certain circles among his people. We must in fact even go beyond Judaism, because, as is the case with the Logos concept which we shall consider later, this concept also was widespread (in different forms of course) in other religions. This might seem to call for a special section devoted to the Son of Man in non-biblical religions. If we nevertheless deal with the question within the framework of our investigation of the Son of Man in Judaism, it is because the non-biblical idea of this figure did not *directly* influence Jesus and the early Church. The debate about the extra-Jewish figure of a 'heavenly man' took place within Judaism, so that the connection between Jesus the Son of Man and the non-biblical Son of Man passes through Judaism.

First we must ask, what is the purely *philological* meaning of the Greek expression υἱὸς τοῦ ἀνθρώπου in the New Testament? We must go back to the Aramaic expression בַּר נָשָׁא (*barnasha*), which corresponds to the Greek phrase. *Bar* is the well-known Aramaic equivalent of the Hebrew *ben*, son. We find it in certain proper names such as Barnabas, Barsabbas, Bartholomew, etc. *Nasha*, man, comes from the Semitic root which in its Hebrew form is *ish*, or *anashim* in the plural. *Bar-nasha* is thus the Aramaic expression behind the Greek υἱὸς τοῦ ἀνθρώπου.

The Aramaic *bar* is very often used in a figurative sense. For 'liar' the Aramaic idiom is 'son of the lie'; sinners are 'sons of sin'; a wealthy man is a 'son of wealth'. The genitive in the construct state following *bar* thus designates the classification to which one belongs. Accordingly, *barnasha* refers to one who belongs to the human classification; that is, it means simply 'man'—like the German *Menschenkind*.[1] Consequently the Greek translation υἱὸς τοῦ ἀνθρώπου is actually inexact because it is too literal. *Barnasha* should be translated simply ἄνθρωπος. This philological consideration does not solve the problem, however. We must still ask in what sense of contemporary Jewish usage Jesus could call himself 'man'.

In 1896 H. Lietzmann dedicated his first work to this question.[2] He thought that 'Son of Man' was not a messianic title in Judaism, and from philological considerations he thus came to a negative conclusion which is no longer generally held. From the correct observa-

[1] The same is true of the corresponding Hebrew *ben adam* (Ezek. 2.1; Pss. 8.4; 80.17).

[2] H. Lietzmann, *Der Menschensohn. Ein Beitrag zur neutestamentlichen Theologie*, 1896.

tion that *barnasha* means nothing more than 'man' he concluded that Judaism at the time of Jesus could not have called the Messiah by this name, that it would have made no sense for Jesus to give himself a designation which was meaningless because it was too general. Lietzmann believed that in Dan. 7.13, where the expression occurs for the first time, it had no messianic character; the term simply distinguished between a human being and the beasts which appeared in the vision. The early Church invented this self-designation of Jesus by giving 'man' a messianic significance and making it a title.

This thesis, which J. Wellhausen with critical reservations also accepted in his *Skizzen und Vorarbeiten*, VI, 1899, pp. 187 ff., has since been rightly rejected.[1] The refutation given by G. Dalman in his *The Words of Jesus* (pp. 234 ff.) is not satisfactory, however, because he tries to show that *barnasha* was not commonly used in the general sense of 'man' in Galilean Aramaic. P. Fiebig, *Der Menschensohn, Jesu Selbstbezeichnung mit besonderer Berücksichtigung des aramäischen Sprachgebrauchs für Mensch*, 1901, proved that Dalman's assertion is untenable: philologically *barnasha* really means only 'man'. But the conclusion which Lietzmann and Wellhausen drew from this, that therefore it was not a messianic title, is not correct.

We must investigate the literature of Judaism to find the answer to the question whether the general expression 'man' did not serve in Jesus' time to designate a particular eschatological redeemer. We discover here that this simple word 'man' is indeed the title of a mediator who is to appear at the end of time.[2]

In Dan. 7.13, where we first encounter the designation, one cannot be certain whether it originally concerned the figure of an *individual* redeemer. The Son of Man is contrasted with the four beasts, which according to the following explanation represent the four rulers of the four world empires. The passage reads:

I saw in the night visions, and behold, with the clouds of heaven there came one like a son of man, and he came to the Ancient of Days and was presented before him. And to him was given dominion and glory and

[1] Lietzmann himself later withdrew it.

[2] See W. Baldensperger, *Die messianisch-apokalyptischen Hoffnungen des Judentums*[3], 1903, pp. 91 ff.; A. v. Gall, βασιλεία τοῦ θεοῦ, 1926, pp. 409 ff.; W. Bousset, *Die Religion des Judentums im neutestamentlichen Zeitalter*[3], 1926; G. Dupont, *Le fils de l'homme*, 1927; C. H. Kraeling, *Anthropos and the Son of Man. A Study in the Religious Syncretism of the Hellenistic Orient*, 1927; H. Gressmann, *Der Messias*, 1929, pp. 343 ff.; R. Otto, *The Kingdom of God and the Son of Man*, ET 1938. An especially valuable newer work is E. Sjöberg, *Der Menschensohn im äthiopischen Henochbuch*, 1946, especially pp. 41 ff.

kingdom, that all peoples, nations, and languages should serve him; his dominion is an everlasting dominion, which shall not pass away, and his kingdom one that shall not be destroyed.

In vv. 15 ff. the apocalyptic writer identifies the Son of Man as the 'saints of the Most High'. We certainly should not lose sight of this identification. Nevertheless we must ask why it is as 'man' that the nation of the saints is contrasted with the four beasts. It has been rightly pointed out[1] that the explanation of the vision contains a certain inconsistency: the beasts are interpreted as kings, as *representatives*, of the world empires, but the 'man' is the nation of the saints itself. The incongruity suggests that the 'man' may also originally have been a representative of the nation of saints. Representation easily becomes identity in Judaism. According to the Jewish concept of representation, the representative can be identified with the group he represents. We have observed this Jewish phenomenon, which is very important for New Testament Christology, in the chapter on the Servant of God,[2] and we shall encounter it again. The Jews of a later period, in any case, thought of the Son of Man in Dan. 7.13 ff. as an individual figure.[3]

He appears as an individual also in other writings of the late Jewish apocalyptic movement. In the apocalypse known as IV Ezra the Son of Man appears as an apocalyptic redeemer rising out of the sea and riding upon the clouds.[4] Verse 26 says of him that the Most High has kept him back for a long time, waiting to deliver creation through him. This writing also speaks of him as the Messiah.

We find the figure of the 'man' in these senses especially in the parables of chs. 37–71 of the Ethiopic Enoch.[5] This late Jewish writing is very important in general for understanding the beginnings of Christianity. It plays a prominent part in R. Otto's last book, *The Kingdom of God and the Son of Man*. Although the figure appears also in other passages, the most important ones for the study of the Son of Man are Enoch 46, 48 f., 52, 62, 69, and 71. We may probably accept as a proven fact that we have to do here with a single personality, not the personification of the people of Israel as in

[1] H. Gressmann, *op. cit.*, pp. 345 ff.
[2] See pp. 54 f. above.
[3] Cf. Justin, *Dial.* 31 f.
[4] II (4) Esd. 13.
[5] See E. Sjöberg, *op. cit.*, pp. 44 ff., concerning the much discussed question whether as R. H. Charles suggests, *The Ethiopic Version of the Book of Enoch*, 1906, pp. 86 f., the demonstrative 'this' referring to the Son of Man in the Ethiopic translation is the pattern for the simple article in the Greek. Sjöberg concludes that 'Son of Man' is a messianic title.

Dan. 7.13. But we must by no means forget that the idea of the Son of Man at its ultimate source also includes the idea that the figure of *the* Man represents all men. The word itself points to this fact.

N. Messel, *Der Menschensohn in den Bilderreden des Henoch*, 1922 was unsuccessful in his attempt to prove a purely collective interpretation. He could carry through his thesis only by considering a number of important texts as Christian interpolations. In a different way also M.-J. Lagrange, *Le Judaisme avant Jésus-Christ*, 1931, pp. 242 ff., attempted to establish the presence of Christian interpolations in Enoch. But this hypothesis is by no means necessary. Scholars in general have appealed to it all too quickly, sometimes for apologetic reasons, in order to distinguish as radically as possible between Jewish writings and those of early Christianity. It is just the recognition of an actual inner relationship which should induce us to seek the newness of the Gospel where it really exists. This principle applies also in our contemporary situation to the comparison of the Qumran texts with the thought of the New Testament.

In the Ethiopic Enoch, the Son of Man is one whose name is named before the Ancient of Days at the beginning of creation; that is, he is created before all other creatures.[1] Just as everything concerning him and the end is a hidden teaching, so he himself is hidden until the end when he will come to judge and to rule over the world.[2] This book also occasionally calls him the Messiah.[3]

This expectation of the Son of Man, then, was apparently common in esoteric Jewish circles. If the falsely named Apocalypse of Lamech, one of the scrolls of the Qumran texts, had really been so closely related to the Book of Enoch as some originally conjectured, it would of course have been extraordinarily important for the question of the origin of the Son of Man idea. Unfortunately, however, this conjecture has not been confirmed. Nor is the Son of Man idea to be found in the published hymns. On the other hand, it is not impossible that the idea of the Second Adam appears in one passage of the Manual of Discipline. We shall see that this figure is a variant

[1] Enoch 48.2, 6.—As Sjöberg, *op. cit.*, p. 94, correctly remarks, the Son of Man in Enoch is thus not merely an angel as M. Werner, *Die Entstehung des christlichen Dogmas*[2], 1953, pp. 302 ff., believes. See also W. Michaelis, *Zur Engelchristologie im Urchristentum*, 1942.

[2] R. Otto, *op. cit.*, emphasizes especially this 'hiddenness', but one can probably not derive the 'messianic secret' from this, as also Sjöberg, *op. cit.*, p. 115, suggests. At most this may be considered a secondary explanation of the 'messianic secret'. For its primary meaning, see p. 124 above.

[3] Enoch 48.10; 52.4. See Sjöberg, *op. cit.*, pp. 140 ff.

of the Son of Man concept.[1] In any case, this expectation of the Son of Man confirms the fact that the religious life of Palestine was much richer and more varied than the usual schematism which differentiates only between the Pharisees and Sadducees leads us to believe. The Book of Enoch acquaints us with a group in which the messianic hope has an essentially different character from that of official Judaism. This group did not expect a political Messiah who would defeat the enemies of Israel in an earthly war and establish a political kingdom, but the supernatural, heavenly 'Son of Man'. He is a heavenly ruler, not an earthly king. We should not be misled by the fact that he is called 'man' and has a human form. His divine majesty cannot be emphasized strongly enough. He is the preexistent heavenly being who lives in heaven from the very beginning of time until he comes to earth at the end of time.

The question naturally arises why this heavenly mediator is called 'man'. A serious consideration of this question by no means represents a departure from the scope of a historical study. On the contrary, it would be intellectually irresponsible simply to be satisfied with stating the fact that there suddenly appeared in Judaism the figure of a redeemer called 'man' or 'Son of Man' which was connected with and yet displaced that of the Messiah. One would expect just such a mediator to have a name indicating his heavenly origin. But he is called simply 'man'. The Jewish texts provide no explanation of this curious fact. But their very silence gives us the strongest proof that there must be some connection here with non-Jewish conceptions of a 'man' who *as man* has a special divine dignity. And in point of fact, we do know of non-Jewish speculations about an 'Original Man', the divine prototype of man.

This is not to say that Judaism took over this concept as an idea completely foreign. There is also an idea in genuine Old Testament thought which points in the same direction and can give depth to the concept: the creation of man in the image of God. On the basis of this we can understand why precisely 'the Man', in so far as he represents the true image of God, is appointed to redeem fallen humanity. It is true that none of the Jewish texts draw these consequences from the fact that man is created in the image of God. We only point out that this Jewish doctrine offers a point of contact for the doctrine of the Original Man.

It is certain that this doctrine of a divine Original Man was wide-

[1] Cf. *Manual of Discipline* 4, 23. E. Dinkler, *Schweizerische Monatshefte* 36, 1956, p. 277, points out the problem of this passage.

spread in the oriental religions of the Jewish environment, and that it was a common feature of all these religions. But it is difficult to say what the developed form of the doctrine was. The representatives of the school of comparative religions may sometimes have gone too far in their constructions,[1] but it cannot be denied that traces of a divine Original Man, the ideal prototype of man, are present in the Iranian,[2] Chaldean, and Egyptian [3] religions; in the cult of Attis; [4] among the Mandaeans [5] and Manichaeans; [6] and in Gnosticism in general. This concept was apparently as universal as that of the Logos. It did not always take the same form, of course, and one need not even postulate as an integrating part of all these religions the idea characteristic of the broad stream of Gnosticism that the Original Man himself must be redeemed in order to redeem mankind.[7]

It would be interesting to assemble all the writings of comparative religion on the Original Man,[8] but we cannot pursue this problem in the present work. The identification of this ideal Heavenly Man with the *first* man, however, is especially important for New Testament Christology. In connection with the conception of the eschatological return of the golden age, this identification leads to the expectation that it is precisely the first man who will come at the end to redeem mankind.

The difficulty of tracing this idea in Judaism lies in the fact that the Jews did not make clear the connection between the idea of the first man on the one hand and that of the eschatological 'Man' or 'Son of

[1] We have the study of comparative religions to thank for pointing out these connections. See especially W. Bousset, *Hauptprobleme der Gnosis*, 1907, pp. 160 ff., 238 ff.; and *Kyrios Christos*[2], 1921; R. Reitzenstein, *Das iranische Erlösungsmysterium*, 1921; R. Reitzenstein and H. H. Schaeder, *Studien zum antiken Synkretismus aus Iran und Griechenland*, 1926; W. Manson, *Jesus the Messiah*, 1946, pp. 237 ff.

[2] See especially Reitzenstein and Schaeder, *op. cit.* In this context they refer particularly to *Gayomart*, the first man in the Iranian religion.

[3] Reitzenstein refers to the *Poimandres*. On this writing see E. Haenchen, 'Aufbau und Theologie des "*Poimandres*" ', *ZTK* 53, 1956, pp. 149 ff. See also C. H. Dodd, *The Bible and the Greeks*[2], 1954, who thoroughly investigates the 'Original Man' of the *Poimandres*.

[4] H. Hepding, *Attis, seine Mythen und sein Kult*, 1903, especially pp. 50 ff.

[5] In addition to the literature cited above see R. Reitzenstein, *Das mandäische Buch des Herrn der Grösse und die Evangelienüberlieferung*, 1919.

[6] W. Henning, *Geburt und Entsendung des manichäischen Urmenschen*, 1933. See also H. Puech, *Le Manichéisme*, 1949, pp. 76 ff.

[7] It is also wrong in the present discussion of the Gnosticism of the Qumran sect to consider the presence or absence of this myth as the criterion of Gnostic character or lack of it.

[8] C. G. Jung has recently applied his theory of 'archetypes' to the concept of the Son of Man.

Man' on the other. It is in fact highly questionable whether they could make the connection clear, since the first man is the source of sin. We shall see how a solution to this difficulty was first reached in Paulinism. But first we must explain why in Judaism the concepts of the Original Man and that of the coming Son of Man developed along two separate lines, so that their original solidarity is no longer apparent. The otherwise completely inexplicable fact that the eschatological redeemer is called 'man' shows that the two concepts really do belong together.

In what follows I shall emphasize the inner necessity for this *separate* development. Otherwise the identification of 'Son of Man' with 'Second Adam' which I wish to show could appear arbitrary. These two concepts are usually not identified on the ground that no Jewish or early Christian text indicates their connection.

The vision of Dan. 7, and especially the Son of Man speculations of IV Ezra and the Book of Enoch, develop only the eschatological aspect, and only here and there take up isolated features of the other conceptions of the Original Man. They also say nothing of the real incarnation; the Son of Man who rises out of the sea and comes on the clouds does not become incarnate in sinful humanity.[1] He does occasionally exhibit attributes of the *ebed Yahweh*, as when he is designated 'Servant' in II (4) Esd. 7.28 and 13.32; 'the Righteous One', or 'the Elect' or 'Light of the People' in many passages of Enoch. But he never assumes the form of the Servant.[2]

But besides the eschatological use of the Original Man concept, Judaism felt it necessary to deal also with the idea stemming from the same root of a perfect *first* man—especially since the biblical statements about the image of God in man come very close to this idea. Thus there arose a special Adam literature in apocryphal and rabbinical-mystical writings.[3] But also in the broad stream of Jewish literature we find traces of the *Adam problem*. The Jews were faced

[1] E. Sjöberg, *op. cit.*, pp. 147 ff., attempts to show that also the identification of the Son of Man with Enoch cannot be considered here, since Enoch originally becomes the Son of Man only after his exaltation.—The question of an incarnation arises at most in the case of the problematic figure 'Metatron'. See H. Odeberg, *Third Enoch or the Hebrew Book of Enoch*, 1928.

[2] J. Jeremias, 'Erlöser und Erlösung im Spätjudentum', *DT* 2, 1929, pp. 106 ff., assumes the suffering of the Son of Man, but this remains questionable. See Sjöberg, *op. cit.*, pp. 116 ff.

[3] See especially *Vita Adae* 12 ff.; Slavic Enoch 30. Rabbinical texts should also be considered. See B. Murmelstein, 'Adam. Ein Beitrag zur Messiaslehre', *Wiener Zeitschrift für die Kunde des Morgenlandes*, 1928, pp. 242 ff.; 1929, pp. 51 ff.

with a dilemma: since the original speculations had done so, they felt the need to identify the Heavenly Man and the first man; but since according to the Old Testament Adam sinned, such an identification seemed impossible. The biblical account reports that the first man is the one who robbed man of his divine character, and that just because of him it became necessary for the Heavenly Man to restore men to the destiny for which God had created them. At this point the extra-Jewish idea of the Original Man was bound to undergo a radical alteration as soon as it came into contact with Judaism. This is the reason why even into the time of early Christianity 'Son of Man' and 'Second Adam' seem to be two different concepts, whereas actually they are internally united and always belong essentially together.

Since 'Son of Man' and 'Second Adam' are two different developments of the same Christological idea, we shall not devote a special chapter to the latter.

The fact that Jesus must be called the second Adam rather than simply Adam shows why a distinction between the two concepts was nevertheless necessary. It also indicates the point at which even Judaism had difficulty in taking over the theologically fruitful idea of the Son of Man. On the one hand, it had to connect the idea of the divine Man, the *barnasha*, with the time of creation; the Heavenly Man is man as God willed him to be when he created man in his own image. But on the other hand, since the biblical creation account is connected with the fall of the first man, it was impossible for Judaism without complications to introduce the divine Man who is identified with the first man into its theology. Is this also the reason for the fact that speculations about the *barnasha* do not occur in official Judaism, but only in esoteric Jewish circles such as we come to know in IV Ezra and Enoch? We can only ask the question. This might also be a reason (besides the hiddenness we have mentioned) why these apocalyptic writers surround these ideas with an air of mystery, and speak of it in veiled, indirect terms.

There were two quite different possibilities of overcoming the difficulty, and both were undertaken simultaneously. One possibility was to place no special emphasis on the identification of the divine Man with the first man; the other was to place no emphasis on the fall of Adam. We have seen that the Son of Man plays a very important role in the Book of Enoch. It is characteristic of this book that it simply ignores the fall of Adam. This might be a coincidence and have no particular significance, were it not true that this very book takes great care to explain the origin of sin. It does so conspicuously without mentioning Adam's fall. Chapters 83–90 give a summary of the world's history from creation to the establishment of the messianic kingdom, but amazingly do not say a single word about the sin of Adam. The Slavic Enoch even emphasizes that Satan tempted only Eve and not Adam. This is certainly not accidental. There is a clear tendency to exempt Adam from the first sin. Enoch uses a different Genesis story, that of the fall of the angels in Gen. 6, to explain the origin of evil. Various passages develop in detail the doctrine of sin based on this source. They describe the consequences of the sinful affairs of the angels: all evil, all violence, all sin and especially all idolatry come from here. It is surely no unjustified argument from silence to make conjectures about Enoch's conspicuous failure to mention Adam's sin. Of all the Jewish writings, this book makes the greatest use of the Son of Man concept, which, as we have discovered, goes back to the universal idea of the Original Man. Has not the author at least unconsciously still remembered that, according to the original conception of the Son of Man taken over from other religions, the *barnasha* who returns at the end is identical with the first man? He probably did know this, but he does not venture to take the decisive step of identifying the Son of Man openly with Adam. He is just as reluctant expressly to deny Adam's fall. He simply remains silent.

The Gnostic Jewish Christians, whose speculations are contained in the Pseudo-Clementine writings, did take this further step.[1] We

[1] In opposition to W. Bousset and to my own thesis, *Le problème littéraire et historique du roman pseudoclémentin*, 1930, H. J. Schoeps, *Theologie und Geschichte des Judenchristentums*, 1949, pp. 305 ff., attempts to dispute the *Gnostic* character of these writings. But his attempt is not successful, for his strong emphasis on the rabbinical source of the Pseudo-Clementine thought forms proves nothing against its Gnostic character. R. Bultmann, *Gnomon*, 1954, pp. 177 ff., correctly replies that Gnosticism penetrated also into rabbinical circles. G. Bornkamm, *ZKG* 64, 1952/53, pp. 196 ff., also rejects Schoeps' argument. See also my essay, 'Die neuentdeckten Qumrantexte und das Judenchristentum der Pseudoklementinen', *Theol. Stud. f. R. Bultmann*, 1954, pp. 35 ff.—Recently Schoeps, 'Das gnostische Judentum in den Dead Sea Scrolls', *Ztschr. f. Religions- u. Geistesgeschichte*, 1954, p. 277, himself admits: 'To me the most important conclusion to date is that "Gnostic Judaism in the pre-Christian period", which in both my books . . . I declared problematic and improbable, really existed.' In view of this, it is strange that in his most recent work, *Urkirche, Judenchristentum und Gnosis*, 1956, he returns to his old position, which is characterized by a greatly narrowed concept of Gnosis, and explains all Gnostic features in Judaism as 'pseudo-Gnostic'.

may speak of this group in our section on the Son of Man in Judaism, because although they acknowledged Jesus as the Christ, in general they were nevertheless more Jewish than Christian. We can understand them almost as a Jewish sect, and their theology without doubt belongs within Judaism.[1] So far as the development of the idea of the Son of Man is concerned in any case, they represent only an internal Jewish development. The way in which they solved the problem of the identity between the divine Original Man and the first man follows directly from the attitude we have just observed in the Book of Enoch.

We have seen that the Pseudo-Clementine *Preaching of Peter* considers Jesus as the True Prophet.[2] But at the same time it identifies this True Prophet Jesus with Adam. The decisive step has been taken; the Son of Man and Adam are one. We remember that for these Jewish Christians the True Prophet has been reincarnated at different times. The first incarnation was in Adam.

But how could they make this identification? How could they accept Adam, whom the Bible reports to have been the first sinner, as the first incarnation of the True Prophet? These Gnostic Jewish Christians dare to go further at this point than the author of the Book of Enoch, to give a much more radical solution than his. Instead of remaining silent about the fall of Adam, they actually declare that this account is a lie! According to their syzygial theory[3] Adam represents the principle of good, Eve the principle of evil. Therefore Adam did not sin at all. The Pseudo-Clementine source bases this bold assertion on its peculiar doctrine of the so-called false sections of the Pentateuch. Lies are said to have crept into the Scriptures through the work of the devil. On the basis of a secret teaching these sections must be extracted from the Scriptures. One of the principal lies is the report of the transgression of the first man Adam. In this way Adam may be identified with the True Prophet Jesus without complication.

These Jewish Christians therefore pay the highest respect to Adam. They glorify him as the devil's opponent. We find a similar glorification of Adam and the same opposition of Adam and the devil in the previously mentioned Jewish Adam-speculations, above all in the *Life of Adam*.[4] But the Jewish Christians developed this whole theory

[1] The connection between the Jewish Christians and the Qumran sect indicated in my essay mentioned above also shows this.

[2] See pp. 38 ff. above.

[3] See p. 41 above.

[4] *Vita Adae* 12 ff., 39; Slavic Enoch 30.11 ff. See also B. Murmelstein, *op. cit.* on p. 144 n. 3 above.

much further; every limitation collapses with the unqualified rejection of the story of Adam's fall.

They teach that Adam was anointed with oil from the tree of life. He is the eternal priest who is reincarnate in Jesus, the perfect man, the prototype of humanity. At the creation of the world God appointed a prototype for each of his creatures: an angel for the angels, a spirit for the spirits, a star for the stars, a demon for the demons, an animal for the animals—and for man he appointed *the* Man who appeared in Adam. This idea actually does lead us to the common root of 'Son of Man' and 'Second Adam'. The Jewish Christians, of course, are not interested in a second Adam, but simply in Adam. Since they deny the fall, they need no second Adam. They say that the first man really fulfilled the role intended for him.

According to this theory salvation consists simply in a complete return of the primeval age. It abandons the biblical linear conception of time for the cyclical Greek scheme, according to which all things recur and there is no real temporal progression. We have already emphasized that the *Preaching of Peter* exhibits Gnostic influence.[1] The Gnostic concept of time is not Jewish but Hellenistic. Like the Son of Man in the eschatology of the Book of Enoch, the Messiah of official Judaism does not limit himself simply to a repetition of the created state, but brings something new. Also from this point of view we see that the Son of Man cannot simply be equated with the first man in Christian thought. According to the Bible, Adam revolted against the destiny God appointed for him, and the golden age so far as man is concerned existed at the beginning only in the intention of God, but not in its realization.

Next we must consider how Philo, the great Jewish philosopher of Alexandria, solved the problem resulting from the introduction of the idea of the Son of Man into Judaism. This concept plays an important part in his thoughts also. We have said that the identification of the Heavenly Man and Adam within Judaism was made possible only by the rejection of the fall of Adam. Philo reaches a less logical and less radical solution to this problem. He too assumes the identification of the Heavenly Man with the first man, but he seeks a solution which will allow him to assert this identity and still retain the biblical account of the fall. Radical solutions such as that of the Pseudo-Clementine writings did not suit his taste. He devoted his entire life's work to harmonizing his philosophy, which was inspired exclusively by Greek thought, with the Old Testament. He never

[1] See p. 146 n. 1 above; also pp. 38 f.

resorts to the desperate solution of eliminating certain inconvenient parts of the Old Testament. When biblical passages trouble him, he uses an allegorical exposition to give them a meaning which agrees with his philosophical convictions. Thus he is able to retain Old Testament accounts and to render them harmless by a kind of 'demythologizing'.

It is with this exegetical method that Philo is able to assert identity between the Heavenly Man and the first man, and at the same time retain the account of Adam's fall. In this case he takes refuge not only in allegory but also in the specifically rabbinical method of contrasting two passages. He distinguishes between two Adams in the biblical account; Genesis thus speaks of two 'first men'. He supports this assertion by a rather arbitrary interpretation of Gen. 1.27 and 2.7. The first passage reads: 'God created man in his own image, in the image of God he created him.' The second reads: 'Then the Lord God formed man of the dust from the ground, and breathed into his nostrils the breath of life: and man became a living being.'

We find speculations about these texts twice in the writings of Philo: in the *Allegory of the Holy Laws* (*Legum allegoria* I, 31 f.) and in the treatise *On the Creation of the World* (*De mundi opificio* 134 ff.). In these works Philo sets the two verses from Genesis in opposition, maintaining that they have to do with different Adams. The Adam in Gen. 1.27 is the Heavenly Man. He is made in the image of God, comes from heaven and possesses the fullness of the Holy Spirit. In him is nothing transitory. He is man as God wills him, man created in God's own image. He is free from sexual desire, beyond the distinction between man and woman. He is simply *the* man, the Heavenly Man. Everything the oriental religions teach about the first man, the perfect being, the divine prototype of man—all that refers to the Adam in Gen. 1.27.

But Gen. 2.7 deals with the creation of another Adam. Everything the Book of Genesis relates about Adam's sin and punishment refers to this Adam, not to the one in Gen. 1.27. The Adam in Gen. 2.7 is really the sinful man, the source of sin. He is not made in the image of God; he does not come from heaven but from earth. God formed him 'of the dust from the ground'. God had to breathe 'into his nostrils the breath of life', for only in this way could the Adam taken out of the earth become a living soul.

Thus, from the fact that Genesis twice reports the creation of man (a fact which modern Old Testament scholarship explains by the existence of two different sources) Philo concludes that God called two Adams to life at the creation. The first, the ideal Heavenly Man, disappears from the story after Gen. 1.27; the second is the transgressor of God's command, the Adam of Gen. 2 and 3.

That Philo developed this theory in two different places indicates that he attributed a special significance to it. We find the theory later also in rabbinical writings, but in a relatively late stratum of this literature. For this reason it is not possible to assert (as the genuinely rabbinical character of his method of proof might suggest) that Philo took it from the Jewish rabbis.[1] However that may be, the theory helps us to understand the development of the concepts 'Son of Man' and 'Second Adam' in the New Testament, for we shall see that the Apostle Paul very probably was acquainted with it.

The advantage of Philo's explanation over the other Jewish conceptions of the relation between the Heavenly Man and the first man lies in the fact that it retains the account of Adam's fall. Nevertheless, even apart from its arbitrary exegetical foundation, it is guilty of the same error which characterizes the Jewish Christian Gnostic theory. It betrays a basically Greek character, and leaves no more room than the Jewish Christian theory for a new action by the Heavenly Man after creation, since he is already there as an ideal figure from the beginning. In fact, there can be no new divine action through this mediator in time at all, because as the Spiritual Man he has already realized the Absolute at the beginning.

Philo knows neither an incarnation nor an eschatological return of the Spiritual Man; for him there can actually be no new divine revelation in time. He cannot conceive of the idea that the Heavenly Man must by his very nature, so to speak, become an incarnate man in history. Thus he cannot conceive of a development, a *history* of salvation.

We come to the following conclusions concerning the Jewish concept of the Son of Man. The Heavenly Man who is also known in extra-biblical religions appears in Judaism in two different forms.

(1) He is a heavenly being, now hidden, who will appear only *at the end of time* on the clouds of heaven to judge and to establish the 'nation of the saints'. We find this exclusively eschatological figure in Daniel, the Book of Enoch, and IV Ezra.

(2) He is the ideal Heavenly Man who is identified with the first man *at the beginning of time*. Philo of Alexandria develops this in-

[1] The utilization of older tradition is not entirely excluded at least for *Leg. Alleg.* I, 31. Cf. H. Lietzmann, *An die Korinther* I/II (HNT)[4], 1949, p. 85.

terpretation, and it also appears in the Pseudo-Clementine *Preaching of Peter* as well as in the rabbinical Adam speculations.

The first form corresponds to specifically Jewish thought, to the Jewish concept of time. The Jewish texts which mention the *future* Heavenly Man do not reflect upon his origin, but they do assume that he exists in heaven and at the end descends from heaven—or rises out of the sea. In any case he is clearly considered as pre-existent. The Book of Enoch says that he was chosen by God and hidden before the creation of the world (Enoch 48.3–6; 62.7; 70.1).

On the other hand, we find the second form primarily in texts of a Hellenistic character. These writings, in accordance with the tendency of philosophy and Gnosticism, are not interested primarily in eschatology, but in the beginning. For this reason they emphasize the identity of the Son of Man and the first man.

In spite of the difference between the two forms, they concern basically the same concept—the 'Man', the Heavenly Man. We encounter the *barnasha* in both categories of texts. Both forms deal with the man who remains faithful to his divine destiny to be the image of God. This is the common root of the two forms. The link between them is revealed by the fact that pre-existence in heaven is presupposed also for the eschatological Son of Man (Daniel, Enoch, IV Ezra). When one thinks of him as existing before the end time, the question of his origin is implicitly raised. But in both cases the idea of an incarnation of the Heavenly Man is foreign to Judaism. Neither for the eschatological texts nor for the Hellenistic and Philonic texts is it necessary that the Heavenly Man himself become a man among men. Even the Son of Man returning on the clouds of heaven does not fully enter into humanity. In the Pseudo-Clementine writings the True Prophet who was first on earth in Adam does appear in several figures of biblical and Jewish history, but as we have seen, this involves the repeated return of the Prophet rather than the incarnation of the Heavenly Man.[1] The concept of the Son of Man is here united with a concept which comes from a completely different conceptual framework.

The oriental syncretism we encounter in extra-Jewish Gnosticism knows still less of a genuine incarnation. True, it does speak of a descent of the Heavenly Man. According to the familiar redeemer myth, expressed for example in classic form in the Naassene hymn (Hippolytus, *Refut.* V, 6-11), the redeemer himself must be redeemed. But it is not his incarnation which is the basis of redemption. He does not leave the mythological sphere to

[1] See p. 40 above.

enter the historical. As R. Bultmann correctly observes in his *Theology of the New Testament* I, pp. 167 f., the mythological Heavenly Man is only 'disguised' as man. For this reason all Gnostics are Docetics.

2. *Jesus and the Son of Man*

The question whether and in what sense Jesus designated himself the Son of Man is one of the most discussed and contested problems of the New Testament scholarship. I have already mentioned the work of Lietzmann, who asserts that Jesus did *not* consider himself the Son of Man.[1] He supports his thesis with the unquestionable philological fact that υἱὸς τοῦ ἀνθρώπου simply means 'man'. But we now know that this by no means excludes the possibility that with this title Jesus could ascribe a special redeeming role to himself, since in Judaism the designation 'the Man' is a title of exaltation and presupposes the quite precise conception of a heavenly being.

Only in one respect can one make a concession to Lietzmann's thesis. There are perhaps one or two sayings of Jesus in which υἱὸς τοῦ ἀνθρώπου does not refer—primarily at least—to himself, but simply designates 'men' in a quite general way. This could be the case in the familiar saying about the sabbath in Mark 2.27. When the Pharisees question whether it is lawful to work on the sabbath, Jesus answers: 'The sabbath was made for man, not man for the sabbath.' The Greek text correctly reproduces the Aramaic root *barnasha* simply with ἄνθρωπος. Jesus' answer obviously refers to men in general, not to the divine Man, the 'Son of Man'. In the following verse we read: 'So the Son of Man (υἱὸς τοῦ ἀνθρώπου) is lord even of the sabbath.' If we had to draw for ourselves an unprejudiced inference from v. 27, we would expect v. 28 also to say that man in general, every man, is lord of the sabbath, since the sabbath was made for his sake. But instead of the simple ἄνθρωπος, man, of the preceding verse, v. 28 has υἱὸς τοῦ ἀνθρώπου, Son of Man. Mark at least understood this verse to mean that Jesus used 'Son of Man' to designate himself lord of the sabbath. Otherwise he would have used the same simple expression also in the second verse. He therefore interpreted this saying in the same sense as John 5.17, in which Jesus does give a Christological foundation for non-observance of the sabbath. But in this case, the logical connection between vv. 27 and 28 of Mark 2 is not perfectly clear. We must therefore at least consider the possibility that, despite the evangelist's interpretation, Jesus

[1] See p. 138 n. 2 above.

himself did not refer to himself in the second sentence. He spoke Aramaic and used the same Aramaic expression *barnasha* in both verses. This suggests that he referred to man in general both times.

I do not say that the interpretation of the evangelist (that Jesus referred to himself in v. 28) is necessarily to be excluded. T. W. Manson, who earlier shared the view that the υἱὸς τοῦ ἀνθρώπου in this verse was the result of a misunderstanding of *barnasha* intended in the general sense, has recently suggested a quite different solution.[1] He postulates that *both* verses have to do with the Son of Man, so that v. 27 too does not speak of man in general but should read, 'The sabbath was made for the Son of Man, not the Son of Man for the sabbath.' But Manson is able to defend this thesis only by giving 'Son of Man' an emphatically collective sense: the 'Son of Man' for whom the sabbath is created and who is lord of the sabbath is Jesus together with his disciples, the 'people of the saints of the Most High'. Although this interesting interpretation can hardly be maintained in such an exaggerated form, there is without doubt a true thought behind it.[2] T. Preiss points in the same direction in his *Le Fils de l'Homme*, 1951, pp. 28 f. He suggests that Jesus intended a double interpretation of the saying, since *barnasha* itself has a double meaning, indicating both every man and the man who represents and stands for the many: 'If man in general is the one for whom the sabbath exists, how much more reason will there be for the Man who came to save men to be Lord of the sabbath.'

The other passage which could perhaps be interpreted in the same way is Matt. 12.31 f. (Luke 12.10), although in this case it is less probable that the evangelist misunderstood the Aramaic word. 'Therefore I tell you, every sin and blasphemy will be forgiven men, but the blasphemy against the Spirit will not be forgiven. And whoever says a word against the Son of man will be forgiven; but whoever speaks against the Holy Spirit will not be forgiven, either in this age or in the age to come.' The question arises in v. 32 concerning the words κατὰ τοῦ υἱοῦ τοῦ ἀνθρώπου. According to the Greek text and the opinion of the evangelist, these words must refer to a sin against Jesus. One concludes that sin against Jesus will be forgiven, but sin against the Holy Spirit will not be forgiven.[3] But

[1] T. W. Manson, 'Mark 2.27 f.', *Coniectanea Neotestamentica* 11, 1947 (in honorem A. Fridrichsen), pp. 138 ff. [2] See p. 154 n. 3 below.

[3] A. Fridrichsen, 'Le péché contre le Saint-Esprit', *RHPR* 3, 1923, pp. 367 ff., considers the saying an invention of the Church and ascribes its origin to the early Church's missionary interest; those who rejected Jesus during his lifetime (i.e., the Jews whose conversion is sought) will be forgiven; those who reject him after his resurrection will not be forgiven.

it is possible that here also Jesus originally meant men in general: if anyone speaks against men he will be forgiven, but if anyone speaks against the Holy Spirit, he will not be forgiven. The Marcan parallel (3.28) speaks in favour of this possibility. In the first sentence we read: '. . . all sins will be forgiven the sons of men, and whatever blasphemies they utter . . .' The Greek text reads υἱοὶ τῶν ἀνθρώπων, sons of men, by which it quite obviously means men in general.[1]

Thus there are two sayings of Jesus in which it is possible that the expression 'Son of Man' does not refer to Jesus but to men in general.[2] This interpretation is excluded, however, as a possible meaning of his other sayings. The evangelists generally made a clear distinction in Greek between Jesus the 'Son of Man' and 'men' in general. They translated the same Aramaic word *barnasha* as ἄνθρωπος when it referred to men; as υἱὸς τοῦ ἀνθρώπου when it referred to Jesus. But since no distinction exists in Aramaic, they may have made a mistake in translating the ambiguous word *barnasha* in the two passages mentioned.

But we must reckon with the possibility that Jesus always used 'Son of Man' in a deliberately ambiguous sense. We recall that in Daniel it has also a collective meaning,[3] and that by virtue of its

[1] Among others J. Wellhausen, *Das Evangelium Matthaei*, 1914, pp. 60 f., and R. Bultmann, *Geschichte der synoptischen Tradition*, p. 138, consider the Marcan version to be the original one, and think that the version in Matthew and Luke which speaks of 'blasphemy against the Son of man' arose out of a misunderstanding of υἱοὶ τῶν ἀνθρώπων in Mark 3.28. Preiss, *Le Fils de l'Homme*, 1951, p. 31, attempts here as in the saying about the sabbath to explain both possibilities as corresponding to the intention of Jesus, who, Preiss believes, always thought at the same time of *all* men and of himself as the representative of humanity.

[2] Matt. 8.20 ('. . . the Son of man has no place to lay his head') has also been explained in this way. R. Bultmann, *Geschichte der synoptischen Tradition*, p. 27, postulates an ancient proverb which speaks of the homelessness of men in general. For my interpretation of this text see p. 162 below.

[3] T. W. Manson especially has repeatedly called attention to and rightly emphasized in many sayings of Jesus the *collective* sense of the Son of Man concept derived from the Daniel passage: *The Teaching of Jesus*[2], 1935, pp. 231 ff.; *The Sayings of Jesus*, 1949, p. 109; the essay mentioned on p. 153 n. 1 above. According to Manson, by this expression Jesus designated himself with his followers as the 'people of the saints of the Most High'. Although this emphasis is legitimate in itself, Manson may go a little too far when in his essay, 'Realized Eschatology and the Messianic Secret', *Studies in the Gospels, Essays in memory of R. H. Lightfoot*, ed. D. E. Nineham, 1955, pp. 209 ff., he explains the messianic secret on the basis of the idea of this 'collective' Son of Man.—In connection with Manson's emphasis see A. E. J. Rawlinson, *The New Testament Doctrine of the Christ*, pp. 247 ff. See also the literature cited on p. 156 n. 1 below.

origin, it includes the idea that perfect humanity is personified in the Original Man.[1] We shall return to this idea, but we mention it now because if this double interpretation is valid, then there is no radical alternative even for the two passages we have just considered.

There are so many passages in the Synoptic Gospels in which Jesus definitely refers to himself as the 'Son of Man' that we need not enumerate them all. Some scholars have asserted that this title as a self-designation by him was an invention of the evangelists based on the theology of the early Church, but this all too simple thesis is disproved by the fact that 'Son of Man' was not at all a common title for Jesus in the early Church. This argument is also relevant to the *ebed Yahweh* title,[2] but it is much more important in the present case. The decisive question is: If the evangelists were really the first to introduce the title, why do they use it only when they represent Jesus himself as speaking?[3] They themselves never call him by this name and they never report another's doing so in conversation with Jesus. This would be completely inexplicable if they were really the first to attribute the title to Jesus as a self-designation. Actually, they have preserved the memory that only Jesus himself used it in this way.

W. Manson in *Jesus the Messiah*, 1946, p. 160, and G. Kittel, 'Menschensohn', *RGG*², III, col. 2119, and others have emphasized this fact. If the evangelists were responsible for the use of the title, Kittel justifiably asks, why did they not, for example, have Peter confess at Caesarea Philippi, 'You are the Christ, the Son of Man'?

At this point we must differentiate between two categories of Jesus' sayings about the Son of Man: first, those in which he uses the title with reference to the *eschatological* work he must fulfil in the future; second, those in which he applies it to his *earthly* task.

The eschatological application represents a pronounced statement of majesty which corresponds to the Jewish view we have found in

[1] Preiss, *op. cit.*, has attempted to follow this idea through to its final consequences.

[2] See pp. 60 f. above.

[3] The fact that in isolated passages (certainly in Matt. 16.13) they do so wrongly does not lessen the force of this argument.—The title Son of Man is applied to Jesus by another only once: in Acts 7.56 by Stephen. The very fact that it is a *Hellenist* who uses this expression seems to me to go back to a correct memory of the author. We greatly underestimate the role of these Hellenists. They seem to me at this point as in other respects to belong to the Jewish circle whose views Jesus himself shared. See p. 184 below.

Daniel, Enoch, and IV Ezra. We have seen that even in these Jewish writings 'Son of Man' indicates the most exalted eschatological function. By means of this title Jesus thus ascribes to himself the highest imaginable role in the eschatological drama. In the light of the collective use of the title in Dan. 7.13 f., it is almost certain that the idea is not completely foreign to Jesus that as the 'Son of Man' he represents the 'remnant of Israel' and through it all mankind.[1] This passage, to which Jesus expressly refers before the high priest, certainly gives this significance to the Son of Man for the nation of saints.[2] Of course Jesus thinks primarily of an individual redeeming figure as do IV Ezra and Enoch,[3] but we must not forget that for Jewish thought the individual interpretation does not *exclude* the collective one.

The eschatological role of the Son of Man is attested by sayings such as those about the 'day of the Son of Man' (Luke 17.22 ff.), 'the coming of the Son of Man' (Matt. 24.27 and 37 ff.), and about his 'coming in the glory of his Father with the holy angels' (Mark 8.38). Anyone who accepts these sayings as genuine but tries to explain them by the theory that Jesus designates someone other than himself as the coming Son of Man, raises more problems than he solves.[4]

Especially important in our present context is Jesus' statement before the high priest in Mark 14.62 and parallels, which we have

[1] T. W. Manson, *The Teaching of Jesus*, pp. 227 ff., emphasizes this aspect very strongly. E. Percy, *Die Botschaft Jesu*, 1953, p. 239 n. 1, disposes of it all too quickly. Others who agree with Manson are V. Taylor, *Jesus and his Sacrifice*, 1948, pp. 24 ff.; M. Black, *ExpT* 60, 1949, pp. 33 f. F. Kattenbusch, 'Der Quellort der Kirchenidee', *Festgabe f. A. Harnack*, 1921, pp. 143 ff., has drawn important implications for Jesus' concept of the Church from this idea.

[2] See pp. 139 f. above.

[3] On the untenable thesis of Messel that the Son of Man is a collective concept in the Ethiopic Enoch, see p. 141 above.

[4] Thus R. Bultmann, *Theology of the New Testament* I, pp. 26 ff., is willing to accept these words as genuine, but he denies that Jesus identified himself with the proclaimed Son of Man. The decisive argument for him is the following: The prophecies of suffering say nothing about the future, and the prophecies about the future say nothing about death. The previous suffering of death, therefore, is incompatible with the expectation of the Son of Man. The eschatological Son of Man expected by Jesus cannot be identical with a man who has already appeared on earth. Only the Church, for which the death of Christ was self-evident, could connect the two kinds of statements and identify the expected Son of Man with the suffering Jesus. But the foundation of this judgment is Bultmann's unproved and simply asserted thesis that all prophecies of Jesus' suffering are *vaticinia ex eventu*. See pp. 60 f. above.

already considered in connection with the Messiah concept.[1] We recall that in this scene Jesus does not accept the title Messiah without qualification, and may even reject it if the Aramaic words 'You have said so' really mean 'No'. We have emphasized the fact that in any case Jesus adds a statement about the Son of Man rather than about the Messiah. In Matthew he even introduces the statement with the strongly adversative πλήν. Jesus quotes the words of Daniel about the Son of Man who will come on the clouds of heaven, and connects them with the saying from Ps. 110 about the 'Lord' who sits at the right hand of God.[2]

In the New Testament as well as in the late Jewish texts (especially in the Ethiopic Enoch) the primary eschatological function of the coming Son of Man is that of *judgment*. This is clearly the Son of Man's function in the important section about the last judgment of the 'sheep and goats' in Matt. 25.31–46. In Mark 8.38 and parallels he is both judge and at the same time, like the angels in the writings of late Judaism, witness against those who have been ashamed of him.[3] The transference to Jesus of judgment, which the New Testament also often ascribes to God himself, is directly connected with the Son of Man concept. Since the designation of Jesus as 'Judge' represents one aspect of the Son of Man idea, we need not devote a separate chapter to it.

In agreement with other New Testament writings, Paul represents God himself also as Judge (I Thess. 3.13; Rom. 3.5; 14.10). But he is nevertheless convinced that we must all appear 'before the judgment seat of *Christ*' (II Cor. 5.10; I Cor. 4.5). Jesus also appears as Judge in the parables of Matt. 25.1–13 and 14–30. In Acts 10.42 he bears the title 'Judge of the living and the dead'. II Tim. 4.8 calls him the 'Righteous Judge'. Acts 17.31 indicates the connection between the old view that God himself exercises judgment, and the view that as Son of Man Christ is the Judge of the world: God appoints Jesus to the judicial office, and he judges in the name of God. The fact that Jesus the Son of Man sometimes appears also as a witness at the

[1] See pp. 117 ff. above.

[2] E. Percy, *Die Botschaft Jesu*, p. 226, very quickly eliminates this saying as not genuine, primarily because it seems to him impossible satisfactorily to explain how the members of the Sanhedrin could have considered it blasphemous. This question is connected with the whole problem of the legal aspect of Jesus' trial. It seems certain to me that the Synoptics (in contrast to the fourth evangelist) have pushed aside the whole legal situation, but this does not affect the genuineness of Jesus' saying. See also O. Cullmann, *The State in the New Testament*, especially pp. 41 ff.

[3] See Preiss, *op. cit.*, pp. 36 f. See p. 183 below.

judgment may be connected with this. Thus in Acts 7.56 Stephen sees the Son of Man standing at the right hand of God instead of sitting there, as the usual expression drawn from Ps. 110 describes the scene.[1] In any case, God confers jurisdiction upon Jesus—just as according to the hymn in Phil. 2.6 ff. he has given Christ the whole dominion. The formula then develops which is included in the ancient confession: 'He will come to judge the quick and the dead' (II Tim. 4.1; Acts 10.42; I Peter 4.5. See also Polycarp 2.1; *II Clement* 1.1).

The function of Jesus as Judge is especially important in the Gospel of John—qualified, of course, by the Johannine idea of judgment. That the evangelist did not forget the eschatological nature of this function is proved first of all by the reference to the 'last day' in 12.48, which (along with other references to the 'last day' in John 6.39, 40, 44, 54) Bultmann without justification simply eliminates.[2] But above all the eschatological character of Jesus' judgment follows from John 5.27, which is particularly interesting to us here: '(God) has given him authority to execute judgment, *because he is the Son of Man.*' Here also the idea of the judge is anchored in that of the Son of Man.

The way in which Jesus took over and reshaped this very idea of judgment shows the new element in his interpretation of the Son of Man. The same Jesus who appeared as a man among men and as such assumed the *ebed Yahweh* role is at the same time the future Son of Man who is Judge of the world. This must give the idea of judgment a fundamentally different character, although the eschatological framework is preserved throughout. On the one hand, the judgment is now closely connected with the atoning work of the Servant of God who cancels sin; on the other hand, the foundation on which the last judgment is accomplished by the Son of Man is man's attitude toward his fellowmen in whom Jesus the Son of Man is present. The Synoptic report of the last judgment in Matt. 25.31 ff. shows this latter fact in an impressive way. In v. 40 we read: 'As you did it to one of the least of these my brethren, you did it to me.' The Son of Man comprehends *all* men. Again in view of this passage no choice is possible between the individual and collective significance of the Son of Man.[3] We see how the New Testament deepens the concept of the Son of Man as Judge: Jesus is both the incarnate man who is the representative Suffering Servant of God, and the future 'Man' who

[1] Similarly also C. F. D. Moule, *SNTS Bulletin* 3, 1952, pp. 46 f.

[2] See R. Bultmann, *Das Evangelium des Johannes*, *ad loc.*

[3] T. W. Manson, *The Sayings of Jesus*, pp. 249 ff., strongly emphasizes this idea in Matt. 25.31 ff. Cf. p. 154 n. 3 above. J. A. T. Robinson, 'The "Parable" of the Sheep and the Goats', *NTS* 2, 1955–56, pp. 255 ff., gives a different explanation.

is the Judge.[1] The connection between the future and the incarnate 'Man' is as close as possible here.

This brings us to the much discussed question whether Jesus could have ascribed the function of the Son of Man to himself within the framework of his earthly life's work. It is just with reference to the idea of judgment that we have already implicitly answered this question in the affirmative. Some scholars have thought that Jesus could have spoken of his role as the Son of Man only in the eschatological sense, because only that sense is present in the Book of Daniel upon which he based his understanding of the role. But we must guard against the prejudice that Jesus could have taught nothing Christologically new over against Judaism. On the contrary, his conviction that with his person the Kingdom of God was already introduced must have had consequences for the role he assumed as the Son of Man. Because he regarded his coming as the dawning of the end time, even the concepts which had an exclusively eschatological character in Judaism had to be transferred into the present when applied to Jesus. Therefore the fact that the Son of Man in Judaism will come only at the end of time proves nothing for Jesus' concept of the Son of Man, for according to his teaching the end has already been introduced. His answer to John the Baptist in Matt. 11.4 ff. shows this clearly: 'Go and tell John what you hear and see . . .' So also his saying in Matt. 12.28 and parallels: 'But if it is by the Spirit ('finger' in Luke) of God that I cast out demons, then the kingdom of God has come upon you.'[2]

In view of this, Jesus can call himself the Son of Man already during his earthly incarnation, although he did not descend to earth 'on the clouds of heaven'. The view then arises which we found nowhere in Judaism that the Son of Man is incarnate in a man in the ordinary human framework, a man among men. This is new not only with respect to Philo and the Jewish Christians, but also with respect to Daniel and Enoch.

[1] T. Preiss especially pursued the legal aspect of the Son of Man idea. After his untimely death, sketches of a study of the Son of Man problem were published in the book I have often mentioned, *Le Fils de l'Homme* (Études Théologiques et Religieuses), Montpellier, 1951 and 1953. In this work precisely the new elements in his point of view could be reproduced only in the context of general expositions of New Testament Christology, and therefore they are not entirely validated. It is unfortunate that he was unable to finish his work. According to Preiss, the identity of the Son of Man with *all men* is the real 'mystery', which was revealed first in Matt. 25.31 ff.

[2] See W. G. Kümmel, *Promise and Fulfilment*, especially pp. 105 ff.

It is true that Jesus never speaks of a 'second' coming of the Son of Man. [1] In the Synoptic Gospels he never says, 'I shall come again.' He takes over from Jewish eschatology its language about the parousia, advent, of the Son of Man, but he does not call his appearance on earth, his birth, a parousia, because the idea of glory is connected with this expression. Just as he does not speculate about his pre-existence, so also he does not speak of his becoming man, nor set the event of his incarnation parallel to the parousia as Christians later did. He also teaches no details about the transition from his earthly life's work, which is to be fulfilled in his death, to the parousia.[2] But if it is true that he regarded himself as the *ebed Yahweh*, then he did conceive of his present and future work as a unity.

As soon as Jesus in decisive passages unites the title Son of Man with the suffering of the Servant of God (i.e., when he relates it to his earthly vocation), his designation of himself as the Son of Man becomes also a declaration of humiliation. Thus he combines *ebed Yahweh* and *barnasha*, the two decisive concepts for his self-consciousness, in a really classical way in Mark 10.45: 'The Son of Man also came not to be served but to serve, and to give his life as a ransom for many.' Jesus explains his human life and death in terms of the work the Servant of God has to execute: 'The Son of Man must suffer many things, and be rejected by the elders and the chief priests and the scribes, and be killed' (Mark 8.31). Here again he combines the Son of Man title with the idea of the Suffering Servant of God.[3] Mark 2.10 also expresses this connection which is quite basic for Jesus' self-consciousness: 'The Son of Man has authority on earth to forgive sins.'[4]

One may ask why Jesus preferred the title Son of Man to that of the *ebed Yahweh* rather than the reverse.[5] This becomes quite understandable

[1] Heb. 9.28 speaks of a *second* appearance, a *return* of Christ. See p. 103 above. We find the idea later in Justin, *Dial.* 14.8; 40.4.

[2] In answer to the high priest in Mark 14.62, Jesus does refer not only to Dan. 7.13, but also to Ps. 110, a passage he had already previously discussed (see p. 131 above). 'Sitting at the right hand of God' could then furnish at least a temporal connection between his earthly life and his coming at the end, although this 'sitting' will of course actually be 'seen' only at the end.

[3] Thus he does more than IV Ezra and Enoch, which only use the *title* of the Servant in this way.

[4] When we remember that we must always consider the collective significance of 'Son of Man', this also casts a light on Matt. 18.18 ff., in which the disciples receive the authority to bind and to loose 'on earth'. See Preiss, *op. cit.*, p. 27.

[5] See also W. Manson, *Jesus the Messiah*, pp. 156 f.

when we consider that the Son of Man idea is more comprehensive. It both refers to Jesus' future work, and at the same time, with regard to his work as the incarnate one, visualizes his humanity as such. It was therefore more appropriate to subordinate the *ebed Yahweh* concept to that of the Son of Man. Jesus did this in such a way that the vocation of the *ebed* becomes, so to speak, the main content of the Son of Man's earthly work. As soon as the Son of Man concept was applied to the earthly life of Jesus (an application which represented a complete innovation in the development of the concept), the two central Christological titles, Son of Man and Suffering Servant of God, had to come into contact.

Both the 'Suffering Servant' and the 'Son of Man' already existed in Judaism. But Jesus' combination of precisely *these* two titles was something completely new. 'Son of Man' represents the highest conceivable declaration of exaltation in Judaism; *ebed Yahweh* is the expression of the deepest humiliation. Even if there really was a concept of a suffering Messiah in Judaism, it cannot be proved that suffering was combined precisely with the idea of the Son of Man coming on the clouds of heaven.[1] This is the unheard-of new act of Jesus, that he united these two apparently contradictory tasks in his self-consciousness, and that he expressed that union in his life and teaching.

One important presupposition for their combination did already exist in Jewish thought: the idea of representation is common to both the *barnasha* and the *ebed Yahweh*. According to its deepest meaning, which is clear from the word itself, 'Son of Man' represents humanity (according to Daniel, 'the nation of saints'); the *ebed Yahweh* represents the people of Israel. In both cases the many are represented by the one. We have shown in the chapter on the Servant of God how this idea contains the meaning of all *Heilsgeschichte*. The principle of representation, then, finds its deepest expression precisely in the two most important and central Christological designations.

We have seen that Jesus contrasts the concept Son of Man with that of the Messiah just at both the points in his life which were decisive for the question of his self-consciousness: in Caesarea Philippi when he asks his disciples the 'Christological' question,[2] and

[1] The connections between Son of Man and Servant of God in IV Ezra and the Ethiopic Enoch are of a formal nature and do not concern suffering. See p. 144 above.

[2] E. Percy, *Die Botschaft Jesu*, pp. 227 ff., like Bultmann, *Die Geschichte der synoptischen Tradition*, p. 276, considers also this account non-historical. In contrast to Bultmann, Percy does believe that Jesus considered himself the eschatological bearer of salvation in the kingdom of God he proclaimed. But he finds only the

before the high priest when he himself is asked the question. It is true that his statement in Caesarea Philippi concerns his earthly life's work, whereas before the high priest it concerns his future work. 'Son of Man' refers to his humiliation in the first case; to his exaltation in the second. But the fact that both times he sets the Son of Man concept in these two quite different senses over against the title Messiah proves that he himself thinks only of two different aspects of the same function.

Classical theology often contrasted Son of Man and Son of God. From the standpoint of the later dogma 'true God—true man', one understood the designation 'Son of Man' only as an expression of the 'human nature' of Jesus in contrast with his 'divine nature'. At that time theologians were not acquainted with the Jewish speculations about the figure of the Son of Man, and did not take into account the fact that by means of this very term Jesus spoke of his divine heavenly character. Reacting against this false understanding of the title, contemporary New Testament scholarship in general rightly emphasizes the intensified claim to exaltation implied by Jesus' consciousness that he was the 'Son of Man'. But perhaps this emphasis is too one-sided. It may be that the earlier use of the expression did contain an element of truth. The idea of 'natures' was of course completely foreign to Jesus. But it seems to me that the application of the title Son of Man to his earthly life does call attention to his humiliation. The presupposition of the Son of Man's incarnation and of the fact that he must suffer many things and be killed—this forces upon us the idea of humiliation as a consequence of the incarnation of the Heavenly Man. This idea certainly lies behind the hymn in Phil. 2.6 ff., which we shall consider in the next section. At this point I am concerned to emphasize that in applying it to his earthly work, Jesus himself also understood the title Son of Man as an indication of his humiliation. This is what he means when he says of himself in Matt. 8.20, 'Foxes have holes, and birds of the air have nests; but the Son of Man has nowhere to lay his head.'[1] His saying about the Son of Man who came 'eating and drinking', in Matt. 11.19 and parallels, also belongs in this context.

following texts to be proof of this: Matt. 11.4 ff. and parallels (the answer to John the Baptist); Mark 2.19 f. (the saying about the bridegroom); and in a secondary sense, Matt. 10.35 ff.; Matt. 12.41 f. and parallels.

[1] On the other explanation (reference to mankind as a whole), see p. 154 n. 2 above. A combination of both explanations, such as Preiss, *op. cit.*, p. 29, undertakes here (also for Matt. 11.19; see *ibid.*, p. 30), is quite possible. Jesus was conscious of representing humanity.

We shall see that Jesus considered himself also the 'Son of God'. Contrasted with this consciousness, the title Son of Man *must* suggest humiliation, despite the exaltation it implies.[1] Along with the technical sense of the term *barnasha* borrowed from eschatological theology, we must not forget completely the etymological meaning of the word—'man' in contrast to God. This is important precisely because Jesus' self-consciousness also includes the consciousness of a quite special relation to God. The term *ben adam*, child of man, which often occurs in the Old Testament (especially in the Psalms, but also elsewhere) points to human weakness or helplessness before God's omnipotence. Jesus cannot have forgotten this idea when he identified in himself the heavenly Son of Man and the Suffering Servant of God.

Again in this particular context we must recall that just like *ebed Yahweh*, 'Son of Man' includes the idea of representation. *The* Man represents all men, and thus precisely as the Son of Man also shares in their weakness.

We recall that while the Jewish texts know no incarnation of the *barnasha* but only his majestic appearance at the end, they do assume his pre-existence. Since Jesus was obviously familiar with the Jewish Son of Man idea, the question arises whether he reflected upon his own pre-existence. We shall have to ask this question in the chapter on Jesus the Son of God, but it arises also here in connection with the Son of Man title. In this context, however, the question is difficult to answer. The technical sense of the formula 'the Son of Man is come' might be at least indirectly significant. Jesus also never expresses himself concerning his relation to Adam. He does seem to be convinced of the general corruption of men when he says, 'You then, who are evil . . .' (Matt. 7.11), but he does not actually say anything about the origin of sin.

We could at most suppose that when he applied the title Son of Man to himself, he did somehow connect his work with the divine creation of man—perhaps even with Adam. When he utilized this title to designate his person and function, he thought of the Son of Man coming on the clouds of heaven, and at the same time of his first coming in lowliness to suffer and to die the atoning death. In view of this we may perhaps assume that he also understood his work

[1] According to W. Manson, *Jesus the Messiah*, pp. 159 f., Jesus also contrasts the 'Son of Man' with the 'Son of God' in the temptation account. Satan says, 'If you are the Son of *God* . . .' Jesus answers with Deut. 8.3, '*Man* shall not live by bread alone'. The Jonathan Targum has *barnasha* for 'man' here.

in the light of God's purpose in creating man 'in his own image'. The idea of a contrast between the disobedience of Adam and the obedience of Jesus at least lies behind the Synoptic report of Jesus' temptation by Satan.

We conclude that, apart from one or two passages in which the term may designate all men, Jesus used the title Son of Man to express his consciousness of having to fulfil the work of the Heavenly Man in two ways: (1) In glory at the end of time—a thought familiar to the expectation of the Son of Man in certain Jewish circles: (2) in the humiliation of the incarnation among sinful men—a thought foreign to all earlier conceptions of the Son of Man.

We can only conjecture about the connection Jesus drew between himself as the Son of Man and the *first* man.

3. *The Place of the Son of Man Christology in Early Christianity*

We have seen that the Son of Man Christology is not that of the Synoptic writers. Although 'Son of Man' occurs 69 times in the first three Gospels (more often than in any other writing of early Christianity), it does not express the authors' personal faith in Jesus. For them Jesus is the 'Christ'. When we read 'Son of Man' in the Synoptic Gospels, the term is always used by Jesus; the writers are simply handing down a tradition which existed already before them. The question then arises: which group in early Christianity saw the solution to the Christological problem in this designation which was so decisive for Jesus' own self-consciousness? E. Lohmeyer seeks a geographical solution to this question in his widely discussed book *Galiläa und Jerusalem*. He thinks there were two forms of early Christianity in Palestine, a Galilean and a Jerusalemite, which produced two separate strands of tradition—and two different Christologies. The Galilean Christology is based on the Son of Man (and the *Kyrios*), the Jerusalemite on the Messiah.

Lohmeyer is certainly correct in distinguishing between different streams within early Palestinian Christianity. Corresponding to the diversity of Palestinian Judaism which we have often emphasized in this work and to which the newly found Qumran texts call attention, there is indeed a diversity within early Palestinian Christianity. The usual distinction between Palestine and the Diaspora is quite insufficient. However, I do not believe that the distinction between the various groups within Palestine can be made geographically as Lohmeyer proposes. His schematic division of early Christian thought into Galilean and Jerusalemite views is too forced and scarcely supported by the texts. The only really demonstrable division of the original Christian tradition in terms of geographical origin in Galilee and Jerusalem has to do with the reports of Jesus' appearances after the resurrection. There is no factual basis for such a distinction between Christological views.

Within the early Church in Jerusalem itself we find the *Hellenists*, a group much more significant for the study of the beginnings of Christianity than is usually realized.[1] Hellenism—or more accurately, oriental-Hellenistic syncretism—did not exist only outside Palestine. The schematism which does not take this fact into consideration is also often responsible for the premature localization of early Christian writings such as the Gospel of John.

At this point, and precisely in connection with the question of the Son of Man Christology, I would like to refer to the Palestinian 'Hellenists'. We know that in various other questions (such as the attitude toward the temple) they represented Jesus' own teachings more faithfully than the other groups.[2] I only provisionally ask the question: May it not be that they remained more faithful also to Jesus' own conception of his person and work than the Synoptic writers? The Hellenists' understanding of the Gospel did not predominate in the early Church; this is one of the reasons why we find only traces of their distinctive views.

We have seen that in Judaism there were already esoteric groups which fostered the expectation of the Son of Man almost as a secret teaching. Jesus must somehow have come into contact with these groups. Did not disciples come to him from them perhaps even during his lifetime? The 'Hellenistic' group certainly did not suddenly appear only after Jesus' death. Its existence very probably extends back into the time of Jesus. If this is true, definite perspectives open up which might throw new light on the connection between certain early Christian movements and those esoteric Jewish

[1] In my essay on the significance of the Qumran texts for the investigation of early Christian literature, *The Scrolls and the New Testament*, pp. 18 ff., I suggest that the connection between the Qumran sect and early Christianity is made by way of these Hellenists. Ἑλληνισταί does not mean 'Greek-speaking' Jews, but those who live in a Greek manner. In the same way, there is no unambiguous text which uses Ἑβραῖοι only as a *linguistic* definition. On the question of the Hellenists in Acts see Foakes Jackson and Lake, *The Beginnings of Christianity* V, 1933, pp. 59 ff. See also pp. 183 ff. below.

[2] See O. Cullmann, 'Samaria and the Origins of the Christian Mission', *The Early Church*, pp. 185 ff. See also my essay mentioned in the previous note.

groups.[1] The name 'Hellenists' is explained by the simple fact that no other expression was available for 'syncretistic Hellenistic Judaism'.

At this point we only suggest the question. Before we very carefully attempt to answer it we must first investigate the form in which the conceptions connected with the 'Son of Man' may be found in the New Testament writings other than the Synoptic Gospels.

4. *Paul and the Son of Man*

The most developed early Christian Christology is found in the writings of Paul. We begin with him even though he does not use the title Son of Man—at least not in the Greek form familiar to us from the Gospels. Of the two Jewish conceptions which stem from the common root of the Original Man idea, Paul appears to use only the one concerning Adam. And in fact, his major interest is in this side of the problem. But on the other hand, his whole theology and Christology is so completely embedded in eschatology that he calls the 'Second Adam' the 'last Adam' (ὁ ἔσχατος Ἀδάμ, I Cor. 15.45) or the 'coming Adam' (ὁ μέλλων, Rom. 5.14). Even if Paul does not directly refer to Dan. 7 in connection with statements about the 'Man', he does share the view that Christ will come on the clouds of heaven. He writes in I Thess. 4.17 that we (together with those who have fallen asleep) 'shall be caught up . . . *in the clouds* to meet the Lord in the air'. This expectation must go back to Daniel's picture of the Son of Man 'coming on the clouds'.

Paul's primary interest, however, is the idea of the incarnate Heavenly Man, the 'Second Adam'. In his situation he looked back to the 'Man' who had already appeared. But he was also concerned about the connection between the Incarnate and the 'Last Man' who comes at the end. This becomes clear in the completely eschatological framework of I Cor. 15.45 ff., which we shall presently investigate.

Paul formulates the Christian solution to the Jewish problem of the relation between the Son of Man and Adam entirely in agreement with Jesus' self-consciousness. He does make use of the Jewish speculations which, by means of the theories we have described above, try to achieve the impossible identification of the Son of Man

[1] See my essay mentioned above, *The Scrolls and the New Testament*, pp. 18 ff., and especially my article 'Secte de Qumran, Hellénistes des Acts et IVe Evangile', in the volume *Les manuscrits de la Mer Morte* (Colloque de Strasbourg 25–27 mai 1955), Paris, 1957, pp. 61 ff., where I have set out my thesis in more detail.

with Adam. But at the same time he shows the only way in which the problem involved in those speculations can be overcome. Above all Paul's radically new idea in contrast to the Jewish speculations is his identification of the Son of Man with a historical man who appeared on earth once at a very definite time and lived in the historical framework. This conception speaks no longer either of the constantly recurring return of the Heavenly Man of the Jewish Christian theory, or of the mythological descent of Gnosticism's heavenly being who is only disguised as man. Thus Paul gives a completely new complexion to the relation between the Son of Man and Adam.

In order to understand fully the originality of Paul's solution to the problem, it is necessary to be acquainted with Philo's theory of the 'two Adams' we have described above. We must therefore keep that theory in mind as we now consider the relevant Pauline texts.

Three Pauline passages are especially important for our question: I Cor. 15.45 ff., Rom. 5.12–21 (which we have already mentioned in the chapter on the Servant of God)[1] and Phil. 2.5–11 (the hymn we treated briefly also in connection with the Servant of God).[2]

I Cor. 15.45–47 reads: 'The first man Adam became a living being; the last Adam became a life-giving spirit. But it is not the spiritual which is first but the physical, and then the spiritual. The first man was from the earth, a man of dust; the second man is from heaven.' It seems clear to me that Paul refers polemically here to a doctrine very similar to that of Philo. How could he have known of it? Had he read it directly in one of Philo's tracts? That is not very probable. It is more likely that he became acquainted with it in rabbinical circles, although, as we have mentioned,[3] we have no evidence of it in the more ancient rabbinical texts.[4] Philo was surely not the only one who represented such a doctrine.

However that may be, it seems certain to me that in this text Paul refers directly to the doctrine we find in Philo,[5] because he attacks all its essential points simultaneously. He speaks of a 'first' and a 'last' Adam (πρῶτος and ἔσχατος 'Αδάμ). Nowhere else do we encounter

[1] See p. 77 above. [2] See pp. 76 f. above.

[3] See p. 150 above.

[4] Strack-Billerbeck III, p. 478. Regarding the assumption of possible earlier traditions see p. 150 n. 1 above.

[5] So also J. Héring, *La première Epître de S. Paul aux Corinthiens, ad loc.*; *Le royaume de Dieu et sa venue*, pp. 153 ff.

the expression 'last Adam'. Paul simply invented it as an analogy to πρῶτος 'Αδάμ. In this antithesis it means practically the same as 'second man' (δεύτερος ἄνθρωπος), an expression we find in v. 47 (ὁ δεύτερος ἄνθρωπος ἐξ οὐρανοῦ). The connection between the incarnate and the future 'Man' is clearly present here. Also v. 48, for the sake of which the whole passage is introduced, shows especially the eschatological connection between the heavenly character of the Son of Man and the men who belong to him.

Paul takes over the speculation about the Heavenly Man, and identifies him with a historical person, Jesus of Nazareth. But what of the *identification of the Heavenly Man with Adam*, which was the subject of the Jewish problem? This is the point at which Paul deliberately abandons—in fact, expressly attacks—the Philonic doctrine. This is clear from v. 46. It is not the spiritual, τὸ πνευματικόν (i.e., not the Pauline 'last Adam') which is first, but the physical, τὸ ψυχικόν (i.e., the first Adam), and then comes the spiritual. This sentence is meaningful only if Paul thinks of a doctrine which asserts just what he denies here.

Paul is saying in other words that the Heavenly Man may not be identified with the first man at creation as in the speculation which Philo advocates—not even in Philo's own modified form of the identification. This is what is new in Paul's doctrine: he accepts the doctrine of the Heavenly Man, and he too establishes a relation (which we shall define more exactly) between the Heavenly Man and the first man. But he rejects the identification of the two. The Heavenly Man was not the first created man at the beginning. Paul rejects this solution to the problem of the relationship between the two. God did not create two first men. There is only one Adam—the one who was unfaithful to his divine destiny, who transgressed the divine command. The ideal divine Man, the Heavenly Man, the perfect prototype of men, does not belong at all in the Genesis account of the creation of man. As incarnate man he came only later, ἔπειτα.[1] Philo's order must be just reversed.

Paul also conceives of the Heavenly Man as pre-existent, of course. We have seen that already in Judaism the Son of Man's pre-existence is

[1] K. Barth, *Christ and Adam. Man and Humanity in Romans 5*, ET 1956, does not sufficiently consider this chronological determination of the relation between Adam and Christ. But otherwise he rightly understands and expresses the significance of the Christ-Adam speculation for Paul's anthropology.—J. Héring, *Die biblischen Grundlagen des christlichen Humanismus* (ATANT 7), 1946, shows very well the theological consequences of the Christ-Adam doctrine.

presupposed everywhere, even in Daniel, IV Ezra and Enoch, which ascribe only an eschatological role to the Son of Man. In Judaism it is just the idea of pre-existence which establishes the connection between the two separated views, the purely eschatological view and that which emphasizes the relation to the first man.[1] But Paul, like the Jewish eschatological texts, does not *speculate* about this pre-existence; he simply takes it for granted. Thus he clearly says that the 'second Adam' comes from heaven, where he exists in the 'image of God'.

Where was the pre-existent Christ before his incarnation? The New Testament does not answer this question with the idea of the Son of Man, but with the related *Logos* concept: according to the Gospel of John, the Logos was 'with God'.[2]

Paul not only denies that Jesus the Heavenly Man is identical with Adam, but says that he actually came to correct Adam's error, that is, to fulfil the task which the first man failed to fulfil. Paul will hear nothing of two first men, one in Gen. 1.27 and a different one in Gen. 2.7. He assumes that both verses speak of one and the same Adam. It is true that he cites only Gen. 2.7, which says that God formed Adam out of the dust from the ground and breathed the breath of life into his nostrils, in order to make him a living being. But it does not occur to Paul to contrast this with Gen. 1.27, which says that man is created in the image of God. There can be no contradiction between the two because the Adam in Gen. 1.27 is not the 'Heavenly Man' who later is incarnate in Jesus, but the Adam who is created in God's image and sins immediately thereafter. Paul does believe that the Heavenly Man Jesus was pre-existent, but he does not believe that the Genesis account concerns Jesus' pre-existence. This attitude is consistent with the New Testament in general, which (except for John 1.1 ff.) rather presupposes than describes this pre-existence. In any case, Paul's opinion, clearly expressed in I Cor. 15.45 ff., is that the Son of Man appeared on earth for the first time in Jesus in the fullness of time, whereas only the one sinful Adam was on earth at the beginning. That Paul thinks of Jesus also as the mediator of creation (I Cor. 8.6; Col. 1.15) is another confirmation of the fact that he does not believe Jesus was already on earth at the beginning as created, incarnate 'man'. Jesus' pre-existence extends beyond creation.[3]

But while an identity between Adam and Jesus the Son of Man does not exist with regard to their persons, there is an identity with

[1] See p. 151 above. [2] See pp. 249 ff. below.
[3] See pp. 176 ff. below on the concept of the 'image of God', εἰκών.

regard to their tasks.[1] They have the common task of exhibiting the image of God. But with regard to the execution of this task there is a radical contradiction between the two. Adam was unfaithful to this mission. He sinned, and following him, all humanity became sinful and no longer bears the image of God. There is only one exception—the Heavenly Man, who already existed at the beginning, but not on earth; who came only much later (ἔπειτα) as an incarnate, earthly 'man'.

He came to earth, of course, in connection with the first man Adam; that is, he came to atone for Adam's sin. This idea is not actually expressed in I Cor. 15.45–47, but it is certainly presupposed. Thus the 'Son of Man' is related to Adam in a twofold way: positively, he shares with Adam the task of exhibiting the image of God; negatively, he must atone for Adam's sin. We must pay attention to both sides of this relationship.

The second side of the relationship just noted is prominent in Rom. 5.12 ff., the second Pauline passage relevant to the idea of the Son of Man. This passage shows especially clearly how Paul solved the Adam—Son of Man problem which Judaism was actually unable to solve either by tracing man's sin to the fall of the angels rather than to the fall of Adam (the Book of Enoch), or by denying the fall of Adam altogether (the Jewish Christians), or by seeking a middle way in presupposing two first men (Philo). Paul alone could give a real solution to the problem, because he understood that Jesus the Son of Man brought something completely new, something which was not a mere repetition of what was already on earth at the beginning. He interpreted the whole of *Heilsgeschichte* on the basis of the Incarnate One, and understood the significance of the Son of Man from that standpoint. He grasped the full meaning of the Heavenly Man's becoming flesh. This allowed him to affirm the relationship between the Son of Man and Adam, but radically to deny their identification. Only at the end time introduced by Jesus' coming does the existence of the Heavenly Man in the image of God become effective for created men, and this happens as atonement for their sins.

The verses in Rom. 5.12 ff. which are important for our question are: 'Therefore as sin came into the world through one man and

[1] K. Barth, in the essay mentioned above, emphasizes that in Romans everything Paul says about Adam only becomes understandable in the light of the second Adam, Christ. This is correct in so far as Paul thinks that in Jesus man appears for the first time really in the image of God.

death through sin, and so death spread to all men because all men sinned . . .' (v. 12). 'But the free gift is not like the trespass. For if many died through one man's trespass, much more have the grace of God and the free gift in the grace of that one man Jesus Christ abounded for many' (v. 15). 'Then as one man's trespass led to condemnation for all men, so one man's act of righteousness leads to acquittal and life for all men. For as by one man's disobedience many were made sinners, so by one man's obedience many will be made righteous' (vv. 18 f.).[1]

In so far as the main emphasis of this passage is on the atoning work of the 'Man' Jesus, we find here the Son of Man and the *ebed Yahweh* very closely related. This is very important, as we have seen, because Jesus himself made the same connection. *Barnasha* and *ebed Yahweh* are the Christological titles which go back to Jesus himself, and their connection represents what is decisively new about him Christologically. The unprecedented thing is Jesus' assertion that the Son of Man who appears on the clouds of heaven in divine majesty must suffer many things.

It is relevant to the much argued 'Jesus and Paul' debate that precisely at this point we find a basic agreement between the two. In this Christologically important passage, Rom. 5.12 ff., Paul united the two basic concepts Son of Man and Servant of God exactly as Jesus united them. One cannot say, as W. Bousset (among others) asserts, that this agreement stems from the fact that both Paul and the evangelists depended upon the theology of the early Church, because the Christology of the Synoptic writers is not based either on the *Pais* or the *Anthropos* concept. The very fact that in spite of this they use the term 'Son of Man' and emphasize the ideas connected with the *ebed Yahweh* when they report Jesus speaking shows that at this point they do not simply reflect the early Church's theology. They preserve the memory of a historical situation. It is therefore all the more noteworthy that the Apostle Paul here interprets Jesus' own thought so correctly.

It might at first appear arbitrary to find any reference at all to the Son of Man concept in Rom. 5.12 ff. We must therefore give attention to what lies behind the Adam-Christ confrontation here. Verse 14b says of

[1] The proposal of J. Héring in his commentary on I Corinthians, and previously in *Le royaume de Dieu et sa venue*, pp. 155 ff., that εἷς . . . εἷς is to be translated 'the one . . . the other' is not clear to me, because this passage deals with the contrast 'the one—the many' and shows that this same contrast is true of both Adam and Jesus.

Adam that he is 'a type of the one who was to come' (τύπος τοῦ μέλλοντος) —that is, the type of the last (ἔσχατος) or second (δεύτερος) Adam. It is clear in this passage that the idea of the 'Second Adam' goes back to the same root as that of the Son of Man concept. We should not allow the terminology to mislead us. It is true that the expression υἱὸς τοῦ ἀνθρώπου does not appear here, but in v. 15 Jesus is called the *one man* (εἷς ἄνθρωπος Ἰησοῦς). We have seen that the simple ἄνθρωπος, just like the evangelists' υἱὸς τοῦ ἀνθρώπου, corresponds to the one basic Aramaic word *barnasha*. Also in I Cor. 15.45 ff., the text we considered just above, Paul uses ἄνθρωπος to discuss the conception of the Heavenly Man. He never uses υἱὸς τοῦ ἀνθρώπου. This expression occurs only in the Gospels, in Acts, and in the Revelation.[1] The reason is that the evangelists (including John) still clearly sensed that Jesus attributed a particular meaning to this expression. They chose the phrase υἱὸς τοῦ ἀνθρώπου whenever it seemed to them that he used *barnasha* Christologically so that they might distinguish between his designation of himself as the 'Son of Man' and the ordinary meaning of the word. But it would be a premature judgment to assume that Paul also excludes the technical Christological understanding of *barnasha* when he writes simply ἄνθρωπος. Perhaps we should also think of *barnasha* in a Christological sense in the phrase δι' ἀνθρώπου ἀνάστασις (by a man resurrection . . .) in I Cor. 15.21. The idea we found in Jesus' sayings that the Son of Man at the same time represents all humanity is so common in Paul's writings that (as was the case in Aramaic) he makes no distinction in Greek between 'man' meaning specifically Jesus and man meaning all men.

We understand how Paul could and must see precisely in the connection of the 'Son of Man' and *ebed Yahweh* concepts the solution to the Son of Man/Adam problem which Judaism could not solve. The idea of representation is common to both concepts. The concept of the Heavenly Man presupposes and is based upon just this idea of representation. The role of the Heavenly Man is to redeem men by making them what he himself is, the image of God. That is his mission. But men are sinful; the first man Adam, the representative of all men, sinned, and redemption from sin requires atonement. The Heavenly Man, the divine prototype of humanity, must therefore himself enter sinful humanity in order to free it from its sins.

In Gnostic Hellenism the Heavenly Man saves other men simply by descending to earth and ascending again (Naassene hymn, Hippolytus, *Refut.* V.6–11). But this is not enough for Jewish and Christian theology. The problem here is not redemption from matter but redemption from

[1] And in one passage in Hebrews, Heb. 2.6, in a citation of Ps. 8.

sin. An 'appearance' on earth is not sufficient to accomplish this. Redemption is a question of atonement by the 'Man'.

At this point it is clear why in a Christian context the Son of Man concept must necessarily encounter that of the *ebed Yahweh*, which rests upon the idea of representation with respect to sin. Paul shows how through his sin Adam too played a representative role—an evil one of course.

Verse 15, which is logically parenthetical, emphasizes the fact that there is a fundamental difference, however, between the representation of Adam and that of Christ. A single man, Adam, sufficed to make all men sinners. The gracious act of Jesus is representative in the same way in that it frees all men from the effects of sin. Here lies the correspondence between the two. But in this verse Paul says further that the power of the atoning act must be greater than the power of sin. Here lies the difference between them. One might clarify the situation by means of a figure of speech: a single spark is enough to set a whole forest on fire, but infinitely greater power is required to extinguish the fire. In the case of the Second Adam's atoning work, one individual brings also this greater power. The one who accomplishes this miracle is precisely the Son of Man.

We have seen that in Judaism too the idea of representation is implicit in the Son of Man concept,[1] although Judaism does not see the connection between human sin and the Son of Man in the same way. In Dan. 7.13 ff. the Son of Man represents the holy people, just as the beasts represent the kings of the world empires. But the author of Daniel thinks only of the Son of Man's redeeming role, not of his atoning role. The idea of Rom. 5.12 ff., on the other hand, is that the one man Jesus comprehends in himself the whole fellowship of those freed from sin. Paul's concept of the Church as the Body of Christ may be in the background here. That concept is also connected with the idea of representation.

The whole of present-day humanity stands between two poles, so to speak—between Adam and Jesus, the first and second Adam. Both the identity and difference between the first man and the Heavenly Man are also clear at this point: identity in that by their actions both comprehend the 'many' in themselves; difference in that one does this through sin, the other through atonement (the power of which must be greater than that of sin). This is how Paul solved the old Jewish problem of the relation between the first man and the Heavenly Man.

[1] And already in the non-Jewish ideas of the Original Man also.

Paul's expositions concerning the 'old' and 'new' man also probably belong in this context. Even if passages in which these concepts occur emphasize only the subjective aspect, the effect on the 'many' or humanity, they do presuppose the idea of Rom. 5.12 ff. that the old man depends upon the first Adam, the new man on the second Adam, Jesus. Paul writes in Col. 3.9 f.: 'Do not lie to one another, seeing that you have put off the old man with its practices and have put on the new man, which is being renewed in knowledge after the image of its Creator.' The expression 'put on the new man', which is completely parallel to 'put on Christ' (Gal. 3.27; Rom. 13.14), shows that Paul thinks also of the objective basis for this transformation—Adam for the old man, Jesus for the new man. The reference to creation in God's image also points to Adam and the Son of Man. Only the one who represents the image of the Creator in complete purity and clarity can renew us in the image of the Creator. The 'Man', who alone is and has remained the image of the Creator, can form us according to this image when we 'put on the new man'. The words κατ' εἰκόνα (according to the image) certainly come from Gen. 1.26. We find an analogous idea in the parallel passage, Eph. 4.24: '. . . and put on the new man, created after the likeness of God . . .' Here again we encounter the expression which corresponds to 'putting on Christ', and the reference to creation in God's image. Thus this verse too points to the memory that Adam—and with him the whole of sinful humanity—has been unfaithful to the task of exhibiting the image of God, whereas Jesus fulfils that task.

We turn to the investigation of Phil. 2.5–11, the third Pauline passage in which the idea of the Son of Man plays a prominent part. This text, which is extremely rich Christologically, unites three concepts: 'Son of Man', 'Servant of God', and *Kyrios*. The last of these will later bring us back to this passage for the third time.

Verses 5–8 are particularly important for the 'Son of Man' concept and its connection with the *ebed Yahweh*: 'Have this mind among yourselves, which you have in Christ Jesus, who, though he was in the form of God, did not count equality with God a thing to be grasped, but emptied himself, taking the form of a servant, being born in the likeness of men. And being found in human form he humbled himself and became obedient unto death, even death on a cross.'

E. Lohmeyer has proposed the hypothesis that Paul is quoting here an ancient Christian Aramaic psalm.[1] This is a very probable thesis,

[1] E. Lohmeyer, *Kyrios Jesus. Eine Untersuchung zu Phil. 2.5–11.* All later exege-

although it cannot be definitely proved. There can be no doubt that the text exhibits Aramaisms.

It has also been suggested that Paul took over a Jewish-Gnostic hymn and fitted it into his Christian theology.[1] If this is true, the Jewish original would have sung of the Heavenly Man's appearance on earth. In any case it seems to me that J. Héring has conclusively shown that the subject is quite clearly the Heavenly Man and his relation to Adam.[2] Héring agrees with Lohmeyer that there is a pre-Pauline hymn present here, and he thinks it comes from Syria. But the way in which the hymn sets the Heavenly Man parallel to the first man Adam, and on the other hand identifies him with the *ebed Yahweh*, corresponds so completely to Paul's discussions in I Cor. 15.45 ff. and Rom. 5.12 ff. that it can be understood only against the background of these Pauline texts. It seems to me that this should be emphasized even if Lohmeyer and Héring and others are right in finding an earlier pattern here, for we have found this form of the theory neither in Judaism nor in the very early Church.

E. Käsemann, '*Kritische Analyse von Phil. 2.5–11*', *ZTK* 47, 1950, pp. 313 ff., emphasizes strongly the anchoring of this text in the thought world of *Hellenism*. He thinks that the hymn can only be understood on this basis: Behind it lies the Hellenistic myth of the Original Man/Redeemer, and this explains the exclusively soteriological (not ethical) orientation of the hymn. On the other hand, its specifically Christian eschatology breaks up the mythical framework.—As we have shown, it is true from the point of view of comparative religion that syncretistic speculations about the Original Man lie in the background. But it does not seem appropriate to me to begin primarily from this point of view, first of all because a *direct* influence of that Gnostic myth cannot be proved; but above all because the thought of Phil. 2.5 ff. relates primarily to the Genesis story and can be understood only by reference to it. The μορφή concept presupposes Gen. 1.26, and it is not necessary to appeal to Hellenistic-Gnostic conceptions in order to explain it. All externally introduced parallels (Herm. 1.13 f., for instance) are indeed interesting from the standpoint of comparative religion, but exegetically they are nevertheless far-fetched.

tical investigation of this text builds on this fundamental work. See also the division of the whole hymn into two stanzas of six groups of three lines. Lohmeyer considers the phrase 'even to death on a cross' in v. 8 a Pauline addition.

[1] P. Bonnard, *L'Epître de S. Paul aux Philippiens* (CNT), 1950, p. 49.

[2] J. Héring, 'Kyrios Anthropos', *RHPR* 16, 1936, pp. 196 ff.; *Le royaume de Dieu et sa venue*, pp. 162 f.; *Die biblischen Grundlagen des christlichen Humanismus*, appendix pp. 29 ff. Héring further develops Lohmeyer's interpretation at least in so far as the explanation of the concept μορφή is concerned.

The expression μορφή (form) firmly establishes the connection between Jesus and the creation story of Adam from the very beginning. J. Héring has correctly pointed out that this Greek word corresponds to the Hebrew דְּמוּת (image) of Gen. 1.26. The Peshitta indicates the same connection in translating μορφή with *demutha* here. Thus μορφή in Phil. 2.6 is immediately related to the concept εἰκών, since the Semitic root word דְּמוּת or its synonym צֶלֶם can correspond to either of the two Greek words.[1] This means that v. 6 does not refer to Jesus' divine 'nature', but rather to the image of God which he possessed from the beginning. We find ourselves, then, completely in a context relating to the Heavenly Man who is the only one to fulfil the divine destiny of being the image of God. This terminology corresponds perfectly to other Pauline statements. We think above all of Col. 1.15, which says that Christ is the εἰκών (image) of the invisible God.[2] We read also in II Cor. 4.4: '. . . the god of this world has blinded the minds of the unbelievers, to keep them from seeing the light of the gospel of the glory of Christ, who is the likeness (εἰκών) of God.' We see that the idea at the beginning of the hymn in Phil. 2.6 ff. is thoroughly Pauline: Christ is the only true likeness of God, the Heavenly 'Man'. It is on the basis of this idea that Paul emphasizes that our renewal can come only through a 'trans-formation' into the image of Christ.

This idea of our transformation (μεταμορφοῦσθαι) into the image of Christ (who is himself the image of God) recurs repeatedly in Paul's writings. It is presupposed in Col. 3.10, which contrasts our 'new man' created in God's image with our 'old man'. The relation between transformation and image is quite clear in II Cor. 3.18: 'And we all, with unveiled face, beholding the glory of the Lord, are being changed (μεταμορφοῦσθαι) into his likeness (εἰκών) from one degree of glory to another . . .' The same idea occurs in Rom. 12.2, where the 'likeness' is not specifically mentioned, but is implied by the verb μεταμορφοῦσθαι: '. . . be transformed by the renewal of your mind . . .'[3]

On the basis of these passages we come to the further idea that our final transformation at the end of days (i.e., our reception of the spiritual body) takes place through our adaptation to the likeness of Christ the Heavenly Man. We read in Rom. 8.29: 'For those whom he foreknew he also predestined to be conformed (σύμμορφος) to

[1] Compare the translation of צלם in Gen. 1.26 with that in Dan. 3.19 (LXX).
[2] See C. Masson, *L'Epître de S. Paul aux Colossiens* (CNT), 1950, p. 98.
[3] See J. Héring, *Le royaume de Dieu et sa venue*, pp. 146 ff.

the image (εἰκών) of his Son, in order that he might be the first-born among many brethren.' It is interesting that we find here the root μορφή closely followed by εἰκών, for this confirms the fact that Phil 2.6 really refers to Gen. 1.26. Similarly we read in Phil. 3.21: Christ 'will change (μετασχηματίζειν; cf. σχῆμα in Phil. 2.7) our lowly body to be formed like (σύμμορφος) his glorious body...' Finally we read in I Cor. 15.49, which is especially important because it follows immediately after the exposition about the two Adams, and thus represents its application to our human body and its transformation: 'Just as we have borne the image of the man of dust (i.e., Adam), so we shall also bear the image of the man of heaven.' Again the word εἰκών refers to the fact that the Heavenly Man bears the image of God.

We should relate all these texts to Phil 2.6. They are far more relevant to its interpretation than all Gnostic parallels. Only from this point of view do we understand that by the 'form' of God in which Jesus Christ existed at the very beginning is meant precisely the form of the Heavenly Man, who alone is the true image of God. Once again we see clearly that the statement 'Jesus is the Son of Man' is primarily an exalted declaration of majesty, not a title of humiliation. Because Christ is the Son of Man, he is the pre-existent Heavenly Man, the pre-existent pure image of God, the God-man already in his pre-existence.

Phil. 2.6 asserts that the Son of Man Christ Jesus possessed this form, this μορφή. The texts we have cited demonstrate that μορφή means this image of God, and is to be understood in the sense of the Hebrew דְּמוּת or צֶלֶם, and the Greek εἰκών. On the other hand, all these Pauline passages presuppose the theological speculation which is probably most clearly developed in Phil 2.6 ff. Also from this standpoint we must emphasize again the Pauline character of this psalm; its content, despite the apostle's use of an antecedent form, corresponds perfectly to Pauline theology.

The difficult phrase which follows this declaration that Jesus was in the form of God, '(He) did not count equality with God a thing to be grasped', can also be explained only on the basis of a contrasting parallel between the Heavenly Man and Adam. Without the background of Paul's doctrine of the two Adams, either these words can scarcely be understood, or we become lost in tangential theological speculations foreign to early Christianity.[1] In order to understand the

[1] P. Henry, 'Kénose', *Dictionnaire de la Bible*, Suppl. vol. V, col. 7 ff. (a Catholic work), gives a good survey of the whole relevant literature.

phrase, we need only think of the promise of the serpent in Gen. 3.5: 'When you eat of it . . . you will be like God.' Adam, tempted by the devil, wanted to be like God. That was his sin, and as a result of it he lost his highest possession, the image of God. The Heavenly Man did not commit this 'robbery' and therefore remained faithful to divine destiny to be the image of God. This is shown precisely by the fact that he 'emptied' himself; that is, that he determined to become *a* man, to enter into the humanity which had lost the likeness of God.

Equality with God is thus considered 'a thing to be grasped' (*res rapienda*).[1] Adam's real fall consists in the arrogance which was not satisfied with the highest task God had conferred upon his earthly image.

In answer to the much discussed question whether the verb ἐκένωσεν ἑαυτόν (he emptied himself) refers to the pre-existent or the incarnate Christ, we may say that this text probably includes both ideas: the idea that *the* Man became *a* Man; and the idea, mentioned in v. 8, that he assumed the role of the *ebed Yahweh*. According to both ideas the Son of Man proved his obedience (ὑπήκοος, v. 8) in contrast to Adam. This obedience is the determining factor, for Adam's sin consisted precisely in his disobedience. This leads us back again to Rom. 5.19, which also characterizes Adam by his disobedience and the Son of Man Jesus by his obedience. Jesus' likeness to God is revealed precisely in his obedience, which expresses itself in a double way: in his becoming man in the flesh, and in his humbling himself unto death (his accepting the role of the *ebed Yahweh*). Jesus must assume the form of fallen man in order to take the μορφὴ δούλου.

The phrase which follows in v. 7, being born 'in the likeness of men' (ἐν ὁμοιώματι ἀνθρώπων), shows that Jesus entered completely into fallen humanity. This understanding of ὁμοίωμα is thoroughly attested.[2] The next sentence accentuates Jesus' complete assumption of incarnate human nature: this is how *the* Man became man. He who by nature was the only God-man, who deserved the designation by bearing the image of God, became man in fallen flesh through obedience, in which he proved himself precisely the Heavenly Man, and by which he accomplished his atoning work.

After Paul has explained the title ἄνθρωπος in its double relation-

[1] The clever conjecture of A. Fridrichsen, *RHPR* 3, 1923, p. 441, that ἁρπαγμόν is to be read ἄπραγμον (pillow) is thus not tenable.

[2] We think for instance of Rom. 5.14: ἐπὶ τῷ ὁμοιώματι τῆς παραβάσεως Ἀδάμ.

ship to the Heavenly Man and to the man incarnate in the humanity corrupted by Adam, he develops and justifies in v. 8 the δοῦλος concept by defining the *ebed Yahweh*'s unique act as the content and climax of obedience: obedience unto death. The phrase 'unto death' is of course not intended chronologically, as though it meant only that Christ was obedient 'throughout his whole life'. Paul considers Jesus' death itself the highest expression of obedience. The words 'even death *on a cross*' indicate that Jesus fulfilled the *ebed Yahweh* role so completely that he accepted the most disgraceful form of death. The cross was to the ancients what the gallows is to us. The greatest σκάνδαλον, the greatest offence, the ignominious death of hanging from the gallows, is precisely the high point of the *ebed Yahweh*'s obedience, as well as the high point of the *barnasha*'s obedience in contrast to Adam's disobedience (Rom. 5.19).

We have emphasized from various points of view that 'Son of Man' and 'Suffering Servant of God' are by their very nature two very closely related concepts, and in this connection we have pointed to the idea of representation common to both. Now we come to the same result from the concept of obedience. By his very nature the Heavenly Man must be obedient, just as the Second Adam must correct the first Adam's sin of disobedience. Adam's sin consisted in disobedience; he was not content to be the image of God. But obedience is also the essential nature of the representative Suffering Servant of God.

We have thus confirmed the fact that this hymn in Phil. 2.6 ff., just as Rom. 5.12 ff., connects the *barnasha* and the *ebed Yahweh* concepts.[1] Apart from Paul only Jesus himself connects the two in this way—although Jesus does not in this way explain the connection theologically. If we agree with Lohmeyer and others that Paul has taken over a psalm of the early Church here, then we must of course also assume that the Church had already made this theological connection. This is not impossible, since the connection as such originates with Jesus. But in any case (and this is what is important), it corresponds to the most essential character of Paulinism.

We have already mentioned that Phil. 2.6 ff. also combines the *Kyrios* concept with that of the 'Son of Man' and the 'Servant of God' so that in these few verses we actually possess a complete

[1] O. Michel, 'Zur Exegese von Phil. 2.5–11', *Theologie als Glaubenswagnis* (volume in honour of K. Heim), 1954, pp. 79 ff., comes to the same conclusion. He begins his proof of this connection with the statement in v. 7 and only touches upon the explanation of v. 6 which I propose.

Christology in condensed form. In the chapter on the *Kyrios* we shall have to speak about the closing verses 9–11 of this passage, which speak of God's conferring the title *Kyrios* on Jesus after his death, with all sovereignty 'in heaven and on earth and under the earth'. But at this point we must mention this basic text's logical connection of the Son of Man and *ebed Yahweh* concepts with that of *Kyrios*. The connection lies in the verb ὑπερύψωσεν in v. 9. Scholars usually consider this verb a sort of rhetorical pleonasm which actually means nothing more than the simple ὑψοῦν.[1] Héring has correctly emphasized, however, that the compound verb ὑπερυψόω signifies more than the simple ὑψόω,[2] so that we should not simply translate it, 'he has highly exalted him', but rather, 'he did *more* than exalt him'.

This 'more' becomes understandable only from the standpoint of the explanation we have given of vv. 6 f., especially from the standpoint of the statement that Christ was ἐν μορφῇ θεοῦ before he 'emptied' himself. If Jesus was already the image of God in his pre-existence and now God has done more than exalt him, this can only mean that after his death Jesus did not simply return to the form of existence he already had as the Heavenly Man in his pre-existence with God before his incarnation. He has now entered a still closer relationship with God; God now confers upon him the title *Kyrios* with full lordship over all. *Kyrios* is the Greek translation of the Hebrew *Adonai*, the designation for God the Father himself.[3] In other words, God confers his own name with his whole lordship upon Jesus because of Jesus' proven obedience as the Son of Man. Christ thus receives the equality with God which in the obedience of the Heavenly Man he did not usurp as a 'thing to be grasped'. God has now given him this equality.

This is not to say that only now is Jesus exalted to deity. We are not dealing in Philippians with the doctrine of Adoptionism, either as it was proposed in antiquity or as it is proposed more recently as a New Testament Christology. It is not as though Jesus received his divine character only on the basis of his exaltation.[4] The idea that he possessed the μορφή of God is not very different from the idea of the

[1] E. Lohmeyer, *Der Brief an die Philipper* (Meyer 9), 1930, p. 97 n. 2, suggests that ὑπερυψοῦν is identical with δοξάζειν (Isa. 52.13; *Test. Naphth.* 5; *Test. Jos.* 10.3).

[2] J. Héring, *Le royaume de Dieu et sa venue*, p. 163.

[3] See pp. 200 f. below.

[4] P. Henry, *op. cit.*, sees only the adoptionist possibility in the assumption that ὑπερύψωσεν means that Christ received more in his exaltation than he possessed

prologue of the Gospel of John that he was with God in the beginning as his 'Word'. Also according to Phil. 2.6 ff. Jesus the divine Heavenly Man was divine already in his pre-existence. Already then he was the highest possible being in his relationship with God—a perfect image or 'reflection' of God, as Paul attests elsewhere. But now, because of his obedience, complete equality with God in the exercise of divine sovereignty is added. We do not have to do here with speculation about 'natures', but with *Heilsgeschichte*. It is only to Jesus' work that something new is added. All the statements of Phil 2.6 ff. are to be understood from the standpoint of the Old Testament history of Adam. Adam was created in the image of God, but he lost that image because he wanted to grasp equality with God. Unlike Adam, the Heavenly Man, who in his pre-existence represented the true image of God, humbled himself in obedience and now receives the equality with God he did not grasp as a 'robbery'. Although he was already υἱός, now he becomes, as Rom. 1.4 puts it, υἱὸς τοῦ θεοῦ ἐν δυνάμει. As Acts 2.36 expresses it, he is 'made' *Kyrios*.[1]

We have seen that in the three passages we have investigated Paul connects the Son of Man concept with his total Christological understanding in a most harmonious way, and that in so doing he agrees with what we call Jesus' self-consciousness.

5. *The Son of Man in the Remaining New Testament Writings*

We have already asked which early Christian group considered the title Son of Man and the ideas related to it as the solution to the Christological problem. However decisive Paul's theological contribution may be to the application of the Son of Man concept to Jesus, we cannot assume that he was the first to build upon Jesus' self-designation in this way. We have seen that there is much to be said for Lohmeyer's thesis that a pre-Pauline hymn of the early Church lies behind Phil. 2.6 ff., which is so important for this question. On the other hand, we could not accept Lohmeyer's assertion that the Son of Man Christology originated in Galilee. We have indicated that the expectation of the Son of Man appears almost as a secret doctrine in esoteric groups on the fringe of Judaism. Jesus must have

in his pre-existence before his incarnation. Therefore he rejects this interpretation. But in reality it does not necessarily lead to the conclusion he fears. We have to do here with a new function in *Heilsgeschichte*.

[1] See p. 216 below.

come into contact with them. Therefore we must probably search for those who first advocated the application of the Son of Man concept to Jesus among those of his disciples who somehow came from these Jewish circles or were at least in some way connected with them. I have suggested that they could be the Palestinian members of the early Church whom Acts calls 'Hellenists'. Is there evidence to support this hypothesis? In order to answer this question we turn to the attitude of the remaining New Testament books toward the 'Son of Man'.

We have mentioned several times that the Son of Man Christology is not that of the Synoptic writers, although they use the expression 69 times—more often than any other New Testament writing. Even if we subtract the parallel passages, approximately half of these occurrences remain. The Gospel of John, on the other hand, uses the expression only 12 times. We have seen, however, that the Synoptic writers introduce the title only when they represent Jesus himself as the speaker. Therefore we should not draw the false conclusion from the statistics that they themselves especially prefer the Son of Man Christology. Unlike the writer of the Gospel of John, who, led by the Paraclete, the 'Spirit of Truth', sought to interpret the Christ of the Church (John 14.26), the Synoptic writers intended primarily only to repeat Jesus' words as he spoke them.[1] At this point they only preserve the tradition of Jesus' sayings. Their own Christology is that of the 'Christ' or the 'Son of God' rather than that of the 'Son of Man'. In view of the frequency of its occurrence, it can be no accident that the Synoptic writers always attribute the term 'Son of Man' to Jesus, never to those who speak with him. They know that from the beginning the title used by Jesus was not common.

We have seen that in their Greek translation of *barnasha* the Synoptic writers distinguish between its technical Christological sense (υἱὸς τοῦ ἀνθρώπου) and its ordinary sense of man in general (ἄνθρωπος). This does not prove much more than that they sensed that Jesus attached to the designation definite views whose familiarity he could presuppose, although they themselves perhaps no longer completely understood it.

[1] This is not to contest the validity of 'form criticism' of the Synoptic Gospels. But the principle of form criticism should not be so misused that it blots out every distinction between the Synoptics and the Gospel of John. Even though the interest of the early Church did influence the Synoptic writers' reports of Jesus' sayings, the influence was in their case rather an unconscious, collective tendency, whereas the writer of John quite deliberately intended to view the incarnate and the exalted Christ together and to let both speak at the same time.

Perhaps Acts could give us a clue which would point to the little known but very important early Christian group of the Hellenists as the circle which fostered the Son of Man Christology. The expression υἱὸς τοῦ ἀνθρώπου occurs only once in Acts—in the first part of the book, which deals with the very early Church. In 7.56 Stephen says before being stoned, 'Behold, I see the heavens opened, and the Son of Man standing at the right hand of God.' The author expressly remarks that Stephen was 'filled with the Holy Spirit' at the moment he spoke these words. Just as Jesus did before the high priest (Mark 14.62),[1] Stephen speaks here of the exaltation of the Son of Man. But whereas Jesus, using the terminology of Ps. 110, speaks of the Son of Man sitting at the right hand of God, Stephen sees him standing (ἑστῶτα). This implies that in contrast to Jesus, Stephen sees the Son of Man not as Judge[2] but as witness or advocate.[3] Thus we should not attribute this reference to the Son of Man to Luke himself; it comes rather from an old tradition about Stephen. Apart from Paul, Stephen was perhaps the most significant man in the early Church. According to the little we know of his theological views, he grasped what was new in Jesus' thought better than almost anyone else. We are not surprised, then, to find that he is the very person who uses the designation for Jesus which Jesus applied to himself. In any case, it is noteworthy that the author of Acts attributes the use of this designation only to Stephen, and that the title occurs only in this one verse in the twenty-eight chapters of the book. We remember that he reports Peter as saying 'Servant of God' when he speaks of Jesus.[4] We conclude that in Peter's case this represents a genuine ancient memory. That could also be the case when Stephen, the Palestinian 'Hellenist', is the only person who speaks of the exalted Jesus as the 'Son of Man'.

This conclusion may seem venturesome, but it gains weight when, even apart from this passage in Acts, we consider the probability that the Palestinian 'Hellenists' were related to that esoteric Jewish group with which we become acquainted in the Book of Enoch and now

[1] In his passion narrative Luke reports Jesus' saying about sitting at the right hand of God without connecting it with his coming on the clouds.

[2] See pp. 157 ff. above.

[3] See also p. 158 n. 1 above. T. Preiss, *Le Fils de l'Homme*, draws far-reaching consequences from this for the whole idea of the Son of Man, which in this way he relates to that of the *Paraclete*. His remark on Acts 7.56, p. 23, is very interesting: at the moment the human judge condemns Stephen, the Son of Man as intercessor entreats God for his justification (see Mark 8.38).

[4] See pp. 74 f. above.

through the Qumran texts. These Hellenists must have played a much more important role in the formation of Christianity than is revealed by the description of it in Acts. As I have shown elsewhere,[1] Luke and the author of the Fourth Gospel are the only New Testament writers who give us a glimpse of their importance. It seems to me that the Gospel of John is actually trying to uphold the honour of these Hellenists when in 4.38 it reports Jesus as emphasizing that the twelve did not found the mission in Samaria, but entered into the work of others (ἄλλοι) there. This points us to Acts 8.4 ff., which reports that the Hellenists were the founders of the Christian missionary activity, whereas the twelve only subsequently sanctioned their work. But if the Gospel of John is particularly interested in these Hellenists and defends them, we may venture the further conclusion that this Gospel probably originates in a circle which is closely related to the Hellenists. This is further confirmed by the fact that the thought of John exhibits a relationship with the esoteric Judaism of which we have spoken.[2]

If we are correct in making the connection esoteric Judaism—Jesus—the Hellenists—Gospel of John,[3] then we can understand the fact that the Son of Man Christology must be especially significant for John—paradoxically, much more so than for the Synoptic Gospels. This brings us to the question of the relation between the author of the Fourth Gospel and the Son of Man concept. We have seen that in this Gospel Jesus calls himself by this title only twelve times, much less often than in the Synoptics. But we have already indicated that we cannot allow these statistics to mislead us, for we know that the fourth evangelist is not concerned to reproduce Jesus' speeches literally, but to give their meaning which is disclosed to him by the Spirit. He thus consciously allows his own personal Christological

[1] See O. Cullmann, 'Samaria and the Origins of the Christian Mission', *The Early Church*, pp. 186 ff.

[2] H. Odeberg, *The Fourth Gospel*, 1929 (a work unfortunately difficult to obtain), was ahead of his time in recognizing this. The Qumran texts have to a large extent confirmed his observations. See also K. G. Kuhn, 'Die in Palästina gefundenen hebräischen Texte und das Neue Testament', *ZTK* 53, 1950, pp. 193 ff., also my articles on Qumran and early Christianity, mentioned on p. 166, n. 1. F. M. Braun, 'Hermétisme et Johannisme', *Revue Thomiste*, 1955, pp. 22 ff., 259 ff., comes to a similar conclusion by reference to the Hermetic material. Cf. also W. F. Albright, 'Recent Discoveries in Palestine and the Gospel of St John', in *The Background of the New Testament and its Eschatology* (Essays in honour of C. H. Dodd), ed. W. D. Davies and D. Daube, 1956, pp. 153 ff.

[3] It seems to me that Ebionite Jewish Christianity yields a further confirmation of this. See pp. 188 ff. below.

convictions to play a much more important part in his formulation of Jesus' speeches than do the Synoptic writers. For this reason we may assume that the Son of Man idea is particularly familiar to him, since he uses the title and concept in decisive passages.[1]

The fact that like the Synoptic writers John uses υἱὸς τοῦ ἀνθρώπου rather than the simple Pauline ἄνθρωπος indicates that at least at this point he knows a tradition in common with the Synoptic writers, the tradition which distinguishes between the technical and general sense of *barnasha* by means of this special Greek translation.

Several passages in which the Johannine Christ designates himself 'Son of Man' thus clearly presuppose the characteristic interpretation of this concept. We read in John 3.13: 'No one has ascended into heaven but he who descended from heaven, the Son of Man.' There can be no doubt that the author is fully aware of what he is saying here, and that he thinks of the descent of the pre-existent divine Heavenly Man who comes to earth, enters fallen humanity and ascends again to heaven in glory. It is characteristic of the Johannine use of the expression that in almost all passages the exaltation of the Son of Man is emphasized, and that the title does not describe him in terms of his natural human weakness. The genuine Johannine view of the unity of the Incarnate and the Exalted One[2] is especially appropriate for expressing the fundamental Christological idea of the connection between the divine Son of Man and the Suffering Servant of God. Thus the very next verse, John 3.14, says that the Son of Man 'must be lifted up'. We know that according to Johannine usage, the verb ὑψωθῆναι means both 'to be raised up on the cross' and 'to be raised up (exalted) to God'.[3]

In John 12.23 and 13.31 Jesus designates himself Son of Man again precisely in view of his 'glorification', although these passages too unite the glorification with his death: 'The hour has come for the Son of Man to be glorified.'

Even the passages which use 'Son of Man' in connection with Jesus' earthly vocation consider it an explicit title of majesty, and thus point to the divine Heavenly Man. We hear in John 1.51 of 'the

[1] This also holds good for S. Schulz, *Untersuchungen zur Menschensohn-Christologie im Johannesevangelium*, 1957. He sees in the extensive use of the Son of Man concept evidence of the later Jewish apocalyptic 'native soil' of the Gospel.

[2] See my *Early Christian Worship*, pp. 38 ff.; *Les sacrements dans l'Evangile johannique*, 1951, pp. 9 ff.

[3] O. Cullmann, 'Der johanneische Gebrauch doppeldeutiger Ausdrücke als Schlüssel zum Verständnis des vierten Evangeliums', *TZ* 4, 1948, pp. 360 ff.

angels of God ascending and descending upon the Son of Man' while he dwells on earth. It is significant that this reference to Gen. 28.12 is applied to Jesus as the Son of Man. The bridge between heaven and earth is no longer geographically defined, but is connected with the person of Jesus Christ. Heaven is 'open' since the Son of Man descended from there to men on earth. Thanks to this man who is the image of God, now men can see into heaven.

John 5.27 mentions the Son of Man's function as judge: the Father 'has given him authority to execute judgment because he is the Son of Man'. Wendt's conjecture that the genitive ἀνθρώπου should be eliminated to make the text read 'because he is the Son' is neither necessary nor convincing.[1] We have seen on the contrary that the judicial office belongs to the Son of Man by his very nature[2] —whether the judgment is future or present or (as in the Gospel of John) both.

The Son of Man appears again in 6.27 and 6.53 as the exalted Lord of the Church, who in the present gives the bread of life in the sacrament of the eucharist. It would be interesting to investigate more closely this idea of the Gospel of John that the Exalted One precisely in his character as the Heavenly Man, the Son of Man, gives his body, the incorrupt divine image, as nourishment.

Having seen that we may follow a specifically Christological use of the designation through the entire Gospel of John, we are not surprised to read in 9.35 that Jesus asks the man born blind, 'Do you believe in the Son of Man?'[3] The question presupposes that the reader knows to whom the title refers. Thus we must assume that the writer of the Fourth Gospel, like Paul, is quite familiar with the Son of Man concept; in fact, that this idea constitutes his fundamental Christological interpretation. This conclusion agrees completely with our conjecture that this Gospel must have originated in an environment where apparently already in Judaism there were reflections about the Son of Man.

The assertion that 'Son of Man' is a basic Christological concept of the Gospel of John will be contradicted by those who from the point of view of the prologue think that this Gospel considers Jesus primarily as the Logos, the Word. We certainly do not wish to underestimate the significance of the Logos concept. We shall devote a chapter to it in which it will receive full appreciation. Nevertheless,

[1] H. H. Wendt, *Das Johannesevangelium*, 1900, p. 121. [2] See pp. 157 ff. above.

[3] Most exegetes agree that the reading υἱὸς θεοῦ is secondary. See J. H. Bernard, *The Gospel According to St John* (ICC), 1928, p. 338.

one cannot deny that the Son of Man concept is much more important than that of the Logos in the Gospel of John as a whole.

Moreover, we see how closely the two concepts are related when we consider that both of them presuppose the idea of pre-existence. The Logos too is with God at the beginning, and he exists with God just as the 'image of God' exists with him. Héring has even asserted, perhaps not incorrectly, that the author of John uses σάρξ instead of the ἄνθρωπος we would have expected in 1.14, because he knew that this 'Word' which was with God in the beginning was already then the divine Man in the sense we have described the term. For this reason the evangelist could not say 'he became man', but wrote instead 'he became flesh'.[1] This thesis would be even more probable if, as has been suggested, a pre-Christian hymn to the Original Man really lay behind the prologue to this Gospel.[2]

At any rate, the closing verses of the prologue, John 1.14–18, seem to refer directly to the Son of Man: 'We have beheld his glory (δόξα), glory as the only Son from the Father.' This verse reminds us forcefully of the Pauline expositions about Jesus as the image of God. Because Jesus Christ is the image of God, we are now able to know God himself. It is God's own glory we see when we see Christ. 'No one has ever seen God; the only Son . . . he has made him known' (v. 18). The same idea also plays an important part in I John.

'Son of Man' occurs twice in the Book of the Revelation: '. . . in the midst of the lampstands (I saw) one like a son of man' (1.13); 'Then I looked, and lo, a white cloud, and seated on the cloud one like a son of man' (14.14). Both passages clearly refer to Dan. 7.13. The word ὅμοιος (like) may indicate the same apocalyptic mysterious character that the Son of Man has in Daniel.[3] An indirect reference to the idea of Jesus as the Second Adam is present in Rev. 12.3 ff., where the dragon's persecution of the mother of the Messiah who is the founder of a new humanity certainly stands in connection with the serpent's seduction of the mother of fallen humanity.

The Epistle to the Hebrews also deserves special mention in this

[1] See J. Héring, 'Kyrios Anthropos', *RHPR* 16, 1936, pp. 207 ff.

[2] R. Reitzenstein and H. H. Schaeder, *Studien zum antiken Synkretismus aus Iran und Griechenland*, 1926, pp. 306 ff.

[3] R. H. Charles, *The Revelation of St John* (ICC), 1920, I, p. 27, emphasizes that ὡς υἱὸς ἀνθρώπου in apocalyptic means the same as ὁ υἱὸς τοῦ ἀνθρώπου in the Gospels and in Acts. I simply raise the question whether there could be a connection between ἐν ὁμοιώματι ἀνθρώπων in Phil. 2.7 and the ὅμοιος in Rev. 1.13 and 14.14. O. Michel, 'Zur Exegese von Phil. 2.5–11', *op. cit.* on p. 179 n. 1, places the use of Phil 2.7 in the framework of 'apocalyptic style of paraphrase' (pp. 91 f.).

context. Simply because of its (generally neglected) relationship to the Gospel of John, we would expect the idea of the Son of Man to be present here. And in fact we read in Heb. 1.3 that the Son is the 'reflection' (ἀπαύγασμα) of the glory of God and bears the very 'stamp' (χαρακτήρ) of his nature. Heb. 2.5 ff. also merits consideration. This passage deals with the superiority of the Son of Man over the angels, and in this connection the author cites the familiar eighth Psalm: 'What is man that thou art mindful of him, or the son of man that thou carest for him?' Hebrews applies the psalm to Jesus as the Son of Man. The author's interpretation of the citation indicates that he apparently had quite precise information about the Son of Man doctrine.

We conclude from this survey that within early Christianity the 'Hellenists' and the group represented by the Gospel of John especially expressed their faith in Jesus (in close connection with his own self-consciousness) by means of the Son of Man concept, and that Paul gave the concept greater theological depth.

6. *The Son of Man in Jewish Christianity and in the Thought of Irenaeus*

Although on the whole we confine ourselves in this work to the books of the New Testament, at this point we should extend our investigation into the second century. Without investigating all the passages in which the expression 'Son of Man' occurs, we shall consider at least two early Christian authors who are significant for the development of this Christology: the Jewish Christian writer, Hegesippus; and Irenaeus, the Church Father of the second half of the second century, who is theologically much more important.

The report of Hegesippus is important because it throws light on the question of the Christian circles in which the Son of Man title as such survived. The text which is preserved in Eusebius' *Ecclesiastical History* (II, 23.4–18) contains the following account: James, the brother of Jesus, was asked to speak to the people. They led him to the battlement of the temple and said to him: 'O just one, to whom we all owe obedience, since the people are straying after Jesus who was crucified, tell us what is the gate of Jesus?' James answered with a loud voice: 'Why do you ask me about the Son of Man? He is sitting in heaven on the right hand of great power and he will come on the clouds of heaven.' The report goes on to say that the Pharisees and scribes threw James down from the battlement of the temple and stoned him. Since he was still alive, a laundryman beat him to death with his club.

What interests us in this story is James' identification of Jesus as the Son of Man by reference to Jesus' own words before the high priest. It is at least certain that the Jewish Christian Hegesippus attributed this saying to James. E. Lohmeyer believes that the passage confirms his thesis that the expectation of the Son of Man was a Galilean one,[1] but there is no clear evidence here to support the thesis. Rather we should ask whether this report also is not the result of a Jewish Christian effort formally to preserve an old tradition without grasping (as Paul did, for example) its deeper meaning. But as we have seen above, we must also consider the fact that Adam/Son of Man speculations (in a distorted form and connected with the idea of the Prophet) play no insignificant role in the Jewish Christian source, the Pseudo-Clementine *Preaching of Peter*. Here Adam is the perfect 'True Prophet', who is repeatedly reincarnated and finally appears in Jesus and in the coming Son of Man. We encounter here Ebionite Christianity, which settled across the Jordan after the fall of Jerusalem and, isolated from the general development of the ancient Church, became reactionary and distorted, on the one hand falling into a rigid legalism, and on the other hand laying itself open to syncretistic and Gnostic tendencies. I have tried to show elsewhere [2] that especially this branch of ancient Christianity adopted features of that esoteric, more or less Gnostic Judaism we have come to know in the Qumran texts. Certainly the Jewish Christian Adam/Original Man speculations are connected with these influences. However, we emphasize again that the Jewish Christians did not develop these ideas theologically in a really Christian sense as Paul did (although he himself does not place the title Son of Man in the foreground of his thought).

We are on an entirely different level when we speak of Irenaeus. He was the only one of the ecclesiastical writers of the second century to grasp the depth of Paul's idea about the Son of Man. His entire Christology is dominated by the contrast between Adam and Christ, and he makes the only attempt in the whole history of doctrine to build a Christology on the concept 'Man'. In his *Adversus Haereses* V, 21.1, having pointed out the exact parallelism between the deeds of

[1] E. Lohmeyer, *Galiläa und Jerusalem*, pp. 68 ff. See pp. 164 f. above.

[2] O. Cullmann, 'Die neuentdeckten Qumran-Texte und das Judenchristentum der Pseudoklementinen', *BZNW* 21, pp. 35 ff.

Adam and Jesus, Irenaeus writes: 'The Lord professes himself to be the Son of Man, comprising in himself the first man . . . so that through a victorious man we may rise again to life, just as through a vanquished man our human race descended into death. As through a man death obtained victory over us, so again by a man we may attain victory over death.'

Irenaeus thinks that in order to understand Jesus' work, we must go back to the story of creation. Jesus completes the divine creation of man. He fulfils the role which God assigned to man at creation and for which he created him. Irenaeus always considered it his primary task to combat the Gnostics by emphasizing the connection between creation and redemption, between the Old and New Testaments. Therefore his Christology too is governed entirely by this motive. But it is precisely the concept of the Son of Man as the Second Adam which establishes the Christological connection with the idea of creation.

Both in his *Adversus Haereses* and in his theological sketch, *The Demonstration of the Apostolic Preaching*, Irenaeus shows how Jesus point by point assumed the work of Adam, but in such a way that he accomplished what Adam did not accomplish and thus restored what was lost in Adam's fall. It is characteristic of Irenaeus, however, that he emphasizes almost exclusively the idea of *fulfilment* to the neglect of the idea of *restoration*. For this reason he speaks of Adam's sin with a certain indulgence, and actually excuses it. In contrast to the apologist Tatian, who taught the eternal damnation of Adam, Irenaeus proclaims the possibility of his salvation. The curse falls on the serpent rather than on Adam. He attempts to represent Adam's sin as a necessity: Adam was like a child; he sinned only because of immaturity. Thus Jesus appears in Irenaeus' thought as the one who fulfils Adam's deficient work rather than as the one who makes good Adam's sin.

Irenaeus also stresses the fact that Adam was made in the image of God more strongly than the fact that he lost this image through sin. In his *Demonstration* he glorifies God's creation of man. God made man with his own hand. He put man on earth as his own image. Then the author describes how God made Adam the lord of the whole creation, and continues: But this task was too great for him. Adam was a child; he lacked maturity. Therefore he fell before the Tempter. We see that Irenaeus, unlike Philo and the Jewish Christians, had a completely linear concept of time in *Heilsgeschichte*: everything strives forward from the very beginning. Redemption at the end is not simply a return to the beginning. Christ brings more than was there at the beginning.

We have seen that the greatness of Paul's conception of Christ the Heavenly Man is his relating without identifying Jesus and Adam. Redemption thus does not consist simply of a return to Adam, since, on the contrary, Jesus brought something entirely new in his incarnation. Irenaeus took up this correct idea, but in such a way that he carries it to excess by a too exclusive emphasis on the continuity of the development of salvation. Despite his greatness, it must be objected that he did not sufficiently consider that it was precisely as the Son of Man that Jesus undertook the *ebed Yahweh*'s role. Irenaeus did not see as Paul did (Rom. 5.12 ff.) that Jesus' task in relation to Adam consists not just in fulfilling Adam's uncompleted work, but in correcting his sin, without which the fulfilment of his task is not possible. Irenaeus did not take seriously enough Adam's sin as an act of revolt. He did not understand that by his sin Adam broke the line of *Heilsgeschichte*, so that it can be continued only when its continuity is restored by the *atonement*.

With this reservation, we may acknowledge the great theological value of Irenaeus' interpretation of Jesus as the Second Adam. He likes to emphasize the complete correspondence of Jesus' life with Adam's (but in such a way that Jesus always fulfils all things). Thus Jesus was born of a virgin just as Adam was formed out of virginal earth (virginal because it had not yet rained). The fall of Adam came from the disobedience of a virgin, Eve; the redeeming work of Jesus came to pass through the obedience of a virgin, Mary. Irenaeus sees a further parallel of a more external kind in the concrete object which drove Adam to sin and the one through which Jesus corrected that sin: the tree of whose fruit Adam ate, the tree of disobedience, corresponds to that other tree in the history of the Second Adam, the cross, the tree of obedience. The fact that Irenaeus adds still other examples in *Adversus Haereses* shows how deeply he was impressed by the idea that Jesus is the Second Adam.

He shows, for example, how the temptation to which Adam fell consisted of a forbidden act of eating, whereas Jesus resisted Satan precisely by refusing to break his fast. The following parallel in *Adversus Haereses* V, 21.2 is theologically more significant: Satan tempts both Adam and Jesus, and the content of both temptations is the same. In the Genesis account, the devil offers Adam equality with God, exactly as he offers it to Jesus in the Gospel story. In both cases he wants to cause the intended victim to transgress the limits set for him by God. The immature Adam lets himself be seduced, but Jesus withstands the temptation of human pride which grasps for equality with God. We have seen that this is the basic idea of the fundamental Christological text, Phil. 2.6 ff. In so far as he made it the foundation of his Christology, Irenaeus grasped this basic idea quite clearly.

After Irenaeus the specific biblical conception of the Son of Man was more and more forgotten. It is true that the expression 'Son of Man' often occurs in later theological interpretations of Christology, but it is used only to indicate the lowliness of Jesus—his 'human nature'. In this later period 'human nature' refers only to Christ's entrance into the flesh, that is, into *sinful* nature. Later writers no longer consider at all precisely the essential idea that Christ was already the Son of Man in his pre-existence, and that he will appear as the Son of Man at his return. It was entirely forgotten that in this sense the designation Son of Man means the same as the assertion that Jesus is the 'image of God'. At best we find here and there in the later history of theology (in Schleiermacher, for instance) weak indications of the idea that Jesus is the 'original pattern of humanity'. In recent times Karl Barth has performed the service of making quite new use of the *imago Dei* Christologically.[1] But we still have no utilization of all aspects of the specific Son of Man concept as it is presupposed in the New Testament. It would be interesting to investigate at least the tendencies toward a Son of Man Christology in the history of Christian doctrine and theology.

It would be still more important if a modern theologian would undertake to build a Christology entirely on the New Testament idea of the Son of Man. Not only would such a Christology be entirely oriented toward the New Testament and go back to Jesus' self-designation; it would also have the advantage of putting the logically insoluble problem of the two natures of Christ on a level where the solution becomes visible: the pre-existent Son of Man, who is with God already at the very beginning and exists with him as his image, is *by his very nature* divine Man. From this point of view the whole toilsome discussion which dominated the earlier Christological controversies actually becomes superfluous.

[1] Especially in *Church Dogmatics* III/1. See the work of the Old Testament scholar, J. J. Stamm, 'Die Imago-Lehre von Karl Barth und die alttestamentliche Wissenschaft', *Antwort* (volume in honour of K. Barth), 1956, pp. 84 ff. In connection with the exaltation of Christ the concept of the Son of Man plays an important role in *Church Dogmatics* IV/2.

PART THREE

The Christological Titles which Refer to the Present Work of Jesus

THE CHRISTOLOGICAL ASPECT we have now to consider is given due value in the theology of the New Testament, but Protestant systematic theologians have neglected it to a large extent. Yet it was this very aspect which was of primary importance, if not in their theological thought, at least in the Church life of the first Christians. We must therefore give special attention to this side of Christ's work. That Christ continues his work since his exaltation is by no means a 'Catholic' invention, but a fundamental idea of the whole New Testament. It was just for this reason, for instance, that the Gospel of John was written. We have seen that some of the titles we have already considered (especially 'High Priest') refer also to the present work of the Christ exalted to the right hand of God. But above all in this context we must speak of a Christological concept which points primarily to the exalted Christ. It is the concept Jesus as Lord. Its importance for early Christianity cannot be overstated.

7

Jesus the Lord

(κύριος)

THIS DESIGNATION expresses as does no other the thought that Christ is exalted to God's right hand, glorified, and now intercedes for men before the Father. In designating Jesus as the *Kyrios* the first Christians declared that he is not only a part of divine *Heilsgeschichte* in the past, nor just the object of future hope, but a living reality in the present—so alive that he can enter into fellowship with us now, so alive that the believer prays to him, and the Church appeals to him in worship, to bring their prayers before God the Father and make them effective. Both the individual Christian and the gathered Church experience in faith the fact that Jesus lives and continues his work. The Church as the Body of Christ is founded on faith in the exalted Christ who still intervenes in earthly events. The first Christians expressed this deep conviction in their confession of faith *Kyrios Jesus*, 'Jesus is Lord'.

1. *The* Kyrios *Title in Oriental-Hellenistic Religions and in Emperor Worship*

Because the designation *Kyrios* for Jesus developed into a Christological title especially in the environment of Hellenism, it is proper that we investigate its secular and religious significance in this area outside Christianity. Since there were quite concrete and generally familiar concepts of the designation here, we must assume from the very beginning that the Christians in Hellenistic areas were conscious of a relation between these conceptions and the title as they used it. We shall see that this is in fact the case. But that is not to say that we can accept the much discussed thesis advocated by W. Bousset in his *Kyrios Christos*[1] that this title for Jesus was adopted only under Hellenistic influence and in a Hellenistic environment. We shall have

[1] W. Bousset, *Kyrios Christos*, 1st ed., 1913; 2nd ed., 1921.

to investigate this thesis in detail. But in any case Bousset has directed our attention to the importance of the *Kyrios* in oriental-Hellenistic religions.

In the first place, we must not forget the obvious fact that in the Hellenistic world too *Kyrios* was used not only in connection with certain *religious* conceptions, but also (as the equivalents of the word in all languages suggest) in the general sense of 'master' or 'owner'. Especially as an address, *Kyrie*, it often became fixed as a mere form of politeness which meant nothing more than the French *Monsieur*. Bousset's thesis suffers because he does not consider the connection between this secular use and the specifically religious use either of the Greek word or of its Semitic equivalents, which we must later investigate. This is why he can deny that there is a bridge from the general expression of the superiority or ownership of a person called *Kyrios* to the absolute concept of the rule of the *one* divine *Kyrios*. In point of fact one does see a development from the first to the second use in the writings of early Christianity. But precisely with regard to these writings Bousset will not recognize a development. He thinks that the absolute use of the title here is something completely unprecedented: *Kyrios* in the absolute sense of a divine ruler (in Luke and Paul, for instance) is to be explained exclusively by the introduction of Hellenism; in Palestinian thought Jesus was called 'Lord' only in the secular, commonplace sense.

We must emphasize already at this point that Bousset's delimitation and sharp separation of the secular and religious use of the title rests on a fully unjustified *a priori*, and that however necessary may be a distinction between them as such, a development from one to the other must be recognized.

It can be shown that in Hellenism itself there were aspects of the secular application which could lead to the concept of a divine *Kyrios*. A comparison of κύριος with its synonym δεσπότης is instructive in this respect.[1] Although δεσπότης did not yet have the connotation of our word 'despot', it did already suggest the idea of arbitrariness, whereas κύριος suggested the idea of legitimate authority. Only κύριος, not δεσπότης, can lead to the concept of *one* divine Lord.

Thus we can understand without trouble how the expression *Kyrios* could designate *deity* with respect to its absolute power or

[1] See R. C. Trench, *Synonyms of the New Testament*[8], 1876, p. 93; W. Förster, *Herr ist Jesus*, 1924, pp. 61 ff.; K. H. Rengstorf, 'δεσπότης', *TWNT* II, pp. 43 ff.

superiority, and how it actually became a name which emphasized divinity in a unique way. The word in this sense occurs very frequently in the oriental-Hellenistic religions of the Roman Empire. Various scholars have collected examples of it.[1] Here we need only mention that it was quite common. Both the national and mystery religions of Asia Minor, Egypt, and Syria call gods and goddesses (such as Serapis, Osiris and Isis, for instance) *Kyrios* and *Kyria*. When Hellenism speaks simply of THE *Kyrios*, it refers to some especially revered divinity.

It is obvious that Christianity outside Palestine would encounter this use of the word and have to deal with it, but if special confirmation of the fact is necessary, we may cite I Cor. 8.5 f.: '. . . there are many "gods" and many "lords"—yet for us there is only one God . . . and one Lord, Jesus Christ.' For the Christian who knows that all power in heaven and on earth has been given to Jesus since his exaltation, the heathen *kyrioi* are no longer absolute lords, for their authority has been absorbed into that of the one *Kyrios*. Behind this statement of Paul lies of course also the faith (of which we must speak later) [2] that all these *kyrioi*, these 'powers and authorities', have been conquered by Christ, are subject to him, and just for this reason can for us no longer be *kyrioi* in the absolute sense. The paradox of Paul's assertion that there *are* many *kyrioi* and yet that there are *not* points to the distinction we have made between the two uses of the word. The *kyrioi* of the heathen, who claim to be that in an absolute sense, are for the Christian *kyrioi* only in the ordinary sense and have no claim to absolute rule over us.

The same is true also of the Roman emperor, the *Kyrios* who demanded special recognition of his 'lordship'.[3] He was called *Kyrios*

[1] See F. Cumont, *Les religions orientales dans le paganisme romain*[4], 1929; art. 'κύριος' in Pauly-Wissowa, *Realencyclopädie*, Vol. 23, 1924, col. 176 ff. (Williger); art. 'κύριος' in W. H. Roscher, *Ausführliches Lexicon der griechischen und römischen Mythologie* II/1, 1890/94; Bousset, *Kyrios Christos*; W. Förster, *Herr ist Jesus*, pp. 69 ff.; *idem*, 'κύριος', *TWNT* III, pp. 1038 ff.

[2] See pp. 233 ff. below.

[3] See A. Deissmann, *Licht vom Osten*[4], 1923, pp. 287 ff. (ET, rev. ed.: *Light from the Ancient East*, 1927, pp. 338 ff.); P. Wendland, *Die hellenistisch-römische Kultur in ihren Beziehungen zu Judentum und Christentum* (HNT)[2, 3], 1912, pp. 123 ff.; K. Prümm, 'Der Herrscherkult im Neuen Testament', *Biblica* 9, 1928, pp. 1 ff; *idem*, *Religionsgeschichtliches Handbuch für den Raum der altchristlichen Umwelt*, 1943, pp. 54 ff., 83 ff.; Förster, *Herr ist Jesus*, pp. 99 ff.; L. Cerfaux, 'Le titre Kyrios et la dignité royale de Jésus. Le titre et les rois', *Recueil L. Cerfaux*, I, 1954, pp. 3 ff. A full bibliography is given by J. Tondriau, 'Bibliographie de culte des souverains hellenistiques et romains', *Bull. de l'Assoc. G. Budé*, n. s. 5, 1948, pp. 106 ff.

primarily in a political-legal sense, of course, and the title does not refer primarily to his divinity.[1]

Also the adjective κυριακός, which is used in a cultic sense in the New Testament (κυριακὴ ἡμέρα, Lord's day; κυριακὸν δεῖπνον, Lord's supper), appears in the technical language of the Roman administration only in the legal sense of 'imperial'. Thus the imperial finances are called κυριακαὶ ψῆφοι; the imperial treasury κυριακὸς λόγος. See W. Dittenberger, *Orientis Graecae Inscriptiones Selectae*, 1903/05, no. 669.

But we also know that long before Roman times oriental rulers were venerated as gods. The Roman emperors inherited divine dignity from them. They were worshipped because they were believed to be of divine origin and nature. At first only dead Roman emperors were worshipped, but later also living ones. The Roman Empire in the East was naturally the centre of this worship. The emperors soon recognized the value it could have for the unity of the empire and began to demand it. Thus divinity assumed a visible character in the person of the emperor—ἐναργὴς ἐπιφάνειά.

When on the one hand the emperor was called *Kyrios* as a sign of his political power, and on the other hand was revered as divine, the title *Kyrios* must automatically take on a religious significance—especially where this name was a common designation for heathen gods.

W. Förster (*Herr ist Jesus*, pp. 103 ff., and *TWNT* III, pp. 1052 ff.) and others are correct in emphasizing so strongly the fact that in secular texts the designation *kyrios* is applied to the emperor only as a political term and not in direct connection with emperor worship. But in the light of what we have just said, one cannot conclude from this that the name *kyrios* applied to the emperor visualizes only the political ruler and not the god. For it is a fact that the emperor was revered as god, and that in the common religious use of oriental-Hellenistic paganism *kyrios* was a designation for gods. How could it have been possible for the absolute religious sense of the term not to suggest itself when the emperor was called by that name?

It is impossible to make a sharp distinction between acknowledg-

[1] W. Förster, *Herr ist Jesus*, and 'κύριος', *TWNT* II, pp. 1038 ff. (following F. Kattenbusch, *Das apostolische Symbol* II, 1900, pp. 596 ff.) emphasizes this strongly. But in thinking that the political use of *kyrios* and emperor worship can be separated, Förster seems to me to fall into the error of distinguishing too sharply between secular and religious use, the very error in Bousset he seeks to combat. See pp. 207 f. below.

ment of political subjection to the emperor and worshipful subordination to him as god. Not only Christians (*Mart. Polyc.* 8.2)[1] but also non-Christians of this time thought of the absolute religious sense of the word when they heard the formula *Kyrios Kaisar.* According to the ancient view, lordship over the world empire indicates lordship over the cosmos. This in itself is an indication of how close the connection between the secular-political and the religious use of the term must have been. The political recognition Κύριος Καῖσαρ (the emperor is lord) was inevitably religiously coloured and approached the confession θεὸς Καῖσαρ (the emperor is god). The latter expression may be the meaning of the number 616 (a textual variant of 666) in Rev. 13.18.[2]

Whether or not the Jews were exempted from the requirement of actual emperor worship (a question not yet definitely settled), they were at least clearly aware of the consequences of the requirement that all those subject to the Roman Empire must recognize the lordship of the emperor. Information we have about the Zealots proves this.[3]

This brings us to the question of the Jewish concept of the word 'Lord' in its Aramaic, Hebrew and Greek forms. Even if it is certain that the Christian confession *Kyrios Jesus Christos* in the New Testament writings is closely related to the designation for both oriental-Hellenistic deities and the Roman emperor, we must nevertheless guard against Bousset's premature conclusion that one cannot find a Jewish influence on the Christian conception of the term.

2. *The* Kyrios *in Judaism*[4]

The Greek word *kyrios* is אָדוֹן in Hebrew and מָר in Aramaic. We now have to ask whether, like their Greek equivalent, the Hebrew and Aramaic words were used in the New Testament period in

[1] W. Förster, *Herr ist Jesus*, p. 106, attempts to apply the thesis that *Kyrios* applied to the emperor referred only to his *political* claim also to *Martyrdom of Polycarp* 8.2, in which Polycarp is asked, 'What harm is there in saying *Kyrios Kaisar* . . .?' But the whole context of the passage shows that Förster's explanation is not possible here. See p. 220 below.

[2] See the plausible suggestion of A. Deissmann, *Licht vom Osten*[4], p. 238 n. 3 (ET, p. 278 n. 3). See also my book, *The State in the New Testament*, pp. 80 ff.

[3] See especially Josephus, *Bell. Jud.* VII, 10.1. W. Förster, *Herr ist Jesus*, pp. 106 f., cites further texts.

[4] See W. Baudissin, *Kyrios als Gottesname im Judentum und seine Stelle in der Religionsgeschichte*, vols. I-IV, 1926/29; O. Grether, *Name und Wort Gottes im Alten*

the absolute sense of '*the* Lord' as well as in the general sense of 'master' or 'owner'. This is the decisive question for our problem.

We need not give examples of the general use of *Adon*. When it is so used, the substantive does not stand alone, but is qualified by another substantive or suffix to indicate which lord is meant. It is also applied in this way to God—for instance, 'my Lord' or 'the Lord of all the earth'.

It is important to note that the Jews did not speak the name of God, JHVH. After a certain time they replaced it with *Adonai* in their services of worship. We do not know exactly when this substitution took place, but *Adonai* was certainly the characteristic Jewish designation for God in the first century before and the first century after Christ. The substitution may have been made even earlier than this, perhaps even before the Greek translation of the Old Testament, the Septuagint. In any case it was certainly accepted at the time of the rise of Christianity,[1] although the use of *Adonai* in this absolute sense did not become part of everyday speech, and so not a common designation for God either. Other indirect designations such as הַמָּקוֹם (the place) or הַשֵּׁם (the name) were usual.

Nevertheless *Adonai* was unquestionably a substitute for the name of God in the Jewish liturgies. It may be that this fact was formerly emphasized too strongly, but it seems to me that in more recent works it has been underrated. Although the absolute sense of the term was limited to liturgical use, one must still ask how it happened that it was in fact *Adonai* that came to replace JHVH. The very fact that this word was chosen presupposes that it suggested a particular significance. Scholars usually say that it was 'only' characteristic of liturgical use; should not one say rather that if the Jews chose it for the highest possible function of replacing the unspeakable name JHVH in the ceremonial reading of the Word of God in the service of worship, they must have considered *Adonai* the unsurpassable majestic name?[2]

Before we speak of the word *mar*, the Aramaic equivalent of *kyrios*, we must mention in the present context the Greek-speaking Jewish Diaspora. In the Septuagint too we find *kyrios* used not only

Testament, 1934; G. Quell, 'κύριος im AT', *TWNT* III, pp. 1056 ff.; for later Judaism generally: W. Förster, 'κύριος', *TWNT* III, pp. 1081 ff.; for the Septuagint and Hellenistic Judaism in particular: L. Cerfaux, 'Le nom divin "Kyrios" dans la Bible grecque', and 'Adonai et Kyrios', *Recueil L. Cerfaux* I, pp. 113 ff., 137 ff.

[1] So also Baudissin, who usually has the tendency to fix dates as early as possible.

[2] This is very important for the explanation of Phil. 2.9, in which the name *Kyrios* is designated the 'name which is above every name'. See p. 217 below.

in the secular sense, but also in the absolute sense actually as the name of God and as the translation for both *Adonai* and JHVH. We do not know exactly how the translators came to use *kyrios* in this way.

There are two major explanations of the fact. According to the first, it happened as a result of the influence of the Hellenistic designation for gods; according to the other, it happened precisely as a result of the influence of the liturgical use of the Hebrew *Adonai* for JHVH. The first explanation is not valid, because we have no evidence of the use of *kyrios* as a designation for gods in the Hellenistic world *before* the time of the Septuagint. The question of date is of course also relevant for the second explanation, which is possible only if *Adonai* was read in place of JHVH before that translation. Whether this is actually the case is a disputed point.[1] However that may be, we have already seen that since *Adonai* was chosen at a certain time for the highest liturgical role, it must long before then have had an especially exalted significance. The translators of the Septuagint must also have known this. For this reason the Greek word *Kyrios* quite naturally suggested itself to them.

Of course the absolute application of *Kyrios* to God did not at first penetrate into the everyday language even of Greek-speaking Judaism. It was understood and respected primarily as a sacral word. We discover it in Josephus, for instance, only in prayers and Old Testament citations; otherwise he does not usually speak of God as ὁ κύριος.[2] This use is more common in the Greek apocryphal and pseudepigraphic writings.

We conclude, then, that *Adonai-Kyrios* was a liturgical designation for God both in Palestinian and Diaspora Judaism of the New Testament period.

What of the Aramaic equivalent *mar*? It is especially interesting to us here, first, because Jesus himself as well as his first disciples spoke Aramaic; and secondly, because the New Testament has preserved the Aramaic liturgical prayer *Maranatha* of the early Church. We must investigate this prayer presently, but first we must ask whether there is evidence that the Aramaic *Mar*, like the Hebrew *Adonai* and the Greek *Kyrios*, was used in the absolute sense of '*the* Lord' (i.e., God) as well as in the general sense of 'master' or 'owner' and in the sense of an ordinary polite form of address. This precise point cannot be affirmed for the pre-Christian period;[3] *Mar* does not occur

[1] Thus above all Baudissin, *op. cit.*, but see W. Förster, *TWNT* III, p. 1082, and the two studies of C. Cerfaux mentioned in the note opposite.

[2] See A. Schlatter, *Wie sprach Josephus von Gott?*, 1910.

[3] G. Dalman, *The Words of Jesus*, pp. 179 ff.

as a divine title in this absolute sense—not even in Dan. 2.47 and 5.23. But every Jew must have known that in Hebrew God is called 'the Lord', *Adonai*. We must on no account forget this. In everyday language *Mari* was a very respectful form of polite address similar to 'Rabbi', which means more than simply 'Teacher' and may be translated as *Kyrie* in Greek. *Mari* expresses even greater respect than 'Rabbi'. It was used to refer to king and emperor, but also to highly respected teachers. The double form 'Lord, Lord' (*Mari*, *Mari*), like double 'Rabbi, Rabbi', indicates very special respect.[1] But even this use is still far removed from the absolute sense.

We have seen that in Hellenistic thought *Kyrios* developed from the general meaning 'lord' to the absolute meaning '*the* Lord'. The same is true of *Adon* in Hebrew thought. If these two words manifest such a development from the one to the other meaning, then such a development cannot *a priori* be excluded for the transition from the Aramaic designation *Mari* (which originally expressed only the relation between Jesus and his disciples during his lifetime) to the one *Kyrios Jesus* (which was characteristic especially for the faith in Christ of Hellenistic Churches). Therefore one cannot too quickly assert, as do W. Bousset and R. Bultmann (who agrees with him completely), that there is no development here, but only an immediate transition under Hellenistic influence to something completely new. That is, one cannot say that Jesus was first *worshipped* as *the* Lord in a Hellenistic environment.

We can prove the existence of such a bridge from the general to the absolute in the case of *mar* only in our next section when we investigate the early Church's post-Easter faith in the exalted Christ. The same disciples who during Jesus' lifetime had expressed only their role as followers with the address 'my Lord'—these disciples encountered him after his death as the exalted Christ who was present in the Church's worship and who demanded absolute devotion of his people. This is the real foundation for a linguistic connection between the Aramaic *Mari* and the Christian conception of the κύριος. In other words, the application to Jesus of the Hellenistic use of the *Kyrios* and of the *Kyrios* passages in the Septuagint does not mean philologically and theologically a new beginning, but is connected with the Aramaic use.

Bousset asserts that the actual foundation for the *cultic worship* of Jesus as *Kyrios* is to be found in a Hellenistic environment (first of all

[1] See the example in Dalman, *ibid.*, p. 325. This is relevant for understanding 'Lord, Lord' in Matt. 7.21.

in Antioch), not in the original Palestinian Church. This assertion is the basis of his rejection on principle of the linguistic derivation of the Greek Κύριος Χριστός from the Aramaic *Mari*. We can therefore take a final position regarding his far-reaching thesis only in our next section when we speak of the faith of the early Church in the exalted Christ. Now we wish only to indicate that the development of the Hellenistic concept κύριος and of the Hebraic concept *Adon* suggests philologically an analogous development from the naive use of the Aramaic *Mar* to the Christian theological significance of the Greek κύριος—with the presupposition, of course, that this *theological* development to a cultic and individual experience and worship of the present exalted Lord had taken place already among the Aramaic-speaking Palestinian followers of Jesus. We shall see that this is in fact the case. The Aramaic prayer *Maranatha* forms both a factual and a philological link between *Mari* and κύριος.

We have still another question to ask concerning 'the Lord' in Judaism: Did the Jews designate the *Messiah* as 'Lord'? We can hardly consider the few rabbinical passages in which the Messiah receives the Yahweh name [1] as examples of such a connection. It seems to me that Jesus' explanation of Ps. 110 in Mark 12.35 ff. and parallels is more important for this question. We have already spoken of this passage [2] and shall speak of it again. Jesus' whole argument rests on the idea that David calls the Messiah his 'Lord'. One may of course not conclude from this that the Messiah bore that title as such in Judaism. Nevertheless the passage in Mark seems to me to confirm once again that already in Judaism the word 'Lord', depending upon the circumstances in which it was used, could be given a special significance which makes possible a development from a secular meaning to the 'name which is above every name'.

3. Kyrios Jesus *and Early Christianity*

It is not necessary for us to devote a special section to the question whether and in what sense Jesus designated himself *Kyrios*. We shall deal with this question in the context of the early Christian faith, for it is certain that the *Kyrios* title applied to Jesus received its full meaning only after his death and exaltation. It is characteristic of the expression *Kyrios Jesus* that it refers to his post-Easter, present work fulfilled in the state of exaltation. The title thus naturally developed

[1] W. Heitmüller, *Im Namen Jesu*, 1903, p. 273.

[2] See pp. 130 f. above.

with the salvation event itself. The first Christians perceived this when they emphasized that God 'has *made* him both Lord and Christ' (Acts 2.36), that only after his obedience as the *ebed Yahweh* God 'more than exalted him' and bestowed upon him this *Kyrios* name, the 'name which is above every name' (Phil. 2.9).

Therefore we do not expect to hear the earthly Jesus using the *Kyrios* designation in its full meaning. It does appear indirectly in the above-mentioned passage, Mark 12.35 ff. and parallels, in which Jesus cites Ps. 110 to show that Davidic sonship is not definitive for the Messiah. It appears directly in Mark 11.3 ('say "The Lord has need of it . . ." ') and in Matt. 7.21 ('Not every one who says to me "Lord, Lord" . . .'). None of these passages indicates the *absolute* use of *Kyrios* as we find it applied to Jesus in early Christianity. On the other hand, we do see in these three examples that the word can be given different meanings according to the context in which it is used. One cannot simply say that in all these cases *Kyrios* means only 'Teacher'.

It is true that the absolute use is not yet present even in Mark 12.35 ff. and parallels. This passage refers to the *Kyrios* of David. Nevertheless the designation takes on a very special importance when it is the foundation of the whole argument to prove the superiority of the Messiah over David the king. The idea is at least in the background that human descent can be of no importance whatever for the Messiah whom David calls *Kyrios*.

Mark 11.3 must be differently evaluated. This passage even uses the article with *Kyrios* (ὁ κύριος), and since it is the only passage in the whole book in which the title so appears, we could say that it is not typical of Mark, but represents the precise memory that Jesus himself used the expression. But even so, we cannot conclude that on this occasion Jesus designated himself *the* divine *Kyrios*. In the first place, the original Aramaic here may have been 'our Lord' or 'his Lord'; and in the second place (the more probable explanation), *mar* may have been used here simply as an expression of the disciple-rabbi relationship.

The same is true of the third example, Matt. 7.21. The genuineness of this saying as such cannot be questioned. We have seen that the doubled 'Lord, Lord' corresponds to the Semitic form of polite address.[1] Like the previous passage, this also probably refers to the address of the disciple to a respected master.

But it is just this last example (along with a similar one in John

[1] See p. 202 above.

13.13: 'You call me Teacher and Lord') which proves that the disciple–rabbi relationship can give the designation *Kyrios* in particular situations a significance which far exceeds the dignity of an ordinary teacher. When this rabbi appears with a special claim on the whole person of his disciple, when he actually makes the disciple his δοῦλος (slave), and by virtue of his special authority compels the disciple to absolute voluntary obedience—then it is clear that the title *Kyrios* goes beyond a polite form of address and actually becomes the expression of an absolute total claim, which correspondingly gives also the concept δοῦλος an absolute meaning. 'Rabbi' and *mari* mean more than just 'Teacher' when, as in the case of Jesus, the rabbi attributes to himself the authority to forgive sins. True, this use of *Kyrios* in terms of the disciple-rabbi relationship is still far removed from the later absolute use, in terms of which the Christians are actually called 'those who call on the name of our Lord Jesus Christ'.[1] Nevertheless the earlier use suggests the possibility of the same development to the absolute use we discovered in the case of the Hellenistic *Kyrios* and the Hebraic *Adon*. When the Rabbi Jesus becomes the object of *cultic veneration*, the Teacher and Lord who speaks and acts with absolute authority becomes the *one* Lord.

Is Bousset right in maintaining that such cultic veneration is possible only in a Hellenistic environment, at the very earliest in Antioch? Is this worship of the 'Lord' really so foreign to the original Palestinian Church? Is it really true that for that Church only the coming Son of Man is of importance, but not the exalted, present Lord? If such were the case, then the indispensable connecting link for the development from the Aramaic *Mar* to the unique *Kyrios* really is missing. For that reason, the Palestinian Church is the key to our problem.

We must come to terms with Bousset, not only because his book *Kyrios Christos* (which has already been more or less put aside) is rightly considered the classical work on the question,[2] but above all because R. Bultmann has again made Bousset's thesis relevant. In his *Theology of the New Testament* I, pp. 52 f., 121 ff., Bultmann accepts the thesis without reservation.

Bousset believes that his thesis (that there is no connection between the Aramaic address for Jesus and the *Kyrios* title) is confirmed by the fact that one can find the absolute application of that title to Jesus

[1] I Cor. 1.2; II Tim. 2.22. Cf. Acts 9.14, 21.

[2] On the question he raises, see also E. v. Dobschütz, 'κύριος Ἰησοῦς', *ZNW* 30, 1931, pp. 97 ff.

only in the early Christian literature characterized by extra-Palestinian influences. It is a fact that in the Synoptics neither Mark nor Matthew ever calls Jesus this (except for Mark 11.3, in which Jesus is called 'the Lord'), whereas Luke, in the very passages peculiar to that Gospel, does so more often. In the same way we find the title used more and more often in the absolute sense in the other early Christian writings which belong in the Hellenistic environment. These observations are correct. But they do not prove that the absolute use of the title was possible only on Hellenistic ground because worship of Christ first began there. Without doubt the Hellenistic belief in divine *Kyrioi* and (for the Jews of the Diaspora) the Septuagint's use of *Kyrios* for the divine name had a strong influence and powerfully demanded that the absolute use of *Kyrios* be applied to Jesus in Christianity. This is the explanation of the more and more frequent designation of Jesus by this title in Hellenistic Christianity. But the designation presupposes that Jesus was already before this the object of cultic veneration.

It can by no means be proved that the Hellenistic Churches were the first to worship Jesus as divine. It can be proved neither by the philological observations we have discussed, nor by the fact that *Kyrios* was a designation for Hellenistic gods. We shall in fact see that precisely a philological consideration clearly contradicts Bousset's thesis. But first we shall investigate the sources at our disposal concerning the history of early Christian worship, in order to see whether it is really true that the earliest Church did not yet worship Jesus. But one cannot legitimately approach these sources with a prejudiced opinion.

It is not a valid procedure arbitrarily and *a priori* to consider all the statements of Acts about the early Church as anachronisms and all the views and experiences ascribed to the Church in Jerusalem as Hellenistic. The manner in which some scholars distinguish between the *kerygma* of the very early Church and that of the Hellenistic Church often rests on a really naive confidence in purely artificial, subjective assumptions and oversimplifications. In this way, for instance, some simply make the very early Church into a Jewish-eschatological sect. Everything which really distinguishes Christianity from Judaism is called 'Hellenistic'. So-called 'consistent eschatology' with its relentlessly applied prejudices has strongly contributed to this scientifically questionable method. The recently discovered Qumran texts are especially valuable for putting an end to such oversimplifications, because Palestinian Judaism itself appears in them less than ever the unified whole which scholars have liked to contrast with Hellenism.

We must above all ask why, after the death of Christ, a particular community was founded at all. If the very early Church really had *only* a future expectation, if only the *coming* Son of Man was Christologically significant for it, then it would be impossible to explain the impulse to form a Church in which enthusiasm ruled and the working of the Spirit determined the whole of life.

It is true that hope for the end was especially intense—more so than at any time in Judaism. But this was true precisely because the community of the disciples was firmly convinced that Christ's resurrection had already introduced the end time. Already realized possession gave their hope for the first time the absolute confidence in the consummation which characterized their attitude. But this was also important for their Christological views. On the basis of the conviction that with Christ's resurrection the end had already begun, the first Christians could no longer think of him only as the coming Son of Man. He must mean something also for the present, for time already fulfilled. The intense hope that the end is near is not the foundation but the consequence of the Easter faith. The resurrection of Jesus stands at the centre of the Christian faith, and who will maintain that this faith came for the first time outside Palestine? But if Jesus is risen from the dead, then death is already overcome and the transition from one aeon to another has taken place.

Even if the first Christians did expect only a short interim between the resurrection and the second coming, they must nevertheless have had a definite understanding of Christ's present, continued work during this short interim. He has died and risen, and he will come again. But he must have a task to fulfil also between these two salvation-events. His work cannot simply cease in the meantime.

Bousset is right in connecting faith in Christ's present lordship with the Church's worship. This is indeed the place where it was revealed to the community of Christians that God not only resurrected him but gave him lordship, 'made' him to be the *Kyrios* (Rom. 1.4; Acts 2.36). But this worship took place in the very earliest Church, and not for the first time in Antioch.

W. Förster, whose works we have already cited,[1] is certainly correct in contesting Bousset's assumption of a Hellenistic origin of the Christian title *Kyrios*. He also correctly emphasizes the significant theological idea

[1] In addition to the work of W. Förster and W. Bousset on the whole complex of the *Kyrios* name, see the various articles of L. Cerfaux now collected in *Recueil L. Cerfaux* (*Bibl. Ephem. Theol. Lovaniensium*, vol. 6–7) I, 1954. See also his article 'κύριος', *Dictionnaire de la Bible*, suppl. vol. V, pp. 200 ff.

of Christ's absolute claim on the disciples. But it does not seem to me that this is enough to explain the origin of the *Kyrios* faith. Förster seems to me to throw out the baby with the bath water when he does not give the foundation of that faith in early Christian worship the attention it deserves. Bousset is not unjustified in seeking in Church worship the origin of the *Kyrios* faith; he is wrong only in his prejudiced assumption that such worship, in which Christ was experienced as *Kyrios*, could have first taken place only in Hellenistic congregations.

Christ's present lordship must be experienced not only as individual revelation, but as Christological revelation of his present form of existence, and this happened in the first gatherings for worship.

In the course of these worship services, in which bread was broken 'with glad and generous hearts' (Acts 2.46), the presence of the risen Christ was experienced ever anew as a reality. The goal of these services was precisely the realization of fellowship with the same risen Christ who had appeared to his assembled disciples at a meal on Easter Sunday. As I have tried to show in various works on early Christian worship,[1] this realization of fellowship was the meaning of public worship in the earliest Church. The 'appearance meals', if we may call them that, helped the early Church to experience always afresh the presence of the Lord, even if not so tangibly as he was experienced during the 'forty days' after Easter.

There is no reason at all, then, for contesting the fact that the very earliest community called Jesus 'the Lord'. He was considered the invisible Lord who rules his Church and appears in worship among the brothers 'where two or three are gathered in his name'—although at the same time he sits at the right hand of God and rules the whole world.

But, as we have already indicated, Bousset's thesis is untenable also from a philological point of view. The oldest liturgical formula we possess contains the title *Kyrios* in its Aramaic form. It is the very ancient prayer of the Church, *Maranatha*, which we find in the New Testament in I Cor. 16.22. The early date of this formula is proved by the fact that the Apostle preserves its original Aramaic form in a letter written in Greek to a Greek-speaking Church. He must have received it through the very earliest Church tradition. In his Greek letters Paul preserves in Aramaic precisely the oldest characteristic prayers of the first Church. Another prayer in Aramaic, *Abba* (Father), occurs twice in theological discussions of prayer (Rom.

[1] See especially O. Cullmann, *Early Christian Worship*, pp. 12 ff.

8.15, Gal. 4.6). This probably refers to the beginning of the Lord's Prayer.[1]

The formula *Maranatha* occurs at the end of I Corinthians in a definitely liturgical context. It is transliterated into Greek. Written in Hebrew characters the word reads מרנאתא. What does this mean? It is certain that it begins with the Aramaic *Mar*, 'Lord'. We have seen that this can be used as a polite form of address, but the context in which the expression is used shows that this cannot be the case here. Before we can say what meaning the word 'Lord' has here, then, we must investigate the framework in which the Aramaic formula is spoken. First we consider the second element of the expression, which is a form of the Aramaic verb 'to come'. A difficulty arises because there are two possible meanings according to the way one analyses the formula. One can propose either of the following divisions:

Maran-atha: מרן אתא

or

Marana-tha: מרנא תא

In the first case the verb form is a third person indicative and the formula should be translated: 'Our Lord comes.'[2] In the second case, it is an imperative and the formula should be translated: 'Our Lord, come!' The first would be a confession; the second a prayer. Both possibilities are grammatically and theoretically correct;[3] in both cases the formula would have a liturgical character.

Nevertheless, the second possibility seems to me the more probable. It is *a priori* easier to understand why a prayer formula should be maintained in the original language than why a liturgical confession should be. A saying of the latter type would more likely have called for translation. We find in fact that in the New Testament the relatively many confessional formulas have been without exception translated into Greek. On the other hand, we have previously mentioned that besides the formula in question here, Paul also preserves in Aramaic precisely a characteristic prayer address: *Abba*, Father.

But there is a further argument which may well be considered decisive. In the last verse but one of the Revelation, a book which in

[1] More particularly, with the simple form of address in Luke 11.2.

[2] See E. Hommel, 'Maran atha', *ZNW* 15, 1914, pp. 317 ff.; E. Peterson, Εἷς θεός, 1926, pp. 130 f.

[3] K. G. Kuhn, 'Μαραναθά' *TWNT* IV, pp. 470 ff., cautiously restricts himself to this conclusion.

general contains an abundance of ancient liturgical material, we find almost certainly the translation into Greek of this ancient formula, and therefore learn this author's understanding of it.[1] The formula in Rev. 22.20 reads ἔρχου κύριε (Come, Lord!). This clearly indicates that the writer understands it as an imperative, a prayer.

We may mention still another argument. The formula appears in its Aramaic form in chapter 10.6 of the *Didache*, the oldest liturgical collection we possess. In this passage the expression concludes a eucharistic prayer.[2] Thus also the collector of these liturgical writings obviously considers it a prayer. Although the preceding prayer is in Greek, the author still preserves the Aramaic form of this exclamation. Apparently the memory remained alive quite long that special respect is due to this prayer because it was spoken in the mother Church by the first Christians—by the very community of disciples to whom the Lord appeared. For this reason one uttered the prayer only with the greatest reverence, and avoided giving it a different form from that it had in the original Church. In any case, the *Didache* also indicates that the formula is a prayer.

H. Lietzmann is probably right in believing that the formula *Maranatha* here is embedded in a eucharistic liturgy in dialogue form:

Leader: May grace come and this world pass away!
People: Hosanna to the Son of David!
Leader: If anyone is holy, let him come; if he is not, let him repent. *Maranatha!*
People: Amen.[3]

Lietzmann is certainly also right in thinking that Paul uses fragments of the oldest eucharistic liturgies in the salutations of his letters because he knows that his letters will be read when the Church gathers for worship and the breaking of bread. Thus we should probably understand the brief section containing *Maranatha* at the end of I Corinthians as a part of a eucharistic liturgy analogous to that in the *Didache*:

If any one does not love the Lord, let him be accursed!
Maranatha!
The grace of the Lord Jesus be with you!

[1] He may have thought that he had to translate it because his whole book is more or less a translation from the Aramaic. When a writer translates everything, he usually forgets that there are individual bits which would better be left in the original language (as actually was done by the Apostle Paul).

[2] ἐλθέτω χάρις (at this point the Coptic translation reads ὁ κύριος, which is perhaps original), καὶ παρελθέτω ὁ κόσμος οὗτος | ὡσαννὰ τῷ θεῷ Δαυίδ | εἴ τις ἅγιός ἐστιν | ἐρχέσθω | εἴ τις οὐκ ἔστι | μετανοείτω | μαραναθά | ἀμήν.

[3] See H. Lietzmann, *Messe und Herrenmahl*, 1926, p. 237.

It is important that *Maranatha* seems to be a eucharistic prayer; this allows us to come still closer to an understanding of both its meaning and of the significance of the title *Kyrios* for the early Church. When we hear this prayer, we think first of an eschatological petition for the coming of the Lord at the end of days. Especially in light of the first part of the Lord's Prayer this meaning forcefully suggests itself. But we know that all worship in early Christianity was considered an anticipation in the present of the Kingdom of God. What will become an enduring reality at the end already happens in the assembled Church now. This connection between present and future reality (a relationship which was of course lost with the passing of time) represents the peculiar character and greatness of the early Church's worship. It is especially characteristic of the 'breaking of bread', the eucharistic celebration. In this meal there takes place an impressive anticipation of Christ's 'coming'—or more accurately, his 'return'—which he had promised. True, he will return to the earth only at the end, but he also comes already now in his Church gathered to break bread. He has promised, 'Where two or three are gathered in my name, there I am in the midst of them' (Matt. 18.20). This relationship between the early Church's eucharist and eschatology also corresponds perfectly to the meaning Jesus himself gave the act of distributing bread and wine at the Last Supper with his disciples. He quite clearly makes an eschatological reference to the end when, according to all three Synoptic reports, he alludes on this occasion to the messianic meal at which he will 'drink of the fruit of the vine new in the kingdom of God' (Mark 14.25 and parallels). Paul's report of the Last Supper (I Cor. 11.23 ff.) does not contain this saying, but the apostle too makes the eschatological connection when he writes in 11.26: 'For as often as you eat this bread and drink this cup, you proclaim the Lord's death *until he comes*.' Finally we should also recall in this context a passage in Revelation, a book which understands what is promised for the future as already partially fulfilled in worship, and therefore makes use of liturgical pictures and formulas and many ancient Christian hymns to describe the essentially indescribable drama of the end. Rev. 3.20 thus probably thinks both of the messianic meal in the kingdom of God and of the cultic meal of the Church: 'Behold, I stand at the door and knock; if any one hears my voice and opens the door, I will come in to him and eat with him, and he with me.' It is an unproven theory that this relationship is only possible in a Hellenistic environment. In reality the cultic experience of the presence of the risen Christ is to be explained by reference to the Jewish hope of the presence of the Messiah at the messianic meal, and by reference to the Easter experience of the Palestinian early Church gathered to celebrate the meal.

Now we understand better the high and strong expectation not only for the future but also for the immediate present which the Church attributed to this fervent cry *Maranatha*, 'Lord, come!' The people call upon the risen Christ to appear again at the table as he did on Easter Sunday, and thus to ensure his early final return. For all those who have experienced his coming to his own during the breaking of bread, the expectation of the final return of Christ is no longer an empty hope, a dogma in which they believe only because of tradition. They themselves have experienced the fact that the Lord can come to earth, and they experience it again every time they come together and fervently pray for the coming of the risen Christ. They know that the Lord will appear on the earth in the same way when he comes to complete all things.

Thus we can quite understand that this ancient prayer *Maranatha* meant, for those who spoke it, both 'Lord, come at the end to establish thy kingdom,' and 'Come now while we are gathered at this meal.' Those who came together for worship may hardly have been conscious of the theological and theoretical distinction we have made between present and future, anticipation and final coming. For them both elements were so intimately related that in the experience of Christ's presence in worship they really experienced in anticipation his final return. When we speak of the early Church's eschatology, we should consider more than is usually done that the early Church not only waited for 'eschatological realization', but already experienced it—precisely in the eucharistic meals. Christian worship is worship in the πνεῦμα (John 4.23), an eschatological element. Thus the working of the Spirit in *glossolalia* is already the 'speech of angels' (I Cor. 13.1)!

Since the Church already experienced Christ's coming to his Church we can also better understand how the early Christians could think of him as both Lord of his Church and Lord over the whole world. We shall later speak of this remarkable paradox, characteristic for the early Christian *Kyrios* conception, that Christ is at the same time Lord of this little community which represents his body on earth, and from that very centre Sovereign over all the world. We grasp this when we consider that his lordship is already experienced every time the little community celebrates the Lord's

Supper. Thus the Church appears in reality as *the centre of Christ's lordship over the whole world.* The typical juxtaposition of Church worship and coming Kingdom of God in the whole thought of the early Church shows that the ancient prayer *Maranatha* really means at the same time both the presence of Christ today and his coming again.

This has implications for the understanding of the concept *Mar* in this formula. We have seen that in the New Testament, translated as *Kyrios*, it can be used more or less colourlessly, or that it designates a rabbi. But after all we have said about *Maranatha* and its place in the life of the early Church, we must exclude such a general use of the term in this prayer. *Mar* must here approach the meaning implied by the formula *Kyrios Christos*; it must mean practically the same as 'divine ruler'. *He* is the one who comes when bread is broken in the assembled Church, the same Lord who will return at the end to complete all things and who already now (invisibly) reigns.

We have seen that the meaning of *Mar*, like that of *Adon* and *Kyrios*, has a capacity for development, and can be defined only in terms of the particular context in which it occurs. That is the reason we had first of all to consider the use of *Maranatha* in early Christian worship. It is absolutely impossible that the word *Mar* in this formula means only a form of polite address or 'rabbi'. A. E. J. Rawlinson rightly points out the impossibility of translating *Maranatha* 'Teacher, come'.[1] Not only is there no proof that Christ was not called upon in the earliest Christian worship; everything in fact speaks against the assertion that he was not—above all the Aramaic form of the liturgical prayer *Maranatha* itself.

This formula has rightly been called the 'Achilles heel' of Bousset's whole thesis.[2] He and Bultmann, who follows the thesis in every detail, simply cannot satisfactorily explain why this prayer in Aramaic form was used even in the Greek-speaking Church. We feel the same embarrassment, already characteristic of Bousset, in Bultmann's *Theology of the New Testament* too. How troublesome the formula is for Bousset is indicated by the fact that in the first edition of his *Kyrios Christos* in 1913 he attempted a rather forced explanation of its Aramaic form which would agree with his theory of the purely Hellenistic origin of the worship of Christ; then, himself probably not convinced of the correctness of that explanation, he replaced it with a still less probable one in *Jesus der Herr* in 1916; and he finally

[1] A. E. J. Rawlinson, *The New Testament Doctrine of the Christ*, pp. 239 ff.
[2] *Ibid.*, p. 235.

returned to his first explanation in 1921 in the second edition of *Kyrios Christos*. Bultmann, apparently not satisfied with Bousset's first and final explanation, adopts in his *Theology of the New Testament* the explanation of 1916—the one Bousset himself did not believe could be maintained! This fluctuation is significant. It shows from the very beginning that it is impossible to explain the Aramaic formula *Maranatha* successfully except in the way which naturally suggests itself when one approaches it without a preconceived opinion: it is an expression of the cultic veneration of Christ by the original Aramaic-speaking Church.

In his first explanation of 1913, to which he returned in 1921, Bousset attempts to avoid this inescapable conclusion by saying that the Aramaic form of the prayer does not necessarily prove its Palestinian origin. One could reckon with the possibility that it originated in the bilingual area of Antioch, Damascus and Tarsus—that is, in a Hellenistic environment.[1] It was not without reason that Bousset once rejected this explanation, and not without reason that Bultmann cannot accept it. It really is not sound. An Aramaic formula originating in a bilingual area would hardly have become so fixed that it would remain untranslated even in a *Greek* text. The only explanation for the reverent preservation of the Aramaic form is that there must have been a memory that its source was the original Church in Jerusalem. It was respected for that reason, just as the Aramaic form of the words '*Abba*', '*Talitha cumi*', and '*Eli, Eli, lama sabachthani*' was respected because one knew that Jesus himself had spoken them in this way.

The following statement of Bousset indicates that even in 1921 he himself was not firmly convinced of the correctness of the original explanation he had taken up again: 'Since all other arguments speak against the Palestinian origin of the *Kyrios* title, the origin of *Maranatha* must also be sought outside Palestine.' That is certainly a clear *petitio principii*.

Bousset's second explanation, which he himself abandoned because of its improbability, and which Bultmann strangely accepts without any attempt to justify it,[2] is completely groundless: *Maranatha* is an oath sworn before God; originally it had nothing at all to do with Christ!

In reality the formula represents the transition from the Palestinian to the Hellenistic faith in Christ the Lord. The assertion of Bousset and Bultmann that there is a complete break between the original Palestinian Church and Hellenistic Christianity is simply a construction which is neither justified by the elements handed down to us

[1] W. Bousset, *Kyrios Christos*[2], p. 84.

[2] R. Bultmann, *Theology of the New Testament* I, p. 52.

from the very early Church, nor able to explain the origin of Hellenistic faith in the *Kyrios Jesus*. It is clear that whenever Paul mentions the confession of Christ as Lord, he draws upon an old tradition and presupposes acquaintance with it as the foundation of all proclamation of Christ.

The non-Christian use of the *Kyrios* name in the Hellenistic world, its relation to emperor worship, and above all its use as the name of God in the Septuagint—all this certainly contributed to making *Kyrios* an actual *title* for Christ. But this development would not have been possible had not the original Church already called upon Christ as the Lord. Bousset is right in saying that the *Kyrios* title goes back to the experience of the Church's worship; but it is the experience of worship in the *original* Church.

There is no reason to believe with Lohmeyer (*Galiläa und Jerusalem*, p. 17) that we must think only of Galilee as the particular region of the title's origin.

Personal prayer to Christ developed from the Church's invocation of the Lord in public worship. We encounter such personal prayer in the writings of Paul, who prayed directly to the Lord Christ at decisive times (II Cor. 12.8; I Thess. 3.12; II Thess. 3.2 ff.). We also find prayers directed to God 'in the name of' Christ or 'through' Christ. This is especially true of the Gospel of John (14.13; 15.16; 16.24 ff.), but Paul also prayed to God 'through' Christ (Rom. 1.8; 7.25; II Cor. 1.20; Col. 3.17). The fact that Christ is both the one to whom and through whom prayers are made is Christologically significant. The theological idea of prayer *through* Christ presupposes that already before this one had prayed *to* him.

We have seen that *Maranatha* is to be interpreted as a prayer rather than as a confession. The *confession* '*Kyrios Christos*' was derived from and is closely connected with the prayer. Early Christianity knew no sharp distinction between the two; every confession was also a prayer, and 'calling upon' (ἐπικαλεῖσθαι) the *Kyrios* also included praying to him. Since the prayer *Maranatha* does so, the confession must also go back to the Palestinian Church—although it must be admitted that it was first in the Greek-speaking Church that the confession achieved its full meaning as a counterpart of the confession of non-Christian *Kyrioi* and especially of the *Kyrios Kaisar*. If Lohmeyer and others are right in maintaining that the Christological hymn in Phil. 2.6 ff. has an Aramaic foundation, we have here a confirmation of the Aramaic origin also of the confession, since this whole hymn reaches a climax in the confession of the *Kyrios Jesus Christos*.

Unlike the prayer, the confession was not preserved in Aramaic, but was translated into Greek. One reason for this is that the prayer was treated with more reverence than the confession. But one must also consider especially the contrast between the Christian *Kyrios* on the one hand, and non-Christian *kyrioi* and the *Kyrios Kaisar* on the other. Translation into Greek was a means of bringing this contrast into focus as sharply as possible, and there was no reason to maintain the original Aramaic form which did not make this visible.

The confession *Kyrios Jesus* is one of the most ancient we possess. This brief formula expresses the whole faith of the early Church with the single word *Kyrios*. This designation of course points primarily only to the present work of Christ, but from this point of view one can visualize the whole work of Christ both in the past (his work of atonement) and in the future (his second coming in glory). Everything is seen, however, in the light of the triumphant certainty that already now, in the present, Christ exercises lordship, although it is invisible and only the faithful recognize it, whereas non-Christians still think that another *Kyrios* rules the world.

We read in Acts 2.36: '... God has made him both Lord and Christ, this Jesus whom you crucified.'[1] This shows clearly that reverence for Jesus as the *Kyrios* after his resurrection was connected with reverence for him as the Messiah. Only now can Jesus be designated 'Messiah' too, for now lordship is actually conferred upon him. It is probably no accident that in this passage the title *Kyrios* comes *before* the title Christ; Jesus can be designated Messiah-King only in view of his invisible lordship as *Kyrios*.

Paul is actually the one who gave the present lordship of Jesus a theological foundation. Rom. 10.9, Phil. 2.9 and I Cor. 12.3 are especially important with regard to the confessional formula as such. In so far as the fact of Jesus' lordship is concerned, however, we have to consider all the passages which speak of his exaltation or of his victory and rule over all powers. We begin with the three passages whose subject is the confession itself.

These three passages show first of all that Paul is not the creator of the idea that Jesus is Lord, but that he took over the confessional formula together with the conceptions related to it from the earliest Church; that is, the passages show that in the final analysis the root

[1] In Phil 2.9 ff also (see p. 217 below) he is *made Kyrios*.

of Paul's own faith in the *Kyrios* is the experience of the Lord in the earliest Church's worship. This is especially clear in the first passage, Rom. 10.9: '. . . if you confess with your lips that Jesus is the Lord and believe in your heart that God raised him from the dead, you will be saved.' Paul expressly connects 'confession with the lips' and 'faith in the heart'. It is significant that to 'confess with the lips' quite self-evidently refers to this one confession, 'Jesus is *Kyrios*.' This is without doubt *the* confession, the 'original confession' which includes all others. When the topic is simply 'confession', this is the formula which forces itself upon Paul's mind. It is thus unquestionable that already before him this formula was in general liturgical use.

We have already considered Phil. 2.6 ff. in detail in the chapter on the Son of Man. We mentioned then that the climax of the whole hymn is the confession that of everything in heaven and on earth and under the earth, 'Jesus Christ is Lord'. The short original formula is so to speak Christologically developed in these verses. In the light of the lordship of Jesus Paul looks back over the whole history of Christ from the very beginning when he was 'in the form of God' in his pre-existence. The whole hymn was composed in view of the *Kyrios* title (although we have seen that it also deals with the two other fundamental titles, 'Son of Man' and 'Servant of God'). Its central point is the fact that God has 'more than exalted' Jesus.

We have seen that ὑπερύψωσεν is not just a rhetorical expression, but that one must understand the prefix ὑπέρ in its full meaning. Christ was 'in the form of God' already at the very beginning. Because he did not disobediently grasp at equality with God, God conferred it upon him on the basis of his obedience 'unto death on a cross'. God has 'made him Lord' (Acts 2.36). Christ's exaltation to equality with God manifests itself in the fact that God now gives him the name above every name, the name *Kyrios*. Why is this a name which cannot be surpassed? It is the name of God himself; *Kyrios* is the translation of the Hebrew *Adonai*. It is quite clear at this point that we have to think of the Hebrew equivalent of the *Kyrios* title. It is difficult to understand how Bousset and many others with him (including W. Förster,[1] who otherwise contests Bousset's thesis) can simply reject this derivation. The bestowal of the divine name, however, does not refer only to the name itself. In Judaism, as in all ancient religions, a name represents also a power. To say that God confers upon Jesus his own name is to say that he confers upon him

[1] W. Förster, *Herr ist Jesus*, p. 122; very decidedly also L. Cerfaux, *Le Christ dans la théologie de S. Paul*, 1951, pp. 347 and 358.

his whole lordship. We shall see that this idea is included in the general early Christian conception of Jesus' exaltation when we speak of the concept of his lordship in the passages which contain the idea but not the actual title *Kyrios*.

The lordship bestowed upon the *Kyrios Jesus*, who is now equal with God, manifests itself especially in the fact that also all the invisible powers of creation are subjected to him, so that now 'every knee should bow in heaven and on earth and under the earth and every tongue confess: Jesus Christ is Lord.' This idea is the foundation of every New Testament passage which actually identifies Jesus with God.

From the point of view of the conviction that 'all power in heaven and on earth' is given to Christ, Paul then looks back over the whole history of the Christ-event to the present. Phil. 2.6 ff. shows that the final lordship of Jesus was prepared from the very beginning through his obedience as the image of God. We shall see that other passages of the New Testament draw another line connecting Jesus' present lordship and his pre-existence. These are the passages which speak of Christ's participation in creation—or more accurately expressed, of his being the Mediator of creation. We shall consider this idea in the last part of our work when we come to the titles referring to Jesus' pre-existence. At this point we only indicate that a backward glance from faith in the present Lord of all creation leads inevitably to the assumption that he was destined for this lordship from the very beginning, and that therefore from the very beginning he was closely related to creation. This suggests another connection with the Genesis story which goes beyond the Son of Man concept.

But before we speak of these consequences which result from the *Kyrios* concept and even lead occasionally to Jesus' actually being designated 'God', we must examine the third Pauline passage in which the confessional formula 'Jesus is *Kyrios*' is present.

Here Paul thinks of the particular situation in the Hellenistic churches, and here the use of the Christian confessional formula is certainly influenced by the thought of those other Hellenistic *kyrioi* and especially of *one* other *Kyrios*. We read in I Cor. 12.3: 'Therefore I want you to understand that no one speaking by the Spirit of God ever says "Jesus be cursed!" and no one can say "Jesus is Lord" except by the Holy Spirit.' This comes at the beginning of a statement about spiritual gifts, and scholars usually relate it to speaking with tongues. On the basis of the context, the verse could be so interpreted. But speaking with tongues is inarticulate speech, whereas both the curse and the confession in this verse have to do with quite intelligible assertions. The situation here is similar to that in Rom. 8, which asserts that the Spirit himself speaks in all prayers. The Romans passage thinks also of the extreme form of the Spirit's speaking in which men speak with tongues, but it nevertheless considers all prayers the work of the Spirit—also those formulated in intelligible words. I Cor. 12.3 speaks not of prayer, but of confession. But in a quite analogous way it considers confession to be the direct work of the Spirit. Although the idea of direct spiritual language, *glossolalia*, may be in the background, all confessions are nevertheless meant, above all the ancient confession formulated in quite coherent words, 'Jesus is *Kyrios*', and its negative counterpart, 'Jesus be cursed!' Both are related to the Spirit, the first proving the working of the Spirit, the second proving the absence of that work.

I believe that the primary theme of the verse is not *glossolalia* but emperor worship and persecution because of the confession *Kyrios Christos*. There is very probably here a reference to a saying of Jesus in which he promises his disciples the inspiration of the Holy Spirit precisely at the moment when they will stand before their judges in times of persecution and be called upon to confess their faith. Matt. 10.17 ff. reads: '. . . they will deliver you up to councils, and flog you in their synagogues, and you will be dragged before governors and kings for my sake, to bear testimony before them and the Gentiles. When they deliver you up, do not be anxious how you are to speak or what you are to say; for what you are to say will be given you in that hour; for it is not you who speak, but the Spirit of your Father speaking through you.'

In connection with I Cor. 12.3 also we should mention the letter of the governor Pliny to the Emperor Trajan describing the procedure used to deal with those accused of being Christians. Here we learn that in order to deny by oath that he was a Christian, it was not enough for the accused to say, 'The emperor is Lord' and to make a sacrifice before the image of the emperor; he had also to curse Christ in order to prove that the sacrifice to the emperor was sincere. The same procedure is presupposed in the *Martyrdom of Polycarp* 8.2 when the Roman official says to Polycarp, 'What harm is there in saying "Caesar is lord" and offering sacrifice and what goes with it . . .?' The last part of the sentence probably refers precisely to the required cursing of Christ. Although these two documents date from the second century, there is no reason to assume that the procedure they describe was different in the first century, a time when emperor worship was also common. We read in Acts 17.7 that in Thessalonica the Jews accused Paul and his followers of 'acting against the decrees of Caesar, saying that there is another king, Jesus'.

In this situation the promise of Jesus to his disciples casts a special light on I Cor. 12.3. Some of the Christians must have weakened before non-Christian judges, made the sacrifice to the emperor and cursed Christ. Afterwards they must have excused themselves to their brothers with an appeal to Jesus' words in Matt. 10.17 ff, saying that it was the Holy Spirit speaking through them at the time of the trial who caused them to say 'Cursed be Jesus!' Perhaps Paul had such people in mind when he reminded the Corinthians that the Holy Spirit who stands by the persecuted is at work only when the confession *Kyrios Jesus* is made. Whoever curses Christ in that situation proves by this very action that he does not have the promised Spirit.

We see therefore that apparently already at a relatively early date the confession 'Jesus is Lord' had a special meaning for the Christians outside Palestine—especially in the face of persecution. Although the idea of the 'lordship' of Jesus was present even earlier as a result of faith in his exaltation and his appearance in the Church, it becomes especially concrete in opposition to emperor worship. In the emperor a person was to be worshipped whose lordship over the world was visible and tangible.[1] This must naturally have contributed to the fact that the idea of the present lordship of Jesus, the only true Lord, assumed more vital form. The state simply could not understand why the Christians were so obstinate at this point. 'What harm is there in saying "Caesar is lord"?' (*Mart. Polyc.* 8.2). But the Christians would rather die than say it. After all, the confession '*Kyrios Christos*' would no longer be valid if there were another *Kyrios* beside him. The Revelation, which is full of allusions to emperor worship, expressly calls Christ the 'Lord of lords' (κύριος κυρίων) and 'King of kings' (Rev. 17.14). *Jesus* is *Kyrios*, not the emperor!

The title 'King' (βασιλεύς) is therefore a variant of the *Kyrios* title, and it is not necessary for us to devote a special chapter to it. We have seen earlier that the idea of the Messiah-King can be

[1] See p. 197 ff. above concerning the problem of the relation between emperor worship and the originally purely political designation of the Roman emperor as *Kyrios*. The recollection that the Romans condemned Jesus himself as a Zealot, as a pretender to the throne, which is shown by the inscription over the cross, must have suggested to the Christians the contrast between Κύριος Χριστός and the Κύριος Καῖσαρ. See O. Cullmann, *The State in the New Testament*, pp. 42 f.

applied only to the lordship Jesus exercises after his resurrection. Jesus' kingdom is of course not the earthly one of the Messiah expected by the Jews, but a 'kingdom not of this world'.

Jesus is designated 'King of the Jews' in the following passages of the New Testament: Matt. 2.2; 27.11, 29, 37; Mark 15.2, 9, 12, 18, 26; Luke 23.3, 37, 38; John 18.33, 39; 19.3, 14, 19 ff. He appears as 'King of Israel' in Matt. 27.42; Mark 15.32; John 1.49; 12.13. Most of these passages refer to the Roman accusation of Jesus. The inscription on the cross gives as the reason for his sentence the charge that he aspired to kingship. The expression is thus used here in the political sense of the Zealots, whereas the first Christians attributed to it a non-political meaning related to the *Kyrios* title.

In order to distinguish between *Basileus* and *Kyrios*, we could perhaps say that the title King emphasizes more strongly Jesus' lordship over his Church, since the Church takes the place of Israel and he fulfils the kingship of Israel. The title *Kyrios* on the other hand emphasizes more strongly Jesus' lordship over the whole world, over all the visible and invisible creation.

Despite the subtle distinction one may make in principle between the application of the two titles to Jesus, they are interchangeable. On the one hand, the lordship of the *Kyrios* includes also Jesus' kingship over Israel and thus over his Church. On the other hand, the title King visualizes also Jesus' lordship over all creation. *Kyrios* is thus equivalent to *Basileus* in all the passages which especially emphasize opposition to the claims of the Roman emperor. And lordship over all is meant when I Tim. 6.15 (similar to Rev. 17.14) designates Jesus King of kings and Lord of lords (βασιλεὺς τῶν βασιλευόντων, κύριος τῶν κυριευόντων). The same is true when I Cor. 15.25 speaks of the kingship of Jesus: 'For he must reign as king (βασιλεύειν) until he has put all his enemies under his feet.' Here also the apostle thinks of Jesus' lordship over all creation, over all invisible powers (the 'enemies' he will 'put under his feet'). As a final proof of the identical meaning of *Basileus* and *Kyrios*, we may point out the fact that the Gospel of Matthew, the Gospel which from the very first chapter emphasizes most strongly Jesus' dignity as 'King of Israel', is also the Gospel which reaches its climax in a statement about the absolute lordship the risen Jesus exercises over all: 'All authority *in heaven and on earth* has been given to me' (Matt. 28.18). We shall see that the juxtaposition of 'lordship over the Church' and 'lordship over the world' is characteristic of the New Testament conception of the κυριότης of Jesus. We have found the explanation for this already in the fact that the first Christians first of all experienced the lordship of Jesus within the small Church fellowship during their meetings for worship.

W. Förster, *Herr ist Jesus*, p. 142, believes we should completely exclude the cosmic significance of the lordship of Jesus from the faith of early Christianity. It is true that in Rom. 10.12 and Acts 10.36 the expression κύριος πάντων refers to lordship over men, and that the Old Testament quotation in I Cor. 10.26 ('the earth is the Lord's') could refer to God's lordship. But we cannot limit ourselves to the consideration only of the passages which contain the *word* κύριος; we must extend our investigation to all the passages which speak of the lordship of Jesus. Förster cannot think of Jesus' lordship over the world because of his thesis that according to the faith of the early Church Jesus is Lord only in so far as he makes a claim of absolute lordship on us.

Now we must speak of the passages which, without necessarily containing the title 'Lord' or 'King', express the theological idea of the rule of the one Lord.[1] Only when we extend the scope of our investigation in this way can we understand the full importance of the *Kyrios* designation for New Testament Christology. We shall see that we are concerned here above all with the *work* of Jesus. In contrast to our usual procedure, we can group the various New Testament books together in considering every aspect of the problem, because at this point there is a far-reaching agreement among the early Christian writers.[2] Paul will naturally have the most important place. We shall devote an independent section only to the Gospel of John, although even his conception does not differ from that of early Christianity in general. This consensus itself indicates the central significance of the lordship of Christ for the faith of early Christianity. The particular question which concerns us now is: To what exact function of the exalted Christ does the *Kyrios* name point?

All the numerous New Testament passages which mention that Jesus 'sits at the right hand of God' and that 'all enemies are subject to him' come into consideration with regard to the 'lordship of Christ'. As we have already seen in the chapter on Jesus the High Priest, these ideas are a messianic application of Ps. 110. Scholars do not usually attribute sufficient importance to the fact that statements

[1] See O. Cullmann, 'The Kingship of Christ and the Church in the New Testament', *The Early Church*, 1956, pp. 105 ff.

[2] H. Conzelmann, *Die Mitte der Zeit*, 1954, pp. 146 ff. (ET, *The Theology of St Luke*, 1960, pp. 170 ff.), believes that Luke is different here. See p. 237 n. 1 below.

about the exaltation of Christ to the right hand of God (which were very early included in the creed) formally go back to this psalm.

Nothing indicates better than the very frequent citation of this very psalm how vital was the present lordship of Christ in early Christian thought. It is quoted not just in a few isolated places, but throughout the whole New Testament. Almost no other Old Testament passage is cited so often. We find it in Rom. 8.34; I Cor. 15.25; Col. 3.1; Eph. 1.20; Heb. 1.3; 8.1; 10.12 f.; I Peter 3.22; Acts 2.34f.; 5.31; 7.55; Rev. 3.21; Matt. 22.44; 26.64; Mark 12.36; 14.62; 16.19; Luke 20.42 f.; 22.69. In the Apostolic Fathers we find it in *I Clement* 36.5 and *Barnabas* 12.10.

The assertion that Jesus sits at the right hand of God in fulfilment of this psalm is only another expression of the early confession *Kyrios Christos*. The idea has become so common that it is repeated even apart from direct reference to the Old Testament psalm. Indeed, already in the New Testament we find it in a developed confessional formula, the ancient formula in I Peter 3.22 which clearly appears as such in contrast with the context: 'Jesus Christ, who has gone into heaven and is at the right hand of God, with angels, authorities, and powers subject to him.'[1] The words 'angels, authorities and powers' refer implicitly to the 'enemies' who Ps. 110 says are made the 'footstool' of the Lord. Whereas the psalm thinks of the earthly enemies of Israel, the first Christians identified them with the unseen powers. It is *their* subjection which shows that Christ is now the only Lord, beside whom there is no other in heaven or on earth. Even if these forces still exist, all power is taken from them.

The importance of this faith for the first Christians is evident from the fact that it is just the oldest formulas of faith as we find them already in the New Testament and in the Apostolic Fathers which regularly repeat the statement that Christ sits at the right hand of God, with all powers subjected to him. Without lordship over these unseen powers Christ would not be the *Kyrios* beside whom there can simply be no other. Thus we read in the confession preserved in I Tim. 3.16, '. . . seen by angels'. Besides the passage in I Peter 3.22, we find also in the background of Phil. 2.9 f. this faith in Christ's lordship over the ἐπουράνια, ἐπίγεια and καταχθόνια. Here it is these powers which confess Christ as *Kyrios* and bow before him. Outside the New Testament the subjection of these powers is expressly mentioned in the confessional formulas cited by Ignatius (*Trall.* 9.1), Polycarp (2.1), and Justin (*Apology* I, 42). In Irenaeus'

[1] See B. Reicke, *The Disobedient Spirits and Christian Baptism*, 1946, pp. 198 ff.

Adversus Haereses I, 10.1 the confession of Christ the 'Lord' is a confession of his lordship over all powers of the whole creation, visible and invisible. I emphasize this point in order to indicate the important place this assertion held in the faith of the first Christians. All these ancient confessional formulas preserve only the most important elements of the early Christian faith. If Christ's lordship over the powers and authorities is regularly mentioned in these short summaries, it must be a quite central article of faith.

This is connected with the constant experience of faith the first Christians had when they gathered to worship. In worship they experienced Christ's presence, his 'lordship', and it is understandable that they saw everything in the light of this lordship. They connected all the events which happened in the world about them with the invisible rule which Christ the Lord already exercises.

We have mentioned several times the remarkable juxtaposition of statements about Christ's lordship over his little earthly Church and statements about his lordship over the whole world, and we have already said that it was the first Christians' experience of the presence of Christ in common worship which naturally led them to connect the one with the other. Now we must ask, however, what the conceptual and theological foundation for this connection was.

First we must establish what these two 'lordships' of Christ (that over the Church and that over the world) have in common. Primarily they both refer to the same limited temporal period, and this distinguishes them from the Kingdom of God.[1] The Kingdom of God will come only at the end of time, but, like the Church itself, the lordship of Christ belongs to the interim between his ascension and return. Thus, as distinguished from the Kingdom of God, the lordship of Christ has already begun: '(God has) transferred us to the kingdom of his beloved Son . . .' (Col. 1.13). With the exception of Heb. 10.13 and I Cor. 15.25, all the texts we have cited concerning Christ's 'sitting at the right hand of God' and the 'subjection' of his enemies presuppose the ascension of Jesus as the chronological beginning point of his lordship. The two exceptions expect the subjection of the powers only at the end of time. The reason for this apparent contradiction is the New Testament's general conception of time, according to which the end phase has already been introduced, but the end itself has not yet come. It is thus possible for one group

[1] Concerning the fact that the distinction between the Father and the Son has significance only from the point of view of *Heilsgeschichte*, see pp. 293 and 325 ff. below.

of passages to assert that the powers have already been conquered, whereas these two other passages still look forward to that victory. To use a metaphor from the Revelation, we could say that these powers are provisionally only 'bound'; they will be finally conquered only at the end.

One can follow the tension created by the juxtaposition of 'already fulfilled' and 'not yet completed' through the whole New Testament. It is characteristic of the New Testament situation. This tension can result in the assertion of I Peter 3.22, for instance, that the subjection of the hostile powers has already taken place, whereas according to Heb. 10.13 the Christ sitting at the right hand of God still 'waits' for this subjection. The same tension explains the relation between the 'subjection' and the 'destruction' of the powers. The verb καταργεῖν, which the New Testament uses in many of these passages, has two meanings: 'to subject' and 'to destroy'. Thus II Tim. 1.10 uses it to describe the victory over death already achieved by the crucified Christ, whereas I Cor. 15.26 uses it to describe the victory which will take place only after the return of Christ at the end. The subject of both passages is victory, but in II Tim. 1.10 the power of death is only 'subjected', whereas in I Cor. 15.26 death is 'destroyed'. What is true of death is also true of the other powers. Between the two victories the powers are subject to Christ, but in such a way that they are only tied on a rope, so to speak, which can sometimes be shortened, sometimes lengthened, so that they may have the illusion that they can free themselves. But it is only an illusion, because in reality they are already conquered. The fact remains that the decision has already been made. All these passages presuppose that the beginning of Christ's lordship has already been introduced. Christ is the Lord already, today, in the present.[1]

Just as this lordship has a beginning, so it has also an end. According to the New Testament, the end cannot be described in terms of a date, but it can be described in terms of an event, the return of Christ. The lordship of Christ began with his ascension and will end with his return. Thus in Acts 1.10 f. the two men 'in white robes' emphasize the external correspondence of the two events which bracket the lordship of Christ: 'This Jesus, who was taken from you into heaven, will come in the same way (i.e., on the clouds) as you saw him go into heaven.'

In Revelation and I Cor. 15.24 the return of Christ and the events immediately following mark the end of his lordship. After the last battle, in which the Son will be victor, 'he delivers the kingdom to

[1] See on this whole question O. Cullmann, *The Earliest Christian Confessions*, and *The State in the New Testament*, pp. 86 ff.

God the Father'. This final act recapitulates in a concentrated and definitive form everything which has already happened before and everything that is taking place in the present—above all the victory over Satan and the 'powers'.

The assertion that the lordship of Christ comes to an end with his return must be slightly corrected in so far as, according to Revelation at least, it extends briefly into the end time, the new aeon, itself. This is the meaning of the concept of the 'thousand-year reign' [1] which occurs only in the Revelation and in this book represents the Church present at the time of the final act of the drama. I do not agree with Augustine (who himself took the idea from the Donatist Tyconius) that Revelation intends to identify this thousand-year period with the whole period of the Church between Christ's ascension and his return. Revelation thinks rather of a specifically eschatological kingdom to be realized only in the future. It is, so to speak, the very last part of Christ's lordship, which at the same time extends into the new aeon. Consequently, the thousand-year kingdom should be identified neither with the whole chronological extent of Christ's lordship nor with the present Church. That lordship is the larger concept; it has already begun and continues in this aeon for an undefined length of time. The thousand-year reign, on the other hand, belongs temporally to the final act of Christ's lordship, the act which begins with his return and thus already invades the new aeon. The very beginning of the Book of Revelation indicates that the lordship of Christ has begun long since. Christ has power over death and controls the place of the dead (1.18); he is the ruler of earthly kings (1.5); he rules the people with an iron rod (12.5); he is 'Lord of lords and King of kings' (17.14).

The period of the Church coincides perfectly with the period of Christ's lordship—also in terms of the characteristic tension between present and future and in terms of what we have said about the invasion of the new aeon. The Church too has a beginning and end. It too presupposes the death and resurrection of Christ as its beginning. True, even the Old Testament knows of a 'Church': the chosen people of God, then the remnant which repents. But the Old Testament offers only an anticipation. The Church exists only as the fulfilment of the Old Testament. It is a reality only since the Holy Spirit became the common possession of all who belong to it; that is, it exists only since Easter and Pentecost. The time of Christ's lordship and of the Church is the time of the Holy Spirit, and the common possession of the Holy Spirit begins only with Christ's glorification (John 7.39). In Matt. 16.18, too, the incarnate Jesus says in the future

[1] On the question of the thousand-year reign see the recent work of H. Bietenhard, *Das tausendjährige Reich*[2], 1955.

tense, 'I will build my Church (οἰκοδομήσω) . . .' This means after his death and resurrection.

In the same way, the end of the Church is the same as that of Christ's lordship; the Church comes to an end with his second coming, but also reaches characteristically into the end time. In the final act Christ will thus be surrounded by those who formed his original Church. The apostles will sit on twelve thrones (Matt. 19.28); they will rule with him (Rev. 5.10; 20.4; II Tim. 2.12). The 'saints' (i.e., all members of the Church) will judge the angelic powers (I Cor. 6.2 f.). The 'thousand-year kingdom' of Revelation will therefore be the Church of that time, the Church of the end time.

The presence of the Holy Spirit, the constitutive element of the Church, is a sign of the tension between the 'already fulfilled' and 'not yet completed' we have mentioned. The Holy Spirit himself is only an anticipation (ἀπαρχή, Rom. 8.23; ἀρραβών, II Cor. 1.22; 5.5; Eph. 1.14) of the end.

But despite this fundamental identity between Christ's lordship and the Church with regard to their temporal nature, there is nevertheless a decisive distinction between them. The difference lies not in the category of time, but of space. The area covered by Christ's lordship is not the same as that of the Church. This spatial distinction allows us to differentiate between the lordship of Christ over his Church and his lordship over the world. In order to understand exactly the character of the κυριότης of Christ, we must give a precise account of this relationship.

The realm of Christ's lordship is much larger than that of the Church. Literally no element of creation is excluded from it: '*all* authority in heaven and on earth has been given to me' (Matt. 28.19); all creatures 'in heaven and on earth and under the earth' must confess Christ as Lord (Phil. 2.10); God was pleased 'through him to reconcile to himself all things, whether on earth or in heaven' (Col. 1.20).

The realm of the present lordship of Christ is thus not limited to visible heaven and earth; Christ rules also over the invisible powers which stand behind empirical situations—above all over the invisible powers behind the *state*.

Along with others, I believe that the New Testament conception of the state may be traced back to the invisible angelic powers designated especially by Paul as ἐξουσίαι. Despite the fact that it has become the fashion to contest this position as more or less 'fantastic', I am more than ever positive that Rom. 13.1 very probably means *both*: the empirical state authority, and the invisible powers behind it. This is suggested also by the late Jewish conception of 'folk angels'. One should emphasize especially that Paul otherwise never uses the word ἐξουσίαι in any other sense, and that the same juxtaposition of invisible powers and their empirical organs is quite common in the New Testament. This is above all true of the 'rulers' in I Cor. 2.8 ff. On this whole question see O. Cullmann, *The State in the New Testament*, pp. 65 ff. In answer to the objections which have been made also to this latest statement of my position on this point, I wish to emphasize the fact that the ἐχθροί of Ps. 110 (i.e., precisely the *political* enemies of Israel) are consistently interpreted by the early Christian writings as invisible 'powers and authorities'. See also R. Morgenthaler's discussion of the temptation story in Luke from this point of view, '*Roma—Sedes Satanae. Röm. 13.1 ff. im Lichte von Lk. 4.5–8*' (*TZ* 12, 1956, pp. 289 ff.; *Festgabe für Karl Barth, 2nd part*).

The lordship of Christ must extend over every area of creation. If there were a single area excluded from his lordship, that lordship would not be complete and Christ would no longer be the *Kyrios*. For that reason the realm of the state also—precisely that realm—must fall under his lordship. Precisely on the basis of the confession *Kyrios Christos* as opposed to the confession *Kyrios Kaisar*, this conviction must necessarily be a central part of faith in Christ as Lord.

Only in one respect must a limitation be made. Although Christ's lordship knows no boundaries, its realm nevertheless does not simply coincide with the realm of creation. That will be the case only for the Kingdom of God after the end. The lordship, already conquered but not yet destroyed, of the 'flesh', of death which is the 'last enemy', is still present in the whole realm of Christ. The Holy Spirit, who is indeed already at work, has not yet transformed earthly bodies into 'spiritual bodies'. That will happen only in the future (Rom. 8.11, 23; I Cor. 15.35 ff.).[1] When we speak of 'limitation' in regard to the realm of Christ's lordship, we do not use the word in the sense of excluding a part of creation from it. We mean rather that although 'flesh' and 'death' have already been conquered, they are still at work within the lordship of Christ. Any part of the realm of that lordship can still apparently break away from it and reject Christ. This is the situation in the case of the state, which can become 'demonic' and seemingly fall away from the rule of Christ.[2]

Colossians and Ephesians describe Christ's lordship over the visible and invisible creation with the figure of the 'Head': Christ is the

[1] See my 'Immortality of the Soul and Resurrection of the Dead: The Witness of the New Testament'.

[2] See O. Cullmann, *The State in the New Testament*, p. 69.

'*head* of all rule and authority' (Col. 2.10); God has chosen 'as a plan for the fulness of time, to unite (ἀνακεφαλαιώσασθαι, 'to bring together under one head') all things in him, things in heaven and things on earth' (Eph. 1.10). But at the same time these two letters describe Christ as Head of the *Church* (Col. 1.18 and Eph. 1.22). This is characteristic of the problem which concerns us now, the problem of the relation between Christ's lordship over the Church and his lordship over the whole world. Christ is Lord over all creation, but he is also Lord over his little earthly Church.

Having defined the spatial distinction between the two areas of lordship, now we must discover the connection between them within the framework of this difference. Their positive relation would not be correctly defined if we simply said that Christ is Lord of the Church only because the Church is a part of the total realm of his lordship; that is, because it belongs to creation. In reality the importance of the Church for the total lordship of Christ is much greater: in a spatial sense, it is the centre, the mid-point from which Christ exercises his invisible lordship over the whole world. It is not only a part, but the heart. In *Christ and Time* I have tried to describe this situation graphically with two concentric circles, the inner representing the Church, the outer representing the total realm of Christ's lordship.[1]

The New Testament expresses the central place of the Church in the lordship of Christ by calling the Church the 'body of Christ'. The Church is the earthly body of the risen Christ, who since his ascension sits in full glory at the right hand of God. But at the same time this Christ is described as 'Head' of all creation and as 'Head' of the Church. The picture results in a certain incongruity, since he is at once Head and body of the Church, and since, moreover, the body 'grows up into him who is the head' (Eph. 4.15). But this apparent incongruity is characteristic precisely of the special relationship between the Church and the lordship of Christ: on the one hand, the Church is only a part of the whole realm whose Head is Christ; on the other hand, he is present in this limited part of his lordship in a very special way, different from the way he is in the other parts. On the one hand, the Church is the body of Christ himself, the highest possible reality on earth; on the other hand, the Church is subjected to Christ its Head just as are all other parts of creation included under his lordship.

In order really to understand the relationship between the two

[1] *Christ and Time*, p. 188.

realms of lordship, we must speak of the distinction between the members of the Church and the members of the total lordship of Christ. The members of the Church know about that lordship; the other members belong to it unconsciously. Since of all the realities of creation over which he has been given power Christ has chosen as the centre precisely the narrowly limited area of the fellowship of the Church, this extreme concentration must have a special meaning also for his whole lordship. The members of this Church must participate in his lordship in a special way. To be a member of a 'lordship' always means both to be ruled and to share in the rule, despite subjection to the head. Here we encounter the major distinction betwen the lordship of Christ and of the Church. We have seen that all creatures in heaven, on the earth, and under the earth belong to that lordship. Thus all invisible powers and authorities together with their empirical organs (the earthly state, for example) are also members of his lordship. They are placed completely within it, and, for this reason, the very people who understand the nature of this lordship, the members of the Church, owe obedience to the powers and authorities (Rom. 13.1 ff.).

Nevertheless, all the powers outside the Church are members of the lordship of Christ only in a very indirect way, for they do not necessarily know the role assigned to them within his lordship. Everything that is said by Paul, and before him by Jesus, about subjection to Caesar and the state refers to a non-Christian state which knows neither Christ and his kingdom nor God the Father of Christ. Even a pagan state like the Roman empire, therefore, can thoroughly fulfil the task assigned it by God in the lordship of Christ when it limits itself to its own quite definite role and allows the Church, the place where Christ's rule has such great significance, to 'lead a quiet and peaceable life' (I Tim. 2.2). A pagan state can play a role in Christ's lordship even though it does not know itself that it belongs to that lordship.

According to the New Testament, therefore, Christian resistance to a state can never be justified simply on grounds that it is a pagan state. Resistance is legitimate only when the state abandons its proper role and deifies itself. The state—even the heathen one—which remains within its limits belongs to the lordship of Christ, even if it is not aware of the fact.[1]

Because only the Christian knows of this subjection of the state to Christ's lordship, precisely in this sense the state has paradoxically a

[1] See O. Cullmann, *The State in the New Testament*, especially p. 51.

greater significance for him than for any other citizen. On the other hand, when a state transgresses its limits, the Christian feels this much more strongly than anyone else, although also non-Christians can also notice the fact itself. The Christian sees especially that the state has denied the lordship of Christ, that a demonic power has freed itself, that the 'beast' has appeared.

The fundamental distinction, then, between all the members of the lordship of Christ and the members of the Church is that the former do not know that they belong to this lordship, whereas the latter do know it. This allows us to define still more precisely the relationship between the lordship of Christ over the whole world and his lordship over the Church. The members of the Church, who know that Christ is Lord, belong consciously to his lordship, and this is how they are distinguished from the other members of that lordship, who serve him only unconsciously. Now we understand how it is that theologically this little fellowship can be the centre of the lordship of Christ over the whole world, over the visible and invisible powers. The apparent disproportion between this little band and its vast significance for the whole world is explained by the principle of representation in terms of which the whole *Heilsgeschichte* develops—the principle we have explained above.[1]

The members of the Church not only recognize the situation of the other members of the lordship of Christ; above all they know what task they themselves have to fulfil as men who believe in that lordship. For this reason, at the final act of Christ's lordship (Rev. 20.1 ff.) they will reign with him and participate in the judgment which will descend upon the other members of his lordship (I Cor. 6.3). In a more exact sense they will 'rule with' Christ, συμβασιλεύσουσιν (II Tim. 2.12). As we have seen, however, this final act only recapitulates what already characterizes the present kingly rule of Christ. Thus already in the present we are to take literally Paul's words about the 'reign of Christians' in I Cor. 4.8, and the words of Rev. 1.6 about our being already a βασιλεία (kingdom).

But we must of course emphasize also the other side:[2] this high vocation includes also the fact that everyone must always be conscious that he is the slave, servant, of the 'Lord' Jesus (II Cor. 4.5). Recognition of the lordship of Christ refers also to the absolute claim the 'Lord' has on our whole existence. Christ is not only the

[1] See pp. 54 f. above.

[2] W. Förster, *Herr ist Jesus*, in contrast to the interpretation given here, regards this side as primary and central.

Lord of the world and the Lord of the Church—he is also *my* Lord. Because he is experienced as Lord of the Church, he is also the Lord of every individual.

The *Gospel of John* especially emphasizes this personal aspect. We devote a special section to this book, although, as we have already remarked, it represents no fundamentally different conception of Christ as lord. Everything we have said about faith in Christ the *Kyrios* in the whole of early Christianity and especially in its Pauline theological expression may be said also for the Gospel of John. We only call attention to several particular points.

The whole Gospel culminates, so to speak, in the confession of Thomas in 20.28: ὁ κύριός μου καὶ ὁ θεός μου ('my Lord and my God'). Thomas, who reached this outspoken conviction after initial unbelief, is also the last of those who have seen the physical form of the risen Christ. Jesus answers him, 'Have you believed because you have seen me? Blessed are those who have not seen and yet believe.' The writer uses these words as an occasion to admonish all future readers to believe in this *Kyrios*. It should be observed that this account about Thomas comes at the end of the Gospel. Chapter 21 is a supplement. The *Kyrios* confession is thus the climax of the book.[1]

We should emphasize especially the genitive μου in this confession. The whole Gospel of John considers the lordship of Christ more strongly than the other New Testament writings from the viewpoint of the individual relationship between the exalted Christ and each of those who belong to him. Thus also Mary Magdalene says in 20.13, 'They have taken away *my* Lord . . .'.

Besides these passages there are several in which the vocative κύριε occurs, but as in the Synoptics it is used simply as a form of politeness which has no theological significance.

But there are other passages in John which, without using the term κύριος, express the idea that since his resurrection Christ exercises lordship already in the present. This actually is the theme of the 'farewell discourses'. After Jesus has left the earth and ascended to heaven, he will not abandon the earth. On the contrary—and this is

[1] Therefore the importance of the *Kyrios* title for the Gospel of John seems to me much greater than R. Bultmann, *Theology of the New Testament* II, p. 36, assumes when he refers to the fact that the title is first used in the Easter account. This is connected with the fact that also according to the fourth evangelist Jesus was first made *Kyrios* on the basis of his resurrection.

the primary idea of these speeches—his action on earth will then be much more effective than it was during the time of his incarnation. In John 14.12 Jesus predicts that those who believe in him will do greater works than he himself has done on earth, 'because I go to the Father'. That is, from now on Christ will work through those who believe in him, and this activity will be even more powerful than that of the incarnate Jesus. 'I go to the Father' thus means 'all power is given me by the Father'. Although this is not said in so many words, it nevertheless is clear that the idea is present in the Gospel of John—precisely in this Gospel—that after his resurrection Christ rules over all things.

After all we have said, the immense significance of the *Kyrios* title for the New Testament faith, and its central place in the theological thought of the first Christians, should have become clear. True, it is not a title which like 'Son of Man' or *ebed Yahweh* goes back to Jesus himself. It is rather an explanation of the person and work of Jesus which already presupposes the conviction of his resurrection.

This title rests upon faith in two essential elements of *Heilsgeschichte*: (1) Jesus is risen; (2) the fact that the decisive event of the resurrection has already happened but that the eschatological fulfilment has not yet happened does not mean that *Heilsgeschichte* has been interrupted. In other words, there is no deep chasm between the resurrection and parousia of Christ. There is no Christological vacuum during the interim in which the world lives between these two events. However long this 'between-times' may last, in any case Christ continues to exercise his role as Mediator.

This interim period is something quite new in comparison with the Jewish scheme of salvation. Contrary to the school of 'consistent eschatology', which continues to assert that it is a solution of 'embarrassment', this interim belongs organically and quite centrally in early Christian thought. As W. G. Kümmel has clearly shown in his *Promise and Fulfilment*, it is also compatible with Jesus' understanding of the pattern of salvation in so far as he too recognized the tension between 'already fulfilled' and 'not yet completed'. In fact, after all that we have discovered, we must actually say that the essentially Christian character of the New Testament conception of salvation consists in the acceptance of this 'between-times'. This is the reason for the importance of the confession *Kyrios Christos*. If the classical systematic Christologies of Protestantism do not give the concept the place it deserves, it is just because Protestant theology has not fully recognized the significance of this interim for New Testament thought.[1]

4. Kyrios Christos *and the Deity of Jesus*

We must speak of one more important aspect of the *Kyrios* concept, and this is also important for the fourth and last part of this book, which deals with the titles referring to the pre-existence of Jesus. Until now we have spoken primarily of the *work* of the *Kyrios Jesus*. But the work and person of Christ always belong together. The faith that with the name *Kyrios* God gave Christ his own authority has far-reaching consequences for understanding the *person* of Jesus—although it must still be emphasized that his *work* is the primary thing.

One consequence of the application of the *Kyrios* title to Jesus is that the New Testament can in principle apply to him all the Old Testament passages which speak of God. This is of course not true of Jesus' own sayings; when he quotes the Old Testament, the word *Kyrios* refers to God. But the New Testament letters quite commonly apply such Old Testament passages to Jesus. As we have seen, the Septuagint translates the name of God with *Kyrios*. The Greek concordance indicates that in the New Testament the Old Testament *Kyrios* passages can automatically refer to Jesus. This is the case, for instance, with Isa. 45.23 ('To me every knee shall bow, every tongue shall swear'), which is quoted in Phil. 2.10 f., the passage we have mentioned so often.

The most striking example is the quotation of Ps. 102.25 ff. in Heb. 1.10 ff.: 'Thou, Lord, didst found the earth in the beginning, and the heavens are the work of thy hands . . .' The Old Testament text obviously speaks of God the Father, the Creator. But as a result of the transfer of the name *Kyrios* to Jesus, the writer of Hebrews does not hesitate to address him with the words of the psalm, and thus to designate him the Creator of heaven and earth. Heb. 1.8 says expressly that the passage refers to the Son.[2]

I do not believe discussions of New Testament Christology have given this passage in Hebrews the attention it demands. We should

[1] This interim may of course not be absolutized at the expense of the eschatological tension as happens in Catholic theology. See O. Cullmann, 'The Tradition', *The Early Church*, pp. 59 ff.

[2] We shall return to this passage when we speak of θεός as a designation for Jesus. See p. 311 below.

generally give much more consideration to the by no means self-evident fact that after the death of Jesus the first Christians without hesitation transferred to him what the Old Testament says about God.[1] This indicates that they had followed through to its final consequences the idea of the present lordship of Christ. The idea in Phil. 2.9 f. that God has 'more than exalted' Christ, given him his own name, and conferred upon him all his authority, must really have been a common factor in early Christian faith.

Faith in the 'deity' of Christ (to use this later theological expression) originates in faith in the ὑπερύψωσις of which Phil. 2.9 speaks. Although Christ was ἐν μορφῇ θεοῦ from the very beginning, he became equal with God for the first time with his exaltation. We shall see that the same idea is also presupposed in Rom. 1.4, a text which also probably repeats an ancient confessional formula. According to this passage, Christ was God's Son already at the beginning, but 'since his resurrection' (ἐξ ἀναστάσεως) he is the 'Son of God in power' (υἱὸς θεοῦ ἐν δυνάμει). 'Son in power' is clearly synonymous with *Kyrios.*

The question of the deity of Christ in the New Testament should be asked in terms of the *Kyrios* title and its implications for the absolute lordship of Christ over the whole world. Only then is the problem considered within a genuinely New Testament framework, whereas the question of the two natures is a Greek rather than a biblical one. The New Testament unquestionably presupposes the deity of Christ, but it does so in connection with faith in the lordship he exercises since his exaltation; that is, primarily in connection with his work rather than with his being.

According to the early Christian faith, this *Kyrios* is of course also pre-existent. If Christ is one with God since his resurrection, he must have been united with God from the very beginning. The early Christian faith in the pre-existence of Jesus (like the existence of the Logos with God at the beginning) should be understood in the light of the present lordship of the *Kyrios* Christ. That is, it should be understood from the point of view of the history of salvation, of the

[1] W. Förster, *Herr ist Jesus,* p. 173, presents a strange argument to weaken the significance of this fact. He concludes from the naive, unreflective way in which this transference takes place in the New Testament that it is not important. He points out than an explanation is added only in I Peter 3.15, where 'that is, Christ' is added. But precisely the opposite conclusion should be drawn from this fact! The self-evidence of this transference proves that the conviction of unity between God and Christ on the basis of Christ's character as *Kyrios* must have been deeply anchored in the consciousness of the early Christian authors.

work of Christ. Thus in Paul's use of the two-part confession in I Cor. 8.6, the pre-existent activity of Christ as Mediator of creation is mentioned only in terms of the *Kyrios* title: '. . . one *Kyrios*, Jesus Christ, through whom are all things and through whom we exist.' Because for us Christ is the one *Kyrios*, the Lord over all things, therefore he must already have been related to all things at the beginning (Rev. 3.14), and this relation in I Cor. 8.6 (as in John 1.1 and Col. 1.16) is that of mediation of their creation. If we are really to grasp the Christology of the New Testament, we must consider the central place in the Church's life occupied by the triumphant certainty that Christ reigns now. Since his exaltation he is the only Lord and King.

If we are to understand the origin and development of New Testament Christology, we must centre our attention on the *Kyrios* title, just as the first Christians themselves placed it at the centre of their confessions and from that centre attempted to understand the other functions of Christ in the total Christ-event.[1]

This is by no means to say that the *Kyrios* Christology was chronologically the first explanation of the person and work of Jesus. Almost all the Christological answers we have investigated in the previous chapters are older. But it is only on this basis of the *Kyrios* Christology that a synthesis was attempted in which all the aspects represented by the other titles we consider in this work found their place in the total history of salvation. It is the great significance of the *Kyrios* concept that it made possible for the first time what we call the Christology of the New Testament. It furnished the foundation for fixing the relationship between the various Christological explanations in *Heilsgeschichte*.[2]

In order to avoid all misunderstanding, therefore, I emphasize that by the 'central place' of the *Kyrios* concept I mean its centrality in the historical development of a total Christological view in the life and thought of the first Christians. The chronological centre of that Christological synthesis itself is of course the death and resurrection of Christ.

The designation of Jesus as *Kyrios* has the further consequence that actually all the titles of honour for God himself (with the exception

[1] It is therefore right that the second article of the so-called Apostles' Creed places the designation *Kyrios* with 'Jesus Christ, his only son', and mentions that he 'sits on the right hand of God'.

[2] E. Stauffer, *New Testament Theology*, p. 114, correctly writes: 'But of all the christological titles the richest is that of "Lord". Its history is a compendium and at the same time a *repetitorium* of NT Christology. For in a few years it passes through the main stages of the development of christological titles, and so takes us once more along the road from the pedagogic and monarchic to the divine honouring of Jesus Christ.'

of 'Father') may be transferred to Jesus. Once he was given the 'name which is above every name', God's own name ('Lord', *Adonai*, *Kyrios*), then no limitations at all could be set for the transfer of divine attributes to him. Thus in connection with the *Kyrios* title we could already speak of the occasional use in early Christianity of the name 'God' (θεός) for Jesus, for this name by no means indicates, as we are inclined to think, a higher dignity than the unsurpassable *Kyrios* designation.[1] Since, however, the title 'God' implies the problem of the relationship between Father and Son and thus of pre-existence, we shall reserve discussion of it until the last part of this work when we discuss the other titles which visualize primarily the work of the pre-existent Christ.[2]

We have already spoken of Christ's work as Judge, another function of God transferred to him.[3] All functions of God were attributed to Jesus—even that of creation.

In close connection with the concept of the present *Kyrios* we now devote a chapter to the designation 'Saviour' (σωτήρ).

[1] According to H. Conzelmann, *The Theology of St Luke*, pp. 170 ff., in Luke this use is more strongly anchored in subordinationism. See p. 313 n. 2 below.

[2] See p. 306 below.

[3] See pp. 157 f. above.

8

Jesus the Saviour

(σωτήρ)

THE LATER DESIGNATION of Jesus as 'the Saviour', especially popular in pietistic circles, has become widespread in all Christian churches. For that reason we are at first surprised to discover that in the early Church it was by no means one of the central titles of honour for Jesus. With the exception of one passage in Philippians, this designation is completely missing from the most ancient of the early Christian writings. It first occurs relatively late in occasional passages in the Gospels of Luke and John; more often in the Pastoral Letters, II Peter, and the letters of Ignatius. Attempting to explain the reason for this, Vincent Taylor has suggested that the title *Soter* was so widespread in the non-Christian environment of the Hellenistic world that it had a bad connotation for Christians.[1] But such an objection would have been applicable to a much greater degree to the *Kyrios* title, and we have seen that it very early became the central expression of all early Christian faith in Christ. It seems to me that the real reason for the late appearance of the title Saviour is connected precisely with the fact that the name *Kyrios* played such a predominant role in early Christianity. 'Saviour', an Old Testament attribute of God, was conferred upon Christ on the basis of faith in him as the risen Lord. But just because *Kyrios* was the 'name above every name', it necessarily overshadowed and took precedence over all other titles which pointed in the same direction. Thus it is not surprising that *Soter* often appears in the New Testament only as a supplement to *Kyrios* (Phil. 3.20; II Peter 1.1, 11; 2.20; 3.2, 18).

It is noteworthy that the Pastoral Letters, which witness most frequently to Jesus as *Soter*, are the very ones that often call *God* 'Saviour' too—sometimes in the same passage in which the title is given to Jesus. This gives us all the more reason to assume that this Christological designation is an Old Testament title of honour for God transferred to Jesus, and confirms our assumption that the name

[1] See V. Taylor, *The Names of Jesus*, p. 109.

'Saviour' (like all the divine attributes) was ascribed to Jesus in connection with his dignity as *Kyrios*. Therefore, without desiring to underestimate the influence of the Hellenistic use of *Soter* upon the Christian utilization of the title, I consider it appropriate to speak of the title first of all in Judaism, and then in the second place in Hellenism.

1. *The* Soter *Title in Judaism and in Hellenism*

The Old Testament calls God 'Saviour'. The Hebrew words יֵשַׁע, מוֹשִׁיעַ, and יְשׁוּעָה, all of which come from the same root, are translated σωτήρ in the Septuagint.[1] The Psalms[2] and all parts of Isaiah[3] give God this title most often, but it occurs also elsewhere and may be traced through the whole of the Old Testament[4] and Jewish[5] literature.

It is certain that the title originally referred to God. But it does also sometimes distinguish definite men of God who by his commission have delivered, are delivering, or will deliver the people. Thus Moses 'saved' the people in the past, and after him other leaders of Israel were called 'saviours'.[6] In connection with this line, the Messiah is seen as the coming saviour who will finally and permanently save his people.[7] Indeed, this designation corresponds perfectly to the function which the Messiah is expected to fulfil. It is surprising that he is not called Saviour more often.[8]

Whereas in the Old Testament and Judaism in general the *Soter* is the saviour of the people, the title has a different meaning in Hellenism.[9] Here gods, but also heroes, and above all rulers are called 'saviours', because they deliver men from all kinds of physical distresses such as sickness and infirmity, dangers such as

[1] In apocryphal and rabbinical writings outside the Old Testament גּוֹאֵל is sometimes used in the same sense, but it is used mostly of course with reference to the Messiah.

[2] Pss. 24.5; 27.1; 35.3; 62.2, 6; 65.5; 79.9.

[3] Isa. 12.2; 17.10; 43.3, 11; 45.15, 21; 60.16; 62.11; 63.8.

[4] Jer. 14.8; Micah 7.7; Hab. 3.18; I Sam. 10.19; Deut. 32.15.

[5] I Macc. 4.30; Wisd. 16.7; Ecclus. 51.1; Baruch 4.22; Judith 9.11.

[6] As Othniel and Ehud, Judg. 3.9, 15. See also II Kings 13.5; Neh. 9.27.

[7] Isa. 19.20.

[8] Could it be because the name 'Saviour' was reserved especially for God?

[9] For the general problem of the *Soter* concept in comparative religions, see W. Staerk, *Soter. Die biblische Erlösererwartung als religionsgeschichtliches Problem*, I (1933), II (1938).

shipwrecks, and especially from the terrors of war and an uncertain existence.

P. Wendland has collected the most important Hellenistic texts which come into consideration here.[1] Asklepios, for instance, is the 'saviour' who delivers from sickness.[2] According to this conception, the idea of 'salvation' approaches that of 'providence', πρόνοια. But above all, σωτήρ is one of the most popular designations for deified rulers. In connection with pagan ruler worship, it is in a certain sense a variant of the title *Kyrios*. The ruler is *Soter* because he brings peace and order.[3] We recall especially Virgil's famous fourth eclogue.

In the mystery cults the *Soter* concept has other aspects. Here the divinity saves from the power of death and matter, and bestows immortality. It is a debatable point whether, as some scholars have asserted,[4] the *Soter* title is of fundamental significance for the mystery religions.[5] Even more questionable, then, is an influence from this source upon the Christian use of the title.[6] In so far as the non-Christian designation may be considered at all influential in the application of the title to Jesus, we must think first of all of its use in ruler worship.

[1] P. Wendland, 'Σωτήρ', *ZNW* 5, 1904, pp. 335ff. See also W. Wagner, 'Über σώζειν und seine Derivate im NT', *ZNW* 6, 1905, pp. 205 ff.; H. Lietzmann, *Der Weltheiland*, 1909; W. Bousset, *Kyrios Christos*[2], 1921, pp. 240 ff.; Dornsieff, 'σωτήρ', Pauly-Wissowa, *Realencyklopaedie*, 2nd series, V, 1927, col. 1211 ff.; E. B. Allo, 'Les dieux sauveurs du paganisme gréco-romain', *Revue des Sciences Philosophiques et Théologiques* 15, 1926, pp. 5 ff.; M. Dibelius and H. Conzelmann, *Die Pastoralbriefe* (HNT)[3], 1955, excursus on II Tim. 1.10.

[2] K. H. Rengstorf, *Die Anfänge der Auseinandersetzung zwischen Christusglaube und Asklepiosfrömmigkeit* (Schriften der Gesellschaft z. Förderung der westfälischen Landesuniversität zu Münster, no. 30), 1953, believes that the Christological use of the *Soter* title began as a conscious rejection of the same title for Asklepios, which the Christians met everywhere.

[3] See A. Deissman, *Licht vom Osten*[4], pp. 311 ff. (ET, pp. 363 ff.); W. Otto, 'Augustus Soter', *Hermes*, 1910, pp. 448 ff.; E. Lohmeyer, *Christuskult und Kaiserkult*, 1919, pp. 27 ff.

[4] G. Anrich, *Das antike Mysterienwesen in seinem Einfluss auf das Christentum*, 1894, pp. 47 ff.; G. Wobbermin, *Religionsgeschichtliche Studien*, 1896, pp. 105 ff.

[5] Thus P. Wendland, *op. cit.*, p. 353. See also the relevant places in the excellent work of K. Prümm, *Religionsgeschichtliches Handbuch für den Raum der altchristlichen Umwelt. Hellenistisch-römische Geistesströmungen und Kultur mit Beachtung des Eigenlebens der Provinzen*, 1943, p. 339 n. 1.

[6] Anrich, Wobbermin, Bousset and F. J. Dölger (*Ichthys* I, 1910, pp. 407 ff.) think such an influence must be taken into account. This is rejected by P. Wendland, *op. cit.*, p. 353, and E. Meyer, *Ursprung und Anfänge des Christentums*, 1923, III, pp. 391 ff.

2. *Jesus the Saviour in Early Christianity*

A one-sided derivation of the designation of Jesus as *Soter* from Hellenism might at first glance seem warranted, because, as we have seen, the title occurs almost exclusively in the later early Christian writings which originated in the Hellenistic environment.[1] Perhaps non-Christian use did in fact further its Christian utilization—just as the non-Christian use of *Kyrios* contributed to the spread of the concept *Kyrios Jesus Christos*. But just as the original source of the *Kyrios* title for Jesus lies primarily in Judaism, so it is more likely that his designation as *Soter* is connected with the Jewish and Old Testament concept rather than with the Hellenistic one. However late their date, the early Christian texts which call Jesus 'Saviour' nowhere exhibit a view of the *Soter* related to the Hellenistic concept. Bultmann also recognizes here an Old Testament as well as Greek influence.[2] It seems to me that the latter is to be considered more with respect to form than to content.

Almost all the passages in which Jesus is called 'Saviour' contain exclusively Christian motifs. This does not mean, of course, as Harnack seems to assume, that the designation may be traced back to Jesus' healing of the sick.[3] Even if the narrower meaning of σώζειν is often 'to heal', none of the Christian *Soter* passages indicate even the trace of a recollection of Jesus' activity as a physician.

Neither by himself nor by others was Jesus ever called *Soter* during his lifetime. Moreover even during the time when the title was occasionally conferred upon him, it was not used to refer to individual functions of his earthly work, but to his total work—and indeed as it was understood from faith in his resurrection and exaltation. Like *Kyrios*, the title *Soter* presupposes the completion of Jesus' earthly work and its confirmation in his exaltation.

We have already mentioned that Jesus is called *Soter* primarily in those writings which bestow this title of honour also upon God.

[1] This argument is emphasized also by the Old Testament scholar L. Köhler, 'Christus im Alten und im Neuen Testament', *TZ* 9, 1953, pp. 42 f. Köhler holds that the origin is purely Hellenistic.

[2] R. Bultmann, *Theology of the New Testament* I, p. 79. H. Gressmann, *Der Messias*, 1929, p. 370, speaking of late Judaism, holds that the Jewish and Hellenistic *Soter* are connected in II (4) Esd. 13. It is impossible to understand why he then rejects such a connection for the Christian use of the concept.

[3] A. Harnack, *Die Mission und Ausbreitung des Christentums in den ersten drei Jahrhunderten*[5], 1915, I, pp. 115 ff. (ET of 2nd ed., *The Expansion of Christianity* I, 1908, pp. 121 ff.). P. Wendland, *op. cit.*, p. 336, rejects this idea also. Harnack's thesis becomes relevant again for K. H. Rengstorf, *op. cit.* (see p. 240 n. 2 above).

This is above all true of the Pastoral Letters, in which God repeatedly appears as Saviour: I Tim. 1.1; 2.3; 4.10; Titus 1.3; 2.10; 3.4. It is also true of the Gospel of Luke in which, quite in the Old Testament style, the Magnificat in 1.47 speaks of God as 'Saviour', whereas the Christmas story proclaims in 2.11, 'To you is born this day a Saviour, who is *Christos Kyrios*.' Again, the final doxology of Jude is addressed to 'the only God our Saviour through Jesus Christ our Lord' (v. 25). It is thus not surprising that II Peter, which is so closely related to Jude, often speaks of the σωτὴρ 'Ιησοῦς Χριστός—and indeed, like Luke 2.11, in connection with the *Kyrios* title.[1] This confirms the fact that the idea of Christ's exaltation to the dignity of divine rule decisively influenced the introduction of *Soter* as a Christological designation. It is certainly not irrelevant, then, to point to the use of the title in Hellenistic ruler worship as a secondary source.

Primarily, however, we are concerned here with the transfer to Jesus of an Old Testament divine attribute. Jesus is the *Soter* because he will save his people from their sins. This is how Matt. 1.21 explains the name Jesus. This proper name is one of the Hebrew forms of the title 'Saviour' applied to God in the Old Testament. At least everywhere in the New Testament where a knowledge of Hebrew may be presupposed, we must therefore take into account the significance of the proper name Jesus for the origin of the title σωτὴρ 'Ιησοῦς. In fact, to Jewish ears 'Jesus' meant the same as σωτήρ, Saviour. The author of Matthew was certainly not the only one who knew this.

But the connection of the *Soter* title with the Old Testament lies above all in the emphasis upon deliverance of the people from sin and death. Whatever may be said about all the many analogies to the terminology of ruler worship (above all about that of the 'epiphany' of the divine ruler),[2] this idea of salvation from sin and death lies behind the statements about the appearance of the 'Saviour' Jesus Christ at his birth (Luke 2.11), after his resurrection (II Tim. 1.10: 'the appearing of our Saviour Christ Jesus, who abolished death'), and at his still awaited coming in glory (Titus 2.13 f.: 'the appearing of the glory of our great God and Saviour Jesus Christ, who gave himself for us to redeem us from all iniquity and to purify for himself a people of his own').[3] It is just when it praises him as the *coming*

[1] See p. 238 above.

[2] Cf. M. Dibelius and H. Conzelmann, *Die Pastoralbriefe*, p. 78.

[3] See pp. 313 f. below for the combination of τοῦ μεγάλου θεοῦ καὶ σωτῆρος ἡμῶν Χριστοῦ 'Ιησοῦ.

Lord that this last passage reminds us (perhaps in deliberate or unconscious opposition to the epiphany of deified earthly rulers) of Jesus' *earthly* work upon which his lordship rests. In a remarkable but characteristic way, Acts 5.31 also connects the already accomplished exaltation of Christ as *Soter* with the statement that this exaltation will bring Israel 'repentance and forgiveness of sins'. We are clearly in the realm of Jewish-Christian thought here: Christ is *Soter*, because he has saved us from sin.

If our reasoning has been correct, this connection between Jesus' lordship and his work of atonement shows us that while the *Soter* title does grow out of the *Kyrios* title, it nevertheless emphasizes an idea which is not a prominent part of the *Kyrios* concept: the idea that the exaltation of Christ to divine *Soter* very definitely presupposes his work of atonement. We are reminded of Phil 2.9: '*therefore* (i.e., on the basis of Christ's obedient humiliation of himself even to death) God has more than exalted him' and given him the *Kyrios* name which is above every name. The designation of Jesus as *Soter* implicitly includes precisely this idea of his atoning work. The Christian inclusion of the concept of reconciliation within the *Soter* title becomes clear also from another fact: the abovementioned doxology of Jude (v. 25), at least, indicates with the words 'through Jesus Christ our Lord' that now, even when God is called *Soter* after the Old Testament pattern, the foundation of all divine salvation is the atoning work of Christ.

Despite this reference to Christ's suffering and death, which mean forgiveness of sins and therefore 'salvation' (σωτηρία), *Soter* is by no means simply a variant of *ebed Yahweh*, as one might be tempted to think. In the concept *Soter* the suffering for forgiveness of sins is understood entirely from the divine ratification of that suffering in Jesus' exaltation to *Kyrios*. Bultmann is right in saying that a change of meaning has taken place in the Pauline idea of justification when the Pastoral Epistles replace δικαιοῦν with σώζειν, and δικαιοσύνη with σωτηρία.[1] Because the designation of Jesus as *Soter* presupposes the Christology of the exalted *Kyrios Christos*, we encounter it relatively late (i.e., in the later New Testament writings and in the letters of Ignatius),[2] but always in such a way that the central Christological idea of atonement is not simply forgotten.

[1] R. Bultmann, *Theology of the New Testament* II, p. 183.

[2] Ign., *Eph.* 1.1; *Magn.* 1.1; *Philad.* 9.2; *Smyrn.* 7.1. See also *Mart. Polyc.* 19.2, and the *Gospel of Peter* 4.13.

The importance of the atonement is also not forgotten in the two Johannine passages, John 4.42 and I John 4.14, which refer to Jesus as the '*Saviour of the world*'. This application of *Soter* formally sounds quite like Hellenistic ruler worship—indeed, it sounds exactly like the formulas applied, for instance, to Hadrian. But one can by no means decide with certainty whether the author was conscious of a parallel to these formulas, or whether here also he was only unconsciously influenced by them. Despite his reference to 'the world', the Johannine writer does not go beyond the general early Christian view of the consequence of Christ's redeeming work. We may recall also his statement about the 'Lamb of God who takes away the sin of the world' (John 1.29).

Finally, despite the fact that its common use was late, we must ask whether the application of the *Soter* title to Jesus was not nevertheless known relatively early. Among the writings attributed to Paul, the Pastoral Epistles are not the first in which we encounter this title. Eph. 5.23, referring to Christ's exaltation, says that he is the Head of the Church and at the same time '*Soter* of the body'. Even if this text is really deutero-Pauline, Phil. 3.20 still remains as the earliest and certainly Pauline use of *Soter*: '(from heaven) we await a Saviour, the Lord Jesus Christ.' Again we note first of all the characteristic connection of *Soter* and *Kyrios*. In contrast with II Tim. 1.10, in which Christ has already fulfilled his role as *Soter*, but in agreement with Titus 2.13, this text in Philippians speaks of Christ's fulfilment of the *Soter* function at the end of days. We have already seen in our investigation of other Christological titles that there is no contradiction here, but that this tension is characteristic of the whole New Testament, and particularly of New Testament Christology. Bultmann rightly observes that in Phil. 3.20 Paul uses an already familiar title, since *Soter* does not otherwise occur in the unquestionably Pauline letters.[1] Thus, it is a pre-Pauline designation, even though it may not be a common one. Further, I Thess. 1.10 corresponds exactly to the thought of Phil. 3.20, although it does not use the *Soter* title itself: we 'wait for his Son from heaven, whom he raised from the dead, Jesus who *delivers* (ῥυόμενον) us from the wrath to come'.

We have seen that the Semitic meaning of the name Jesus naturally suggested reference to the Old Testament title 'Saviour', and that Matthew (1.21) was certainly not the first to see the connection. On the other hand, it is also clear that 'Saviour' could not possibly

[1] R. Bultmann, *Theology of the New Testament* I, p. 79.

become a special title of honour for Jesus in Palestine, because one would simply have had to repeat the proper name 'Jesus'. '*Jesus Soter*' would have been '*Jeshua Jeshua*'. For this reason Jesus could only be called Saviour where Greek was spoken. But this certainly happened very early, especially since the idea was surely already present in the earliest Church that Jesus is not only *named* but *is* Saviour.

As we have seen, a full theological development of the *Soter* concept came only in the time of expanding Christianity. In connection with other important titles added to the name Jesus, it later became a part of the ancient Christian ΙΧΘΥΣ creed: Ἰησοῦς Χριστὸς Θεοῦ Υἱὸς Σωτήρ.[1]

[1] See F. J. Dölger, *Ichthys* I, 1910, pp. 248, 259, 318.

PART FOUR

The Christological Titles which Refer to the Pre-existence of Jesus

THE CHRISTOLOGICAL CONCEPTS 'Logos', 'Son of God', and 'God' remain to be investigated in this fourth and last part. We have already seen that on the basis of the *Kyrios* title, the first Christians could apply all statements about God also to Jesus. We would oversimplify the problem, however, and fall into a heresy condemned by the ancient Church if we were to attribute to the New Testament a complete identification between God the Father and Jesus the *Kyrios*, and maintain that the faith of early Christianity made no distinction at all between the two. The ancient two-part confession in I Cor. 8.6, to which we have already referred in another context, indicates that the early Church by no means forgot the distinction—not even when Christ was recognized as the mediator of creation: '. . . for us there is one God, the Father, from (ἐξ) whom are all things and for (εἰς) whom we exist, and one Lord, Jesus Christ, through (διά) whom are all things and through whom we exist.' The use of prepositions makes clear the distinction: ἐξ and εἰς with reference to God; διά with reference to Christ. We shall seek in vain for a more precise definition of the original relationship between God the Father and Christ the *Kyrios*.

Even with the titles 'Logos' and 'Son of God' we approach a closer definition of this relationship only in so far as they refer directly to the pre-existence of Jesus, his being 'in the beginning'. But we shall see that these names too do not indicate unity in essence or nature between God and Christ, but rather a unity in the work of revelation, in the *function* of the pre-existent one. As we have seen, this is also the meaning of the transfer of the divine *Kyrios* name to Jesus. God and the exalted Jesus are one with regard to world dominion, which is one aspect of God's self-revelation. It is true that *Kyrios* has to do primarily with the divine rule of Jesus in the present phase of *Heilsgeschichte*. But I Cor. 8.6 and Heb. 1.10 ff., for instance, extend the scope of this title to include also Jesus' original function as mediator of creation.

If in the case of the *Kyrios* title this extension must be derived from faith in the present Lord, the situation is different with the Logos title. By its very nature it traces all the revelatory work of God in Christ back to the 'beginning' of all things, to the pre-existent divine work of Jesus. The Logos concept as such closely relates redemption and creation—the work of the Christ who was incarnate, is still present, and will come again; and the work of the Christ who was the 'Word', the pre-existent mediator of creation. With this concept emerges—in a quite marginal way—the question of the essential relationship between God and the pre-existent Jesus. But it is significant that this question is not answered ontologically, not in the sense of a speculation about 'natures', but once again strictly with reference to the history of revelation. In a similar way the 'Son of God' concept also implicitly raises beyond the question of the incarnation that of the essential relationship of Father and Son, and here also the question is answered only in the sense of a unity of revelatory action in *Heilsgeschichte*.

We do hear concerning the Logos that 'In the beginning *was* the Word . . . the Word *was* with God, *was* God.' But, almost as if the writer of the prologue of John feared further ontological speculation, he moves immediately from *being* to the *act* of revelation: 'All things were *made* through him . . . and the Word *became* flesh.' The situation is similar with the Son of God concept. Looking at the end rather than at the beginning of time, Paul leads us in I Cor. 15.28 to the very threshold of a complete eschatological absorption of the Son in the Father: 'When all things are subjected to him, then the Son himself will also be subjected to him who put all things under him, that God may be all in all.'

It is possible to speak of the Son only in connection with the revelation of God, but in principle at least one can speak of God also apart from revelation. But the New Testament is interested only in revelation. This is the source of the New Testament paradox that the Father and Son are at once one and yet distinct—a paradox which the later Christian theologians could not explain because they attempted to do so by speculative philosophical means.

As we investigate in this last section the titles which refer to the pre-existence of Jesus, therefore, we shall have to free ourselves from all the questions asked by later theologians, even though such questions may be indirectly suggested.

9

Jesus the Word

(λόγος)

ALTHOUGH Logos became the predominant designation for Jesus in the classical Christology of the ancient Church, and to a great extent was even considered the essential content of all Christology, we find it as a Christological title only in one group of New Testament writings, the Johannine. Even there it occurs only in a few passages: the prologue to the Gospel of John, the first verse of I John, and Rev. 19.13. It is a common error to think that the Logos designation dominates the Gospel of John. In fact, as we have already seen, the title 'Son of Man' occurs much more frequently. Because the Logos title does not appear in the body of this Gospel, A. Harnack actually maintained that the prologue does not really belong to it at all, but was added later.[1] In this form his thesis is hardly tenable, but one cannot overlook the fact that the title does appear only in the first verses.

On the other hand, the point at which the author of John makes use of the Logos concept shows that the title is indispensable for him when he wishes to speak of the relationship between the divine revelation in the life of Jesus and the pre-existence of Jesus. He does not, like Mark, identify the 'beginning' (ἀρχή) of the history of Jesus with the appearance of John the Baptist. For him the beginning lies in the pre-existence of Jesus, which directs our attention to the absolute beginning of all things. In order to avoid all the misunderstanding which arose in the later Christological discussions of the ancient Church, however, we must emphasize at once that the evangelist is not interested in a speculation about this pre-temporal existence of Jesus. He speaks of this 'beginning' only in the closest connection with what he says of the further work of Christ. He who was 'in the beginning with God' is just the same one whose story the whole Gospel tells, whose life 'in the flesh' is the centre of the history of divine revelation and salvation. This one person who in

[1] A Harnack, *ZTK* 2, 1892, pp. 189 ff. See also E. Käsemann, 'Aufbau und Anliegen des Johanneischen Prologs', *Festschrift F. Delekat*, 1957, pp. 75 ff.

the flesh accomplished the decisive act of revelation was (as the prologue already clearly suggests) [1] at work in the history of Israel, and this one person will continue working in the Church after his death (as his parting words foretell).

With this in mind, however, we must recognize the special significance the evangelist attaches to the pre-existent being of Christ. The Incarnate One, the Son of Man as he appeared in the flesh, is the centre of *all* history. Therefore the question of his pre-existent work arises too. The one who is the centre of the whole *Heilsgeschichte* cannot simply have appeared from nowhere. Therefore the Gospel of John emphasizes very strongly the participation of the pre-existent Christ in creation—even more strongly than the other New Testament writings in which we have found the same idea. The creation belongs to divine revelation just as does salvation through him who became flesh.[2] We must not overlook the fact that the Gospel of John begins with the same words as the first book of the Old Testament. If we, like the first Christians of the Diaspora, were accustomed to read the Old Testament in Greek, this would immediately attract our attention. Genesis begins with the words ἐν ἀρχῇ; John 1.1 begins with the words ἐν ἀρχῇ. We read in the Old Testament: 'In the beginning God created the heavens and the earth.' In the Gospel of John we read: 'In the beginning was the Word, the Logos . . . all things were made through him.' The evangelist gives a new Genesis account, now presented in the light of the Mediator of revelation.[3]

Since 'Logos' is a concept which was widespread both before and contemporaneously with Christianity, we must first of all discuss

[1] C. H. Dodd, *The Interpretation of the Fourth Gospel*, p. 284, correctly emphasizes that the prologue speaks at the same time of the Logos who was not received by the world (the creation) and who was rejected by Israel.

[2] C. H. Dodd, *ibid.*, pp. 277 ff., and M. E. Boismard, *Le prologue de S. Jean*, 1953, point out that in Rom. 1.18 ff. Paul speaks in a very similar way of unbelievers' rejection of the divine revelation in creation. Although Rom. 1.18 ff. does not expressly connect the revelation of God in creation with Christ, it is certainly incorrect to interpret this passage as if creation by God and salvation by Christ were to be separated. We already know that for Paul too Christ is the mediator of creation. W. Bauer, *Das Johannesevangelium* (HNT)[3], 1933, p. 6, rightly says that Paul develops views very similar to the Gospel of John about the Christ who was pre-existent, with the Father, of the same nature, and active in creation. See also p. 267 below.

[3] Both in his commentary on John, p. 6, and in his *Theology of the New Testament* II, p. 64, R. Bultmann recognizes this relation to the Old Testament Genesis story, but he still does not appreciate its full significance.

its place in Hellenism and then in Judaism. The Johannine writer was perhaps by no means unconscious of the fact that he was making use of an extra-Christian concept. It is quite possible that he was familiar with its non-Christian use and believed that the concept was fulfilled only in Jesus. We shall speak in this context of the nature of the Johannine Christological universalism which is expressed in the Logos designation.

1. *The Logos in Hellenism*

We cannot give here a full history of the Logos concept. There are already many works on this subject,[1] and both the older and the more recent commentaries have for the most part adequately dealt with its occurrence and role in Hellenistic philosophy and Hellenistic-oriental religions. I am concerned only to indicate that in the ancient world it was a common concept,[2] the use of which could not have been unfamiliar to the author of the Gospel of John. It is important to know this if one is to understand the full significance of the sentence, 'The Word became flesh.'

The 'Logos' occurs in the earliest period of Greek philosophy in Heraclitus,[3] and then especially in Stoicism.[4] Here it is the cosmic law which rules the universe and at the same time is present in the human intellect. It is thus an abstraction, not a hypostasis. Therefore, although the Stoics too spoke of the Logos, and although they too could say that the Logos was 'in the beginning', nevertheless, with their impersonal, pantheistic World Soul they meant something quite different from the Johannine Logos.[5] Platonism also uses the concept. Its view of the 'real' being (in the Platonic, idealistic sense, of course) may come nearer the Johannine view, but it still has nothing to do with a hypostasis, and the idea of the Logos' 'becoming

[1] See the full list of literature on this subject given by H. Leisegang in Pauly-Wissowa, *Realencyklopaedie*, Vol. 25, 1926, pp. 1035 ff.; and in *TWNT* IV, p. 70 For an older work see A. Aall, *Geschichte der Logosidee, I: in der griechischen Philosophie*, 1896.

[2] C. H. Dodd, *The Interpretation of the Fourth Gospel*, p. 265, thinks that the conception of the Logos as a hypostasis, a mediator, was not so widespread in the Orient as is usually thought. In view of the extensive material from the study of comparative religions, can one really say this?

[3] H. Diels, *Die Fragmente der Vorsokratiker*[5], 1934, Fr. 1 and 2, pp. 150 f.

[4] See K. Prümm, *Der christliche Glaube und die altheidnische Welt* I, 1935, pp. 227 ff.; M. Pohlenz, *Die Stoa*, 1948, I (see index); R. Bultmann, 'Der Begriff des Wortes Gottes im Neuen Testament', *Glauben und Verstehen* I, 1933, pp. 274 ff.

[5] This is recognized also by R. Bultmann, *Das Evangelium des Johannes*, p. 9.

flesh' is quite unthinkable for the Platonist. We must guard against being led by the terminological analogy to read into Greek philosophy the late Jewish or Johannine understanding of the Logos. Augustine well knew that the complete entrance of the Logos into history and humanity is utterly foreign to Platonism, although formal similarities did lead him to remark that with somewhat different expressions the Platonic books say the same thing about the original Logos that John teaches in his Gospel (*Confessions*, 7.9). Actually, of course, the similarity between the two is more one of terminology than of content itself.

Nevertheless this philosophical Logos concept does have a vital place in the long and complicated history of the Logos inasmuch as it did at least formally influence Jewish and pagan conceptions of a more or less personified Logos. Mythological motifs may indeed have had a stronger influence, but the philosophical Logos doctrine does remain one root of these later conceptions. This is especially true of Philo of Alexandria, whose discussions of the Logos occupy so much space in the commentaries on John. Although he does already conceive a personified intermediary being, still the connection between his thought and Greek philosophical teachings is more than evident. The whole discussion whether Philo's Logos is personal or impersonal should not be considered in terms of an alternative, as if only one root were possible.

Only with this reservation can we agree with R. Bultmann, who finds within paganism what he believes to be a more direct preparation than the Greek philosophical for the Jewish and Johannine Logos concept. It is the influence he calls 'Gnostic'. In Gnosticism the Logos is a mythological intermediary being between God and man. He is not only creator of the world, but above all revealer, and as revealer also redeemer. Gnosticism even believed that the Logos temporarily became man, but only in a mythical and docetic sense, never in the historical sense of a real incarnation.[1] Bultmann finds here the myth of the descent and ascent of the redeemer who saves the world in saving himself. This Logos is the same figure we find in non-Christian speculations about the 'original man'.

It is more than probable that there was such a mythological Logos figure already in non-Christian thought, although it is very difficult to find sources to prove its existence. As he himself admits on p. 11 of his

[1] R. Bultmann in his commentary on John, p. 10, rightly uses for this the expression 'disguise'.

commentary on John, Bultmann can only point to later texts from Christian times, even though the ideas in them may be older than the texts themselves. In any case, the explanation he gives of the Gnostic and mythological Logos (pp. 10 ff.) [1] without doubt accurately describes conceptions existing in pre-Christian paganism. But Bultmann assumes too quickly that the pre-Christian Gnostic teaching was a fixed and completely apprehensible entity when he considers its Logos doctrine as the one and only source of the Johannine Logos concept as well as of the Alexandrian Jewish Logos and wisdom teaching as expressed in Philo, the wisdom literature, and in rabbinic texts. The connections between pagan and Jewish Christian thought seem to me too complex for such a schematic explanation as Bultmann's to be valid (see for instance his commentary on John, p. 8).

These conceptions of a personified revealer and redeemer Logos are foreshadowed in ancient religions. Hermes [2] and the Egyptian God Thoth,[3] for instance, were both called 'Logos'. Originally this was only a way of giving an allegorical, philosophical explanation to myths about the gods, and thus giving them a pantheistic meaning. But it did make easier the personification of the Logos, especially for popular religious understanding. Thus arose the voluminous Hermetic literature.[4]

The primary names for this redeemer are *Logos* and *Nous*, but other titles are also given him, above all that of 'man'. The Mandaean texts also speak of the 'Word' in this connection.[5] The relationship between the Logos and Original Man concepts in paganism is all the more noteworthy because we find it also in early Christian usage (although it can hardly be explained here by the influence of pagan mythology).

We must emphasize already at this point that what is true of

[1] Following R. Reitzenstein, *Das iranische Erlösungsmysterium*, 1921; Reitzenstein and Schaeder, *Studien z. antiken Synkretismus aus Iran und Griechenland*, 1926; H. Jonas, *Gnosis und spätantiker Geist*, 1934, I, pp. 260 ff.

[2] Plato, *Cratylus* 407 E ff.; Hippolytus, *Refut.* V, 7.29; O. Kern, *Orphicorum Fragmenta*, 1922, 297a; cf. R. Reitzenstein, *Poimandres*, 1904, p. 88.

[3] Plutarch, *De Iside et Osiride*, 54 f.

[4] See the critical edition of the *Corpus Hermeticum* by A. D. Nock and A. J. Festugière, Paris, 4 vol. completed, 1945–1954. On the problem of the Hermetica cf. J. Kroll, *Die Lehren des Hermes Trismegistos*, 1914; K. Prümm, *Religionsgeschichtliches Handbuch*, pp. 535 ff.; more recently, especially A. J. Festugière, *La Révélation d'Hermès Trismegistos* (Etudes Bibliques) I–IV, 1944–54; *idem*, *L'Hermétisme*, 1948; C. H. Dodd, *The Interpretation of the Fourth Gospel*, pp. 10 ff.

[5] *Ginza* (ed. Lidzbarski, 1925), p. 295. See W. Bauer, *Das Johannesevangelium*, p. 10.

paganism is even more characteristic of Judaism and early Christianity: the Logos concept was so widespread in ancient religious life that many different lines meet here without one being an extension of another. Of course, this does not relieve us of the responsibility for investigating these different lines and discovering which of them more immediately influenced the Christian view. But we must ask especially to what extent Christianity introduced completely new elements and freshly interpreted the Logos concept. We shall see that the Gospel of John did not derive from the widely spread Logos idea a doctrine of general, not exclusively Christian revelation; but that on the contrary it completely subordinated the extra- and pre-Christian Logos concept to the one revelation of God in Jesus of Nazareth, and in this way completely re-formed it.

2. *The Logos in Judaism*

At the very beginning we must distinguish between two different expressions of the Logos in Judaism: (1) the later Jewish form, which conceived the 'Word' as a hypostasis, even a personified mediator, and was certainly more or less influenced by the pagan conceptions we have discussed; (2) the genuine Old Testament form, which, going back to the first chapter of Genesis, conceived the Word of God (*debar Yahweh*) in its original sense, and then on this basis occasionally developed it also into the conception of a divine hypostasis. This distinction remains fully valid even when we recognize that one form influenced the other. Thus the later Jewish form is certainly not to be considered without reference to the Old Testament form. The otherwise useful works on comparative religion we have mentioned, and especially the conclusions Bultmann has drawn from them, have recognized the necessary distinction between these two lines of thought, but they have tended so to exaggerate their difference that no common denominator is left. There is, however, a common denominator in the concept of revelation, and it is no accident that both strains of Judaism chose the same designation, 'Word'.

It is therefore an incorrect procedure in investigating the early Christian Logos concept to consider only the later Jewish doctrine of a divine hypostasis on the ground that only later Judaism (in common with the Gospel of John and the pagan redeemer myth) knew a more or less personified mediator. Even if it is proved that certain circles of early Christianity were familiar with the Logos concept of later

Hellenistic Judaism—and perhaps paganism—the Old Testament understanding of the Word of God may still have directly and significantly influenced the early Christian conception. We can of course say whether this is actually the case only when we investigate the Johannine statements about the Logos. But in any case we should not *a priori* discard the Old Testament tradition as unimportant in our consideration of the question of the Logos in Judaism.

This is what in fact happens in most of the so-called 'critical' commentaries on the Gospel of John. On the other hand, the 'conservative' interpretations often consider only the Old Testament conception of the Word of God. In the article 'λέγω (λόγος)' in the *Theologisches Wörterbuch* one-sidedness in either direction is avoided, thanks to the fact that the material is distributed among several scholars (*TWNT* IV, pp. 69 ff.; the authors are G. Kittel, A. Debrunner, H. Kleinknecht, O. Procksch, G. Quell, and G. Schrenk). In any case, we ought to stop designating an interpretation as 'critical' or 'conservative' simply because it emphasizes either the Old Testament or the Hellenistic Jewish (or pagan) Logos concept. This question of scholarly investigation ought not to involve theological position.

There are many passages in the Old Testament in which, following the first chapter of Genesis, the 'Word of God' is made the object of independent consideration because of its powerful effect, even though it may not yet be personified.[1] These passages are connected above all with the creation story, in which everything happens as a result of the word which God speaks. 'Let there be light, and there was light.' When one reflects on this, the idea comes that every creative self-revelation of God to the world happens through his word. *His word is the side of God turned toward the world.* Thus we hear in Ps. 33.6: 'By the word of the Lord the heavens were made.' After the creation too, God's command calls nothingness to life. Therefore the Psalms often speak of the word of God as the mediator. We read in Ps. 107.20: 'He sent forth his word and healed them.' And in Ps. 147.15: 'He sends forth his command to the earth; his word runs swiftly.' In Isa. 55.10 f. we come very near a personification: 'For as the rain and the snow come down from heaven, and return not thither but water the earth . . . so shall my word be that goes forth from my mouth; it shall not return to me empty, but it shall accomplish that which I purpose.'[2] We are not far here from the Wisdom of

[1] See O. Grether, *Name und Wort Gottes im Alten Testament*, 1934, especially pp. 150 ff.

[2] For parallels from the ancient East, see L. Dürr, *Die Wertung des göttlichen Wortes im AT und im Alten Orient* (Mitt. d. Vorderas. Gesellschaft, 42, 1), 1938.

Solomon, which belongs within the Alexandrian environment. In 18.15 of this book we read: 'Thine all-powerful word leaped from heaven down from the royal throne, a stern warrior . . .' We should also mention here the expression *memra deyahweh*, the Aramaic designation for 'word of Yahweh' found in the Targums.[1] The fact that *memra* can be used instead of the divine name presupposes a special reflection about the 'word of God' as such. Of course, there are no such explanations of the *memra* of God in the rabbinical texts as we find elsewhere of the personified Logos or personified Wisdom.[2]

We first meet the Logos and Wisdom in really hypostatic form in an Alexandrian environment, in Hellenistic Judaism. Here we must without doubt reckon with extra-Jewish influences of a mediator figure of pagan mythology.[3] Nevertheless here too we must take into consideration the reflection about the operation of the word of God as it is expressed in the above-mentioned Old Testament passages in connection with the first chapter of Genesis. We must do so even when we hear no longer of that 'Word of God', but only of '*the* Word'; no longer of the 'Wisdom of God', but only of 'Wisdom'.

Although Philo's Logos doctrine lacks unity and has various roots,[4] the Stoic conception of the Logos as the principle of reason in the world[5] prevails in his writings. This conception has only an indirect significance for us, but, as a result partly of Platonic and partly perhaps of mythological influences, Philo too prepares the way for the conception of a personified mediator.[6]

More important for early Christian thought about the Logos are the Jewish speculations concerning *Wisdom*. Since the studies by J. Rendel Harris,[7] these speculations have rightly been considered

[1] V. Hamp, *Der Begriff 'Wort' in den aramäischen Bibelübersetzungen*, 1938.

[2] Besides this, the question of date is difficult to answer. It is not certain whether this conception belongs in pre-Christian times. See on this Strack-Billerbeck II, pp. 302 ff.

[3] Thus R. Bultmann on John, p. 8.

[4] This is correctly seen by W. Bauer, *Das Johannesevangelium*, p. 8. On the many passages which come into consideration here, see A. Aall, *Geschichte der Logosidee*, 1896, I, pp. 184 ff. See also E. Bréhier, *Les idées philosophiques et religieuses de Philon d'Alexandrie*[2], 1925, pp. 83 ff.; H. A. Wolfson, *Philo*, 1948, I, pp. 200 ff.; 325 ff.

[5] See p. 251 above.

[6] On the whole question of Philo and the Gospel of John, see C. H. Dodd, *The Interpretation of the Fourth Gospel*, pp. 54 ff.

[7] *The Origin of the Prologue to St John's Gospel*, 1917; 'Athena, Sophia and the Logos', *BJRL* 7, 1922/23, pp. 56 ff.

parallels of primary significance.[1] Harris' theory that the prologue of John goes directly back to a hymn to Wisdom has not been proved, but in any case there is materially a very close similarity here—so close that *Logos* and *Sophia* are almost interchangeable. We cite only a few of the especially characteristic statements from the extensive body of relevant material.[2] In Prov. 8.22–26 Wisdom itself speaks: 'The Lord created me at the beginning of his work, the first of his acts of old. Ages ago I was set up, at the first, before the beginning of the earth. When there were no depths I was brought forth, when there were no springs abounding with water. Before the mountains had been shaped, before the hills, I was brought forth; before he made the earth with its fields, or the first of the dust of the world.' We find the same conception in Ecclus. 1.1 ff. and 24.1 ff., and in other places in Jewish literature.[3] According to Wisd. 7.26, Wisdom is 'an image of his eternal light'. In view of the prologue to John it is informative to note that there are many passages which speak of the world's 'hatred' of Wisdom (Prov. 1.28 ff.; cf. Ecclus. 24.7).

Rabbinical texts identify pre-existent Wisdom with the Torah, which in this way also becomes a hypostasis, mediatrix of creation, 'daughter of God'.[4] These speculations are only secondarily derived from the Jewish understanding of 'Wisdom',[5] but they indicate how common in later Judaism was the idea of an intermediary figure who belongs to God as a divine hypostasis.

We may also mention a Qumran text (*Manual of Discipline* 11.11) in which the 'divine thought' is the origin of all that is.

We have distinguished two basic lines of thought in Judaism: first, the specifically Old Testament line of the Word of God (*debar Yahweh*); and second, the later Jewish line simply of *the* Word, which developed under the influence of extra-Jewish sources. The concept of divine revelatory action is common to both. But still

[1] C. F. Burney, *The Aramaic Origin of the Fourth Gospel*, 1922; R. Bultmann, 'Der religionsgeschichtliche Hintergrund des Prologs zum Johannesevangelium', *Eucharisterion* 2 (Forschungen zur Religion und Literatur des Alten und Neuen Testaments), 1923, pp. 3 ff.; C. Spicq, 'Le Siracide et la structure littéraire du prologue', *Mémorial Lagrange*, 1940, pp. 183 ff.; C. H. Dodd, *op. cit.*, pp. 274 ff.

[2] Further passages are given in the literature mentioned on p. 256 n. 4 above. Rabbinical texts are given by Strack-Billerbeck II, pp. 356 f.

[3] Cf. Philo, *Leg. Alleg.* II, 49.

[4] See Strack-Billerbeck II, 353 ff.; III, p. 131.

[5] So correctly R. Bultmann on John, p. 8.

foreign to both is the idea that this revelatory action, this speech of God to the world, happens finally and definitely in the historical framework of an earthly, human life.

3. *The Logos Concept Applied to Jesus*

We have already seen that the title Logos as a designation for Jesus occurs in the Gospel of John only in the prologue, and in only two passages in the other Johannine writings. It is used as a title for Jesus in no other New Testament writing and in no other early Christian literature except that of Ignatius of Antioch, in which it probably has no connection with the Gospel of John.[1] One might think, therefore, that the Logos is not a central concept of the New Testament. It is in fact certainly not so significant as the titles 'Son of Man' or *Kyrios*, for instance. Nevertheless this title expresses very forcefully an important aspect of New Testament Christology—the unity in historical revelation of the incarnate and the pre-existent Jesus. In connection with this, it also clarifies the relation between Christ and God as it is understood in the New Testament (in contrast to the later Christological discussions).

As in the case of the important title *Kyrios*, Jesus was of course identified with the Logos only after his death. But while the *Kyrios* title has its origin in early Christian worship, the Logos designation is without doubt the result of theological reflection, which, of course, presupposes the experience of the *Kyrios* in worship. Since the Logos title was used more consciously than other titles in connection with extra- and pre-Christian parallels, we must reckon more strongly with these parallels here, even though the connection with them remains primarily a formal one.

But on the other hand, it would be methodologically wrong to allow this undeniably reflective theological character of the Logos concept to focus our attention only on its connection with oriental-Hellenistic statements about the Logos, as if the Johannine theological interest were exhausted thereby. Today we know that despite, and precisely because of, its Hellenistic elements, the Gospel of John belongs to the broad category of syncretistically influenced Palestinian Judaism, an outline of which we are beginning to know better

[1] Ignatius, *Magn.* 8.2. See especially H. Schlier, *Religionsgeschichtliche Untersuchungen zu den Ignatiusbriefen* (BZNW 8), 1929. C. Maurer, *Ignatius von Antiochien und das Johannesevangelium* (ATANT 18), 1949, believes that Ignatius knew the Gospel of John, but he admits that Ignatius' 'Logos' in this passage does not necessarily go back to John (pp. 41 f.).

through the Qumran texts.[1] Therefore to a much greater extent than has hitherto been the case, the Hellenistic elements must be seen in their connection with genuine Old Testament conceptions, and we must give priority to the question of the Old Testament roots of the Logos concept.

Further, it is methodologically essential to keep in mind early Christian thought in general—and not simply for the purpose of immediately setting up an antithesis. Even if the title Logos is completely lacking except in the few Johannine passages, we must nevertheless ask whether we cannot find in the other New Testament writings the thought of the pre-existent Jesus and of the specific relationship between God the Father and Jesus characteristic of the Johannine Logos. We shall discover that the prologue of John does in fact teach nothing essentially different at this point from what we have found in Paul's writings in connection with other titles. And we shall ask whether the 'Son of God' designation, which was already known to the oldest Synoptic tradition, did not to a certain extent contain similar conceptions.

First of all, however, we must examine the extent to which the ordinary, not immediately Christological, use of the word 'logos' in the Gospel of John itself and then in the other New Testament writings could also be a root for the application of the concept to Jesus.

This aspect of the question has rightly been considered in the lexicographical articles of the *Biblisch-theologisches Wörterbuch des neutestamentlichen Griechisch* by Cremer-Kögel, 11th ed., 1923; in Kittel's *TWNT*; in C. H. Dodd, *The Interpretation of the Fourth Gospel*, pp. 265 ff. See also J. Dupont, *Essais sur la christologie de S. Jean*, 1951, pp. 20 ff.

The word of Jesus—the word he preached—plays such an important part in the whole Gospel of John that one can hardly assume the evangelist did not think also of this 'word' when in the prologue he identified Jesus himself as the Logos. The supposition that he did so is suggested even more strongly by the basic Johannine thought that Jesus not only *brings* revelation, but in his person *is* revelation. He brings light, and at the same time he is Light; he bestows life, and he is Life; he proclaims truth, and he is Truth. More properly expressed, he brings light, life and truth just because he himself is Light, Life, and Truth. So it is also with the Logos: he brings the word, because he is the Word.

[1] See pp. 183 f. above.

The concordance shows that the word 'logos' occurs extraordinarily often in the Gospel of John, and in the sense of the 'spoken, proclaimed word' is actually one of its central concepts. In common use λόγος means nothing more than the concrete word heard with the ear (John 2.22; 19.8). But there is also a specifically theological use: the λόγος which Jesus proclaims is at the same time God's eternal revelation, which beyond simple hearing requires the understanding of faith. Really to hear (ἀκούειν) includes this understanding.[1] This second use is intended whenever we hear of 'continuing in the word' (John 8.31), 'keeping the word' (8.51); or when we hear of the word which gives eternal life when heard in faith (5.24). In this sense the word proclaimed by Jesus is identical with the concept of the *kerygma* which is so popular in modern theology. In the Gospel of John it is identical with the 'Word of God' (17.14; 5.37 ff.). It is *the* truth as such (17.17). It is more than simply φωνή (voice). When in John 1.23 the Baptist, referring to Isa. 40.3, designates himself as a φωνή, the author surely thinks of the immediately preceding prologue, which speaks of one who is the Logos and as such is expressly distinguished from the Baptist (1.8).

In the Gospel of John a direct line leads from the theologically charged concept of the proclaimed word to the Logos who became flesh in Jesus. This is indeed the meaning of the Gospel: it intends to show that the total human life of Jesus is the centre of the revelation of divine truth.

The word of God which is identical with Jesus' proclaimed λόγος is 'truth' (17.17); but Jesus himself is the truth in person (14.6). Thus in this respect the ordinary Johannine use of the word λόγος directly clarifies the designation of Jesus as Logos. This explanation is of course not enough in itself, but it indicates a line of thought which in any case ought not to be ignored.

While the absolute meaning of λόγος as 'revelation' is nowhere so strongly emphasized as in the Gospel of John, it may be seen as common to all the New Testament writings. Beyond the typical Old Testament use of the 'word of God' (*debar Yahweh*) to indicate the individual, ever repeated instructions of God to the prophets in particular situations, the New Testament usually intends ὁ λόγος τοῦ θεοῦ to mean the proclamation of salvation as such. Thus many passages speak in an absolute sense, without a genitive, simply of 'the word' as the preaching of the Gospel. We can trace this use through

[1] C. H. Dodd, *The Interpretation of the Fourth Gospel*, p. 226, emphasizes the distinction between λαλία and λόγος in John 8.43.

all the books of the New Testament.[1] Sometimes it is qualified by a genitive which specifies the content of the proclamation: the 'word of the cross' (I Cor. 1.18), the 'word of proclamation' (II Cor. 5.19). In these instances also the Logos is the final definitive revelation as such.

The prologue of the Epistle to the Hebrews clearly defines the distinction between this 'word' and the isolated word to men of God under the old covenant: 'In many and various ways (πολυμερῶς καὶ πολυτρόπως) God spoke of old to our fathers by the prophets; but in these last days he has spoken to us by a Son.' A clear parallel to the prologue of John becomes obvious here when we consider that the author mentions in the same sentence the creation of the world through the Son, and in the next verse says this Son 'reflects the glory of God' and 'bears the stamp of his nature'. The word λόγος as such is missing, but this passage, exactly like John 1.1, connects the divine word in the Son with the creation of the world, and defines the eternal relationship of the Son to God the Father. This is actually a much more direct parallel than many others usually cited to clarify the Johannine Logos concept. Whether Heb. 1.1 ff. is earlier or later than John 1.1 ff., one must in either case notice that it connects the Old Testament word of God with *the* revelation which is the Son himself as the reflection of the glory of God. But then we must consider as the connecting link the New Testament use of the word λόγος in the sense of the final, definitive proclamation of salvation.

Although Heb. 1.1 ff. says only that God has spoken *through* or *by* the Son,[2] it does raise the question of the relationship between this Son and God, and it gives an answer similar to that of the prologue of John, even though it does not directly identify the Son and this definitive 'speaking of God'. Hebrews does not call the Son 'Logos'. The first chapter of John does so because it is a prologue to a life of Jesus, which in itself is the starting point for all further Christological reflection. God's revelation is presented in this life not only in the words but also in the actions of Jesus. Jesus himself *is* what he *does*. The Hebrew term *debarim* (words) can also mean 'history',[3] and when one thinks primarily in terms of the life or 'history' of Jesus, it becomes natural to identify Jesus with the Word.

[1] For example Gal. 6.6; Col. 4.3; Mark 2.2; 4.14 ff.; 8.32; Luke 1.2; Acts 8.4; 10.44; 16.6.

[2] The instrumental ἐν.

[3] See O. Procksch, *TWNT* IV, pp. 91 ff.

Thus, although the Johannine designation of Jesus as 'the Word' is related to pagan and late Jewish thought, it nevertheless rests upon a direct reflection about the close connection between the origin of all revelation and the historical life of Jesus. The 'speaking' of God is recognized here as God's action, and therefore it is natural to refer to his creative word, through which he communicated himself already at the 'beginning'. When in this way we ask about the ultimate origin of divine self-revelation, our thoughts must necessarily go back beyond the word through the prophets to the word of God at the creation of the world. Preparation for this conception is made by the above-mentioned Old Testament texts which, with reference to the Genesis story, already conceived the word of God almost as a hypostasis.[1] The speculations of Hellenistic Judaism also make use of the story of creation to support their ideas about the original divine hypostasis. But the prologue of John does not trace only an indirect line through Hellenistic and later Jewish texts to Gen. 1; it is also interested in the direct connection between the history of Jesus and the Genesis story. The Johannine writer begins his whole presentation of the life of Jesus with the words of the Old Testament creation story. For him this connection is so significant that every other point of contact can only be of secondary importance.

As we have already mentioned, both in his commentary on John, p. 6; and in his *Theology of the New Testament*, II, p. 64, R. Bultmann formally acknowledges this connection with the first chapter of Genesis. But it plays only a very subordinate part in his actual explanation.

If the utterance of God which called the world into existence ('and there was light') is the same which speaks to us in the life of Jesus, then the identification of Jesus with the divine Logos itself is obvious. Then creation and the life of Jesus have the same denominator, 'Word', 'Revelation'. And that in turn implicitly raises the question of the relationship between Jesus and God, and answers it as does the prologue of John on the basis of Gen. 1.1 ff.

The prologue of John also belongs within the framework of Old Testament thought[2] in speaking of the rejection of revelation. As

[1] See p. 255 above.

[2] H. Sahlin, *Zur Typologie des Johannesevangeliums*, 1954, maintains that not only the prologue but the whole Gospel of John in general must be understood as a conscious typological parallel to Old Testament thought, and especially to the Exodus tradition. But Sahlin's own attempt (pp. 60 f.) to fit the prologue of John into the Exodus scheme is by no means convincing.

the revelation in creation was not accepted (Rom. 1.18 ff.),[1] so has Israel rejected the word of God spoken through the prophets. It is the disobedient people of God who are the ἴδιοι ('his own') [2] in John 1.11.

The Johannine statements about the Logos are the result of deep theological reflection about the life of Jesus as the central revelation of God. In finding the answer to the question 'Who was Jesus?' the evangelist was certainly helped by the speculations of Hellenistic Judaism which began, not with the consideration of the life of a man appearing in history, but with a definite philosophical and mythological idea. But the Johannine reflection had a quite different beginning point: a concrete event, the life of Jesus. This gives the early Christian statements about the Logos a radically new character in every respect.

R. Bultmann rightly observes that the Johannine prologue does not speak of the 'Word of God', but simply of *the* Logos, *the* Word, without the genitival qualification, as if the evangelist were dealing with a generally known figure. This does of course raise the question whether the evangelist did not quite consciously make use of ideas already familiar to Hellenistic Judaism, or even to the pagan Hellenistic world—ideas about a logos conceived as a hypostasis.[3] It is difficult to answer this question with complete certainty in the affirmative. But it is quite probable that the evangelist did in fact think of the personified Logos common in syncretistic Hellenism and Hellenistic Judaism, and that he very deliberately made formal reference to such conceptions without having a particular text in mind. In designating the historical person Jesus of Nazareth as the Logos, the author who placed this prologue at the beginning of his Gospel knows that he is proclaiming something so radically new that he need not fear a speculative philosophical misinterpretation. He can confidently make use of all sorts of ideas taught by non-Christian authors before and during his time concerning a Logos.

It is by no means impossible (if not actually certain), as many scholars believe, that the evangelist did indeed use a hymn to

[1] See p. 250 n. 2 above.

[2] So also C. H. Dodd, *op. cit.*, pp. 270, 272, who in general emphasizes very strongly the Old Testament roots of the prologue.

[3] The above-mentioned (p. 260) New Testament use of the noun λόγος without closer definition must also be considered here, but it does not give sufficient clarification. That has to do only with proclamation, whereas John's use of the expression here is based on theological reflection and thus goes far beyond mere proclamation.

Wisdom[1] or a Mandaean pattern[2] when he wrote his prologue. But when two people say the same thing, they do not always mean the same—and in this case they certainly do not. 'Logos' in the Gospel of John means the incarnate Jesus of Nazareth, the Word who became flesh, who is God's definitive revelation to the world in this human life. This is an unheard-of thought outside Christianity, even if non-Christian thinkers sometimes *say* some things about the 'Logos' which may sound the same.

By asserting the same thing about his 'Logos' which pagan and Jewish authors say about theirs, the evangelist calls attention not only in the prologue but throughout his whole Gospel to the shockingly new message he will proclaim. His subject is different, even though in form it remains the same and the terminology is unchanged. He does not speak of an abstract stoic or mythological Logos, but of a Logos who became man and who is the Logos for that very reason.

Here is a really genuine Christian and not a syncretistic universalism. Unlike some modern theologians of the 'comparative religion school', the evangelist does not recognize first a general revelation which is common everywhere, then finally point to a special Christian revelation which is added to the other. Such an approach would completely misunderstand the Johannine prologue. If the author takes over many statements about the Logos from Hellenism as well as from the Old Testament, he does not mean to say thereby that the Greeks, for instance, because they spoke of the Logos, already possessed true knowledge. That would be a modern way of thinking. This is what the evangelist is saying: The Greeks spoke of the Logos without knowing him; they did not speak of the Logos who became flesh. What they taught about him was, however, formally correct. The universalism of the Gospel of John consists in the fact that where non-Christians spoke truth, the evangelist sees Christ, the same Christ who at a concrete, particular time became man.

Although I certainly favour reference to parallels drawn from the study of comparative religion, my understanding of the role these parallels play in explaining the Johannine Logos concept is essentially different from

[1] Thus J. Rendel Harris. See pp. 256 f. above.

[2] Reitzenstein-Schaeder, *op. cit.*, pp. 306 ff., and R. Bultmann in his commentary on John, pp. 5 ff. See also the article of Käsemann cited on p. 249 n. 1 above. R. Schnackenburg, 'Logoshymnus und johanneische Prolog', *Biblische Zeitschrift*, N.F. 1, 1957, pp. 69 ff., suggests a *Christian* Logos hymn from Asia Minor as the pattern.

that of R. Bultmann. I seek the biblical and Christian character of the prologue in its starting point, not only in a subsequent demythologizing process set in opposition to the mythological view which the evangelist is assumed simply to have accepted. Exactly contrary to Bultmann's way of thinking, the character of the Johannine universalism can be understood only by explaining the non-Christian parallels, not as the source of the evangelist's inspiration, but as foreign elements secondarily utilized by him.

In order correctly to understand the first verse of the prologue, we must keep in mind v. 14, which speaks of the Word become flesh. Although the prologue begins by referring to the *being* of the Word with God even before the time of creation, the evangelist is already thinking of the *function* of this Word, his *action*. The essential character of the Logos is action; God's self-revelation consists in action. Even if the author does make several marginal references to the being of the Logos, he nevertheless knows that there is such a being only in view of his action, that in the final analysis by his very nature the being of the Logos *is* his action.

Nevertheless we do have here one of the few New Testament passages which speak in this sense of the 'being' of the pre-existent Word. We are actually told something about the source of the divine action of revelation, and the author's purpose is specifically to nip in the bud the idea of a doctrine of two gods, as if the Logos were a god *apart from* the highest God. The 'Word' which God speaks is not to be separated from God himself; it 'was with God' (ἦν πρὸς τὸν θεόν). There is thus nothing here either of the Arian doctrine of the creation of the Logos from nothing, or of Origen's doctrine of an emanation.[1] The 'Word' of God is rather *with God himself*. Nor is the Logos subordinate to God; he simply belongs to God. He is neither subordinate to God, nor a second being beside God. Bultmann rightly emphasizes that the subject and predicate of John 1.1 cannot be reversed.[2] One cannot say θεὸς ἦν πρὸς τὸν λόγον (God was with the word), because the Logos is God himself in so far as God speaks and reveals himself. The Logos is God in his revelation. Thus the third phrase of the prologue can actually proclaim καὶ θεὸς ἦν ὁ λόγος (and the Word was God). We ought not to reinterpret this sentence in order to weaken its absoluteness and sharpness.

[1] Thus R. Bultmann, *op. cit.*, p. 16, whose explanation of this point is especially enlightening.
[2] *Ibid.*

There have been and still are many attempts to do this. θεός has been interpreted as if it were θεῖος: 'The Logos was *like* God.' This interpretation is hardly possible, and R. Bultmann too has rejected it in his commentary on John (p. 17). If the author had intended to say this, the adjective θεῖος was at his disposal; it occurs elsewhere in the New Testament (Acts 17.29; II Peter 1.3).—It is also not feasible to weaken the statement as Origen attempted to do by arguing that in omitting the article before θεός, the author intends to say that the Logos is not actually God but only of divine nature, a divine emanation.

The evangelist means it literally when he calls the Logos 'God'. This is confirmed also by the conclusion of the Gospel when the believing Thomas says to the risen Jesus, 'My Lord and my God' (John 20.28). With this final decisive 'witness' the evangelist completes a circle and returns to his prologue.

In order to avoid the erroneous assumption that there is no distinction at all between God and the Logos, however, the evangelist repeats with emphasis in the prologue: 'He was in the beginning with God.' We can say of this Logos, 'He *is* God'; but at the same time we must also say, 'He is *with* God.' God and the Logos are not two beings, and yet they are also not simply identical. In contrast to the Logos, God can be conceived (in principle at least) also apart from his revelatory action—although we must not forget that the Bible speaks of God *only* in his revelatory action.

We must allow this paradox of all Christology to stand. The New Testament does not resolve it, but sets the two statements alongside each other: on the one hand, the Logos *was* God; on the other hand, he was *with* God. The same paradox occurs again in the Gospel of John with regard to the 'Son of God' concept. We hear on the one hand, 'I and the Father are one' (John 10.30); and on the other hand, 'the Father is greater than I' (John 14.28).[1]

The Logos is the self-revealing, self-giving God—God in action. This action only is the subject of the New Testament. Therefore, all abstract speculation about the 'natures' of Christ is not only a useless undertaking, but actually an improper one. By the very nature of the New Testament Logos one cannot speak of him apart from the action of God.[2] One can say of the being of the Logos only what the Johannine prologue says and no more: he was in the beginning with

[1] Here too I agree completely with the discussion of R. Bultmann, *op. cit.*, p. 18.

[2] This is emphasized with gratifying clarity also by Catholic exegetes such as J. Dupont, *Essais sur la Christologie de S. Jean*, p. 58, and M. E. Boismard, *Le prologue de S. Jean*, p. 122.

God, and he was God. The prologue itself moves from there immediately to the action of the Logos: 'All things were made through him.' The self-communication of God occurs first of all in creation. That is why creation and salvation are very closely connected in the New Testament. Both of them have to do with God's self-communication. Thus the Logos who appeared in the flesh as a human mediator is the same Logos who was already the mediator of creation. Just because the Gospel of John sees the central revelation of God in human life, it takes very seriously the fact that from the very beginning all revelation is an event, an action of God—and *vice versa*, that all divine revelatory action is a Christ-event. In other words, creation and redemption belong together as events of salvation.

We have often mentioned that this connection is characteristic also of Paul's thought, and I have referred especially to the very ancient two-part confession in I Cor. 8.6, which is probably even earlier than Paulinism. Already here Christ is mediator of creation. He appears as such also in Col. 1.16, Rev. 3.14, and Heb. 1.2. Thus reflection about Christ as mediator of all revelation, even the very first, is not originally Johannine. By means of the concept of the Logos, understood in its full profundity, the Gospel of John did of course carry this reflection through to its final consequences. Earlier ideas of a divine hypostasis facilitated the evangelist's bold identification of revelation (λόγος) with the person of Jesus. But his beginning point lies in the specifically early Christian certainty that the human, earthly life of Jesus is the centre of divine revelation. The word of God *proclaimed* by Jesus is at the same time the word *lived* by him; he is himself the Word of God.

This identification is the final consequence of the recognition that Jesus' life represents God's decisive revelation. Just as the experience of the *Kyrios* in worship led to faith in the deity of Christ, so theological reflection about the revelation in Jesus led to the conviction that from the very beginning Jesus Christ was God in so far as God reveals himself to the world. If God has so revealed himself in the life of Jesus that in this life the whole fullness of the divine glory (δόξα) itself has become manifest (John 1.14 ff.), then Jesus must also previously have been God's revelation to men. Therefore he is God in so far as God communicates himself. Therefore from the very beginning when one thinks of God, he must also think of Christ.

We have seen that the Epistle to the Hebrews, which also establishes a relationship between Jesus and the creation of the world from the point of view of the 'Speech' of God, designates Jesus as the 'reflection' and 'stamped image' of God. Here also reflection leads to a specific definition of the relationship between God and Jesus, and here also it is done in such a way that the deity of Jesus is asserted without his being simply identified with God.

We find a very similar evaluation in Paul's designation of Jesus as the 'image of God'. This leads us again to the Son of Man concept as we have found it presupposed in Phil. 2.6 ff. We recall how significant there is the contrast between the obedience of Christ as the pre-existent image of God and the disobedience of Adam, who was created in the image of God. The concepts 'Son of Man' and 'Logos' are thus very closely related. The former shows rather wherein consists salvation through the 'Man' Jesus; the latter emphasizes more strongly the idea of revelation as such. The divine glory itself, the manifestation of which was formerly limited to Bethel (cf. John 1.51), or to the temple at Jerusalem (John 4.21), has now become visible in a 'man' (John 1.14: ἐσκήνωσεν ἐν ἡμῖν;[1] 2.19 ff.).

No other early Christian writer so carefully follows through to its final consequences the thought that God has revealed himself in the Christ become flesh. Nevertheless, this thought is common to all early Christianity. Its importance in the history of revelation is, so to speak, the presupposition of all the Christological concepts we have investigated—those which seek to express the work of the incarnate Christ as well as those which express his future and present work. The viewpoint of revelatory history is central also in I John, in which Jesus is not absolutely designated as the Logos, but given the attribute 'Logos of life' (I John 1.1); and in Revelation, in which Christ is called the 'Logos of God' as eschatological revelation. This view dominates the whole Gospel of John, but the prologue leads us back in the direction of the very beginning to the farthest limit of revelatory history in the past, when already before creation the Logos was with God. In the same way Paul leads us with his Son of God concept in I Cor. 15.28 in the other direction forward to the farthest limit of revelatory history at the end, when the Son, having subjected all things to the Father, subjects also himself, so that God becomes 'all in all', and it is no longer necessary to distinguish between the Father and his Word of revelation.

By way of summary we may say that the following elements constitute the New Testament Logos Christology: (1) Primarily: the

[1] This relationship is especially clear if H. H. Schaeder is correct in saying that the sound of the Greek verb ἐσκήνωσεν here points to the 'Shekina'.

understanding of the life of Jesus as the centre of all divine revelation; the understanding that in his very person Christ *is* what he brings in proclamation and teaching; the theological reflection upon the origin of all revelation in connection with the Old Testament story of creation through the 'Word'. (2) Secondarily: the utilization of contemporary speculations about a divine hypostasis to express not a syncretistic but a genuine Christian universalism.

10

Jesus the Son of God

(υἱὸς τοῦ θεοῦ)

LATER theology usually considered this title also solely in terms of the problem of the two natures of Christ. 'Son of God' was said to designate his divine nature; 'Son of Man', his human nature. We have already seen that this point of view does not do full justice to the latter title: when we think of Dan. 7.13, in fact, we see that 'Son of Man' must be understood first of all as a title of majesty. On the other hand, we shall see that while 'Son of God' does indeed point to the divine majesty of Jesus and his ultimate oneness with God, it also essentially implies his obedience to the Father.

The designation 'Son of God' does make the Father–Son relationship between God and Christ a special and quite unique one. In this respect theologians of the ancient Church were to a certain extent right in using the title in their Christological arguments. But we must guard against ascribing also to the first Christians—much less to Jesus himself—the intention of using the Son of God designation to say something about the Son's identity of substance with the Father. The New Testament title does point to Christ's coming from the Father and his deity, but not in the sense of later discussions about 'substance' and 'natures'.

Once again we must ask first of all what the title we are discussing meant to the Jews and pagans of the New Testament period. It was common in both environments. The problem of the influence of Jewish and pagan use upon the Christian use is similar to the problem of such an influence upon the *Kyrios* title.[1] We shall ask, once again without prejudice, whether the assertion that Jesus is the Son of God is more closely connected with the Jewish or the Hellenistic concept of the Son of God. Above all we must avoid being so fearful of falling back into an uncritical conservatism that we rule out entirely *a priori* the possibility that the first Christians—and perhaps even Jesus himself—could have filled an old expression with a completely

[1] With the difference, of course, that in the case of the title Son of God we must ask whether Jesus gave himself this title.

new content. The dogmatic exclusion of such a possibility would be just as unscholarly as conservative dogmatism.

1. *The Son of God in the Orient and in Hellenism*

It is all the more necessary to investigate the Son of God concept in Hellenism because in his *Theology of the New Testament*[1] R. Bultmann follows the theses of W. Bousset with regard to this title just as he does in the case of the *Kyrios* title. With Bousset, Bultmann holds that the application of the 'Son of God' to the earthly Jesus can be traced back neither to Jesus himself, nor to the original Palestinian Church, but only to Hellenistic Christianity, which accepted the general meaning of the concept in the Hellenistic environment.

According to Bultmann, *Theology of the New Testament* I, p. 50, the early Church, with reference to Ps. 2, applied the Son of God title only to the risen Christ. Bultmann finds proof for this assertion especially in Mark 9.7 in the voice at the Transfiguration, which he says is actually an Easter story projected into the past; further, in the ancient confession cited by Paul in Rom. 1.3, in which Jesus is said to be the Son of David according to the flesh, and since the resurrection the Son of God in power according to the Spirit.

The distinguished work of G. P. Wetter on the Son of God[2] contains copious material from the comparative study of religions about the 'sons of gods' in Hellenism. The origin of the 'son of God' concept lies in ancient oriental religions, in which above all kings were thought to be begotten of gods. This belief was especially common in Egypt: the rulers, or Pharaohs, were all considered to be the sons of the sun god Re.[3] The same belief may be less clearly found in Babylonia and Assyria. The Uppsala School, which we have mentioned before,[4] connects the idea of the divine parentage of kings

[1] R. Bultmann, *Theology of the New Testament* I, pp. 128 ff.

[2] G. P. Wetter, *Der Sohn Gottes. Eine Untersuchung über den Charakter und die Tendenz des Johannesevangeliums*, 1916. See also W. Grundmann, *Die Gotteskindschaft in der Geschichte Jesu und ihre religionsgeschichtlichen Voraussetzungen*, 1938. For an older work see P. Wendland, *Die hellenistisch-römische Kultur in ihren Beziehungen zu Judentum und Christentum*[2, 3], 1912, pp. 123 ff.; H. Usener, *Religionsgeschichtliche Untersuchungen I, 1: Das Weihnachtsfest*[2], 1911, pp. 71 ff.

[3] Cf. C. J. Gadd, *Ideas of Divine Rule in the Ancient East*, 1948.

[4] See p. 23 n. 2 above.

with ancient oriental enthronement ceremonies. In the New Testament period also the Roman emperors were entitled *divi filius.*[1]

But in Hellenism the expression is by no means limited to rulers. Anyone believed to possess some kind of divine power was called 'son of God' by others, or gave himself the title. All miracle workers were 'sons of God', or, as one also said, θεῖοι ἄνδρες: Apollonius of Tyana, for instance, whose life is described by Philostratus in a form which is often reminiscent of our Gospels; or Alexander of Abonoteichus, whom we know through Lucian.[2] Used in this sense, the title was quite common. In the New Testament period one could meet everywhere men who called themselves 'sons of God' because of their peculiar vocation or miraculous powers. The designation thus did not have the connotation of uniqueness which is characteristic of New Testament use. We learn in Origen's *Against Celsus* (7.9) that there were people in Syria and Palestine who said of themselves, 'I am God; I am the Son of God; or, I am the Divine Spirit . . . I wish to save you.'[3] Bultmann emphasizes very strongly the similarity between these θεῖοι ἄνδρες and Jesus as the 'Son of God'.

The claim of these men to be 'sons of God' rests solely upon their possession of 'divine powers'. The Hellenistic concept is so deeply rooted in polytheistic thought that it can hardly be transferred to a monotheistic framework. It lacks Jesus' extremely intense consciousness of complete, unique unity of will with the one God in executing the divine linear plan of salvation. In the mystery religions, too, in which the initiate can become a 'son of God', we find ourselves on a quite different level from that of the New Testament. Without anticipating ourselves, we must question from the very beginning whether the monotheistic Old Testament religion does not perhaps have a 'Son of God' concept which, although it may not be identical with the Christian concept, yet might be considered a more likely point of contact for the Christian title.

2. *The Son of God in Judaism*

In the Old Testament we find this expression used in three ways: the whole people of Israel is called 'Son of God'; kings bear the

[1] See A. Deissmann, *Licht vom Osten*[4], pp. 294 f. (ET, pp. 346 f.); E. Lohmeyer, *Christuskult und Kaiserkult*, 1919.

[2] Lucian, *Alexander* 11 ff. Cf. also W. Bauer, *Das Johannesevangelium*, p. 37.

[3] According to C. H. Dodd, *The Interpretation of the Fourth Gospel*, p. 251 n. 1, these were *Christian* ecstatics. Thus this passage would not be relevant to Hellenism.

title; persons with a special commission from God, such as angels, and perhaps also the Messiah, are so called. The fact that the same designation is used for the whole people and for its representatives reminds us of the similar discovery we made in our investigation of the *ebed Yahweh* and *barnasha* concepts.

We consider first the most important texts in which the *people* are addressed as 'Son of God'. In Ex. 4.22 f. Moses is commanded to say to Pharaoh, 'Israel is my first-born son . . .'. In Hos. 11.1 Yahweh says, 'Out of Egypt I called my son.' In Isa. 1.2 and 30.1 the Israelites as a whole are called 'sons'. In Jer. 3.22 the people are called 'faithless sons'. In Isa. 63.16 the Israelites say to God, 'Thou art our Father,' and they mean this in a peculiar sense, because Israel is the 'Son of God' in a unique way. One might mention in this connection also Jer. 31.20; Isa. 45.11; Ps. 82.6; Mal. 1.6.[1] In all these texts the title 'Son of God' expresses both the idea that God has chosen this people for a special mission, and that this his people owes him absolute obedience.

This is also true of the way in which *kings*, the representatives of the chosen people, are addressed by God as 'son'. 'I will be his father, and he shall be my son' (II Sam. 7.14). 'You are my son, today I have begotten you' (Ps. 2.7, a passage from the royal psalm often cited by the Christians). 'He (the king) shall cry to me, "Thou art my Father, my God, and the Rock of my salvation"' (Ps. 89.26). The king too is 'son' as one specially chosen and commissioned by God. We need not investigate here to what extent foreign oriental ideas of divine parentage influenced this idea of the king.[2] The primary thought in these texts is the same as that in the designation of the people as 'Son of God'. The king is son of God because the nation is.

In the passages where angelic beings appear as 'sons of God' (partly, no doubt, after the pattern of mythological ideas—cf. the 'sons of God' in Gen. 6.2), the Old Testament writer always thinks they are commissioned by God.[3]

The question whether the *Messiah* bears this title in Judaism has

[1] The good Israelite is called 'Son of God' in Ecclus. 4.10; Psalm of Solomon 13.9. The whole people as 'righteous Israel' is called this in Psalms of Solomon 17.27; 18.4.

[2] This would have to do primarily with the royal ritual of enthronement. G. von Rad, 'Das judäische Königsritual', *TLZ* 72, 1947, pp. 211 ff., and A. Alt, *Kleine Schriften z. Geschichte des Volkes Israels* II, 1953, 133 f., emphasize the connection between the coronation ritual and the adoption of the king as 'Son of God'.

[3] Job. 1.6; 2.1; 38.7; Ps. 29.1; 89.6; Dan. 3.25, 28.

been often considered but not yet clearly answered. The difficulty lies in the fact that no known ancient text definitely calls the Messiah 'Son of God'. The Ethiopic Enoch 105.2 is probably a later interpolation.[1] The passages in II (4) Esd. (7.28 f.; 13.32; 37.52; 14.9) can hardly be considered as examples, because they point to the παῖς in the sense of the *ebed Yahweh* and do not refer directly to sonship.[2] It is thus understandable that G. Dalman and W. Bousset [3] flatly deny that 'Son of God' was a Jewish designation for the Messiah, and that W. Michaelis [4] maintains for this reason that the New Testament designation of Jesus as 'Son of God' is something really new. Although we have no unambiguous proof-texts, it is nevertheless difficult to assume that this royal attribute should not occasionally have been transferred also to the Messiah [5] when we consider how closely related were the Jewish expectation of a Messiah and the idea of the king. A clear indication of this is the fact that the royal psalms were related to the Messiah.[6] The New Testament identification of Messiah with Son of God (Mark 14.61; Matt. 16.16; Luke 1.32) could also point in this direction. It is of course a dangerous procedure to refer too readily to these New Testament passages. We shall see that the Synoptic designation of Jesus as Son did not grow out of his messianic dignity, and it could be that the connection between Messiah and Son of God (which occurs only in a few passages) simply resulted from the fact that early Christians saw in Jesus both figures at the same time, but from two different points of view. In any case, we must carefully distinguish between Messiah and Son of God in the New Testament. Therefore, if in Judaism the Messiah was possibly given the title 'Son of God', this could have happened

[1] See G. Dalman, *The Words of Jesus*, pp. 269 f. The probability is strengthened by the fact that the passage is missing in a Greek Enoch fragment (see C. Bonner, *The Last Chapters of Enoch in Greek*, 1937).

[2] B. Violet, *Die Apokalypsen des Esra und des Baruch in deutscher Gestalt*, 1924, *ad loc.*

[3] G. Dalman, *op. cit.*, p. 272; W. Bousset, *Kyrios Christos*², pp. 53 f.; E. Huntress, '"Son of God" in Jewish Writings Prior to the Christian Era', *JBL* 54, 1935, pp. 117 ff.

[4] W. Michaelis, *Zur Engelchristologie im Urchristentum*, 1942, pp. 10 ff.

[5] R. Bultmann, *Theology of the New Testament* I, p. 50, reckons with this possibility. Also J. Bieneck, *Sohn Gottes als Christusbezeichnung der Synoptiker* (ATANT 21), 1951, p. 25, although he incorrectly considers the question unimportant. C. H. Dodd, *The Interpretation of the Fourth Gospel*, p. 253, considers this assumption probable if not certain.

[6] But G. Dalman, *op. cit.*, pp. 219 ff., emphasizes that Ps. 2, which is particularly important here, was seldom interpreted messianically.

only in connection with the same idea of election which is of constitutive significance for the Son of God designation of the king.

In conclusion: the Old Testament and Jewish concept of the Son of God is essentially characterized, not by the gift of a particular power, nor by a substantial relationship with God by virtue of divine conception; but by the idea of *election* to participation in divine work through the execution of a particular commission, and by the idea of strict *obedience* to the God who elects.

3. *Jesus and the Son of God Designation*

Did Jesus understand himself to be the 'Son of God'? Anyone who, with W. Bousset and R. Bultmann, traces every occurrence of this New Testament designation for the earthly Jesus [1] to the *Hellenistic* use of the title will have to answer negatively from the very beginning. We must therefore first of all investigate this thesis. But even if it should prove untenable, we shall have to consider the possibility that it was the early Church under the influence of *Old Testament* thought which first viewed Jesus as the Son of God, without Jesus himself having actually given himself this name. And if the question is put in this way, then we must as always first attempt to discover in terms of form criticism whether 'Son of God' was a common designation for Christ for early Christianity itself. At the same time we must also ask whether the Old Testament use alone (that is, without reference to Jesus himself) suffices to explain the rise of the conviction among the first Christians that he is the Son of God.

But even if such considerations justified ascribing to Jesus the personal consciousness of being the Son of God, the question would still remain in what sense he used this title. At present we can say only this much: in any case—whether Jesus called himself Son of God or not—according to the witness of the whole Gospel tradition, the 'Son of God' title as applied to Jesus expresses the historical and qualitative uniqueness of his relation to his Father.

W. Grundmann [2] has suggested that Jesus thought himself to be the son of God in the very general sense in which we are all 'children of God'.

[1] According to Bultmann the designation of the *risen* Christ as 'Son' can be explained from Judaism. See p. 271 above.

[2] See W. Grundmann, *op. cit.* on p. 271 n. 2; though according to a more recent statement ('Sohn Gottes, ein Diskussionsbeitrag', *ZNW* 47, 1956, pp. 113 ff.) he seems to have revised this thesis considerably.

Only later was this general sense of being a child of God made into a unique 'sonship'. In this case, so far as Jesus himself is concerned, the Son of God designation would have no particular Christological significance at all. But such a cheap simplification cannot solve the problem. It rests solely on a hypothesis and has no textual foundation. The Synoptic writers (above all Mark) use 'Son of God', whether spoken by Jesus himself or by others, in such a way that it is impossible to interpret the original sense to mean being a child of God in this general sense. Even Paul, who in Gal. 4.4 ff. and Rom. 8.14 ff. actually does speak of *our* 'sonship', derives it from the unique sonship of Jesus. The theological reasoning of Paul is thus just the reverse of Grundmann's.

We begin with the question of Hellenistic derivation—especially as this thesis has become widespread today on the authority of Bultmann's *Theology of the New Testament*.[1] We have already indicated that the Hellenistic understanding of the designation 'Son of God' can hardly be separated from the polytheistic background of pagan antiquity, and that the idea simply of the gift of divine powers (such as those of the θεῖοι ἄνδρες, the miracle workers, some of whose biographies we still possess) is not applicable to the Gospel tradition of Jesus as the Son of God. The most important passages of the Synoptic Gospels in which Jesus appears as the Son of God show him precisely not as a miracle worker and saviour like many others, but as one radically and uniquely distinguished from all other men. He knows that he is sent to all other men to fulfil his task in complete unity with the Father. This distinction, this isolation, means to Jesus not primarily miraculous power, but the absolute obedience of a son in the execution of a divine commission. This is the Synoptic emphasis. As we have already seen in our investigation of the *ebed Yahweh*, the heavenly voice at Jesus' baptism (Mark 1.11 and parallels) speaks of the Son in terms of the introductory verse of the Old Testament songs about the Suffering Servant of God. Probably the Hebrew text of Isaiah itself implies the idea of a Son. Without a doubt the Synoptic writers emphasize precisely at the baptism of Jesus the connection of the Son concept with the concept of the Suffering Servant; that is, its connection with Jesus' death.

The temptation story, which comes immediately after that of the baptism,[2] sets Jesus even more radically apart from all Hellenistic 'sons of gods'. According to Matthew the first two temptations

[1] See pp. 271 and 275 above.

[2] It is certain that the two accounts were already connected in the oral tradition (despite R. Bultmann, *Geschichte der synoptischen Tradition*, p. 270).

begin significantly with the phrase 'If you are the Son of God . . .' (Matt. 4.3, 6; cf. Luke 4.3, 9).[1] We have seen that Satan attempts to force upon Jesus a political messianic role which would prevent his suffering. Now we note that Satan chooses as his beginning point precisely Jesus' consciousness of being the Son of God, which is not necessarily identical with his messianic consciousness.[2] It is highly significant that Jesus rejects as satanic also the suggested 'Hellenistic' conception of his divine sonship in the sense of miraculous powers. The point of the first two temptations is not whether Jesus believes that God's miraculous power is present in the Son, but whether he will be disobedient to his Father by attempting to use that power apart from the fulfilment of his specific commission as the Son.

In his investigation of the Son of God passages in the Synoptic Gospels J. Bieneck comes to the conclusion, therefore, that they give a 'completely un-Greek picture' of the Son of God. The only story in which Jesus is called 'Son of God' in a sense which corresponds to the Hellenistic concept is Matthew's version of Jesus' walking on the sea, after which the disciples cry out as a result of the miracle, 'Truly you are the Son of God' (Matt. 14.33). Not to mention the fact that Mark gives a quite different conclusion to this story, we note that even within Matthew itself it has no special significance whatsoever.[3]

Otherwise the witness of the Synoptic writers is unequivocal. Jesus is the Son of God not as a miracle worker, but in the obedient fulfilment of his task—precisely his task of suffering. We shall come back to the individual passages, but at this point we call attention to the fact that both in Peter's confession (Matt. 16.16) and in the centurion's confession at the cross (Mark 15.39) [4] the Son of God title is

[1] J. Bieneck, *Sohn Gottes als Christusbezeichnung der Synoptiker*, 1951, p. 64 n. 18, correctly explains the reason why the phrase 'If you are the Son of God' is not repeated with the third temptation in Matthew: Satan demands an act of subjection here, whereas in the first two temptations he demands an act of power.

[2] Neither are the two necessarily connected in the question of the high priest (Mark 14.61), in which both titles are mentioned at the same time, or in the mockery reported in Mark 15.20 ff. and par.

[3] There is in fact a certain difficulty here: it seems inconsistent that this recognition should come in Matt. 14.33, when, according to the structure of the Gospel of Matthew, the disciples actually first recognized Jesus in Matt. 16.16. J. Bieneck, *op. cit.*, p. 56, attempts to explain this by saying that Matt. 14.33 has to do with an imperfect recognition. This explanation is worth consideration, but it is somewhat forced.

[4] As opposed to J. Bieneck, *op. cit.*, p. 55 (following Schlatter and Zahn) I do not consider the parallel passage in Matt. 27.54 to be the original version. It seems to me rather to belong somewhere near Matt. 14.33.

connected with suffering. The title is also proclaimed in the transfiguration story (Mark 9.7 and parallels) as confirmation of Jesus' divine commission and his complete oneness with the Father in its performance. This very close relationship is also expressed in the much debated statement in Matt. 11.27 about the Son whom 'no one knows except the Father'.[1] This statement does indeed have its parallels in the Hellenistic mystery cults,[2] but in the framework of the Synoptic Gospels it is connected with the specific view that the relationship of Jesus with the Father is his exclusive secret, the perception of which demands a supernatural knowledge which can only be given to a man from outside himself—either from the Father, as in the case of Peter (Matt. 16.17); or from Satan, as in the confession of those possessed by demons (Mark 3.11; 5.7).

With regard to the Synoptic Gospels, therefore, one cannot maintain the thesis of the Hellenistic origin of the designation of Jesus as Son of God. On the basis of this fact, at least, one cannot *a priori* doubt the genuineness of the few sayings in which Jesus calls himself 'Son'. It could be, of course, that the Palestinian early Church first put the designation in Jesus' mouth. 'Son of God' is indeed one of the means by which the first Christians expressed their own faith in Jesus. We shall see that there was in fact a short confessional formula: 'Jesus is the Son of God.' The title is one of the fundamental Christological concepts in the Gospel of John and in the Epistle to the Hebrews. Paul also uses it, although much less often than the title *Kyrios*. We have already seen that in the Synoptics it does not occur only as a self-designation of Jesus; Mark above all seems to consider it especially significant, since, according to some ancient texts, he introduces his book as 'the beginning of the gospel of Jesus Christ, the Son of God'.[3] Thus the situation with this title is different from that in the case of 'Son of Man' and 'Servant of God'. We could answer affirmatively the question whether or not Jesus attributed to himself the title 'Son of Man' and the role of the 'Suffering Servant', because we saw on the basis of form-critical investigation that the Church did not express its own faith in Jesus by means of these conceptions. The Synoptic writers use the expression 'Son of Man'

[1] See pp. 286 ff. below for the exegesis of this saying.

[2] W. Bousset, *Kyrios Christos*², pp. 48 f., cites among other examples a prayer to Hermes in the Magical Papyrus, Lond. 122.50: 'I know you, Hermes, and you know me; I am you, and you are I.'

[3] See p. 294 n. 3 below.

only when Jesus speaks of himself, never when they themselves or others speak of him. Faith in Jesus as the 'Son of God', on the other hand, is part of the Christological conviction of the Church and therefore also of the early Christian writers.

Theoretically, therefore, it is possible that the early Church did later put this designation in Jesus' mouth, that Jesus himself did not actually call himself by this name. Nevertheless we should note that according to the Synoptic writers Jesus was recognized by others as the Son of God only in exceptional cases, and then because of a special supernatural knowledge. He was recognized as such by Peter, to whom 'flesh and blood' had not revealed it (Matt. 16.17), by Satan (Matt. 4.3, 6), by demons (Mark 3.11; 5.7). Otherwise it is either the divine voice which addresses him as 'Son' (baptism, transfiguration), or Jesus who calls himself that.[1] This compels us to ask whether the Synoptic writers did not in fact preserve the recollection here that it is the *Son of God* concept more than any other understanding of Jesus which goes back to Jesus himself and to its attestation during his earthly life.[2] At this point we can only ask the question; these observations do not in themselves provide proof for such an assertion.

It seems to me that the decisive consideration is that on the basis of the Old Testament and later Jewish views there is no apparent ground whatever for the early Church to designate Jesus as the Son of God. Even if theoretically we must reckon with the possibility that in connection with the conception of the king, the Jewish Messiah was now and then called 'Son of God', the complete lack of proof for his being given such a title indicates at least that it was not an essential attribute of the Messiah. Moreover, in the New Testament itself—even in the question of the high priest—the Son of God title is never the consequence of Jesus' messianic calling.

In Mark 14.61 the high priest does ask, 'Are you the Messiah, the Son of the Blessed?' In Matt. 26.63 the question is similar: 'I adjure you by the living God, tell us if you are the Messiah, the Son of God.' It may be that this connection was made first by the evangelists, for whom Jesus was both the Messiah and the Son of God from two different points of view.

[1] Mark 14.61 and Matt. 27.43 do not come into consideration here because neither the high priest nor those who mock him at the cross really believe that Jesus is the Son of God.

[2] O. Bauernfeind, *Die Worte der Dämonen im Markusevangelium*, 1927, pp. 78 ff., makes the point that reference to the witness of the demons contradicts Wrede's theory of the messianic secret.

But it is certain that they did not derive the second from the first. Luke may have followed a better tradition here when he separated the question concerning the messianic claim from that concerning the claim to be the Son of God, and divided the hearing into two different questions (Luke 22.67 ff.).

Peter's confession indicates a connection between Messiah and Son of God only in Matthew (Matt. 16.16: 'You are the Christ, the Son of the living God'). Mark and Luke speak only of the Messiah (Mark 8.29; Luke 9.20). J. Bieneck[1] correctly shows that the words in Matt. 16.17 (... 'flesh and blood has not revealed this to you, but my Father who is in heaven') which, with the sentences about the foundation stone of the Church and binding and loosing, are found only in Matthew, refer only to the confession of the Son of God, but not to the identification of Jesus as the Messiah. Mark and Luke, in which Peter confesses only the Messiah and not the Son of God, do not mention the answer of Jesus about the direct divine inspiration of Peter's confession. Indeed, we have seen in our investigation of Jesus' attitude toward the title Messiah[2] that according to Mark's interpretation he really had no reason to say of Peter at this time that he was inspired by God. Precisely as an answer to Peter's false understanding of the Messiah Jesus says to him sharply, 'Get behind me, Satan.'

I should like to go still a further step in this explanation of Peter's confession. J. Bieneck has correctly related the blessing of Peter and Jesus' saying about the direct revelation (Matt. 16.17) only to one element of the confession as Matthew reports it, the confession of the 'Son of God'. As I have indicated in my book on Peter, I am of the opinion that Matt. 16.17–19 actually belongs in a different context.[3] I believe these verses contain Jesus' answer to a quite different confession of Peter (a parallel of which is John 6.69), in which Peter says only 'You are the Son of the living God.' Whereupon Jesus blesses

[1] J. Bieneck, *op. cit.*, p. 50 n. 15.

[2] See pp. 122 ff. above.

[3] See O. Cullmann, *Peter: Disciple, Apostle, Martyr*, pp. 170 ff., and especially my essay, 'L'apôtre Pierre, instrument du diable et instrument de Dieu: la place de Matt. 16.16–19 dans la tradition primitive', in *New Testament Essays: studies in memory of T. W. Manson*, ed. A. J. B. Higgins, 1959, pp. 94 ff. As I had anticipated, my daring to accept this passage as genuine has earned me much pedantic censure. But the question of genuineness has attracted so much attention that there has been hardly any comment on my essential thesis, namely, the attempt to place Matt. 16.16–19 at another time in the life of Jesus on the ground that it did not originally belong in the context of Caesarea Philippi (Mark 8.27 ff.) at all.

him because God has revealed this to him—just as in Matt. 11.27 he says that only the Father knows the Son.

I should even say that only the event reported in Matt. 16.16–19 is a real 'confession of Peter'. Mark 8.27 ff. obviously has a completely different point. It has to do not with a confession of Peter, but on the contrary with a reprimand of Peter because of his false understanding of the Messiah. As he so often does, Matthew has combined here two different events between which he sees a connection from a particular theological point of view.

The observation that according to the Synoptics 'Son of God' and 'Messiah' must be separated is of the greatest importance for our question whether Jesus considered himself to be the Son of God. If the early Church did not derive the Son of God designation for Jesus from his messianic calling, what did cause it to attribute to Jesus the claim to be the Son of God? The obvious answer can only be that Jesus called himself by this name.

In his 'Das Gleichnis von den bösen Weingärtnern', *Aux sources de la tradition chrétienne* (volume in honour of M. Goguel), pp. 120 ff., W. G. Kümmel thinks that it must be denied that Jesus told the parable of the evil tenants above all because of the Son designation. But he gives no satisfactory explanation for the origin of the title in the early Church. He agrees that the Jewish messianic concept does not lead to the Son of God concept, but for that very reason he is not convincing when he derives the idea of Jesus as the Son of God solely from an early Christian use of Ps. 2.7.[1] One must still explain the motivation for reference to this passage.

It is certainly significant that W. Bousset and R. Bultmann must point to the really somewhat far-fetched derivation from Hellenistic biographies of all kinds of miracle workers in order to explain the origin of the Son of God designation for the earthly Jesus. They too see no possibility of making the early Church responsible for this. W. Grundmann, who also wants to discard the offence of Jesus' consciousness of being the Son of God in a unique and exclusive sense, does at least think it is necessary to go back to Jesus himself in order to support his somewhat naive thesis that Jesus thought of himself only in terms of being a child of God in general.

In view of the special importance and difficulty of the problem, it was necessary that we consider the above questions before we now

[1] *Op. cit.*, p. 131 (following C. H. Dodd).

ask in what sense Jesus considered himself to be the 'Son of God'. Earlier we saw that Jesus consciously avoided, if not actually rejected, the title 'Messiah' for himself. He did not avoid the title 'Son of God', but he used it so seldom that we can hardly consider it a typical self-designation like 'Son of Man'. And yet the conviction that in a unique way he was 'God's Son' must belong to the very heart of what we call the 'self-consciousness' of Jesus. W. Wrede's thesis seems to me unsatisfactory also at this point. It is true that we cannot speak of a 'Son-secret' as we have spoken of the 'messianic secret', but if we look back to Jesus himself here also, the explanation is similar to the one we have given of the messianic secret. Jesus usually prefers the title 'Son of Man' to 'Son of God' because the former expresses in a more unmistakable way what is important to him in the latter; that is, 'Son of Man' also points to the complete identity of Jesus' will with that of the Father as expressed in his obedience to the divine plan, but unlike 'Son of God' it is not so likely to be wrongly understood by the disciples and the people as a majestic claim only.

But there is another reason for Jesus' reserve in using the title 'Son of God'. It does indeed contain a statement of majesty, but it expresses the very essence of Jesus' self-consciousness in a way quite different from the majesty implied by 'Son of Man' or even 'Messiah'. 'Son of God' expresses Jesus' constant experience of complete unity of will with the Father, the full perception of revelation, which makes itself known to him as a unique recognition of himself by the Father. This is more than simply the prophetic consciousness of a man who knows himself to be God's instrument; more than the 'compulsion' which the Apostle Paul feels when he cries, 'Woe to me if I do not preach the gospel' (I Cor. 9.16). God acts not only through him, but with him. Thus he can presume to forgive sins—an act promptly interpreted as blasphemy by the scribes, who were at least correct in seeing that this meant a conscious identification with God: 'Who can forgive sins but God alone?' (Mark 2.7). Jesus does carry out God's plan as does the prophet or apostle, but in so doing he experiences oneness with the Father. This experience is Jesus' secret, and here lies the explanation of the fact that (analogous to his withdrawal in solitude to pray: Mark 1.35)[1] he speaks of himself as the 'Son' very infrequently, and then usually in such a way that he does not openly proclaim but only suggests the secret hidden from human understanding. Even in antiquity ordinary human under-

[1] This parallel shows that Wrede's explanation of Jesus' reticence is unnecessary.

standing must consider such a Son-consciousness as Jesus' to be an exaggerated peculiarity in contrast to that of the large class of miracle workers who could openly proclaim themselves as such to be 'sons of God'. This is the reason for Jesus' reserve: he did not want his consciousness of sonship to be included among analogous psychiatric 'cases'.

Therefore, in the few Synoptic passages (we shall speak later of the Gospel of John) in which Jesus speaks of himself as the 'Son of God' or simply as the 'Son', these two aspects always appear: first, the obedience of the Son in fulfilment of the divine plan; second, the profound secret that Jesus has been aware of since his baptism and constantly experiences in executing his obedience, the secret that he is related to God as no other man is.

If the expression 'Son of God' occurs to Jesus himself to describe his experience from his baptism onwards, we know now that this does not follow from the Jewish concept of the Messiah, but from the Old Testament use of the name 'Son of God'. We have seen that as the instruments chosen to fulfil the divine plan of salvation, the people of Israel and their king bore this name. The connection between Jesus' consciousness of sonship and this Old Testament view becomes clear when we remember that this consciousness expresses itself as obedience. On the other hand, precisely in executing this obedience Jesus has also this new experience, bound only to his person, of the complete unity of will with the Father. Even the Old Testament 'Son of God' offers no parallel to this experience. But the fact that in using the title 'Son' Jesus makes use of an Old Testament name for the whole people of Israel does open up a perspective which makes visible an important characteristic of this title in common with other Christological titles essential to his self-consciousness: like the 'Son of Man' and *ebed Yahweh* concepts, 'Son of God' expresses the idea of representation which we have seen to be the principle of all New Testament *Heilsgeschichte*.[1]

We have already spoken of the close relationship between 'Son of God' and 'Servant of God'. This becomes all the more significant when we note that during Jesus' life his *baptism* is the beginning point for the twofold consciousness that he must fulfil the *ebed Yahweh* role and that he stands in a unique Son–Father relationship with God. It is true that the introductory verse of the *ebed Yahweh* songs (Isa. 42.1), which contains the words spoken by the voice from heaven at Jesus' baptism, does not use the Hebrew word *ben*, 'son'. But it

[1] See O. Cullmann, *Christ and Time*, pp. 115 ff.

has been pointed out that the expression used instead, *bechiri* (my beloved, ἀγαπητός), implies the idea of sonship—and indeed, in the sense of an *only* Son.[1] This may account for the fact that the Septuagint translates *ebed* not as δοῦλος but as παῖς, which means both servant and son.[2] In any case, the voice from heaven at Jesus' baptism emphasizes both ideas: you are my only Son; you must fulfil the role of the *ebed Yahweh.* It is just this connection with the Suffering Servant of God which shows that the Synoptic Gospels think of the Son of God not only in terms of exaltation, but also in terms of obedience.[3]

Jesus' baptism experience stands at the beginning of both Mark and John. It provides the introduction to an understanding of the whole life of Jesus—and of all Christology. Who is Jesus? At this moment the answer is directly revealed to Jesus himself together with the passion mandate. From this moment on he never loses the double consciousness of his complete oneness with the Father and of his clearly defined task. The temptation story shows this immediately: 'If you are the Son of God . . . ,' says Satan. But Jesus resists temptation, for he knows that just because he is God's Son, he cannot be a miracle worker like the Hellenistic 'sons of God'[4] or a world ruler like the political messiah. Just because he is 'Son', he can depend upon miraculous divine power only if he is obedient to his divine commission, but not if he throws himself from the pinnacle of the temple. Thus understood, the temptation of Jesus as the Son represents a parallel to Adam's temptation. We have seen the same parallel in Phil. 2.6 ff. Jesus' being in the form of God did not lead him to 'steal' equality with God as Adam tried to do when he was tempted, but to obey God even to death on a cross. In the same way, the meaning of the temptation story is that, for Jesus, to be the Son of God is always to be obedient.

On the other hand, from the moment of his baptism the consciousness of the closest oneness with the Father always accompanies Jesus. It is certainly no accident that the words from heaven at the transfiguration[5] partially repeat those of the heavenly voice at the

[1] See G. Schrenk, *TWNT* II, p. 738; W. F. Arndt and F. W. Gingrich, *A Greek-English Lexicon of the New Testament*, p. 6.

[2] So also L. Cerfaux, *Le Christ dans la théologie de S. Paul*, p. 340.

[3] J. Bieneck, *Sohn Gottes als Christusbezeichnung*, has made this admirably clear.

[4] See G. Delling, 'D. Verst. d. Wunders im NT', *Zeitschrift für die systematische Theologie*, 1956, pp. 265 ff.

[5] There is no reason to consider this story as an appearance of the risen Christ projected back into the life of Jesus as do J. Wellhausen, *Das Evangelium Marci*,

baptism. Just as the moments of his life when for him the barriers between heaven and earth disappear briefly, Jesus hears the address 'Son of God'. But also, apart from these moments, he experiences continuously his oneness with the Father.[1] This is why he knows that it requires superhuman understanding when others (Peter and the demons, for example) perceive his unique sonship.

It is certainly not by chance that besides 'Son of God' the demons in the Synoptic Gospels use only one other title for Jesus: 'Holy One of God' (Mark 1.24). This name closely resembles that of Son.[2] It too describes the unique distinction of Jesus from all other creatures. We need therefore consider it only briefly in the present context.

Apart from Mark 1.24 the designation occurs precisely in the Johannine parallel to Peter's confession: 'We have believed and have come to know that you are the *Holy One of God*' (John 6.69). Apparently the same tradition which Matt. 16.16–19 places in the context of Mark 8.27 ff. is repeated here. We see here that 'Son of God' and 'Holy One of God' are almost interchangeable. John 10.36 is probably to be explained on this basis: 'Whom the Father *made holy* and sent into the world is the Son of God.' Finally, we find the same connection in Gabriel's proclamation to Mary: 'He will be great, and will be called the *Son of the Most High*' (Luke 1.32); '. . . the child to be born will be called *holy*, the Son of God' (Luke 1.35). As M.-J. Lagrange, *L'Evangile selon S. Marc*[2], 1947, p. 22, and R. Bultmann, *Das Evangelium des Johannes*, p. 344, have correctly noted, 'the Holy One' is not a messianic designation, and thus also in this respect belongs with 'Son of God'. See also J. Bieneck, *op. cit.*, pp. 46 ff.

1909, p. 71; R. Bultmann, *Geschichte der synoptischen Tradition*, p. 278; and others. A. Harnack, 'Die Verklärungsgeschichte Jesu', *SB d. preuss. Ak. d. Wiss.*, 1922, pp. 76 ff., and E. Meyer, *Ursprung und Anfänge des Christentums*, 1921, I, pp. 152 ff., maintain on the contrary that the transfiguration story is a genuine tradition, and even assume that this event in the earthly life of Jesus is the reason for the vision of Peter after the death of Christ. E. Lohmeyer, 'Die Verklärung Jesu nach dem Markusevangelium', *ZNW* 21, 1922, pp. 185 ff., also contests the derivation of the transfiguration from a later appearance of Jesus, although he does not believe the story to be historical, but rather one originating from Jewish views. H. Riesenfeld does the same thing in his study, *Jésus transfiguré*, referring above all to the Jewish Feast of Tabernacles.

[1] This awareness does not leave him even in Gethsemane, although just as in Matt. 4 he must once again guard his obedient sonship against the final temptation. Only in the moment of death (which for him, as for Paul, is the 'last enemy' which he will conquer in his resurrection) does he cry out, 'My God, my God, why hast thou forsaken me?' But this cry too is completely understandable only on the basis of his sonship. On this point see my *Immortality of the Soul or Resurrection of the Dead?*

[2] According to G. Friedrich, *ZTK* 53, 1956, pp. 275 ff., *both* designations belong to the realm of the conception of Jesus as the messianic High Priest.

Jesus' answer to Peter in Matt. 16.17 'Flesh and blood has not revealed to you (that I am the Son of God)', must be counted as one of his declarations about his being the Son of God. Here we see again the strict reserve with which Jesus speaks of this his deepest secret, and now we understand better why the name 'Son of God' occurs so very seldom as his self-designation. On the other hand, just for this reason one should not too quickly deny the genuineness of these few passages, especially when a passage is marked by the same reserve as Matt. 16.17.

This must be said above all of the familiar saying of Jesus in Matt. 11.27: '. . . no one knows the Son except the Father, and no one knows the Father except the Son and anyone to whom the Son chooses to reveal him.' Of the few Synoptic passages in which the earthly Jesus calls himself 'Son'[1] (only Mark 13.32 and Mark 12.6 = Matt. 21.37 remain to be mentioned), the genuineness of this one is most strongly doubted. The fact that the 'Son' designation occurs just in this very problematical passage may be the reason why many New Testament scholars deny that Jesus ever used the title at all. There is hardly a single commentary which does not emphasize the 'Johannine' character of this saying. Already in the last century K. von Hase called it a 'meteor from the Johannine heaven'.[2] In itself this observation is quite true. Anyone who knows anything at all about the Gospel of John will immediately recognize here one of its major themes. We have emphasized again and again in earlier chapters that the fourth evangelist, on the basis of his conviction that he himself is possessed by the Paraclete, often expresses his own Christological understanding in the form of words he attributes to Jesus. He does this, certain that the Holy Spirit teaches him and brings to his remembrance all that Jesus said (John 14.26); sure that only this spiritual understanding 'guides into all the truth', since during Jesus' lifetime the disciples 'could not yet bear many things' (John 16.12). There is no doubt that from this point of view the author exhausted only a few elements of the life and teaching of Jesus, but he developed these in their full richness and ultimate refinement.[3] But this does not justify the usual assumption that it is self-deception of the evangelist to think that in this way he still remained close to the roots of Jesus' gospel as we know it in the Synoptic writings. This assumption is

[1] The command to baptize (Matt. 28.19 f.) is to be added as a saying of the risen Christ.

[2] K. v. Hase, *Geschichte Jesu*, 1876, p. 422 (following his *Leben Jesu*, 1829).

[3] See O. Cullmann, *Early Christian Worship*, pp. 38 ff.

one of those dogmas held by scholars as tenaciously as many Church dogmas. In view of the deliberately chosen perspective of the fourth evangelist, we certainly would not look first of all to his Gospel for the foundation of a representation of the life and teaching of Jesus, nor have we done so anywhere in the present work. Nevertheless a careful examination of John's major themes shows that while their arrangement usually does reflect the particular Johannine perspective, they are not simply externally imposed upon the life of Jesus.

Now it is true that the particular theme of the Son's complete unity with the Father in his revelatory action toward the world is very prominent in the Gospel of John. We shall say more about this later. But even apart from the passage in Matt. 11.27, can we not find a relationship at this point to the Synoptic witness? Or does this theme contradict the Synoptics? To be sure, the reserve with which Jesus speaks of his sonship in the Synoptics disappears in John. But the reason for this is that the Paraclete who speaks through the evangelist now proclaims openly everything the disciples 'could not bear' before. Moreover, the Johannine thought that only higher revelation leads to perception of Jesus' sonship is by no means a contradiction of the Synoptic tradition. We have found the same thought to be characteristic of Matt. 16.17. Although this verse also is usually believed not to be genuine, no one has called it 'Johannine'. At this point the 'Johannine heaven' is really no different from the Synoptic heaven, although it does of course appear from a different point of view. In any case, I see no reason to deny that Jesus spoke the words of Matt. 11.27 simply because of their close resemblance to a favourite theme of John.[1]

We cannot give a detailed exegesis here. (Concerning the more recent explanations, see J. Bieneck, *op. cit.*, pp. 75 ff.) The passage presents also a problem in the history of the text. A different order, according to which the phrase 'no one knows the Father except the Son' begins the sayings, is attested by writers of the second and third centuries in opposition to the manuscript tradition (see A. Harnack, *Sprüche und Reden Jesu*, 1907, pp. 196 ff.). With A. Schlatter, *Der Evangelist Matthäus*, 1929, *ad loc.*, J. Schniewind, *Das Evangelium nach Matthäus* (NTD), 1937, p. 147, and others, it seems to me (in opposition to M. Dibelius, *From Tradition to Gospel*, 1934, pp. 279 ff.) that the manuscript reading is the *lectio difficilior*, since the idea that God is unknowable is much more common to later

[1] So, among others, also A. Schweitzer, *Geschichte der Leben-Jesu-Forschung*², 1913, p. 310; V. Taylor, *The Names of Jesus*, p. 64.

thinkers than Christ's unknowability. For the same reason one must reject the suggestion of A. Harnack, *Sprüche und Reden Jesu*, pp. 189 ff., and of T. W. Manson, *The Sayings of Jesus*, 1949, p. 80, that the part of the saying in which the Son is the object should be eliminated and only the saying about the Father retained.

If the saying in Matt. 11.27 is genuine, then we must with caution consider the question we have already asked before and in our consideration of other titles answered rather negatively: Did Jesus himself reflect upon his *pre-existence*? Of course, in the case of the 'Son of God' concept also we have to do primarily with revelatory *action* in which Jesus continuously experiences his oneness with the Father. Nevertheless, as A. Schweitzer has correctly suggested, one must consider seriously the 'powerful hymn Matt. 11.25–30', and v. 27 may indeed 'be spoken from the consciousness of pre-existence'.[1] The exegete and historian as such can say no more than that. For in the sayings of Jesus relative to this question in the Gospel of John[2] the evangelist further develops the idea on the basis of his conviction of being led by the Paraclete into 'all truth'. Such an extension of the secret of sonship was foreign to the historical Jesus. Nevertheless, also here the fourth evangelist bases his extension on the momentary flashes of Christological perception which according to the Synoptic writers appear here and there already in the life and speech of Jesus himself.

Jesus also calls himself 'Son' in Mark 13.32 (Matt. 24.36), and here also we have to do with the relationship between Father and Son in view of the redemptive event: 'But of that day or that hour no one knows, not even the angels in heaven, nor the Son, but only the Father.' In the final analysis this saying presupposes the conviction of the complete unity of Father and Son and becomes really meaningful only on that basis. It indicates the single point at which during the incarnation a gap appears in this unity: knowledge of the date of the end. Other New Testament passages also indicate that the determination of this date is the most sovereign act of God the Father; by his own authority (ἐξουσία) the Father fixes the time (Acts 1.7). Mark 13.32 is much more difficult to explain as a later invention of the Church than as a genuine saying of Jesus. Precisely when one accepts as genuine Matt. 11.27, which points to Jesus' omniscience, does the saying in Mark 13.32 with its limitation of that omniscience become understandable as a saying of Jesus. On the other hand, it is questionable whether the early Church could have invented a saying

[1] A. Schweitzer, *op. cit.*, p. 310. [2] John 8.56 ff.

of Jesus which in this way limits his unity with the Father at such an important point.

In point of fact the genuineness of this saying is much less often contested than that of Matt. 11.27 (although W. G. Kümmel does so in his article, 'Das Gleichnis von den bösen Weingärtnern'). However, there is a plausible reason here for the subsequent invention of the Church: the attempt to justify the delay of the parousia by appealing to Jesus himself. On the other hand, could we consider the 'Church' capable of introducing such a bold assertion? Luke omits the saying, and it is often deleted in the manuscripts of Matthew, obviously because the idea was offensive. A case such as this, in which good arguments may be presented for both sides, ought to lead us to raise the question of genuineness only when there is actually a text-critical or material necessity.

Whether in the parable of the evil tenants (Mark 12.1 ff.) Jesus spoke of himself as the 'Son' depends upon the critical evaluation of the whole parable. There seems to me to be no convincing reason to deny it.[1] Here also the Son concept is related to Jesus' commission which brings about the historical act of salvation. Here also Jesus designates himself as the Son only indirectly, only in terms of a parable in which the expression first of all serves simply to make clear pictorially the special and unique relationship of the last messenger to the 'owner' of the vineyard.

If Jesus' consciousness of sonship really has such great significance for the understanding of his person and work, then once more we may not limit ourselves to the few sayings in which the word 'Son' itself occurs. We must also consider above all the way in which Jesus speaks of God as 'Father'. He always says 'my Father' or 'your Father', but never 'our Father'. The prayer which according to Matthew begins with the last phrase is not spoken by Jesus with the disciples, but is part of the prayer he taught them to pray: 'When *you* pray, pray like this' (Matt. 6.9: οὕτως προσεύχεσθε ὑμεῖς). It is just the more unconscious way in which Jesus thus sets himself in a special Son-relationship with the Father without directly stating it which confirms the fact that he understands this as his innermost secret, knowable only through special knowledge. At the same time, it also explains why he uses the expression 'Son' only in exceptional cases.

Finally we may refer once again to Jesus' attitude toward the Son

[1] As opposed to W. G. Kümmel, 'Das Gleichnis von den bösen Weingärtnern', *Aux sources de la tradition chrétienne*, pp. 120 ff.

of David question. In considering Mark 12.35[1] we said that this saying does not actually deny the fact that he is the Son of David, but does certainly deny the basic importance attached to that title by the Jews in view of the Messiah they expected. Similarly, in Mark 3.31 ff. Jesus' family relationship with mother, brothers and sisters is of no primary significance to him. Jesus asks the Jews, 'How is he (the Christ) his (David's) son?' That necessarily raises the question whether he does not so speak from the conviction that only his other sonship, his being the Son of God, is of real importance. We may only conjecture whether this idea was at the back of Jesus' mind here. If it was, then the question would form a bridge to the Johannine discussion of the origin of Jesus: he comes not from men, but directly from God (John 7.14 ff.; 8.12 ff.).

Jesus' primary designation for himself is not 'Son of God' but 'Son of Man'. But when we attempt to speak of Jesus' self-consciousness, the Son of Man title must be supplemented not only by that of *ebed Yahweh*, but also by that of 'Son of God'. We said at the beginning of this chapter that both 'Son of Man' and 'Son of God' are at once statements of humiliation and of exaltation. Now we add that like his consciousness of being the Son of Man, Jesus' consciousness of being the Son of God refers both to his person and to his work: his work of salvation and revelation shows that the Father and the Son are one. This conception of the Son of God is also the foundation of the faith of the first Christians, who in the light of the experience of Easter confessed him as the 'Son'.

4. *The Faith of Early Christianity in Jesus the Son of God*

The first 'witnesses of the resurrection' no longer had any cause for restraint in proclaiming Jesus as the only Son of God. The knowledge which 'flesh and blood' cannot reveal (Matt. 16.17) had been confirmed to them by Christ's resurrection, and now had to be proclaimed to everyone. 'Jesus is the Son of God' is therefore certainly one of the most ancient *credal statements* of the early Church. It was quite probably used in the earliest baptismal liturgy, traces of which appear in Acts 8.36–38. To the question 'What is to prevent my being baptized?'[2] Philip answers in v. 37, 'If you believe with all your heart, you may.' Then the eunuch makes a confession which has a quite liturgical character: 'I believe that Jesus is the Son of God.'

[1] See pp. 130 ff. above.

[2] See O. Cullmann, *Baptism in the New Testament*, pp. 71 ff.

Even if this verse, which is omitted by some manuscripts, is an interpolation, it is doubtless a very early addition.

It is perhaps not accidental that this creed, one of the earliest we know, is a part of a *baptismal* liturgy. Does not this preserve the recollection that Jesus' own consciousness of his sonship goes back to the revelation he received at his baptism in the Jordan? Whereas at other times the Church used the brief formula 'Jesus is the *Kyrios*,'[1] baptism gives special occasion to confess Jesus as 'Son of God'.

We may recall that the demons (Mark 3.11; 5.7) and Peter (Matt. 16.16) also used this formula as a confession even during Jesus' lifetime.

I John actually uses this formula as a basic affirmation: 'Whoever confesses that Jesus is the Son of God, God abides in him and he in God' (I John 4.15). Although the writer does make the title Son of God serve his Johannine ideas, he is clearly quoting here an ancient creed of the Church. We shall speak later of the relation he establishes between Jesus' sonship and that of the disciples mediated by faith in Jesus the Son. The writer obviously uses this ancient creed also to support his polemic against Docetism. It seems to epitomize for him the perfect expression of all confession. I John 2.23 expressly makes knowledge of the relation between the Father and the Son dependent upon 'confession': 'No one who denies the Son has the Father. He who confesses the Son has the Father also.' Although the Gospel of John does not directly quote the formula,[2] we shall see that it develops this idea in liturgical fullness. When we consider that this Gospel always strives to relate its presentation of the life of Jesus to early Christian worship,[3] we could actually think of this development as a commentary on the ancient liturgical confession of the Son.

The existence of such a formula in the very early Church is further shown by the fact that Hebrews designates Jesus 'Son of God' in the context of 'holding fast our confession' (Heb. 4.14). Beyond this, we also find evidence of faith in the 'Son of God' in the Pauline confessional passage, Rom. 1.3 f. This is a confession which Paul has certainly further developed, but it still must be very old. The 'Son'[4]

[1] Concerning the various occasions on which confessions were repeated see O. Cullmann, *The Earliest Christian Confessions*, pp. 18 ff.

[2] Nevertheless it is quoted by Jesus' opponents (John 10.36).

[3] See O. Cullmann, *Early Christian Worship*, pp. 38 ff.

[4] Later in connection with the description 'only begotten' taken from the Gospel of John. See pp. 298 ff. below.

is then always mentioned in the later creed,[1] beginning with its very early forms such as the formula used by Irenaeus in *Adversus Haereses* I, 10.1.[2]

According to Rom. 1.3 f., in which Paul obviously quotes a text already formulated and handed down,[3] the Son of God was descended from David according to the flesh, and 'designated Son of God in power according to the Spirit of Holiness by his resurrection from the dead'. We have pointed out earlier[4] that the phrase ἐν δυνάμει (in power) is especially important here. Jesus is the 'Son of God' from the beginning. At least this appears to be Paul's understanding when in v. 3 he makes 'Son' the subject of the whole two-part confession. But since the resurrection, the eternal divine sonship manifests itself ἐν δυνάμει; the Son of God becomes the *Kyrios*. Further, Paul connects the divine sonship 'according to the Spirit' with Davidic sonship 'according to the flesh'. Whereas in Mark 12.35 ff. (if our earlier conjecture is correct),[5] Jesus himself devaluated Davidic sonship in favour of divine sonship, the two are united here—without their being considered of equal value, of course. What Jesus is according to the πνεῦμα still has greater significance than his lineage according to the σάρξ, though that is also important.

When we turn from the Church's confession cited by Paul to the apostle himself, we note first of all that he also uses 'Son of God' in passages not dependent on older tradition. The title 'Son' does of course occur much less frequently in his writings than the title *Kyrios*. He is obviously most interested in the 'Son of God in power'. Nevertheless Paul does know that Jesus is the *Kyrios* only because, as the 'Son of God' from the beginning, he has been obedient to the Father's plan of salvation. Thus we find that he very strongly emphasizes precisely a side of the 'Son of God' concept which is also characteristic of Jesus' sayings: the Son of God carries out the divine plan of salvation in his life, but above all in his death. God did not 'spare' his own Son, writes Paul in Rom. 8.32, recalling the story of Abraham's sacrifice of Isaac, which also later became the common

[1] Already in the formula ΙΧΘΥΣ, which also represents a confession. See the investigations of F. J. Dölger, *Ichthys*, 1910.

[2] Ignatius' failure to mention the 'Son' in the confessional texts of his letters (although he does elsewhere apply also the title 'Son' to Jesus) may be connected with the fact that in the introductions to the formulas in *Smyrn.* 1.1. and *Eph.* 18.2 he calls Jesus θεός. See p. 314 below.

[3] O. Cullmann, *The Earliest Christian Confessions*, pp. 55 ff. R. Bultmann, *Theology of the New Testament* I, pp. 50 f., also acknowledges the pre-Pauline origin of this text.

[4] See p. 235 above.

[5] See pp. 131 f. above.

type for the sacrifice of a son.[1] To be God's Son means to suffer and to die. Here again we are worlds apart from Hellenism's 'sons of gods'. God 'sent' his Son in order to redeem us (Gal. 4.4). 'We were reconciled to God by the death of his Son' (Rom. 5.10). We 'wait for his Son from heaven' (I Thess. 1.10), who also executes God's future work of salvation.

The goal of reconciliation toward which the 'Son' leads us is his making us to be 'sons'.[2] Using 'son' and 'heir', the same pair of concepts which are found in the parable of the evil tenants (Mark 12.1 ff.), Paul shows in Rom. 8.14 ff. (cf. Gal. 4.6 ff.) the way in which our sonship depends upon Jesus' unique sonship. We are called to κοινωνία (fellowship) with the Son of God (I Cor. 1.9).

In connection with this goal Paul does mention also the other side of the Son of God, the majesty which is shown by his origin. As 'the Son' he is the image of God from the beginning (Col. 1.15 ff.). Therefore God predestined us 'to be conformed to the image of his Son' (Rom. 8.29). Here Paul has combined the concepts 'Son of God' and 'image of God'. The latter, as we have seen, is basic to the meaning of 'Son of Man'.

But in I Cor. 15.28, a very important passage for Christology, we see that Paul speaks of the unity of Father and Son only in the closest connection with *Heilsgeschichte*, that is, with the Son's obedience. Here Paul uses the concept Son to lead us to the very farthest limit of divine revelatory action at the end of time, just as the Gospel of John uses the concept Logos to lead us to the farthest limit at the beginning. 'Son of God' signifies God's redemptive action, the Son's obedience to the end. It is thus very significant that the final fulfilment of all redemptive activity is described precisely as a final 'subjection of the Son' to the Father: 'When all things are subjected to him, then the Son himself will also be subjected to him who put all things under him, that God may be all in all.' Here lies the key to all New Testament Christology. *It is only meaningful to speak of the Son in view of God's revelatory action, not in view of his being*. But precisely for this reason, Father and Son are really one in this activity. Now

[1] So most recently O. Michel, *Der Brief an die Römer, ad loc.* Concerning the connection between Rom. 8.32 and Gen. 22, which was repeatedly made already in the ancient Church, see D. Lerch, *Isaaks Opferung, christlich gedeutet* (Beiträge zur historischen Theologie 12), 1950.

[2] Thus Paul understands the relation between our sonship and that of Jesus in a way just the opposite of the thesis of W. Grundmann (see pp. 275 f. above): only because Jesus is *the* Son in a way entirely different from the way we are can he make us to be sons.

we can say of the 'Son of God' what we said earlier of the Logos: he is God as God reveals himself in redemptive action. The whole New Testament speaks of the redemptive action. Therefore the kingdom in which we live now, before the end, is the 'kingdom of the Son' (Col. 1.13).[1]

In the section on Jesus and the Son of God concept we have already discussed in general the theological position of the Synoptic writers with regard to this title. Now we are interested in the peculiar attitude each of them takes toward 'Son of God'.

'Son of God' appears to have an especially prominent place in Mark's Christological thought. As scholars have often observed,[2] the intention of the whole Gospel is apparently to show in all the events it reports that Jesus is the (first of all hidden) Son of God. In opposition to Wrede's thesis, we have shown that this hiddenness can be explained by Jesus' own reserve. The very first verse designates Jesus 'Son of God',[3] and at the end the centurion at the cross confesses: 'Truly this was God's Son' (Mark 15.39). The writer's very infrequent use of the title in spite of this fundamental attitude toward it confirms our previous conclusions: Mark apparently has a very special understanding of the fact that it expresses the most secret and final revelation of the person and work of Jesus. Therefore he tries to respect Jesus' own reserve in this matter by carefully leading the reader by a historical presentation alone to the centurion's confession.

Matthew and Luke are distinct both from Mark and from John, which proceeds in an entirely different way.[4] They do not display Mark's reverent reticence to penetrate more deeply into the mystery of Jesus' sonship. Conscious that their task is to proclaim Jesus openly as the only Son of God to the whole world, they try by means of the infancy narratives to *explain* Jesus' sonship, and to lift the veil from the question 'how' the Father begets the Son.[5] Independent of one

[1] See O. Cullmann, 'The Kingship of Christ and the Church in the New Testament', *The Early Church*, pp. 109 ff.

[2] Thus for instance E. Lohmeyer, *Das Evangelium des Markus*, pp. 4, 348.

[3] It is true that this phrase is missing from many manuscripts, but good witnesses (including above all the Western text) have the following reading: Ἀρχὴ τοῦ εὐαγγελίου Ἰησοῦ Χριστοῦ υἱοῦ (τοῦ) θεοῦ.

[4] See pp. 297 ff. below.

[5] With their completely philosophical approach the later Christological speculations tried to explain this 'how' in a different way.

another, they obviously use certain traditions which had in the meantime been circulated about Jesus' birth—traditions which in turn utilized familiar oriental and Hellenistic themes. But the evangelists' narrative interest is quite secondary to the theological concern to report only so much as seems necessary to demonstrate the unique conception of Jesus by the Holy Spirit. Nothing shows this more clearly than a comparison of the New Testament accounts with the apocryphal infancy gospels which were written over a long period of time.[1]

As soon as the 'how' of Jesus' divine sonship is reported in terms of the *virgin birth*,[2] the problem arises of harmonizing this idea with the Church's pre-Pauline confession of the Davidic sonship 'according to the flesh' (Rom. 1.3 f.).[3] There was no such problem for this ancient creed, because, without asking about the 'how' of Jesus' origin, it mentions in addition to 'carnal' Davidic sonship only the 'spiritual' divine sonship 'in power' on the basis of the resurrection. But since the genealogies of Jesus presented in Matt. 1.1 ff. and Luke 3.23 ff. run through Joseph, the father, and yet these two gospels at the same time report the tradition of Jesus' birth without a human father, the problem does clearly arise here. Matthew and Luke tried to solve the problem by interpreting the human descent from David to mean Jesus' *adoption* into Joseph's Davidic family. Luke begins his genealogy with the formula: ὡς ἐνομίζετο, '. . . being the son (*as was supposed*) of Joseph . . .' (Luke 3.23). Matthew, according to the text which is probably the oldest, closes his genealogy with the statement: '. . . Jacob the father of Joseph the husband of *Mary, of whom* Jesus was born, who is called Christ' (Matt. 1.16).

The explanation of the two evangelists does not seem to have proved satisfactory, for very early there arose an entirely different attempt to relate Jesus' Davidic sonship and the virgin birth. Descent from David was traced through Mary instead of Joseph; not only Joseph but also Mary was said to have descended from David.[4] Thus later but still early manuscripts substitute αὐτούς for αὐτόν in Luke 2.4 (and others make it even clearer with ἀμφοτέρους, 'both'): '. . . because *they* were of the house and lineage

[1] On this point see the introduction to my contribution, 'Apokryphe Kindheitsevangelien', to the forthcoming 3rd ed. of E. Hennecke, *Neutestamentliche Apokryphen* (ed. W. Schneemelcher).

[2] On the problems involved in the assertion of the virgin birth see the extensive work of J. G. Machen, *The Virgin Birth of Christ*, 1930. The author's systematic concern is to prove that belief in Jesus' virgin birth was an original article of the Christian faith and thus binding also today.

[3] See also pp. 129 ff. especially pp. 134 f. above.

[4] Cf. pp. 128 f. above.

of David.' This assertion of the Davidic descent of Mary also later occurs in the apocryphal *Protevangelion of James* 10.1; Justin Martyr, *Dialogue with Trypho* 43, 45; Irenaeus, *Adversus Haereses* III, 21.5; III, 9.2; and Tertullian, *Against Marcion* III, 17.20. But it must extend back to the beginning of the second century, for Ignatius of Antioch utilizes an ancient formula which like Matthew and Luke combines Davidic sonship with the virgin birth as a weapon against *Docetism*. Thus he cannot, like the evangelists, have understood κατὰ σάρκα to mean *adoption*, but must have thought that Jesus' Davidic sonship is to be traced physically through Mary. The later creeds, probably as a result of this difficulty, then completely omit reference to Davidic sonship. Thus we can trace the following development: originally Davidic sonship κατὰ σάρκα and divine sonship κατὰ πνεῦμα were contrasted without further attempt to explain the latter (Rom. 1.3 f.). The writers of Matthew and Luke, on the other hand, combine the two by using the virgin birth to explain *how* Jesus is the Son of God, and by understanding Davidic sonship κατὰ σάρκα as Jesus' adoption. Beginning with the early second century, writers tend again to interpret κατὰ σάρκα literally, but then the genealogy of Mary must be traced to David if the statement of the virgin birth is still to be maintained.

It is impossible to determine the exact age of the tradition concerning Jesus' virgin birth used in Matthew and Luke, but we can say with certainty that these two gospels provide our earliest and only first-century evidence.[1] All attempts to find the tradition expressly stated or unquestionably presupposed in other books of the New Testament are too artificial to be convincing. 'Born of woman' in Gal. 4.4 can be said of everyone and in context is intended only to underline the Son of God's complete entrance into humanity. Even if the ancient reading (found primarily in Western texts) is original,[2] the *qui natus est*, 'who *was* born', in John 1.13 by no means proves that the author thinks here of the virgin birth. The following translation results from this interpretation: 'He gave power to become children of God to those who believe in the name of him who was

[1] Already at the beginning of the second century, of course, we find the tradition concerning the virgin birth in the passages from Ignatius cited above. It is mentioned together with the Davidic sonship in ancient formulas used by Ignatius which were certainly known in Antioch earlier, that is, at least at the turn of the century.—There have been attempts to discover a common literary source for the canonical infancy narratives: L. Conrady, *Die Quelle der kanonischen Kindheitsgeschichten*, 1900; A. Resch, *Das Kindheitsevangelium* (Texte und Untersuchungen 10, 5), 1897. Also Machen, *op. cit.*, would like to assume that the birth stories of Matthew and Luke go back to an already fixed tradition about the virgin birth, but this can hardly be proved.

[2] The Bodmer Papyrus II, published in 1956, reads the plural.

born not of blood, nor of the will of the flesh, nor of the will of man, but of God.' This is a typical Johannine idea, expressed also by Paul: *our* sonship is grounded in the sonship of *the* Son and becomes a reality through faith in him.[1]

I would therefore not reject this reading so decidedly as does R. Bultmann, *Das Evangelium des Johannes*, p. 37 n. 7. He thinks that modern exegetes prefer it only because they wish to find the virgin birth in the Gospel of John. Even though this may be true of many exegetes, it is nevertheless just as wrong to reject the reading because of the idea that it originates solely in the ancient effort to introduce the virgin birth into this passage. Being born 'of the will of man' means simply 'human descent', which John 1.13 contrasts with 'born of God'. This contrast regarding Jesus' origin runs through the whole Gospel of John and has nothing at all to do with the virgin birth. The relation of the rebirth of the faithful to the birth of him who 'descended from heaven' (John 3.13) also forms the basis of the dialogue with Nicodemus. With reference to John 1.13, I would not too quickly reject the suggestion of C. F. Burney, *The Aramaic Origin of the Fourth Gospel*, 1922, p. 34, that the plural can be explained by going back to the Aramaic. There are, however, other possible explanations (as opposed to W. Bauer, *Das Johannesevangelium*, p. 22) for the replacing of an original singular with a plural, since the plural does yield a clear, 'easier' context. A. Loisy, *Le quatrième Evangile*², 1921, *ad loc.*, regards the singular as original, but he wishes, certainly unjustifiably, to deduce that the author thereby *rejects* the virgin birth. This shows only that the question of the original reading has nothing at all to do with the problem of the virgin birth. Besides the commentaries, in which the older works on this question are named (see particularly W. Bauer), a more recent monograph is that of F. M. Braun, '*Qui ex Deo natus est*', *Aux sources de la tradition chrétienne*, pp. 11 ff. After citing all the evidence Braun maintains that the singular is original, but he does think that this attests the virgin birth. C. H. Dodd, *The Interpretation of the Fourth Gospel*, p. 260 n. 1, and C. K. Barrett, *The Gospel according to St John*, pp. 137 f., like the majority of scholars, reject the singular.

In explaining Jesus' divine sonship by asserting his virgin birth, Matthew and Luke separate themselves not only from all other New Testament writings, but also from Mark, for whom faith in Jesus the Son of God is basically far more central, but who consciously respects the mystery with which Jesus himself surrounded this title.

We have seen that the Gospel of John, like Mark, does not try to explain *how* the Father begets the Son by referring to the virgin

[1] See p. 293 above.

birth.[1] But like Mark the writer of the Fourth Gospel nevertheless places faith in the 'Son of God' at the centre of his Gospel.[2] For him also it is not an *explanation* of the divine conception in a human setting that is essential, but the *fact* that Jesus comes from God in a special way and thus is uniquely one with the Father. As C. H. Dodd has correctly observed,[3] the preposition ἐκ characterizes Jesus' specific origin in God. Ἀπό or παρά is used in referring to all God's other 'ambassadors'. The author of John so strongly emphasizes the fact of Jesus' origin in the Father that he never even asks whether it is compatible with human birth of known parents (John 7.27) from Nazareth (John 1.45; 7.41 f.).[4] For him Jesus' direct birth from God stands above his earthly birth.

The uniqueness of Jesus' sonship is not thereby in any sense weakened in comparison with its treatment in Matthew and Luke; on the contrary, it represents the main theme of the discussion, so important for John, of the oneness of the Father and the Son. In order to stress this uniqueness, the author uses the word μονογενής, 'only begotten', which later became a part of the creed. It occurs twice in the prologue (John 1.14, 18)—although the second time it is connected with θεός, according to the better reading.[5] The word corresponds to the Hebrew יָחִיד and means 'only', but also 'beloved'. As in the Synoptics, we encounter here the Jewish idea that the Son of God is chosen from the very beginning. Μονογενής is thus not essentially different from ἀγαπητός, especially since both words occur as translations of יָחִיד. Judaism could also apply this adjective to the whole people of Israel,[6] and this agrees with what we have said about the 'Son of God' in general. We find the word applied to Jesus only in the Johannine writings: in the prologue to the Gospel of John; in John 3.16, 18; and in I John 4.9.[7]

We have found that in the Synoptics the title 'Holy One of God'

[1] Nor by a speculation about 'substance' or 'natures'.

[2] This is also correctly seen by R. Bultmann, *Theology of the New Testament* II, pp. 33 ff. On the question of 'Son of God' in the Gospel of John see also W. Lütgert, *Die johanneische Christologie*[2], 1916; and more recently C. H. Dodd, *The Interpretation of the Fourth Gospel*, especially pp. 250 ff.

[3] C. H. Dodd, *op. cit.*, p. 259.

[4] According to R. Bultmann, *Das Evangelium des Johannes*, p. 37 n. 7, and C. H. Dodd, *op. cit.*, p. 260, the virgin birth is actually excluded by the Gospel of John.

[5] See pp. 309 f. below.

[6] Cf. Psalms of Solomon, 18.4; II (4) Esd. 6.58.

[7] Concerning μονογενής and the significance of this expression in the comparative study of religions see R. Bultmann, *op. cit.*, pp. 47 ff.

is practically a synonym for 'Son'.[1] We have already mentioned its use in the Johannine versions of the confession of Peter (John 6.69), and we have explained John 10.36 in the light of it. This expression also emphasizes the distinction between Jesus and all other creatures.

But the Johannine proclamation of the Son of God does differ from that of Mark in one essential point, for although it does not explain Jesus' conception, it proclaims the *fact* of his divine sonship without any restraint to believing Jews as well as to the disciples. The Johannine Christ, through whom the Paraclete proclaims even those things the disciples could not 'bear' during Jesus' lifetime (John 16.12), has no further reason to speak in veiled or reserved terms of his oneness with the Father. In no other early Christian writing is the divine sonship so openly proclaimed, despite the opponents and sceptics who will not accept Jesus' witness to himself. In this regard the fourth evangelist differs not only from the Gospel of Mark, but also from the historical Jesus himself.[2] But although he thus consciously speaks of all the actions and words of Jesus from a post-Easter perspective, we must ask whether he actually proclaims a materially different conception of the Son of God.

We have previously seen that the saying in Matt. 11.27, whose 'Johannine' character has always been noticed by exegetes, fits perfectly into the Synoptic view of Jesus' consciousness of sonship. Now we shall see that the two themes, obedience and unity in revelatory action, are also present in the 'Son of God' concept in the Gospel of John. The fourth evangelist does, of course, emphasize the second theme more strongly than do the Synoptic writers. This is related to the fact that the Gospel of John as a whole emphasizes the idea of revelation in divine redemptive action. At this point the concepts 'Son of God' and 'Logos' meet. In the Logos doctrine, Jesus' oneness with God is based entirely upon the Christ-*event*, above all on the life of Jesus reported in the Gospel. Similarly, the unity of the 'Son of God' with the Father is based on the fact, expressed also by Jesus himself, that he is the only and beloved Son just because he obediently fulfils the Father's commission for the world: 'I can do

[1] See p. 285 above.

[2] A certain parallel to the Synoptic idea (especially Matt. 16.17; see p. 279 above) that it requires special revelation to attain recognition that Jesus is the Son of God can be found in the Gospel of John in the lack of understanding on the part of those with whom Jesus discusses his unity with God. Cf. R. Bultmann, *Theology of the New Testament* II, pp. 47 f., and pp. 301–302 below, besides traces of a messianic secret in John 10.24.

nothing on my own authority; . . . I seek not my own will but the will of the one who sent me' (John 5.30). A oneness of essence exists because there is a complete oneness of will. 'My food is to do the will of the one who sent me, and to accomplish his work' (John 4.34). The picture is especially graphic: as the human body cannot live without nourishment, so it is Jesus' very nature that he must do what God does.

This 'must' is not to be compared with the prophetic or apostolic 'compulsion', for the relationship of the Father's work to that of the Son is quite different from its relationship to the work of the prophets and apostles, who can only be his instruments. The Johannine Christ's answer to the accusation that he breaks the Sabbath provides a very typical illumination of this state of affairs: 'My father is working still, and I am working' (John 5.17).[1] Jesus cannot rest because God's saving work has not yet reached the Sabbath rest in the eschatological sense of Heb. 4.3 ff. His time is God's time. John 9.4 contains the same thought: 'We must work the works of him who sent me, while it is day.'

The oneness of will and work extends even to the Son's participation in the Father's most peculiar work, the creation of life. As the Son is the mediator of creation at the beginning, so he is able in fellowship with the Father to raise the dead. Jesus says after the raising of Lazarus: 'Father, I thank thee that thou hast heard me. I knew that thou hearest me always' (John 11.41 f.).

We have seen that for both the Synoptics and Paul the work of the Son who is united with the Father relates especially to Jesus' suffering and death. We might be inclined to expect that just this theme would not be prominent in the Gospel of John. But we have discovered that John by no means lacks the idea that Jesus' suffering and death are his central work.[2] So, for example, the familiar John 3.16, which stresses precisely the uniqueness of the 'only' or 'beloved' son,[3] also points to his 'being delivered' to die: 'For God so loved the world that he gave his only (beloved) son.' I have elsewhere shown that the verb ἔδωκεν has here the double meaning 'send' and 'deliver up to die'.[4] If we presuppose the twofold significance of the word μονογενής,

[1] On the relation of this saying to the day of resurrection see O. Cullmann, 'Sabbat und Sonntag nach dem Johannesevangelium. Ἕως ἄρτι (John 5. 17)', *In memoriam E. Lohmeyer*, 1951, pp. 127 ff.

[2] See pp. 70 f. above.

[3] Μονογενής. See p. 298 above.

[4] See O. Cullmann, 'Der johanneische Gebrauch doppeldeutiger Ausdrücke als Schlüssel zum Verständnis des vierten Evangeliums', *TZ* 4, 1948, pp. 360 ff.

it seems to me unquestionable that John 3.16, like Rom. 8.32, alludes to the sacrifice of Isaac.

What applies to Jesus' works applies also to his teaching, for teaching and work belong together. The Father and the Son reveal themselves in both; I 'speak thus as the Father taught me' (John 8.28); 'My teaching is not mine, but his who sent me' (John 7.16; see also John 14.10b).

In this context 'Father' is often accompanied by the participial phrase ὁ πέμψας με (he who sent me), which by itself can actually be a synonym for 'Father'. This shows once again the close relationship between sonship and assignment to execute the divine plan. But again the Son is not simply 'sent' as were the prophets and later the apostles. We have already referred to the preposition ἐκ, which fulfils an important diacritical function in this regard. The sending of the Son 'from the Father' rests first of all on the assumption that the two belong together from the beginning. It is especially clear from John 5.19 f. that we are not concerned here with a prophet's consciousness of mission: 'For whatever (the Father) does, that the Son does likewise, for the Father loves the Son.' This indicates the ultimate root of the unity in revelatory action.[1]

Thus we repeatedly hear that Jesus came from the Father: 'I proceeded and came forth from God; I came not of my own accord, but he sent me' (John 8.42). But his return to the Father also expresses this oneness: 'I came from the Father and have come into the world; again, I am leaving the world and going to the Father' (John 16.28). Therefore, he is not 'alone' during his revelatory activity on earth, but in everything he does the Father works—not through him but with him: '. . . for it is not I alone that judge, but I and he who sent me' (John 8.16); '. . . you will leave me alone; yet I am not alone for the Father is with me' (John 16.32).

The fourth evangelist never forgets that the Father is greater than the Son (John 14.28)—greater only in so far as the Son goes forth from the Father and returns to the Father. But on the other hand we hear such impressive sentences as: 'I and the Father are one' (John 10.30); '. . . the Father is in me and I am in the Father' (John 10.38). These lines recall the statement about the Logos in the prologue. The Johannine Christ thus openly declares his pre-existence: '. . . before Abraham was, I am' (John 8.58).

[1] At the same time it recalls the voice which, according to the Synoptics, at Jesus' baptism both addressed him as the 'beloved Son' and implicitly commissioned him to assume the role of the *ebed Yahweh*.

Nevertheless, just as do the Synoptics, the Gospel of John knows that this claim is unacceptable from the standpoint of human knowledge: 'You say,' Jesus tells the Jews, '"You are blaspheming," because I said, "I am the Son of God"' (John 10.36). The fourth evangelist certainly appeals to an old tradition here when he sees the 'blasphemy' not in the messianic claim but in Jesus' claim (veiled though it may be) to sonship. His messianic claim was really offensive only to the Romans.[1] To the Jews, on the other hand, the claim to sonship in the particular form represented by Jesus' self-consciousness gave the most offence, for they correctly interpret Jesus' claim to be 'Son' as identification with God: '... you, being a man, make yourself God' (John 10.33).[2]

But the Jews reproach him above all for appealing only to his own testimony to support such a vast claim. The Johannine Christ answers those attacks (John 5.30 ff.; 8.13 ff.) by trying to show that his testimony is true, and he tells how this revelation is to be known. At this point the fourth evangelist proceeds differently from Matthew and Luke, who, with the help of the assertion of the virgin birth, report 'objectively' how Jesus is begotten by God. The Fourth Gospel does not explain *how*, but maintains firmly *that* the Son goes forth directly from the Father. But it supports and fortifies this 'that'. In chs. 5 and 8, Jesus' arguments with the Jews, the Fourth Gospel actually presents a kind of 'Christological epistemology'.

While witnesses can and must be produced to support other assertions, there can be no question of human witness for Jesus' claim to be the Son of God. God himself is the only possible competent witness. Only he can validate this claim of oneness with himself. The claim to be the Son of God so bursts all human bonds that only this circular explanation is possible: the Father himself must attest that Jesus is the Son; on the other hand, this divine testimony must be given precisely in the Son. This Gospel, then, knows only two means of apprehending God's revelation that Jesus is the Son of God. First, one must know the Father and do his will: 'If any man's will is to do

[1] See O. Cullmann, *The State in the New Testament*, pp. 24 ff. Conversely, the claim to be the Son of God is of no interest to the Romans and therefore not offensive to them.

[2] This same interpretation is presupposed in John 8.53: 'Who do you claim to be?'—See also the Mandaean text R. Ginza I, 200, which contains a polemic against Jesus: 'He says: I am God, the Son of God, whom my Father has sent here' (M. Lidzbarski, *Ginza*, 1925, p. 29). To the extent that the claim to sonship means identification with God it does indeed fall under Jewish condemnation. See Ezek. 28.2 ff.; Dan. 6; Acts 12.20 ff.; Mark 2.7 ff.

his will, he shall know whether the teaching is from God or whether I am speaking on my own authority' (John 7.17). Secondly, one must see Jesus' works: 'If I am not doing the works of my Father, then do not believe me; but if I do them, even though you do not believe me, believe the works, that you may know and understand that the Father is in me and I am in the Father' (John 10.37 f.).

We have no other evidence for any Christology today either, nor can we ever have. Only when we ourselves become 'sons' by accepting in faith Jesus Christ's witness to his sonship, and by doing his divine will, can we know that Jesus is *the* Son. Only in this way can we ever be able to testify with the apostles that 'the Father has sent his Son as the Saviour of the world' (I John 4.14). 'Whoever confesses that Jesus is the Son of God, God abides in him, and he in God' (I John 4.15). This last verse, which uses a very early creed of the Church,[1] places that creed completely in the framework of the Johannine Christological epistemology. The parallel with John 10.38b is obvious. What Jesus says here of himself can thus also be extended to include those who believe in his sonship.

In conclusion we can say that the Gospel of John as a whole penetrates more deeply than Matthew and Luke into the ultimate mystery of Jesus' consciousness of sonship as we believed we could and should infer it from the Synoptics. Although John openly proclaimed what the historical Jesus only referred to with veiled allusion, he very impressively expressed, in their very solidarity, the two sides of Jesus' Son-consciousness: obedience and oneness with the Father.

The remaining books of the New Testament use the title relatively seldom. As we have seen, faith in the 'Son of God' is very important for Mark, but, following Jesus' own attitude, he speaks of it with a certain reticence. Paul writes *Kyrios* more often, although the idea of divine sonship has great significance for him also. Surprisingly, the designation is not mentioned at all in the Pastoral Epistles or in James and I Peter.[2] It occurs only once in Revelation (2.18) and twice in Acts (9.20; 13.33). Thus it seems that a large part of the Church very early more or less lost the deeper understanding of what the

[1] See p. 291 above.

[2] In II Peter 1.17 the title is only a quotation from Ps. 2.7 which is used to refer to the transfiguration.

consciousness of sonship means as the explanation of Jesus' person and work.[1]

The 'Son of God' concept dominates the Christology of Hebrews all the more in contrast. After we have repeatedly established the close relationship between the Fourth Gospel and Hebrews in all essential Christological views, we are not surprised that 'Son of God' is also very prominent here.[2] The author of course dwells longer upon the High Priest concept. It is his own very personal contribution to the solution of the Christological problem that he attempts to group statements concerning faith in Christ around this concept, and we have shown the advantages of this solution. On the other hand, we have also indicated in this context that precisely in view of Jesus' pre-existence the author is interested in connecting 'High Priest' very closely with 'Son of God', for he quotes the confessional formula and makes it expressly recognizable as such: 'Since then we have a great high priest . . . Jesus, the Son of God, let us hold fast our confession' (Heb. 4.14).

Without doubt the writer of Hebrews grasped the deeper content of this confession. On the one hand, he sees that Jesus' divine sonship rests on his mission, that it means imparting the divine revelation. He understands that this provides something in common with the Old Testament prophets. But for this very reason he is concerned to show that this mission is more than that of the prophets. As in the Gospel of John, so in Hebrews Jesus' mission rests on the unique oneness of the 'Son' with the 'Father'. Thus at the very beginning this book distinguishes Christ from the prophets as 'the Son': 'In many and various ways God spoke of old to our fathers by the prophets; but in these last days he has spoken to us by a Son' (Heb. 1.1 f.). Then follow attributes reminiscent of the prologue to John which express the Son's complete participation in the deity of the Father.[3]

In order to demonstrate the Son's uniqueness, Hebrews uses Old Testament quotations to show that the Son is above all beings: above all angels (Heb. 1.5 ff.) and above Moses, who is only a 'servant'

[1] Therefore I do not believe that V. Taylor, *The Names of Jesus*, p. 57, adequately explains the fact that some writings strongly emphasize the title Son of God, whereas others do not use it at all. Taylor thinks that where 'Son of God' is prominent, a pedagogical interest is active; where it is lacking, there a liturgical interest has replaced the pedagogical.

[2] If I am correct in classifying the author of the Gospel of John as one of the Palestinian 'Hellenists' of Acts (see pp. 183 f. above), then Hebrews as well as I John must come from the same group.

[3] See p. 261 above.

(Heb. 3.5 ff.). Thus, as we have often emphasized before, Jesus' deity is more powerfully asserted in Hebrews than in any other New Testament writing, with the exception of the Gospel of John. Hebrews understands 'Son of God' to mean 'one with God', just as does John 10.33, 36. The Old Testament psalms (for example, Pss. 45.6 f.; 102.25 ff.) are applied to Jesus so that he can be addressed directly as 'God' (Heb. 1.8 f.), and the creation of the world ascribed to him (Heb. 1.10 ff.). We should note especially the introductory formula in this passage: 'But of the Son he says . . .'. 'Son of God', then, means complete participation in the Father's deity.[1]

The Christology of the High Priest is combined with that of the Son of God throughout Hebrews. The writer does not forget that the theme of *obedience* belongs with the idea of Jesus' sonship, especially since it can be related easily to the High Priest concept. The author expressly emphasizes that Jesus' learning obedience through suffering and his being the Son (καίπερ ὢν υἱός) are really not contradictory (Heb. 5.8).

Finally, especially significant is the connection of the central figure of the priestly king Melchizedek with the 'Son' in Heb. 7.3: ἀφωμοιωμένος τῷ υἱῷ τοῦ θεοῦ. Hebrews' close relationship with the Gospel of John is again apparent when the same verse says of this mysterious ruler that he is 'without father, without mother'. Human conception is unimportant; Jesus is born of God. The addition of 'without mother' verifies the assertion that one can hardly find evidence for the virgin birth in the environment of this writing. In any case, it is as true for Hebrews as for the Gospel of John that the impressive thing about the confession of the 'Son of God' is the fact as such that the only Son who participated in creation and goes forth directly from the Father nevertheless participates as man, as the true High Priest, in human infirmity.

According to the Gospel of John, the Son of God is God in his self-revelation. According to Paul, he will be absorbed in God when redemptive action has reached its goal. And now we hear in Hebrews: he is also the one through whom God in his self-revelation to the world 'created the world', since from the very beginning he 'reflects God's glory' (Heb. 1.2b, 3; see also John 17.5).

[1] On the direct designation of Jesus as 'God' see the following chapter.

11

The Designation of Jesus as 'God'

(θεός)

OUR INVESTIGATION of the Christological utilization of *Kyrios*, 'Logos' and 'Son of God' has already shown that on the basis of the Christological views connected with these titles the New Testament *could* designate Jesus as 'God'. This is true for each title in a particular sense: the *Kyrios* is the present divine ruler who since his exaltation rules the Church, the world, and the life of each individual; the 'Logos' is the eternal revealer, who communicates himself since the very beginning; the 'Son of God' is the one who wills and works in complete oneness with the Father, from whom he goes forth and to whom he returns. In fact, even the concept Son of Man ultimately led us to Jesus' 'deity' since it shows Jesus as the only true 'image of God'. The fundamental answer to the question whether the New Testament teaches Christ's 'deity' is therefore 'Yes'. But to this 'yes' we must further add: 'on condition that we do not connect the concept with later Greek speculations about substance and natures, but understand it strictly from the standpoint of *Heilsgeschichte*'. Without a divine *Heilsgeschichte* it would not make sense to speak of Jesus' 'deity'. He would then simply be one of the heroes of history—nothing more. Conversely, it would likewise be senseless without *Heilsgeschichte* to distinguish God the Father from the Logos, his revelation, his 'Son'.

The fact that *Heilsgeschichte* is strictly definitive for Christology also determines the specific subordination in the New Testament of Jesus Christ to God—not in the sense of later so-called 'subordinationism', but in the sense that Jesus Christ is God only in his revelation of himself. This is the only dimension which the Old and New Testaments consider, but it does not exhaust the nature of God the Father. The later confusion of the Father and the Son, which the Church rightly condemned in its various heretical guises,[1] is foreign

[1] Such a confusion is nevertheless often characteristic of practical popular Catholic piety. Despite its official condemnation, Monophysitism still dominates the religious thinking of the average Catholic. Jesus and God are often no longer

to early Christianity precisely because its thinking is determined by *Heilsgeschichte*. The danger of such confusion arises only when one tries to solve the Christological problem with speculations about substance and natures.

Since it is clear that the New Testament arrives at the conception of Jesus' deity in the sense indicated from the standpoint of a group of basic Christological ideas, the question whether it also actually designates him 'God' is only of secondary importance. We shall therefore examine the texts relevant to this question with the explicit presupposition that Jesus' 'deity' by no means stands or falls with them. If the investigation should show that the New Testament did not call Jesus 'God', that would have no effect on our previous conclusions. But if, as I believe, the exposition of these passages demonstrates that Jesus was occasionally designated 'God', this can only again confirm our earlier statements.

It is regrettable that also in this purely exegetical question the decision usually depends upon the 'theological standpoint' of the scholar; and here again it is not only the 'conservative', but also just as much the opposite attitude which often influences exegesis.

Actually, the passages which confer upon Jesus the title *Kyrios*, the name of God, are at least as important as those in which he is directly addressed as 'God'—and in some cases the former are even more important. We have seen that on the basis of the designation *Kyrios* early Christianity does not hesitate to transfer to Jesus everything the Old Testament says about God. It is surprising that scholars do not give more consideration to such an important fact.[1] We have also seen in the preceding chapters that without being contradicted Jesus' opponents understood 'Son of God' to mean identification with God.[2]

Passages which apply the designation 'God' to Jesus are not numerous, and some of them are uncertain from the viewpoint of textual

distinguished even by terminology. The question has rightly been raised whether the need for veneration of Mary has not perhaps developed so strongly among the Catholic people just because this confusion has made Jesus himself remote from the believer.

[1] The transference of the description of the 'Ancient of Days' in Dan. 10.5–7 to the Son of Man in Rev. 1.13 ff. should also be mentioned in this context. The fact that the author of Revelation does not hesitate to describe his vision of Christ exactly as Daniel described his vision of God is Christologically at least noteworthy.

[2] See pp. 301 f. above on John 10.33, 36; 8.53.

criticism. Even in ancient times some people apparently attributed undue importance to the question whether or not Jesus was to be called 'God'. Especially in connection with the Christological controversies the designation θεός in certain passages was sometimes considered dangerous, sometimes necessary. This explains the many textual variants precisely in the passages to which we now turn.

By their very nature the Synoptic Gospels drop out of consideration here. Just as Jesus did not call himself κύριος, neither did he call himself θεός, and the evangelists also seem unwilling to do so. The Gospel of John and Hebrews provide the clearest and least ambiguous evidence of the attribution of θεός to Jesus. In the Gospel of John there are at least two indisputable passages: John 1.1, καὶ θεὸς ἦν ὁ λόγος (and the Word was God); and John 20.28, Thomas' confession, ὁ κυριός μου καὶ ὁ θεός μου (my Lord and my God). We have already spoken of both these passages.[1] They frame the whole Gospel. The incident involving Thomas closes the Gospel of John proper (since ch. 21 is a supplement), and at the same time marks its final and climactic confession. The last words of the risen Christ, 'Blessed are those who have not seen and yet believe', refer also to all future readers of the Gospel. They should all believe without having seen. The evangelist's witness to the life of Jesus is intended to lead them precisely to *this* confession of Jesus: 'My Lord and my God.'[2] If therefore the whole Gospel culminates in this confession, and, on the other hand, the author writes in the first verse of the first chapter, 'And the Logos *was God*,' then there can be no doubt that for him all the other titles for Jesus which are prominent in his work ('Son of Man', 'Son of God', 'Lord', and in the prologue, 'Logos') ultimately point toward this final expression of his Christological faith.

We have said that the statement of John 1.1 may not be weakened to mean: 'The Logos was "divine".'[3] Besides, this explanation would be impossible in the confession of Thomas. On the other hand, we have seen that the Gospel of John says not only that the Logos is God, but also that he is with God. With R. Bultmann we concluded that the Logos Jesus Christ can therefore not be a second God beside God, nor an emanation of God, but God only in his

[1] See pp. 265 f. above.

[2] The Old Testament sometimes connects κύριος and θεός as a designation for God. See for example II Sam. 7.28; I Kings 18.39; Jer. 38.17; Zech. 13.9. In the New Testament cf. Rev. 4.11.

[3] See pp. 265 f. above.

self-revelation. This is the only sense which expresses the intention of the statement in John 14.28 that the Father, to whom Jesus returns after he completes his life's work, is 'greater' than he.

We must begin with these two certain passages in order to judge the third, John 1.18, in which not all the manuscripts read μονογενὴς θεός. The later Greek Fathers, the Latin Fathers and also the Curetonian Syriac read ὁ μονογενὴς υἱός. The reading θεός is unquestionably better attested, as every critical edition of the text makes immediately clear. If in spite of this some exegetes, R. Bultmann among them,[1] prefer υἱός, it is primarily because of the difficulty caused by θεός in this context. θεός requires the following translation: 'No one has ever seen God. The only begotten, God, who is in the bosom of the Father, he has made him known.' But precisely because of this 'difficulty', this reading is the *lectio difficilior*, which was later supposed to have been made more understandable by the substitution of υἱός for θεός. On the other hand, it is not evident how a later copyist, in order to confer on Jesus the divine name, could have undertaken to change υἱός to θεός without eliminating the words 'who is in the bosom of the Father'. If we take θεός as original, its connection with the context does prove difficult for later Christians to understand, but it is by no means impossible in the framework of the other statements in the prologue. In the final analysis, the 'difficulty' lies basically in the same Christological paradox which is present in John 1.1 and is characteristic precisely of this Gospel. We read in the prologue, 'The Logos was with God, and the Logos was God.' This means nothing other than that God was with God. If this is true, it corresponds fully with the Johannine idea that no one has ever seen God (the Father) but that God as the μονογενής reveals him (himself) in the life of Jesus, the record of which is to follow. Therefore, following the best attested reading and with the majority of recent investigators, we add this third Johannine passage to the other two.

The same conclusion is reached, above all by W. Bauer, *Das Johannes-evangelium*, pp. 29 f.—C. F. Burney, *The Aramaic Origin of the Fourth Gospel*, pp. 39 f., also thinks that the reading θεός is original, but he believes it should be explained as a mistranslation of the Aramaic original, according to which the noun should have been in the genitive case (θεοῦ):

[1] R. Bultmann, *Das Evangelium des Johannes, ad loc.* Although they do not completely exclude the other possibility, also H. Cremer-Kögel, *Wörterbuch des neutest. Griechisch*[11], 1923, p. 490; C. K. Barrett, *The Gospel According to St John*, p. 141.

'the only begotten of God'. After what we have just said, this explanation seems to me unnecessary.—The fact that the acceptance of the reading θεός means that μονογενής is used substantively should create no problems in view of the texts from the study of comparative religions cited by R. Bultmann, *Das Evangelium des Johannes*, pp. 47 ff.

Since the Johannine witness is quite clear, it is in order to agree with Windisch and Preisker[1] that the saying in I John 5.20 refers to Christ: 'And we know that the Son of God has come and has given us understanding, to know him who is true; and we are in him who is true, in his Son Jesus Christ. *This* (οὗτος) *is the true God* and eternal life.' This explanation is convincing not only philologically but also materially, for we find here the Christological circle which is grounded in fact and which determines Johannine thinking.

Again, it is not surprising that outside the Johannine corpus only Hebrews unequivocally applies the title 'God' to Jesus, since Hebrews actually belongs to the Johannine environment. It is true that the designation occurs twice in consecutive verses (Heb. 1.8 f.) only in a quotation from Ps. 45.6 f.: 'Thy throne, O God, is for ever and ever' (v. 8); and '. . . therefore thy God, O God, has anointed thee . . .' (v. 9). But the psalm is quoted here precisely for the sake of this address, and the author remarks explicitly that it refers to the Son of God: πρὸς τὸν υἱόν (v. 8). The address is thus very important to him. Here, as in the Gospel of John, Jesus can be addressed as God just because of the unique sonship which implies his deity. This agrees completely with the final conclusions of our preceding chapter. But at the same time we also see here that the distinction between the Father and the Son is not simply effaced, even when Jesus is designated 'God'. According to the Christian interpretation of the statement in Heb. 1.9, the word 'God' as the subject refers to the Father; as the object (in the vocative) to the Son: 'Thy God (the Father) has anointed thee, O God (the Son).' Behind this statement lies a royal psalm in which God addresses the king by the title 'God'. In the Old Testament, too, the title 'Son of God' for the king[2] leads to his being addressed as 'God' (see also Isa. 9.6). With this twofold use of the word 'God' Hebrews, like the Gospel of John, thus bears witness to the paradox of all Christology. We have seen this paradox expressed at the beginning of the prologue of John, which says of the

[1] H. Windisch and H. Preisker, *Die Katholischen Briefe* (HNT)³, 1951, p. 135.
[2] See pp. 272 f. above.

Logos Jesus Christ that he is at the same time with God and yet is himself God.

The continuation of these verses in Hebrews confirms what we said earlier about the relation between the title *Kyrios* and Jesus' deity.[1] Heb. 1.10 quotes Ps. 102.25 ff., which contains the address 'Lord' (*Kyrie*) instead of 'God'. However, this title is used to prove exactly the same thing as the psalm quoted in Heb. 1.8 f.: the Son of God is above the angels because he is addressed as *God*. There is no essential difference between *Kyrios* and 'God' as a form of address. This follows also from the content of the psalm quoted. The *Kyrios*, here identified as the Son Jesus Christ, is addressed as the creator of heaven and earth: 'Thou, Lord, didst found the earth in the beginning, and the heavens are the work of thy hands.' Just as the prologue to the Fourth Gospel says, '. . . *all* things were made through him,' so Hebrews also does not distinguish between the Creator and the Redeemer. We have emphasized from the beginning that this later distinction, which is encouraged by the threefold division of the Church's creed and which still persists today in most theologies,[2] is not a New Testament one. The distinction between the Father and the Son does not mean a distinction between creation and redemption, but between God in so far as one *can* theoretically speak of him also apart from his revelation, and God in so far as the New Testament *does* speak of him only as the one who reveals himself. This is just what Hebrews means also.

The direct designation of Jesus as 'God' is less clearly attested in the writings of Paul than in the Gospel of John and in Hebrews. But we must again recall our introductory statement. The predilection of the Pauline letters for the title *Kyrios* leaves no room to doubt that, on the basis of this concept and of course only in the sense thus determined, the apostle could call Jesus 'God'. Of the many relevant passages, I Cor. 8.6 *could* be mentioned. Or again, the phrase ἐν μορφῇ θεοῦ ὑπάρχων in the hymn to Christ in Phil. 2.6 ff. also points in this direction, for the designation 'image of God' (Col. 1.15) with which we connected it [3] implies Jesus' deity just as clearly as does the title Logos in John 1.1. Paul also says unambiguously in Col. 2.9 that 'the whole fulness of deity dwells bodily' in Jesus. However this passage may be related to Gnostic speculations, it is clear that such a text, like the preceding ones, is just a step from directly designating

[1] See pp. 234 ff. above.

[2] K. Barth, *Church Dogmatics*, is an exception to this.

[3] See p. 176 above.

Jesus 'God'. Further, the fact that Paul prays to Christ (II Cor. 12.8) [1] also proves that on occasion he really could call Jesus θεός. It is not certain, of course, whether he actually did. But even if this should be the case, it is certain that he does so only as an exception. This is not surprising, just because for him Jesus is the *Kyrios*, and because this name, which is 'above every name', clearly expresses Jesus' deity precisely from the aspect of his present lordship which is especially important to Paul.

From the unquestionably genuine letters of Paul, Rom. 9.5 is the principal passage to be considered. It is the last part of a list of all the prerogatives of the chosen people of Israel: ἐξ ὧν ὁ Χριστὸς τὸ κατὰ σάρκα ὁ ὢν ἐπί πάντων θεὸς εὐλογητὸς εἰς τοὺς αἰῶνας. ἀμήν. There are two possible translations, depending upon how we punctuate the phrase. Either we place no punctuation marks after σάρκα (or at most a comma), or we place a full stop there. If there is no full stop the following translation results: '. . . of their race, according to the flesh, is Christ, who is over all, God, blessed for ever.' But if we place a period after σάρκα, the following sentence which contains θεός is grammatically independent of Χριστός. Then we have one of those doxologies which Paul sometimes interjects at high points in his expositions, and which would be addressed to God the Father, not to Christ. After an enumeration of the gifts of grace bestowed upon Israel, chief of which is the birth of Christ according to the flesh, God (the Father) is then praised for all of them: 'God, who is over all, be praised for ever. Amen.'[2]

Without giving any sort of preference *a priori* to either of these possibilities on the basis of theological consideration, we must say that while the second cannot be excluded, it is hardly the one suggested by a philological and material consideration of the context.[3] First, independent doxologies are differently constructed. They begin with the predicate nominative εὐλογητός (cf. II Cor. 1.3; Eph. 1.3),[4]

[1] See p. 215 above, where we pointed out the ἐπικαλεῖσθαι of the *Kyrios* or of his name. This is of course on the boundary line between prayer and confession, and certainly implies both.

[2] Among others J. J. Wettstein (18th century) and Karl Barth, *The Epistle to the Romans*, ET 1933, pp. 330 f. n. 4, have conjectured that instead of ὁ ὢν ἐπὶ πάντων θεός, we should read ὧν ὁ ἐπὶ πάντων θεός. This is improbable, since it results in the somewhat artificial meaning that in addition to the previously mentioned gifts, the almighty God also belongs to Israel.

[3] For the history of the exegesis of this verse see O. Michel, *Der Brief an die Römer*, pp. 197 f. Michel himself decides for the Christological interpretation.

[4] In the Old Testament Ps. 66.20 only seems to be an exception. See M.-J. Lagrange, *S. Paul, Epître aux Romains*[2], 1922, *ad loc.*

whereas in Rom. 9.5 the subject stands at the beginning—as is always the case wherever we find not a true independent doxology but a doxological apposition, which follows an immediately preceding relative pronoun. God is praised in this way, for example, in Rom. 1.25 and II Cor. 11.31. Besides this, however, the structure of the preceding clause concerning Christ κατὰ σάρκα both formally and materially requires a continuation which goes beyond κατὰ σάρκα.[1] (See the analogous formula in Rom. 1.3 f.) The words ἐπὶ πάντων also make better sense in the context if they refer to Christ. They are then more than a mere rhetorical formula, and in this case the enumeration of the signs of Israel's election reaches a climax in the statement that from Israel comes one according to the flesh who is simply 'over all'. We conclude that it is quite probable, if not certain, that Paul designates Jesus Christ as 'God' in Rom. 9.5.

From the standpoint of textual criticism, the statement in Col. 2.2 is uncertain: '. . . knowledge of the mystery τοῦ θεοῦ Χριστοῦ, in whom are hid all the treasures of wisdom and knowledge.' Nevertheless, a majority of investigators consider this reading to be original, especially since the following relative clause (v. 3), which certainly refers to Χριστοῦ, ascribes to Christ what otherwise is said to be true of God.

On the other hand, the formula in II Thess. 1.12 (κατὰ τὴν χάριν τοῦ θεοῦ ἡμῶν καὶ κυρίου 'Ιησοῦ Χριστοῦ) can hardly be considered as implying a single article and thus as referring only to Christ, although this possibility cannot be excluded. The analogous formula in II Cor. 1.2, 'Grace and peace ἀπὸ θεοῦ πατρὸς ἡμῶν καὶ κυρίου 'Ιησοῦ Χριστοῦ', seems to prove that Paul speaks first of God, then of Christ.

Titus 2.13 is also an uncertain passage, but it is probable that Christ is called 'God' here:[2] '. . . awaiting our blessed hope, the appearing of the glory τοῦ μεγάλου θεοῦ καὶ σωτῆρος ἡμῶν Χριστοῦ 'Ιησοῦ, who gave himself for us to redeem us from all iniquity and to purify for himself a people of his own.' The phrase θεὸς καὶ σωτήρ is often used as a formula referring to God,[3] and it is probably not to be torn apart. This suggests that 'God' is not to be distinguished from

[1] H. Cremer-Kögel, *op. cit.*, p. 448, refers here to the Old Testament contrast *basar–elohim*.

[2] As opposed to M. Dibelius and H. Conzelmann, *Die Pastoralbriefe*, *ad loc.*, who maintain that we find ourselves here (as in Luke) in a stage of development which, despite the application of the attributes of God to Christ, is characterized by strict 'subordinationistic' thinking.

[3] This is also the case precisely in the Pastoral Letters. Cf. I Tim. 1.1; 2.3; 4.10; Titus 1.3; 2.10; 3.4. See also Luke 1.47.

'Saviour Jesus Christ' here.[1] In addition, the following clause, which (like that in Col. 2.2 f.) certainly refers to Christ, also points to a function which is otherwise attributed only to God.[2] Finally, a simultaneous 'appearing' of God and Christ does not correspond to the usual expectation.[3]

We should make a similar decision in the case of II Peter 1.1, which also contains the phrase θεὸς καὶ σωτήρ: ἐν δικαιοσύνῃ τοῦ θεοῦ ἡμῶν καὶ σωτῆρος Ἰησοῦ Χριστοῦ. The expression κύριος καὶ σωτήρ, which is used as a designation for Jesus in the same book (II Peter 1.11; 2.20; 3.2, 18), indicates that θεός belongs with σωτήρ as an attribute of Jesus Christ. We see here too that the Christological designation θεός is a variant of the more common κύριος.

When the author of Revelation says in 19.12 of the Horseman called 'Logos', 'Faithful' and 'True' that he has another name which 'no one knows but himself', this may allude to the divine name.

We may exclude Acts 20.28, where the reading τοῦ θεοῦ is too uncertain.[4]

We come to the conclusion that in the few New Testament passages in which Jesus receives the title 'God', this occurs on the one hand in connection with his exaltation to lordship (Paul's letters and II Peter), and on the other hand in connection with the idea that he is himself the divine revelation (Johannine writings and Hebrews). Thus this designation does not basically go beyond what we have already recognized in preceding chapters as the essential meaning of Jesus' other titles of honour.

By way of contrast, Ignatius of Antioch, in whose writings the title θεός for Jesus occurs much more often (*Smyrn.* 1.1; *Eph.* 1.1; 7.2; 15.3; 19.3), uses it in such a way that he tends to move away from the New Testament use in the direction of the later Christological controversies. Of course, he also makes the distinction between the Father and the Son (cf. *Smyrn.* 8.1; *Magn.* 13.2).

[1] As a parallel to the adjective μέγας, which then designates Christ, we may cite the occurrence in II Peter 1.16 of μεγαλειότης, which also is attributed to Christ.

[2] Cf. Ex. 19.5; Deut. 7.6; 14.2.

[3] A further passage in the Pastoral Letters, I Tim. 3.16, is excluded since the reading θεός here is obviously a later correction of the more difficult ὅς.

[4] κυρίου is supported by equally good evidence. It is hard to tell which is the *lectio difficilior*. Most scholars seem to decide for θεοῦ, since ἐκκλησία τοῦ κυρίου is a more common equivalent for *qehal Yahweh* (although Neh. 13.1 also speaks of the *qehal ha-elohim*). E. Haenchen, *Die Apostelgeschichte*, 1956, p. 531 n. 1, gives a plausible explanation of the later alteration from θεοῦ to κυρίου: one related the τοῦ ἰδίου to αἵματος, and therefore made the change from θεοῦ to κυρίου in order to avoid the appearance of Patripassianism.

CONCLUSION

Perspectives of New Testament Christology

WE BELIEVE that the overall organization which we have chosen for the presentation of the New Testament Christology has demonstrated its validity. The Christological lines of connection have become visible precisely in the successive treatment of the titles grouped in relation to *Heilsgeschichte*. Above all, the central line of redemptive and revelatory history has also become visible. Because we have not tried to impose an external dogmatic scheme upon the Christology of the New Testament, but have instead followed each title through all the New Testament books, we believe we have done justice to the material. The New Testament itself offers no synthesis but sets out to apprehend the object of revelation from different starting points, in each case from a fresh point of view. But the result of this procedure is not simply a mosaic formation without continuity and unity. Each different concept seeks to arrive at a total understanding of the puzzle of Jesus' person and work, and yet the total pictures thus obtained are mutually influential. Therefore we believe we have escaped the danger which readily attends this kind of organization, namely that of collecting a series of isolated independent monographs. The connection between the various parts may in this way have in fact appeared more sharply and convincingly.

Thus it is in the analysis of the different concepts that the first Christians themselves present what we might call the synthesis of the Christological revelation. They approach the solution of the question 'Who is Jesus?' by a number of paths marked by various titles.

For this reason the cyclic method offers advantages for a 'Christology of the New Testament'. This method draws lines from each of the concepts treated to all segments of the *Heilsgeschichte*, although any one concept may illuminate only one—or only a single point—of these segments. We have coupled this cyclic method with the historical-chronological method by successively investigating within each chapter the relationships revealed by the study of comparative religions, the Jewish roots, Jesus' attitude (as far as the material allowed), and finally the attitude of the early Christian writers considered separately. The simultaneous use of both methods discloses the bridges which connect the different solutions to the Christological problem.

If in these last pages we attempt in a brief summary to speak of the common elements which we have already pointed out in our investigation of each concept, we do so with express warning against the false idea that we wish now at last to offer a synthesis—as if in these few pages we would still attempt to do precisely what the New Testament authors did not do. In reality the true synthesis we believe we have seen will be discovered only by him who has the patience to consider and investigate each of the New Testament Christological titles for its own sake.[1] If with this reservation we may now discuss two main ideas which have emerged repeatedly, this proves that also the principle which we chose for grouping the individual titles (those concerning the incarnate, the returning, the present, and the pre-existent Christ) is not some sort of externally imposed scheme. It is a principle which actually corresponds to the innermost nature of all New Testament Christology which has forced itself on us as we collected the material. It is the principle of *Heilsgeschichte*. In spite of, and precisely through, the cyclic method, a clear line, a movement, does appear. Perhaps we should therefore speak of a spiral rather than a cyclic method.

The variety which results from the plurality of the Christological titles and solutions; the discovery that each of the temporally different Christological functions can first of all be the object of a particular title; the discovery that connection with other titles only gradually appears, and that with it a perspective of *Heilsgeschichte* arises—all this proves that the question about Jesus was not answered by early Christianity in terms of a mythology already at hand, but in terms of a series of real facts. These facts were events which happened in the first century of our era, facts which were unnoticed by those who at that time 'made history' and which today can still be interpreted differently, but are not for this reason less historical. They are the events of the life, work, and death of Jesus of Nazareth, and the experience of his presence and continuing work beyond death within the fellowship of his disciples.

[1] Therefore I emphasize again that this book is not primarily intended to be a reference work on the 'Christology of the New Testament'. It should be used for reference only after it has first been carefully worked through as a whole.

The Christology of the New Testament was conceived on the basis of these events, and the view of Jesus' person and work from the standpoint of *Heilsgeschichte* arose out of this context. It is not a myth which was externally imposed on an essentially non-historical *kerygma*. The way in which the first Christians worked out the various Christological concepts, whose development and theological significance we have investigated in the preceding chapters, proves that the opposite is true. The New Testament authors may have used many elements from the Hellenistic environment in presenting the Christological *Heilsgeschichte*—and we have in fact found a great number of such elements. But one element is not among them: the understanding of Christology as a redemptive history which extends from creation to the eschatological new creation, the centre of which is the earthly life of Jesus.

But if the process of arriving at Christological understanding took place in early Christianity in connection with those central events of the first century, we can say that this process itself belongs within the *Heilsgeschichte*.

Once we are clear about the fact that Christological understanding arose only gradually, primarily as a result of definite historical occurrences, then we can better comprehend that the Christology itself was understood as an event.

Therefore, before we speak of the common characteristics of these concepts, we shall attempt on the basis of the results obtained from our work, to give in rough outline a history of the origin of the first Christians' Christological perception.[1]

All Christology is founded upon the life of Jesus. Although this assertion appears to be a truism, yet it must be emphasized—and not only against those who question Jesus' historical existence. The question 'Who is Jesus?' did not emerge for the first time with the early community's experience of Easter. The life of Jesus already provided the starting point of all Christological thought in a double way: in Jesus' own self-consciousness and in the concrete presentiment his person and work evoked among the disciples and the people.

From the moment of his baptism, Jesus himself was conscious of carrying out God's plan. He knew first that he must accomplish the forgiveness of sins through his death in fulfilment of the prophecy

[1] Again I emphasize as a precautionary measure that this can only be a general *summary*. It can hardly have any meaning for those who have not read the preceding chapters.

about the 'Suffering Servant of God'; and he anticipated this goal already during his life by preaching and healing the sick. He knew in the second place that he had come to introduce the Kingdom of God as the 'Son of Man' whom certain Jewish groups expected soon to come on the clouds of heaven; and he anticipated this goal too already in his human life with its human lowliness. But, finally, he was conscious of fulfilling this double function of the 'Servant of God' and the 'Son of Man' in the complete and unique oneness with God which he experienced continually and in a manner beyond all human possibilities as the 'Son'.

The few sayings in which Jesus spoke with deliberate reserve about this 'self-consciousness' of his did not directly cause the disciples to raise the Christological question already during his lifetime. Neither the people nor the disciples immediately understood Jesus' more or less veiled allusions. Rather it was simply acquaintance with him and with the teaching and activity they witnessed which led them to ask what kind of man he was and what his actions signified. But this means that the Christological problem was bound to force itself upon them if they did not consider Jesus mentally ill, as his family and others actually did. The evangelists effectively expressed this Christological premonition when, in order to describe what the eye witnesses felt in the presence of Jesus, they spoke of his 'authority' and of men's 'astonishment'[1] akin to fear before it: '. . . as one who had authority and not as their scribes' (Matt. 7.29).

At first, of course, they were able to find the answer only in the conceptual categories of official Judaism's expectation of the 'eschatological Prophet' or the political Messiah-King, which did not correspond to Jesus' own 'self-consciousness'. Only in quite isolated cases did the disciples display a higher perception, of which Jesus says in Matthew that 'flesh and blood' had not revealed it to them. Extraordinary occurrences, such as the one reported in the story of the transfiguration, may have provided the visible framework of such direct revelations. But apart from such clues, they had no understanding of what Jesus meant by calling himself 'Son of Man'.

The problem of Jesus in its full theological scope was recognized only in the light of the new events of his death on the cross and the

[1] See ἐκπλήσσεσθαι: Matt. 7.28; 13.54; 22.33; Mark 1.22; 6.2; 7.37; 11.18; Luke 4.32; 9.43. θαμβεῖσθαι: Mark 1.27; 10.24; 10.32; Luke 5.9. εξίστασθαι: Matt. 12.23; Mark 2.12; 5.42; 6.51; Luke 2.47; 8.56. θαυμάζειν: Matt. 8.27; 9.33; 15.31; 21.20; 22.22; Mark 5.20; Luke 4.22; 9.43; 11.14. φοβεῖσθαι: Matt. 9.8; Mark 4.41; 5.15.

experience immediately following of his resurrection. These events caused those momentary glimpses of recognition during Jesus' earthly life to stand in the bright light of perception, and at least a few came to understand those indirect references of his which had found no open ears during his lifetime.

As had been true for Jesus himself, the expectation of what he was to be in the future still remained the centre of Christological interest. The early Church now awaited the appearance of Daniel's 'Son of Man' on the clouds of heaven concretely in the form of a return of Jesus. On the basis of the cross and the Easter experience which placed the person of Jesus in a completely new light, even the messianic conceptions which had previously been falsely applied to him could now be purified and validly used in a higher sense (although the messianic ideal rejected by Jesus still often persisted).

In any case, however, this expectation of Jesus' second coming had to be connected with an explanation of his first coming. In fact even in the early Church not the second but the first coming became the real theological problem, and it is simply false when it is asserted again and again in interpretations of New Testament theology that the early Church was only interested in the *coming* Son of Man or Messiah. As if there were no essential difference at all between the Jewish and the Jewish Christian conceptions of the Messiah! As if the early Church's messianic thinking were utterly untouched by Jesus' first coming, his life and death! As if the question concerning the meaning of Jesus' earthly life and death were asked first among later Hellenistic churches and by Paul! This oversimplified, unproblematical view of the early Church's thought really should be abandoned.

In actuality, as soon as any one now spoke of the parousia, he had to raise the question of its connection with Jesus' first coming and its significance. But this means that already in this respect Christology took on the form determined by *Heilsgeschichte*. Christ was no longer only the one who was to come, but also the one who had come. The fact that he who would appear in glory had previously suffered death had to have a meaning, however, and this called for investigation.

Thus, remembering a number of Jesus' decisive sayings, the early Church formulated an *ebed Yahweh* Christology which understood Jesus' death Christologically. At least Peter, who during Jesus' lifetime had struggled against the idea of the necessity of suffering and death, seems after Easter to have attributed special significance to it. Other circles sought the solution by reference to Jesus' designation of himself as 'Son of Man'. This is probably true especially of the Palestinian 'Hellenists' (Acts 6–8), who were possibly related to Jewish esoteric groups, and to whom also the author of the Fourth Gospel may have belonged. It was precisely the Son of Man title which allowed them to connect Jesus' second coming with his first. The views related to it were not only eschatologically oriented in the sense of Dan. 7; under the influence of Jewish-oriental speculations about Adam and the Original Man, these views could also lead to the conception of Jesus as the *second Adam*, the man from heaven, the uncorrupted 'image of God'. This concept was, of course, really developed first by Paul.

But all these attempts were placed in the right light only by the great perception that Jesus rules as the present Lord over his Church, over the world, over the life of each individual. It was the experience of his lordship which first gave the real impetus to a consistent formulation of Christology in terms of *Heilsgeschichte*.

This new understanding was given to the first Christians in *common worship*, above all in the common meals, and confirmed in the various expressions of their life together. Together with Jesus' earthly work and the experience of Easter, the main root of New Testament Christology is this experience in worship of Jesus as the present Lord, who was now prayed to (*Maranatha*) and confessed (*Kyrios Christos*). From this beginning point the connections given by *Heilsgeschichte* could be extended and developed in all directions, for the new revelation imparted to the first Christians in that experience consisted in the realization that the present Lord is identical with the Jesus of Nazareth who appeared on earth and was crucified, and with the Son of Man who will one day come on the clouds of heaven. Thus the faith which was gained in common worship and in the daily life of the community, faith in the Lord upon whom 'all power in heaven and earth' is conferred, had to stimulate further reflection.

The connection between the present Lord and the earthly Jesus was understood on the basis of Ps. 110, to which Jesus himself had already referred, as the 'exaltation' of the risen Christ 'to the right hand of God'. The frequency with which the early Christians quoted this psalm shows how important it was for them to be assured in this way of the identity between the present and the incarnate Christ. The Christ-line in the *Heilsgeschichte* stood out with ever increasing clarity. All theology became Christology. If Jesus was the *Kyrios*, then this influenced all other titles: every single one was now related either explicitly or implicitly to the whole of the *Heilsgeschichte*. That

Jesus had fulfilled the task of the *ebed Yahweh*, that he was Israel's promised Messiah, that he came and will come as the 'Son of Man'—all this was maintained, but it now appeared in an entirely new light.

But there was still another result of the Christological reflection about the 'Lord' which took place in constant connection with the experience of his presence and therefore was felt to be inspired by the Holy Spirit. The one upon whom all power was conferred, to whom all the Old Testament passages which speak of God could be applied, must have been at work already before his earthly life. If this life was now conceived as the decisive revelation of God's redemptive will, then the redemptive line must also extend in the direction of past history to his pre-existence. Jesus was recognized as the Revealer as such: wherever God has revealed himself, there is Christ. And in this context the question arose concerning the way in which the *Heilsgeschichte* connects the incarnate and the pre-existent Christ. This led to the recollection of Jesus' words about his unique sonship.

Jesus' earthly activity as the central event consequently became the temporal centre of a line of salvation running both forward and backward.[1] Since it represents the highest form of God's self-communication, all other divine revelations must be related to it, for there can be no revelation of God essentially different from the revelation in Christ. Thus along many avenues Christology approached what later theology—not always in the New Testament sense of the term, of course—called the 'deity' of Christ. The paths which lead to it are Jesus' 'self-consciousness' as 'Son of God', the experience of the Lord in common worship, and the conception of the 'Logos' in theological reflection. The Gospel of John, the letters of Paul, and Hebrews, despite all differences, are not far apart in their ultimate Christological understanding precisely in this aspect.[2] Also other Christological concepts which one would not at first expect to do so (for example the 'Son of Man') point in the direction of Christ's character as the 'image of God' and his identity of form with God (Phil. 2.6).

The whole development of Christological perception progressed parallel to the missionary work of early Christianity. It was greatly endangered by contact with the Hellenistic-syncretistic thought of its environment. Christians established contacts with this thought and

[1] What H. Conzelmann, *The Theology of St Luke*, demonstrates for Luke is not only true for the author of the Third Gospel.

[2] See W. Bauer, *Das Johannesevangelium*, p. 6.

borrowed certain concepts, even mythological features, from it. Faith in Jesus as the *Kyrios* was thrown into sharp relief because the pagan world possessed a clearly formulated *Kyrios* concept, and because the emperor caused himself to be venerated as *Kyrios*. Also the Son of Man idea, which was rooted in ancient conceptions of a divine original man, had been further developed already in the Jewish and pagan Hellenistic world (in an entirely different way, of course). One met speculations about the 'Word' of God everywhere in pagan religions and especially in Hellenistic philosophy and philosophical religion. All this influenced the development of Christology. But one cannot assert that the view of Christology sketched above from the standpoint of *Heilsgeschichte* as such also originated from these influences; that is, that it rests on a Gnostic myth. To do so is to preclude any insight into the deeper character not only of the origin but also of the nature of New Testament Christology. Anyone who approaches the text with this premise, which is so popular today, inevitably becomes blind to the inherently Christian themes, to the significance of early Christian events for Christological thinking, and above all also to the correctly understood relationship between Christology and the history of religion. Syncretistic elements, even myths, were indeed appropriated, but they were subordinated to a Christological structure which received its character not from syncretism, not from Hellenism, not from mythology, but from the *Heilsgeschichte*. It is characteristic of this structure that from the very beginning it centres in a real history.

The principal themes of the New Testament Christology were already known and developed by the earliest Church. As ancient confessions and hymns of the early Church prove, it gained all of the important Christological perceptions in connection with the events which followed the death of Jesus. It is true that for the most part the various Christological solutions were first developed in detail and in depth in the letters of Paul, in the Gospel of John and in Hebrews—writings which originated in contact with the Hellenistic environment. One should not forget, however, that Hellenism was not effective only outside Palestine, but that, through Judaism, it was already at work in the original Church on Palestinian soil. The recently discovered Jewish Qumran texts, which on the one hand clearly betray syncretistic influence and on the other hand display marked similarities to the New Testament thought-world, show us how certain groups within Palestinian Christianity (the 'Hellenists' in Acts, for example) could have been in contact with Hellenistic thought from the beginning. It is increasingly acknowledged that the Gospel of John comes from this environment.

We must, then, completely discard the rigid scheme, Judaistic original Church—Hellenistic Christianity. It is not possible to distinguish so sharply as is usually done between a theology of the Hellenistic Church and that of the original Church. Not only do we lack the texts which would allow us to fix the boundary lines, but, more important, it has been demonstrated in the meantime that such an abrupt contrast does not exist at all. This must also be brought to bear on Christology. Of course we by no means thereby dispute the fact that the influence of Hellenistic concepts was much stronger in the pagan environment than in the original Palestinian community.

We too speak of a process of origination of Christological perception. But the essential factor in this process is not the transition from the original community to the Gentile Christian mission Church, however important that may also have been for the development of the different Christological elements. Essential for the achievement of Christological perception are rather the following stages: Jesus' life and death, and his own allusions to his self-consciousness; the Easter experience of the disciples; the experience of the presence of the Lord; the reflection, conscious of the leading of the Holy Spirit, upon the connection in the *Heilsgeschichte* between the chronologically separated functions of Christ, which from the point of view of revelation can be extended back to creation.

This development itself is bound up with the central facts of the Christ-event and therefore can itself be considered as belonging to the history of revelation.

As we now attempt to distinguish the common characteristics of New Testament Christology, we must first of all mention the point of view defined by *Heilsgeschichte*. It is true that this is not followed through to the same extent for all Christological concepts. Often only one of the Christological functions is illuminated from all sides, or the line to other functions is only briefly extended. But nevertheless the other functions too always remain in the field of vision (except in the case of the concept of the eschatological Prophet). There is always in the background the implicit presupposition that the decisive temporal centre of the whole Christ-event lies in Jesus' incarnation, his life, suffering, dying and rising again. Whatever particular function may be under consideration, the identity of the pre-existent, present, or coming Christ with Jesus of Nazareth is certain only when it is recognized that the real centre of all revelation is the Incarnate One. Without this relationship there would be nothing at all to prevent degeneration into Docetism and syncretism. Jesus would become a philosophical-religious principle, his historical life a mythological cloak.

Therefore Docetism (i.e., the Christological solution in which Jesus' historical work as such is not the centre of God's whole revelation) is branded already in the New Testament as the fundamental Christological heresy. Anyone who does not confess that Jesus Christ has come in the flesh belongs to the Antichrist (I John 4.2 ff.). As soon as the centre of revelation is no longer the Christ who appeared in the flesh, we cease to move on the level of New Testament Christology. This connection with *Heilsgeschichte* is not lacking in any New Testament passage, not even passages such as the prologue to the Gospel of John which seem to belong to the realm of speculative thought. Everything that is said in the Johannine prologue about the beginning of all things is seen from the perspective of the decisive statement, 'And the Word became flesh and dwelt among us' (John 1.14). When this temporal occurrence is retained as the centre of the Christ-event, then it is also possible to speak of the pre-existent Christ and his relation to God, and of the invisible present 'Lord', without being in danger of falling immediately into syncretistic-Gnostic speculation. On the other hand, these connections with the concept of the pre-existent Christ, with the title *Kyrios* and with God must be made, for all other revelation of God must be related to the decisive centre.

This view of Christology from the standpoint of *Heilsgeschichte*, which leads us from creation through the reconciliation in the cross and the invisible present lordship of Christ to the still unaccomplished consummation in the new creation, is defined by two essential aspects which we have repeatedly encountered in our investigation of the various solutions to the problem of Christ: the principle of *representation* according to which this whole history occurs; and the idea of *God's self-communication*, which connects the various phases of the history so that (from the common point of view of revelation) Christ as the mediator of creation can be placed on the same level with the crucified Jesus of Nazareth.

In *Christ and Time* I have shown in detail that the principle of representation determines the movement of *Heilsgeschichte*. The path leads first of all from the many in progressive reduction to the one, and from this one, who represents the centre, back to the many. It leads from creation to humanity, from humanity to Israel, from Israel to the 'remnant', from the 'remnant' to the incarnate Christ; then it leads from the incarnate Christ to the apostles, from the apostles to the Church, from the Church to the world and to the new creation. But the one who 'became flesh' at the centre of time is also representatively at work before and after the event of his incarnation. Thus we have repeatedly found the idea of representation contained in the decisive Christological titles: in the Suffering Servant of God, the High Priest, the Son of Man, the Son of God. It is seen in each case, of course, from a particular point of view.

The second of the two principal ideas we wish to emphasize in our retrospective summary is that of Christ as God's self-communication. It especially characterizes the Christological solutions investigated in the last chapters (Logos, Son of God, God). It is, however, by no means limited to these, but in the final analysis is fundamental to all Christological concepts: first of all to those which, like the *ebed Yahweh* and to a certain extent the Son of Man, clarify Jesus' earthly work. In the life of the incarnate Christ God's revelation actually became tangible: we have seen his glory, which is the glory of God himself (John 1.14); we could apprehend it with all our human senses (I John 1.1 ff.). If this human life, Jesus' atoning death, those events which can be chronologically dated, present the revelation of God as his decisive action, then it is just this concept of revelation which demands a Christology from the standpoint of *Heilsgeschichte*. Then all of God's revelation on both sides must be related to this centre in Christ, to this earthly Jesus of Nazareth, the crucified and risen.

The Gospel of John, Paul, and Hebrews follow this idea of revelation through to its logical conclusion: *Jesus Christ is God in his self-revelation*. The Gospel of John makes this ultimate Christological conclusion in identifying Jesus with the word of revelation through which God communicated himself already in creation and in all further redemptive events. Paul does this when he looks upon Jesus as the *Kyrios* who rules the universe. Hebrews does so when it gives Jesus Christ the name 'God'. The first Christians know no dualistic view of revelation in creation and redemption.

The faith which regards Jesus Christ as the Revealer as such implies of course also a statement not only about his work but also about his person. But it does so in such a way that one can speak of his person only in connection with his work. Melanchthon's familiar statement that to know Christ is to know his benefits may certainly not simply be understood as suggesting that the New Testament Christology does not also concern Jesus' person. Rather, the statement must also be read in reverse: the person (i.e., his unique relation to God) must be known in the work. If at the peak of New Testament Christological thought Jesus Christ is God in his self-revelation, then we can neither simply speak of the person apart from the work or of the work apart from the person. From the very beginning all Christology shows both aspects—even when the ultimate logical conclusions have not yet been drawn. Jesus himself knows that as the Son of Man he must take upon himself the suffering of the Servant of God and that just in this way he is uniquely one with the Father as *the* Son of God.

Because the first Christians see God's redemptive revelation in Jesus Christ, for them it is his very nature that he can be known only in his work—fundamentally in the central work accomplished in the flesh. Therefore, in the light of the New Testament witness, all mere speculation about his natures is an absurdity. Functional Christology is the only kind which exists.

Therefore all Christology is *Heilsgeschichte*, and all *Heilsgeschichte* is Christology. This is the reason for the strict Christocentric construction of the earliest confessions of faith, which as yet make no distinction between God as the Creator and Christ as the Redeemer, since creation and redemption belong together as God's communication of himself to the world. When we carry to its conclusion the concept of revelation on the basis of Jesus' human work, we find that creation and redemption cannot be separated. Christ's atoning death has cosmic results (Col. 1.20; Matt. 27.51), and the present *Kyrios Christos* reveals himself not only as Lord of the Church but also as Lord of the cosmos. In view of revelation, therefore, there can be only *one* Logos, only *one* Lord, only *one* God. The New Testament of course maintains the distinction between the Father and the Son even when these last conclusions are made. It is not, however, the distinction between Creator and Redeemer, but between Source and Goal on the one hand (ἐξ and εἰς: I Cor. 8.6) and the Mediator on the other hand (διά: I Cor. 8.6); between God and his Word, which as such is God himself, and yet is not God himself but 'with him' (John 1.1); or, as we have also said, between God as he exists independent of his redemptive revelation directed toward us, and God as he reveals himself to the world. The Father and the Son can be meaningfully distinguished only in the time of revelatory history, that is, in the time which begins with the creation of the world and continues until the end (or rather extends into the time *after* the final event). Where there is no revelation, it is pointless to speak of God's word of revelation, his Logos. The writings of the first Christians of course speak only of the God who reveals himself and is turned toward the world. They speak only of the history which lies between the 'beginning' of John 1.1 and 'God's being all in all' of I Cor. 15.28; between the point at which the Word began to go forth from God as his word of creation, and the point at which the Son, to whom the Father has subjected all things, subjects himself to the Father.

The New Testament neither is able nor intends to give information about how we are to conceive the being of God beyond the history of revelation, about whether it really is a being only in the philosophical sense.[1] It intends rather to report the great event of God's revelation in Christ. The reticent allusions to something beyond revelation are made on the periphery of the New Testament witness and serve solely to point to the simultaneous distinction and unity of the Father and the Son, and thus to remind us that all Christology is *Heilsgeschichte*.

Can the truth of this revelation given to the first Christians be visibly and comprehensibly demonstrated to later men? Can it be logically proved that the centre of all divine revelation is found in Jesus' earthly life and death, and that in this light all revelation is to be considered a redemptive history which began before the incarnation and continues until the end? Even today there is no other 'method' of Christological perception besides the one given in John 5–8. It was just as difficult for the men of that time as it is for us today to believe in what was a *skandalon* to the Jews and 'foolishness' to the educated Greeks. It must be stressed again and again that the difficulty in believing this does not lie in the Bible's outdated 'mythological cosmology'. The technical progress of our time with its electricity, radio and atom bomb has not made faith in Jesus Christ as the centre of the divine redemptive history one bit more difficult than it was for the ancients. Rather, the *skandalon*, the foolishness, lies in the fact that historically datable events ('under Pontius Pilate') are supposed to represent the very centre of God's revelation and to be connected with all his revelations. That was just as hard for men of that time to accept as for us today.

[1] Criticism of my description of the New Testament understanding of time (*Christ and Time*) has almost without exception not understood this.

We have seen that the first Christians achieved this perception in a threefold way: through the acceptance of the witness given in the *life of Jesus* with the events of Good Friday and Easter; through the powerful experience, both personal and in common worship, of the *presence* of the *Kyrios*, who is identical with the incarnate Jesus, as the 'Lord' of the Church, the world, and the life of each individual; through the *reflection*, carried out in faith in the present Lord and the crucified Son of Man, concerning the relation of this Jesus Christ to all the rest of God's revelation. These are the sources of early Christian Christological conviction. For the modern man there are no others. But all three in mutually clarifying interaction are indispensable for answering the question about Jesus.

Epilogue

APART from correction in matters of detail, this second English edition, based on the third German edition, remains on the whole unchanged, though the criticisms to which the book has been subjected may make it desirable for me to define my standpoint and rectify misunderstandings.

In general the criticisms are concerned with questions of method, which relate not only to this book, but to my whole conception of work on the New Testament. I am thinking here particularly of the arguments that have come from the Bultmann school against my *Christology*, arguments which, as a matter of course, dismiss as 'uncritical' every view that discusses, even as a possibility, whether Jesus may have applied to himself decisive titles of honour, and whether in consequence the connection between Jesus and primitive Christianity might be determined otherwise than by the 'call to decision' or 'faith' or 'attitude' of Jesus. Ferdinand Hahn's dissertation, *Christologische Hoheitstitel*, which is to appear shortly and which is not yet available to me in printed form, seems—as far as I can judge from the publisher's announcements—to take this view against my researches. H. E. Tödt has already tried to do the same for the title 'Son of Man'.[1] My answer to the objection raised will be found in my essays on hermeneutics in the collection now being printed and entitled *Geschichte und Glaube*, but especially in my next book, which will deal with the question as a whole in connection with my view of *Heilsgeschichte*.

I was careful to point out on pp. 8–9 that the bestowal of titles of honour in the *Heilsgeschichte* cannot be entirely satisfactory, and that some overlapping cannot be avoided. Nevertheless people have found fault with me over this, and I can only answer that there is no classification that remains uncontested, and that I have merely chosen the one that seems to me to reduce the number of difficulties to a minimum. But the fact that in general I presented the Christology of the New Testament within the framework of the titles of honour at all was also felt to be a defect, on the ground that this plan

[1] In *Der Menschensohn in der synoptischen Überlieferung*, 1959 (ET in preparation); but on this see E. Schweizer, 'Der Menschensohn', *ZNW* 50, 1959, pp. 185 ff.

allows no systematic survey. I am afraid that if I had proceeded differently, I should have been reproached with too much 'constructing' and with not allowing analysis its due. Moreover the final chapter (pp. 315 ff.) contains no attempted synthesis—there is no such thing in the New Testament—but tries to set out the common essential features of all New Testament Christology, and to present briefly the history of its development within the New Testament. In this attempt it has appeared that a characteristic of the Christological view within the New Testament is that it *develops* in the sense of the *Heilsgeschichte*—a conception that is fundamental to my whole outlook—that this development is, so to speak, an essential part of the Christology of the *Heilsgeschichte*, and that accordingly the common principle underlying all New Testament Christology is that of the *Heilsgeschichte*.

Thus we have additional and positive justification for the classification—first chosen more on practical grounds—of the titles of honour according to Christ's functions in the *Heilsgeschichte* in respect of past, present, future, and pre-existence.

That, indeed, puts the great emphasis on the functional nature of New Testament Christology, and it is mainly here that Catholic theology finds the stumbling-block. I am convinced, however, that in the case of many of its representatives some of the attacks that have been made—I am thinking particularly of those of C. Journet[1] and P. Gaechter[2]—rest on a misunderstanding of my book, and partly on a non-observance of the limits of the two disciplines of exegesis and dogmatics. In view of all the Catholic critics[3], however, I felt it necessary to set out clearly my standpoint on the relation of the work and person of Christ. This has been done in my reply to G. Bavaud.[4]

The book has been subjected to criticism of a quite different kind by E. Fascher in a scholarly critical review.[5] In this essay Fascher, as the title suggests, represents the view that the Christological question in the New Testament must be solved on the lines of belief in God's fatherhood, as Christology merges in theology. It is

[1] *Nova et Vetera* XXXV, 1960, pp. 1–8.

[2] *Zeitschrift für Katholische Theologie*, 1960, pp. 88 ff.

[3] Cf. also J. Frisque, *Oscar Cullmann. Une théologie de l'histoire du salut*, 1960.

[4] In the Fribourg Catholic periodical *Choisir*, No. 9–10, 1960, pp. 20 ff. It will appear in German in the collection mentioned above.

[5] 'Christologie oder Theologie? Bemerkungen zu O. Cullmanns *Christologie des Neuen Testaments*', *TLZ* 87, 1962, No. 12, cols. 881–910.

certainly true that for the first Christians faith in Christ did not discount belief in the fatherhood of God. But the expression of the New Testament message, going back to apostolic times, as it exists in the earliest credal formulas, shows us that faith in God was merely assumed as self-evident, and that all the faith and thought of the primitive Church is directed to Christ.

Finally I would point out a misunderstanding that concerns the problem of primitive Christianity viewed from a scholarly and academic standpoint. Since my first sizeable publication, in 1930, on the Pseudo-Clementines, I have not forgotten the question of esoteric Judaism as the cradle of primitive Christianity; and the new discoveries, notably at Qumran, as well as more recent researches, are particularly illuminating in this field. I therefore cannot understand why some people have not noticed at all that my relevant researches on the previous history of certain titles of honour in the comparative study of religions belong to this set of problems, and that I agree with Bultmann precisely on this point. Some saw in my interest in esoteric Judaism only a wish to eliminate pagan influences. In fact, such influences may very well have worked on primitive Christianity *via* this nonconformist Judaism. But on the basis of that simplification it is all the easier to label me 'conservative' in this connection too. The use of theological labels and catchwords does not lead to clarification, but merely to forced simplification of matters that are really complex.

Basel, March 1963 O. CULLMANN

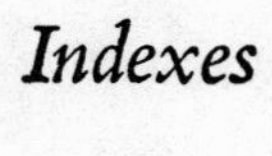

Index of Authors

The number of the page on which a work is cited for the first time appears here in italics.

Index of References

OLD TESTAMENT

EXTRA-CANONICAL WRITINGS

* Serek ha'eda.
† Manual of Discipline.

NEW TESTAMENT

NEW TESTAMENT APOCRYPHA

APOSTOLIC FATHERS

PSEUDO-CLEMENTINE WRITINGS